National Museums Scotland

 S IL er

Made in Scotland

GEORGE DALGLEISH
HENRY STEUART FOTHRINGHAM

With contributions by John Burnett,
Colin T. Fraser and Amanda Game

First published in 2008 by
NMSE – Publishing
a division of NMS Enterprises Limited
National Museums Scotland
Chambers Street
Edinburgh EH1 1JF

Revised reprint 2008

Text and photographic images © 2008
(as credited: and see Image Credits below)

Catalogue format and additional material
(as credited)
© Trustees of the National Museums of
Scotland 2008

The right of all contributors to be identified as
the authors of this book has been asserted by
them in accordance with the Copyright,
Designs and Patents Act 1988.

**British Library Cataloguing in
Publication Data**
A catalogue record for this book
is available from the British Library.

ISBN: 978 1 905267 13 2

Publication layout and design by
NMS Enterprises Limited – Publishing.
Cover design by Mark Blackadder.
Cover photograph by NMS Photography;
artwork by NMS Design.
Printed and bound in the United Kingdom
by Cambridge Printing.

For a full listing of NMS Enterprises Limited –
Publishing titles and related merchandise:

www.nms.ac.uk/books

IMAGE CREDITS

*Acknowledgements for use of source
material, loans and photographs within
this publication. No reproduction of
material in copyright permitted without
prior contact with the publisher or owner
of copyright.*

By courtesy of the Trustees of the
Jackson Collection: Image © National
Museum of Wales [Amgueddfa Cymru –
National Museum Wales]
www.amgueddfacymru.ac.uk

Aberdeen City Council
www.aberdeencity.gov.uk
© Aberdeen Art Gallery and Museums

Angus Council Cultural Services
www.angus.gov.uk
Aberdeenshire Heritage

© Aberdeenshire Council
www.aberdeenshire.gov.uk

Courtesy of Edinburgh City Libraries
The City of Edinburgh Council
Edinburgh Central Library
www.edinburgh.gov.uk

Dumfries Museum
www.dumgal.gov.uk [or]
www.dumfriesmuseum.demon.co.uk/
dumfmuse.html

Glasgow Museums and Art Galleries
Kelvingrove, Glasgow
www.glasgowmuseums.com
© Culture and Sport Glasgow

Hunterian Museum and Art Gallery,
University of Glasgow
www.hunterian.gla.ac.uk

Courtesy of the Huntington Library,
Art Collections, and Botanical Gardens
San Marino, California
www.huntington.org
© Huntington Library

The Incorporation of Goldsmiths
of the City of Edinburgh
www.incorporationofgoldsmiths.co.uk

© Inverness Museum and Art Gallery

Los Angeles County Museum
Photo © 2006 Museum Associates/
LACMA

Manchester City Galleries
www.manchestergalleries.org

The Metropolitan Museum of Art
New York: www.metmuseum.org
The Metropolitan Museum of Art, The
Jules S. Bache Collection, 1949: Image
© The Metropolitan Museum of Art

Museum of Fine Arts, Boston (MFA)
www.mfa.org: Photo © 2008 Museum
of Fine Arts, Boston

© National Archives of Scotland

National Galleries of Scotland
www.nationalgalleries.org
© The National Gallery of Scotland

Perth Museum and Art Gallery
Perth and Kinross Council
www.pkc.gov.uk

The Royal Collection © 2007
Her Majesty Queen Elizabeth II

© South Lanarkshire Council

Stewartry Museum, Kirkcudbright
www.dumgal.gov.uk [or]
dumfriesmuseum.demon.co.uk/
stewartry.html

University of Aberdeen,
Marischal College
www.abdn.ac.uk/marischal_museum/

© University of Edinburgh

University of St Andrews –
Museum Collections
www.st-andrews.ac.uk/
services/muscoll/museum.html
© Reproduced courtesy of the
University of St Andrews

The Collection of the Worshipful
Company of Goldsmiths
www.thegoldsmiths.co.uk

Contents

Dedication   iv

Exhibition and Publication Sponsors   v

Acknowledgements   vi

Foreword   vii

Interpretation   viii

New Attributions   ix

CHAPTER 1   Set in Silver   1

CHAPTER 2   The Science of Silver and 'The Lovable Craft'   11

CHAPTER 3   Surviving the Melting Pot   29

CHAPTER 4   Edinburgh: The Golden Age   55

CHAPTER 5   Making their Mark:
             Burgh Silver   87

CHAPTER 6   Fashioned in Silver   123

CHAPTER 7   Kirk Silver   141

CHAPTER 8   Ceremonial and Presentation Silver   161

CHAPTER 9   Sporting Glories   181

CHAPTER 10   Silver Now   201

Biographical Notes   217

Selected Glossary   228

Bibliography and References   231

This book is dedicated with gratitude and affection to Stuart Maxwell, who from 1948 to 1982 was the Deputy Keeper of the National Museum of Antiquities of Scotland. His constant encouragement of researchers included an extraordinary generosity with the fruits of his own discoveries. In 1975 he delivered a ground-breaking series of papers on Scottish silver, for the Rhind Lectures. He was the driving force behind the exhibition and catalogue 'The Lovable Craft' in 1987.

He is the giant on whose shoulders we have been privileged to stand. We hope that he will enjoy this exhibition and this publication, knowing that they reflect his wisdom and knowledge, and that they have come about in large part because of his inspirational teaching and encouragement.

George Dalgleish and Henry Steuart Fothringham
1 DECEMBER 2007, FEAST OF ST ELOI

Exhibition and Publication Sponsors

EXHIBITION SPONSORS

LYON & TURNBULL

Established in 1826 Lyon & Turnbull is Scotland's longest established auctioneers. We are proud to be co-sponsors of this prestigious exhibition and our support of the exhibition follows on from the many successes we have had over the years promoting and selling Scottish silver and accessories to collectors and institutions.

Our continuing aim is to encourage a new generation to collect and take an interest in Scottish silver; not only from an aesthetic viewpoint but also to recognise its important place in the social history of Scotland.

Trevor H. Kyle
DIRECTOR, SILVER AND JEWELLERY DEPARTMENT

HAMILTON & INCHES

Hamilton & Inches has been hand-making prestigious silver in its own workshop continually since 1866. It is the only Scottish jewellery business to have made silverware throughout its history and today the workshop is recognised as one of Europe's leading exponents in the field, designing and making unique commissions.

Scotland has been prominent in making silverware for many centuries and this exhibition, curated by the National Museums Scotland, celebrates hallmarking in Scotland from 1458. Hamilton & Inches is delighted to be a sponsor and we are also excited to see the 'Silver of the Stars' initiative, which was established by the Incorporation of Goldsmiths to demonstrate the vibrancy of Scottish silversmithing, included as part of the exhibition.

Denzil Skinner
DIRECTOR, HAMILTON & INCHES

PUBLICATION SPONSORS

We are also grateful to the following for their support with this publication:

- The Incorporation of Goldsmiths of the City of Edinburgh
- The Worshipful Company of Goldsmiths of the City of London
- The Silver Society
- Marc Fitch Fund
- Nicholas Shaw Antiques

THE INCORPORATION OF GOLDSMITHS OF THE CITY OF EDINBURGH

Acknowledgements

EXHIBITION CREDITS:

Silver: Made in Scotland
National Museums Scotland, Edinburgh
25 January to 27 April 2008

We are grateful to HRH The Princess Royal for consenting to open this exhibition and for being patron of the 'Silver of the Stars' charity.

Exhibition project team:

Maureen Barrie	Jane Carmichael
George Dalgleish	Michelle Forster Davies
Irene Mackay	Jackie Moran
Sarah Saunders	

Exhibition design: Studio MB

With thanks to colleagues in Conservation, Design and Technical Support, Development, Loans, Marketing and other staff within National Museums Scotland who have contributed to this project.

PUBLICATION CREDITS:

Publication management:
NMS Enterprises Limited – Publishing

Layout and design:
Lesley Ann Taylor
Marián Sumega   Isabelle Van Geet

With text contributions by:
John Burnett   Colin T. Fraser
Amanda Game

Additional assistance:
NMS Design and Technical Support
NMS Enterprises Limited
NMS Library and NMS Photography (in particular Joyce Smith, who has produced some spectacular photography of a notoriously difficult subject)

Many people have given generously of their knowledge, time, wisdom and experience to make this exhibition and book possible. In particular, many happy hours of discussion and exchange of ideas with Stuart Maxwell, William Fortescue, John Hyman, Nicholas Holmes and Virginia Glenn, have provided both delight and enlightenment.

We have also benefited immeasurably from the enthusiasm and knowledge of our brethren in the Incorporation of Goldsmiths of the City of Edinburgh, particularly the deacon Michael Laing, the past deacon Harry Tatton, assay-master Scott Walter, secretary Mary Michel, and archivist Elspeth Morrison.

National Museums Scotland has been lucky in a series of very able interns from sister academic institutions: Megan Brett and Tawney Paul from the University of Edinburgh, and Dorit Kupfer and Kate Neitopiel from the Humboldt University Berlin, have contributed some outstanding research work.

Many other individuals have contributed their knowledge unstintingly to this project. Some are mentioned below, but we thank them all: Dr David Bertie, Vanessa Brett, Dr Iain Gordon Brown, Dr Patrick Cadell, Alistair Cunningham, Maria Devaney, Alastair Dickenson, Kirkpatrick Dobie, Professor and Mrs R. R. Dietert, Richard Edgecome, Helen Edwards, Phillipa Glanville, Richard Hunter, Trevor Kyle, Gordon MacGregor, Andrew McLean, Sandra Olm McRae, Sandra Martin, Jean Munro, Tessa Murdoch, Estelle Quick, Rosemary Ransome-Wallis, Christine Rew, Robin Rodger, David Scarratt, Fraser Simm, Fiona Slattery, Rosemary Watt, Clara Young.

We would also like to thank staff at the National Archives of Scotland, National Library of Scotland, National Galleries of Scotland and Edinburgh Central Library.

We are grateful to a wide range of public institutions and private individuals, both here and abroad, who have generously lent items to the exhibition: each is individually acknowledged as they wished in the text. And, as is traditionally the case, the authors alone are responsible for all errors of omission and commission.

Foreword

The collection of Scottish silver held by the National Museums Scotland is one of the richest areas of its specialist collections. It demonstrates the history of the craft and the different uses of silver, and many pieces have strong associations with major Scottish figures. The collection ranges from the earliest surviving hallmarked spoons, through the 18th-century elegance of goldsmiths like James Ker, up to the modern craft of Malcolm Appleby.

The Museum collection was the starting point for this publication and the exhibition of the same name. With help from many United Kingdom institutions, plus the generosity of private lenders and assistance from American museums, a wonderful array of material has been assembled for display and for study. This comprehensive book with its superb detailed illustrations is the result, and we hope it will provide a lasting legacy. We are very grateful to all of those who have contributed.

Dr Gordon Rintoul
DIRECTOR, NATIONAL MUSEUMS SCOTLAND

Interpretation

BIOGRAPHY AND GLOSSARY

Brief biographical notes on some of the goldsmiths mentioned in the text can be found at pp. 217-27, and a Selected Glossary appears at p. 228.

DATES

All dates are rendered in new style. Note that the calendars of Scotland and England were different from 1600 to 1752. In Scotland, by decree of the Privy Council, the year began on 1 January, as from 1 January 1600, while in England the new year continued to start on 25 March until 1752.

The Edinburgh assay-year usually began in mid-September from 1583 until 1974, before which period the elections of deacons often took place at the Beltane quarter (1st week of May) or at other random times of the year. Thus the date-letters (introduced in 1681) ran from September to September with few exceptions. In this catalogue we have identified Edinburgh and Glasgow date-letters by both the calendar years in which they fall, e.g. 1788-89. As from 1 January 1975, the Edinburgh date-letters coincide with the calendar year and they are identical to those used at the three surviving English assay offices.

SURNAMES

The spelling of early surnames is often very inconsistent in the records, mostly according to the whim of the clerk in an age when spelling was not standardised. We have taken the view that some traditionally accepted spellings of individuals' names should be allowed to stand, but in less clear cases we have been guided by Dr George F. Black's *The Surnames of Scotland* (1991). Less familiar names have been modernised, e.g. Veitch instead of Vaiche, except where some superior logic should prevail.

MARKS

When marks are arranged around a central point (as on the base of a teapot) the maker's mark is read first and then the others follow clockwise. If struck in a line, they are read in order of appearance from left to right.

On pre-trefid spoons it is stated whether the marks are being read from the bowl end or the terminal end of the stem; all marks on spoons are on the back of the stem unless otherwise stated. No known early Scottish spoons are marked in the bowl.

MEASUREMENTS

All dimensions are given in centimetres.

D = diameter   Dp = depth
H = height   L = length
W = width

The order in which they appear depends on the type of object.

WEIGHTS

Wt = weight

Weights are in troy ounces, usually to the nearest whole 100th of an ounce. Where materials other than precious metals and enamel are included in the weight, the term 'all-in' has been added in brackets.

Where scratch weights are given, these are usually in ounces and drops; there were 16 drops to the ounce. Scottish goldsmiths did not adopt pennyweights until well into the 18th century.

NOTE: One troy ounce is equal to 31.1 grams or thereby. One gram equals 0.03215oz troy.

New Attributions

This catalogue includes a number of attributions which are either altogether new or which contradict those already in print. Some of the earlier cases are of the first importance [such as nos 3.2, 3.7 and 3.9]; others are less so. A few have been known to specialists for a long time but have not appeared in print until now. Where we have arrived at new conclusions, we have given our reasons for doing so.

In the cases of the Fergusson Mazer [3.6] and the Cowcaddens Mazer [3.9] the usual order of Edinburgh marks (maker, castle, deacon) appears, from circumstantial evidence, to have been reversed (deacon, castle, maker). This should alert one to the possibility that the order of some other marks may also have been reversed and that perhaps the usual sequence was not as universally observed as was once thought.

During the preparation of this publication some old certainties have been overturned and some uncertainties have been resolved. At the same time, a few new problems of attribution have arisen, which we have done our best to explain.

In addition to these attributions we have dared to include very tentative suggestions about the possible authorship of three other early pieces, two of which are marked and one unmarked: the Bute Mazer [3.1]; Methuen Cup [1.2]; and the Watson Mazer [3.2]. Further work needs to be done on them before anything more definite can be determined.

George Dalgleish
Henry Steuart Fothringham

proūerb·22

Ane·good·mane
is·to·be·chosen·
Aboūe·great·riches
And·loūing·faūour
Is·aboūe·silūer
And·aboūe
Moste·fyne
golde
1569

Set in Silver

Introduction

This verse (opposite), from the Book of Proverbs (22:1), is engraved in the centre of the Galloway Mazer, one of the finest surviving examples of the Scottish goldsmith's art [no. 3.4]. It tells us something important about ourselves and about the subject of this book. It teaches us to admire and to use the beautiful and practical works of the goldsmiths' 'Lovable Craft', not with the envy of desire or the self-satisfaction of ownership, but with an uplifting joy and wonder. But the heart of man is easily corrupted, particularly where gold and silver are concerned, and laws were needed to prevent fraud and deception. The potential honesty of man is above the purity even of gold, but in an imperfect world corrupt men produce corrupt metals. The proverb suggests that the purity of gold and silver are benchmarks against which to measure the honesty of man. Hallmarks guarantee the honesty of the metal and its maker alike, and this book celebrates five and a half centuries of their application in Scotland.

Gold has been used in Scotland for some 4000 years to fashion jewellery and vessels, while the mining and working of silver arrived with the Romans in the 1st century AD. Silver pennies were first minted in Scotland in the 1130s and goldsmiths are frequently referred to as working in the Mint in various capacities. However, it is not until the 16th century that pieces survive by identifiable makers. This is because they are stamped with marks that tell us who made them, and also when and where they were made. This book, and the exhibition that inspired it, is concerned not only with silver and gold vessels, from the earliest surviving marked examples right up to pieces made today, but also with the people who made them and the people for whom they were made.

The reason we know so much about these individuals is simply because of 'hallmarking' – the practice that assured customers that all gold and silver sold in this country was of a certain minimum quality, guaranteed by the marks stamped on the wares. As we will see, the first Scottish legislation enforcing this earliest form of consumer protection dates from 1458. Throughout this book we will try to explain how we know about the objects and their makers. There is good documentary evidence for the independent testing process to determine the quality of metal (known as 'assaying'), and for the stamping of the marks by the maker and the assayer (known as 'hallmarks' because they were applied in the goldsmiths' own meeting-place or hall). The organisation of goldsmiths into trade bodies, known in Scotland as 'incorporations' (not 'guilds'), is chronicled in great detail in their own minute books and other records.

Ane good mane is to be chosen above great riches and loving favour is above silver and above moste fyne golde …

{PROVERBS 22:1}

{opposite page}
3.4 THE GALLOWAY MAZER, 1569

Careful correlation between these sources and the surviving examples of goldsmiths' work can throw fascinating light on the history of the craft. It can also illuminate the lives of the people who made and used silver and gold in Scotland in different ways throughout the centuries.

This book, and the exhibition, are divided into various themes to provide an insight into this remarkable heritage over 550 years. We start by looking at the raw materials themselves, their need to be alloyed or mixed with less valuable metals to make them useable and the subsequent need for testing, along with a look at how the craftsmen who worked in gold and silver organised themselves in 'The Science of Silver and "The Lovable Craft"'. Very little domestic silver and gold has survived from before the Restoration of the Monarchy in 1660, so 'Surviving the Melting Pot' suggests some explanations for this and brings together for the first time virtually all the known remaining pieces. We then investigate 'Edinburgh: The Golden Age'; the capital has always been the major centre of the craft. In 'Making their Mark: Burgh Silver' we look at the work of craftsmen in the rest of Scotland; their history is, in some instances, as old, if not older, than that of Edinburgh. The development of particular styles and the changing demand for silver throughout Scotland dominate 'Fashioned in Silver'. A series of 'case studies' looks at particular types and uses of silver in 'Kirk Silver', 'Ceremonial and Presentation Silver' and 'Sporting Glories'. We are particularly fortunate to have a veritable galaxy of first-class artists and craftspeople working in Scotland at the moment. 'Silver Now' looks at this phenomenon and finishes, in a blaze of glory, with the ground-breaking contemporary initiative of the Incorporation of Goldsmiths of the City of Edinburgh's 'Silver of the Stars'.

Silver and gold have been used to make coinage, medals, clothing, jewellery, scientific instruments, ornaments, spoons and practical vessels for church, state and domestic use. This first small section looks at a few of the wide range of important pieces from the 16th to the 20th centuries; an 'overture' to the full display of *Silver: Made in Scotland*.

1.1 'GARTER SUIT' OF DOUBLET AND HOSE

Suit made of silver tissue for the 6th Duke of Lennox, *c.*1661

Doublet (chest) 89 cm; hose (waist) 83 cm

NMS A.1947.257; donated by Hon. Lady Hersey Baird of Lennoxlove; conserved for display with a generous bequest from the late Margaret Swain

The remaining part of a suit, or uniform, of the Most Noble Order of the Garter, England's premier chivalric order. Worn under the mantle, the suit belonged to Charles Stuart, 6th Duke of Lennox and 3rd Duke of Richmond (1639-72). King Charles II reinvigorated the Order on his Restoration in 1660, and is said to have influenced the design of the highly fashionable uniform himself. The Duke of Lennox, a favourite of the King, was created a Knight of the Garter in 1661 when, presumably, he had this suit made. His career was turbulent and often attended by scandal. In 1672 he was made ambassador to Denmark, but died after falling into the freezing sea attempting to board his ship. He was survived by his wife Frances Teresa Stuart, known as 'La Belle Stewart', reputedly the model for the portrait of Britannia used on coins. Having no children, she instructed her trustees to purchase Lethington House near Haddington for her cousin Lord Blantyre, and to rename it 'Lennoxlove' in their memory.

The doublet and hose are made of plain weave silk with an additional weft of thin silver foil strips to make a fabric sometimes known as 'silver tissue'. The applied silver lace is made of silver foil wrapped around silk fibres. Research in the National Museums Scotland's analytical laboratories shows that the silver used to make these materials is of exceptionally high purity, probably because 'fine' or nearly pure silver like this is soft and easy to beat flat to make into

3.4 (detail)

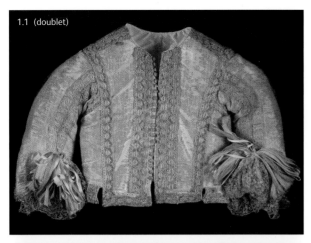

1.1 (doublet)

1.1 (hose)

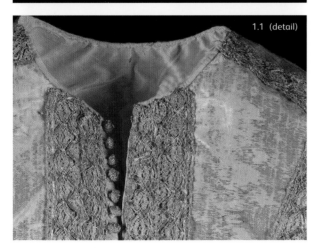

1.1 (detail)

thin foil. It is, however, extremely fragile, and it is only through extensive and painstaking work by the Museum conservators that this rare survival can be safely displayed and preserved for the future.

Not all items made of silver are vessels or jewellery. The Garter Suit shows an unusual use of fine silver in a garment that epitomised high fashion, wealth, power and status.

1.2 THE METHUEN CUP

Possibly John Veitch, Edinburgh, *c*.1530

Marks (struck three times, on cover flange, inside bowl and on underside of foot): 'Vh' in a shield (possibly John Veitch)

H (max.) 17.8 cm; D (rim) 11.5 cm; D (foot) 6.7 cm

Lent by Los Angeles County Museum of Art, William Randolph Hearst Collection

Provenance: by descent to Field Marshall Lord Methuen GCB; Christie's sale, London, 25 February 1920, lot 87; Crichton Brothers, London; William Randolph Hearst Collection

References: Eeles (1920), pp. 285-89; Finlay and Fothringham (1991), pp. 58-60; Norman-Wilcox (1961), pp. 10-15; Schroder (1986), pp. 406-08

Shallow silver-gilt bowl, with octagonal-section rock crystal stem with central band, attached to bowl and foot by notched collars, each with four scrolls; the low-domed foot is edged with a finely-milled band; the double-domed cover has a crystal finial carved with six bosses, held by an open serpent-shaped ring.

Henry Steuart Fothringham has tentatively suggested that one possible candidate for the maker of this beautiful little cup could be John Veitch, goldsmith in Edinburgh. If one were to accept this suggestion, then the Methuen Cup would be the earliest surviving marked example of Scottish silver.

The notched collars and 'milled' edge of the foot are similar in design and construction to the lower rim-band of the Bute Mazer [3.1]; this perhaps further strengthens the case for a Scottish origin. There has been considerable discussion about the use of the cup – whether for secular or for religious purposes.

The use of rock crystal in highly prestigious and talismanic objects was fairly common in Scotland, from simple mounted balls of rock crystal to the magnificent mounted crystal Lochbuie, Lorne, Ugadale and Ballochyle Brooches [see 3.13].

1.2

1.2

1.2 (detail)

1.3 (detail)

1.4

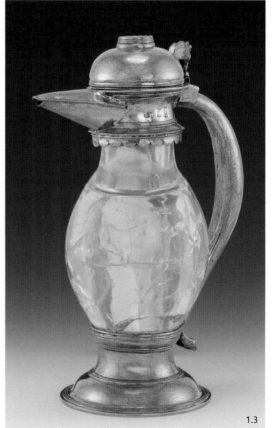

1.3

1.3 THE ERSKINE EWER

James Cok II, Edinburgh, 1565-68

Marks (on lid, inside top, on side of top mount and on side of foot, with visible assay-scrape above each mark): 'IC' (maker James Cok II); castle (Edinburgh); 'GH' monogram with cross (deacon George Heriot II)

H 24 cm; D (foot) 10 cm; L 15.5 cm; Wt (all-in) 43.33 oz

Lent from a private collection at Mount Stuart

Provenance: by descent to Sheriff Erskine Murray; Christie's sale, 1904, Lord Swaythling

References: Finlay and Fothringham (1991), pp. 63, 68-69, pl. 22; Lenman (1995), pp. 159-77; *EGM* (2006), A19; Jackson (1911), p. 185; RSM (1948), no. 3; Dalgleish and Maxwell (1987), no. 1; *Scot. Nat. Mem.* (1890), p. 298

Baluster-shaped body of polished rock crystal with several natural flaws; engraved with stylised vines. The silver-gilt mounts consist of a plain stepped foot connected by a seamed hollow scroll handle to the scalloped neck-band, which has a large beak-like spout. The hinged domed lid has a cast Bacchanalian thumb-piece and is inset with a small disc engraved with the arms of Erskine and Murray.

The unique and somewhat ungainly form of this ewer or wine jug has led past commentators to suggest it might be a later composite, cobbled together from disparate sections. However, this appears to be disproved by the fact that several of these sections have identical assay-scrapes (see pp. 15-16) and repeated full marks. Clearly both maker and deacon were taking care to ensure that the letter of the law was complied with.

This was not the case a few years later when James Cok became heavily involved in the political troubles that beset the latter part of the reign of Mary, Queen of Scots. A supporter of the Queen's Party in the ensuing civil war, he was besieged in Edinburgh Castle and later executed, along with his 'brother goldsmith' James Mosman, in 1573. Traditionally this extreme punishment was said to have been handed down because they were minting coins for the Queen's Party. A more recent survey suggests that the real reason was that both men were actively pawning jewels gathered from supporters, and using the resulting cash to prolong the war.

Another tradition holds that the ewer was a gift from Queen Elizabeth I to John, 6th Lord Erskine, on the baptism of one of his children. Erskine, a Protestant, was friendly towards England, and for a year before his death in 1572 was Regent for the young King James VI. It is, however, unlikely that Elizabeth would have given a piece by a Scottish goldsmith. More probably Erskine himself commissioned it to commemorate his elevation to the Earldom of Mar in 1565. With its stylised vine-leaf engraving and Bacchus mask, this suggests a vessel more suited for holding celebratory wine than baptismal water.

1.4 PEG TANKARD

Edward Cleghorne I, Edinburgh, 1663-65, 1671-73 or 1679-81

Marks (on base): 'EC' in monogram (maker Edward Cleghorne I); castle (Edinburgh); 'EC' in monogram (deacon Edward Cleghorne I); prominent assay-scrape towards edge of base (not above marks); large cursive 'P' engraved on base

H (max. to top of thumb-piece) 18.3 cm; D (rim) 12.5 cm; Wt 25.11 oz

Lent by Glasgow Museums and Art Galleries; gifted in 1966 by Mrs Anne Maxwell Macdonald and family in memory of Sir John Stirling Maxwell; part of a gift of Pollok House and Estate to the City of Glasgow

Provenance: Stirling Maxwell Collection, Pollok House

References: Finlay and Fothringham (1991), p. 121, pl. 49; *Empire Exhibition* (1938), no. 59, pl. 25; RSM (1948), no. 24

Raised body, set on three claw and ball feet; junctions with panels of repoussé decoration of foliage and fruit, highlighted with pricked tendrils spreading from them. Hinged cushion lid has a plain central circular boss surrounded by a band of repoussé foliage and fruit. S-scroll handle terminates in an acanthus leaf and scroll openwork thumb-piece. Inside the body, to the reverse of the handle, are four equally spaced domed pegs.

A good example of the Scandinavian influence migrating to Scotland through many economic, military and cultural connections during the 17th century, this tankard is however a rare survival. The form is known as a 'peg tankard' because of the series of spaced pegs inside the body; this marks the amount of liquid consumed before being passed on during a communal drinking session.

1.3 (three marks)

1.4 (three marks)

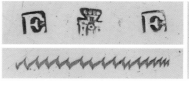

1.5 MONTEITH

Colin McKenzie, Edinburgh, 1698-99

Marks (on base): 'MK' conjoined (maker Colin McKenzie); castle (Edinburgh); 'JP' in monogram (assay-master James Penman); 'S' (date-letter 1698-99)

H 23.2 cm; D (rim) 35.7 cm; D (foot) 20.7 cm; Wt 73.1 oz

Lent from a private collection at Mount Stuart

References: *See below: we are indebted to Dr Iain Gordon Brown for this reference

The bowl is in eight lobed panels on a stippled background, the notched rim with cast and applied foliate and scroll edge, on a circular gadrooned stepped foot, with two opposed ring- and knop-drop handles each issuing from a grotesque mask. The central panel was later engraved with a demi-lion rampant, with a motto in a riband above 'NOBILIS IRA', all below a marquess's coronet.

This example is the joint-earliest recorded Scottish monteith; the other is also by Colin McKenzie [4.7]. Used to cool or rinse wine glasses (which hung by their feet from the notched rim into the bowl filled with ice or water) before they were brought to the table, the origin of their name sounds somewhat apocryphal. According to the *Diary of Anthony Wood* (December 1683), the name derives from a 'Monsieur Monteigh ... a fantastical Scot' at the court of King Charles II, who wore a cloak with a notched or scalloped hem akin to the rim of the vessel. Despite this apparently Scottish origin myth, monteiths are actually comparatively rare in Scotland.

Like many other vessels, they may have a variety of uses. In 1704 John Clerk of Penicuik (1676-1755) described this and their scarcity eloquently: 'a mintieth, which is a bigg loom ['lume' or 'loom', an open container, tub or bowl] that stands upon a table by way of a cobler ['coble', a vat, pond or watering place], and upon occasion by the help of some gymcrack about it can be metamorphosed in 3 other shapes, *viz.* a cadel ['caddel' or 'caudle', scrambled eggs] dish, a milck dish and a bassoon .... Ther's none of them to be found ready made because few people have them, wherefore I have bespoken Mr Law ...'.*

1.6 SLAVE OR DOG COLLAR

Robert Luke, Glasgow, engraved '1732'

Marks: 'RL' twice (maker Robert Luke); tree, fish, bell, etc. (Glasgow); 'S'

H 2.8 cm; D 15 cm; Wt 5.06 oz

Lent by Glasgow Museums and Art Galleries; purchased Sotheby's sale, London, 24 July 1980, Important English Silver, lot 29

Circular narrow band, with adjustment slots, and fixed ring; engraved 'John Crawford of Miltoun Esqr: Owner 1732'. Collars such as these generally survive as dog collars, sometimes given as prizes for races. Collars used to denote ownership of slaves are much rarer, but undoubtedly did exist from the 17th century: several 18th-century paintings show black household servants with such collars. Glasgow in the 18th century, with its growing commercial links with America, the West Indies and Africa, was undoubtedly involved in the slave trade; many merchants made their fortunes out of this traffic in human misery.

The owner of this collar, John Crawford of Milton, was a successful Glasgow merchant, and may well have had a slave or a personal servant. The only other Scottish parallel is a brass collar in the National Museum of Scotland, dated 1701, worn by a convicted criminal who was given as a 'perpetual servant' or serf to Sir John Erskine of Alva. Serfdom was not abolished in Scotland until 1799.

1.7 COFFEE URN

James Weems, Edinburgh, 1738-39

Marks (on base): 'IW' (maker James Weems); castle (Edinburgh); 'AU' (assay-master Archibald Ure); 'I' (date-letter 1738-39)

H 33 cm; W (across handles) 26 cm; Wt 45.08 oz

Lent from a private collection

Reference: *Empire Exhibition* (1938), no. 10, lent by G. E. P. How

Plain egg-shaped body, on three closely-set scroll legs with shell feet, two opposed handles shaped as mythical serpents; lift-off cover with ball and button finial, mouth flat-chased with alternating bands of shell and scrolling foliage, wooden spade-shaped spigot tap.

This uniquely Scottish design was used for coffee [see 4.40-47]. This must have been an ambitious piece for a relatively young goldsmith. James Weems was apprenticed to William Aytoun, a maker of at least two such urns [see 4.40]. He was obviously influenced by his master's work, virtually copying the cover finial, shell feet and serpent handles. However, the legs of the urn are less assured.

1.7

1.5

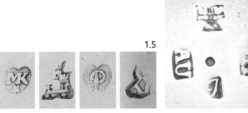

6

1.5

1.5 (detail)

1.6

1.10

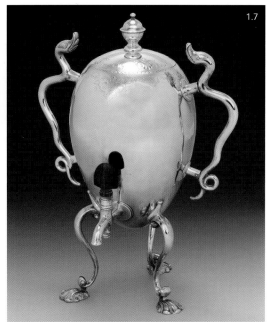

1.7

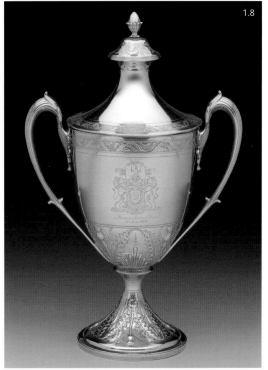

1.8

1.11

1.8 TWO-HANDLED CUP AND COVER

W. & P. Cunningham, Edinburgh, 1799-1800

Marks (on foot edge): 'WPC' (maker William & Patrick
Cunningham); castle (Edinburgh); thistle (standard mark);
'T' (date-letter 1799-1800); king's head (duty mark)

H (max.) 42.5 cm; D (rim) 15.1 cm; Wt 71.68 oz

NMS K.1998.419; purchased in 1998

Vase-shaped body is set on spreading foot, chased
with thistles; two opposed reeded looped handles;
trumpet-shaped cover with acorn finial; the cover
and body rims have bands of bright-cut thistles.
The body is engraved on one side with the full Royal
Arms for Scotland and 'From a Sincere Friend / 3rd
June 1800', and on the other with arms for Arthur
Forbes of Culloden (1760-1803).

The use of the Royal Arms on this exceptionally
fine example is unusual, and it indicated that the cup
was possibly a gift from either a member of the Royal
Family or from an officer of state who was permitted
to use the Royal Arms.

1.9

1.9 THE BREADALBANE TARGE

Designed by James Gillespie Graham; made by Mackay
& Cunningham, Edinburgh, 1835-36

Marks: castle (Edinburgh); king's head (duty mark); 'J.Mc' (maker
James Mackay of Mackay & Cunningham); thistle (standard mark);
'D' (date-letter 1835-36)

D 49.8 cm

NMS H.MEQ 1514; purchased in 1982

Circular silver-gilt shield, following the form of a
Highland targe; four loops on the back for leather
supporting straps; border of applied scrolling foliage,
the domed centre engraved with flowers on a mottled
ground with applied stylised flower heads; applied cast
arms for Campbell of Breadalbane in the centre.

The back is inscribed: 'This shield is presented
to / The Most Noble John Campbell Marquess of
Breadalbane, Earl of Ormelie, Viscount Glenorchy
&c, &c,. / By the Liberal Electors of Perthshire; /
As a testemony of their esteem for his private worth,
their admiration of his public principles / and their
gratitude for his distinguished services in the Great
Cause of Liberty and / as their representative in the
First Reformed Parliament of the United Kingdom,

to which he was triumphantly returned on the XXIXth
of December MDCCCXXXII by a Majority of 543. /
Presented in the name of the subscribers / By the
Hon^{BLE.} Fox Maule / Member of Parliament for the
County of Perth / Under Secretary of State for the
Home Department / Designed by James Gillespie
Graham of Orchill Esq. / Executed by Messrs
Mackay & Cunningham Edinburgh 1836.'

As this spectacular piece indicates, its recipient,
John Campbell, 2nd Marquess of Breadalbane, continued his family's support of Whig politics, becoming
the first Liberal Member of Parliament for Perthshire
(while still the Earl of Ormelie) after the introduction
of the great Reform Act in 1832. On the death of
his father in 1834, he succeeded to the marquessate,
becoming a member of the House of Lords, which
no doubt led to the presentation of the targe by his
supporters.

Campbell employed the architect James Gillespie
Graham to 'gothicise' his vast Perthshire home, Taymouth Castle; this is no doubt the reason the architect
was chosen to design this 'targe'.

1.8

1.9

1.10

1.10 INKSTAND

John Muirhead & Son, Glasgow, 1885-86

Marks (on base): 'J. Muirhead & Son/Glasgow' (maker); lion rampant (Glasgow sterling standard mark); queen's head (duty mark); tree, fish, bell, etc. (Glasgow); 'O' (date-letter 1885-86)

H 9 cm; L 24.9 cm; D 17.6 cm

Lent by Her Majesty The Queen/The Royal Collection, Palace of Holyroodhouse

Rectangular casket, with console corners and hinged hipped lid, elaborately cast and chased with views of Glasgow. Centre of lid inset with an oval shield bearing the City of Glasgow arms, while other panels show views of the River Clyde with the bridges of Glasgow; Dumbarton Castle and rock; University of Glasgow at Gilmourhill; the City Chambers of Glasgow, George Square; depiction of a steamship with shipyard behind; the Royal Exchange Square; Glasgow Cathedral; and an industrial scene of a locomotive to the fore and blast furnaces behind. The inside of the box is plain, with insets for two glass inkwells.

1.11 THE EDINBURGH GOLD CUP

Smith & Rait, Glasgow, 1902

Marks (below rim): 'S&R' (makers Smith & Rait); '18' within shield (18-carat gold standard mark); tree, fish, bell, etc. (Glasgow); lion rampant (standard mark); 'F' (date-letter 1902-03)

H 15.3 cm; L 36.7 cm; W 27.5 cm; Wt 40.5 oz

Lent by Glasgow Museums and Art Galleries; purchased at Christie's sale, Glasgow, 5 March 1985, lot 164

Reference: Frank (1985), p. 104, illustrated

Cup is in the form of a fruit basket in Art Nouveau style, applied cartouches engraved 'EDINBURGH / . GOLD . / CUP / 1902' and 'WON BY. / St. HUBERT / THE / PROPERTY OF / ALEX E. McKINLAY'.

The Edinburgh Gold Cup of 1902 was run at Musselburgh Race Course, near Edinburgh, on Friday 3 October. The winner, 'St Hubert', was the mount of Mr Trigg and owned by Mr A. E. McKinlay. It was a handicap race over one and a half miles with £200 to the winner. The Musselburgh Races are the direct descendant of the earlier Leith Races (see pp. 192-93). What the Edinburgh goldsmiths thought of the Edinburgh Gold Cup commission being given to a Glasgow firm is not recorded.

1.12 CUP AND COVER

Malcolm Appleby, Edinburgh, 1990

Marks: 'MA' in monogram (maker/designer Malcolm Appleby); castle (Edinburgh); lion rampant (sterling standard mark); 'Q' (date-letter 1990); signed and dated 22 March 1990

H (overall) 58.5 cm; W 37 cm; D 29 cm; Wt 8 kg

NMS A.1990.23 (a-p); commissioned from maker by NMS

Cup and cover of partly gilt silver, rock crystal and enamel; pierced and engraved decoration. Design and decoration by Malcolm Appleby (b.1946); raising by Peter Musgrove; casting by Danuta Solowicji; gilding by Parker Finishing of London; and enamelling by Maureen Edgar.

A tour-de-force of one of the most talented and innovative artist-craftsmen working in Scotland in recent times, this monumental cup, commissioned by National Museums Scotland, exhibits his virtuosity and wit as a designer, engraver and storyteller in metal. It also demonstrates the extent to which others, apart from the original begetter, can be involved in the making of a complex object.

1.12

The Science of Silver and 'The Lovable Craft'

Introduction

Gold or silver out of God's treasury-house,
to witt the Earth ...[1]

Gold and silver engenders with the heate
of the sonne and moone ...[2]

Gold and silver have, from time immemorial, been highly valued in many cultures. Their beauty, utility and unchanging nature, combined with both practical and mystical properties, have meant that man has sought them out and coveted them. Frequently, they have formed the basis of currencies. When alloyed, gold and silver have certain shared properties which make them ideal for use in making vessels that are both beautiful and useful. They are reasonably strong without being brittle; they are ductile, i.e. they will stretch without immediately breaking; they will become softer and will eventually melt when heated, allowing them to be used in casting and to be fused or welded together. They can be hammered, cut, drilled, engraved or carved to form virtually any desired shape. Then, finally, they can be treated in a variety of ways to achieve a finish that can range from a high glittering polish to a subtle matt sheen.

Gold

I have devised a plott how the gold mines
may be sett open ...[3]

Gold does not tarnish and is inert to most chemicals. This immutability has led to the metal being credited with mystical powers and is one reason why it has always been so highly valued. It has been mined in almost every country in the world at some time or another.

The principal use of gold since antiquity has been as currency, but its use in jewellery has been almost as important. It is too soft to be used in a pure state, but has the remarkable quality that even when alloyed with large proportions of baser metals (e.g. silver and copper), to a considerable degree it still retains its colour and resistance to tarnish. Degrees of alloying is referred to as the 'carat system' where 24 carat is pure gold, whereas 9 carat is 9/24th pure gold or 375 parts per thousand.[4]

Gold is found all over Scotland, but normally in very small amounts.

His dark
materials ...

{MILTON: *PARADISE LOST*}

{opposite page}
2.20 **THE ARMORIAL BADGE OF THE OFFICER OF THE INCORPORATION OF GOLDSMITHS, 1725-26**

In the 16th century significant deposits were found in the Crawford Muir region, Lanarkshire; so much so that King James V was said, probably apocryphally, to have given each guest at his wedding to Mary of Guise in 1538 a cup filled with 'bonnet piece' coins minted from Crawford gold with the story that this was 'the finest fruits of a barren moor'.[5] However, most gold used in the period covered by this book was probably imported from either Europe or the New World, and has always been in much shorter supply than its sister metal, silver. The men who were proud to call themselves goldsmiths, from their earliest appearance in the records up to the 18th century, actually worked mainly in silver. They preferred the status conveyed by the nobler metal.

2.1 GOLD CASKET

Unmarked, 1881
Casket: L 5.9 cm; H 4 cm; Dp 3.2 cm; Wt 1.98 oz
Nugget: Wt 0.37 oz / Lent from a private collection

Constructed in the form of a 'treasure chest', containing a nugget of gold from the mines at Leadhills, Lanarkshire. Engraved with the arms of Hopetoun and 'Presented To / JALH / Earl of Hopetoun / By the Leadhills Miners / on attaining his majority / 25th September 1881 / (1000 Grains Gold)'.

The mines in this area were referred to in the 16th century as 'God's treasure house on earth' and passed into the ownership of the Edinburgh goldsmith Thomas Foulis, and thence by marriage to the Earls of Hopetoun. The recipient of this 21st-birthday gift was John Adrian Louis Hope, 7th Earl of Hopetoun, later to become the 1st Marquess of Linlithgow.

2.2 GOLD IMPRESSION OF A JAMES V SILVER GROAT

Edinburgh Mint, 1526-39, struck with the mark of
Gilbert Kirkwood, goldsmith / NMS H.C142

King James ordered a coinage of *silver* groats, worth 18 pence, to be issued by the Edinburgh Mint between 1526 and 1539. It is not known why or when this gold impression was struck. Generally the punches and tools for any given coinage were destroyed after the period of issue, so it is probable that this gold version was made at about the same time as the silver coinage. It may have been something to do with the use of native gold in the coinage, as James V also ordered ducats, or 'bonnet pieces', to be minted in the late 1530s and '40s from Crawford Muir gold. Why this coin should have an impression of the maker's mark of the Edinburgh goldsmith Gilbert Kirkwood, who did not become a master of the Incorporation until 1609, is unknown. It is possible that he was asked to assay the impression during his period as deacon in 1623-25 and to stamp it with his mark.

Silver

The greatest quantity of Silver that ever was gotten ...[6]

Pure unalloyed silver, next to gold, is the most malleable of all metals and can be worked or beaten almost as fine as gold. Pure silver can be drawn out into the finest wire or beaten to the finest foil (like that used to make the silver tissue cloth of the Duke of Richmond's Garter Suit [see 1.1]. Pure silver melts

2.1

THE MARTIN NUGGET

Wt 1.33 oz / NMS G.1994.20.4

A nugget of naturally occurring gold from Straightsteps, Wanlockhead, Dumfriesshire. Nuggets of this size are very rare.

2.2 GOLD IMPRESSION OF A JAMES V SILVER GROAT

Edinburgh Mint, 1526-39
NMS H.C142

A groat struck with the mark of Gilbert Kirkwood, goldsmith.

at 960.5°C. It is resistant to most acids and therefore can be used for vessels for eating and serving food and drink. Unlike gold, it is attacked by sulphur compounds which cause tarnishing. Much admired for its lustrous colour and beauty, the lust for it has occasionally driven men mad. Like gold, it is held to have mystical properties and was used as a charm against the evil eye and witchcraft. It was often seen as a symbol of purity, which may derive from its natural oligodynamic properties, as it kills certain bacteria and will purify water stored in vessels made from it.

Generally silver is found as a compound sulphide ore, and is refined to produce the pure metal. In Scotland it is found in lead ore, galena, or as 'native' silver, particles of silver metal adhering to another mineral matrix. Silver, like gold in its pure form, is too soft for most practical purposes, and must be alloyed with another metal, usually copper, to give it enough hardness and durability for use in vessels or ornaments.

Silver is found in many parts of Scotland, frequently associated with lead deposits. Major deposits were found in the Leadhills area from early times, but especially from the 16th century; in the 17th and 18th centuries silver was found in the Bathgate hills, on Islay, and in the Ochills near Alva. However, Scottish-mined silver only ever provided a very small proportion of the raw material needed to supply the demand for vessels, ornaments and coinage. The vast majority of virgin silver bullion came first from Europe and then from the tremendously lucrative mines in the Spanish colonies in the Americas. A major source for new vessels, however, was always reused old silver, either in the form of vessels and jewellery which was melted down, or by melting down coinage. (The latter was to the detriment of the availability of currency and many Royal proclamations and Acts of Parliament sought to prevent this; nevertheless it continued whenever the comparative price of bullion and the value of the currency made it profitable for silversmiths to melt down coins.)

Historically, the main financial value of silver and gold vessels and jewellery was in the actual weight of metal as bullion, while the worth and expense of the workmanship was very much a secondary consideration. This can be seen in many surviving bills and accounts, where goldsmiths sold items by weight of metal, with the cost of workmanship noted separ-

ately. In a period when many people held their available assets in the form of silver and gold plate, the purity of the metal was of paramount importance: 100 ounces of silver of only 80% purity was worth much less than the same weight of 91.6% purity (the traditional Scottish standard). The need to be able to count on this purity led to assaying and hallmarking, as shall be seen later (p. 15). When John Clerk (1611-74), merchant and art-dealer in Paris and later 1st Laird of Penicuik, bought silver for the Earl of Lothian, he summed up the situation neatly. In 1644 he bought a silver salt for the Earl which was 'a verie daintie piece and shall be extraordinarlie weill made. We must not spare the silver – silver is ay silver'.[7]

2.3 DAVID I SILVER STERLING OR PENNY

Minted by Erebald at Edinburgh, 1136-53 / NMS H.C668

This is the first known coin minted for a Scottish king. When David I of Scots captured Carlisle in 1136 he took over the English king's Mint that had been operating there. Erebald was the Mint master and was possibly brought to Edinburgh to coin silver pennies with the head of David I. These were based on the

SAMPLE OF GALENA

Lead ore, also containing silver, from Wanlockhead, Dumfriesshire
NMS G.45.85

Silver was often found associated with lead ore; it could be removed by a refining process called 'cupellation'. When smelted in a furnace, the base metal was absorbed into a bone ash container or 'cupel', leaving the pure silver. This was essentially the same process that was used for assaying gold and silver until the 20th century. There is no evidence of silver having been mined or processed in Scotland until Roman times. The Traprain Treasure, dating from the 1st century AD, is the earliest wrought silver in Scotland.

good quality English pennies known as 'sterlings'. They were produced at a finesse of 925 parts per thousand and this became known as the 'Sterling standard'. The origin of the term 'sterling' is thought to relate to the craftsmen, known as 'Easterlings', imported from the Continent to work the coinage in England. Scottish coins remained at the same fineness and value as English until well into the 13th century.

2.4 SALVER

Hamilton & Inches, Edinburgh, 1909-10

Marks (on base): 'H&I'; 'HAMILTON & INCHES/EDINBURGH' (maker Hamilton & Inches); castle (Edinburgh); thistle (standard mark); 'D' (date-letter 1909-10)

D 26.1 cm; H 3.2 cm; Wt 18.26 oz / Lent from a private collection

Circular salver with shaped and moulded rim, set on three hoof feet. The upper face engraved 'L' over a marquess's coronet for the Marquess of Linlithgow; the base engraved 'To / The Most Hon The Marquess of Linlithgow, / from / the Village of Leadhills. / 19th April 1911' and '(Made of Silver from Mines / on the Hopetoun Estate)'. The maker of this salver is the only Scottish firm of silversmiths founded in the 19th century to survive to the present day. It was presented to Victor, 2nd Marquess of Linlithgow, who succeeded his father in 1908.

2.5 LADLE

William Ged, Edinburgh, c.1720

Made to accompany The Royal Company of Archers Prize Monteith

Mark (on ladle rest): 'WG' only (maker William Ged)

L 33 cm; D (bowl) 6.8 cm

Lent by the Queen's Bodyguard for Scotland, the Royal Company of Archers

References: Balfour Paul (1875), p. 323; Moreton (2007), p. 65

Plain hemispherical bowl with baluster handle with knop end and rim-rest to underside; bowl engraved 'Regal Sagittariorum Cohorti Ex Fodinis Suis Argenteis donavit Johanes Areskinus ab Alva Esq: Auratus die Decem 20:1720', a loose translation of which is '[Made] from his own silver and given to the Royal Company of Archers, by Sir John Erskine of Alva, 20 December 1720'.

As part of his general 'improvement' to his estate of Alva in the Ochills, Sir John Erskine undertook some speculative mining in an area that came to be called the Silver Glen. His miners 'struck it rich' late in 1714. Although Sir John became caught up in the Jacobite Rebellion of the following two years and removed to the Continent, exploitation of the rich vein of silver ore was continued by his wife. Sir John was effectively excused for his part in the Rebellion on condition that he pay the Government a percentage of

2.4
2.5

2.6

14

his profits from the silver mine. In the period 1719-20 a quantity of ore was recovered and refined into silver. Sir John (a member of The Royal Company of Archers in Edinburgh) caused some of the silver to be made into a punch ladle to accompany the Archers' recently acquired prize monteith punch-bowl, also made by William Ged [see 9.8].

2.6 GOBLET

Adam Graham, Glasgow, c.1780

Marks (on underside of foot): 'AG' twice (maker Adam Graham); tree, fish, bell, etc. twice (Glasgow)

H 17.5 cm; D 9.6 cm; Wt 10 oz

Lent by Glasgow Museums and Art Galleries; purchased at Christie's sale, London, 24 June 1986, lot 43, with the aid of the Local Museums Purchase Fund

Provenance: John Noble Collection

References: Finlay and Fothringham (1991), p. 183; *Empire Exhibition* (1938), no. 101, pl. 41; RSM (1948), p. 220

Classical-shaped goblet, the interior gilt, with bowl engraved with crest and motto 'IN ALTUM' for the Alston family; set on a square foot, the underside engraved freehand 'Ilay Silver'.

Made from silver from mines on the island of Islay. Situated between Port Askaig and Ballygrant, lead mines had been worked intermittently on Islay from at least the 14th century. In the later 18th century they were operated by a group of Glasgow merchants, and silver was being extracted as a valuable by-product. According to Thomas Pennant, Islay lead provided 40 ounces of silver from a ton of the base metal. No doubt it was at this time that the maker, Adam Graham, acquired the raw material for the goblet.

The occurrence of native silver on Islay was recorded by the geologist Robert Jameson in 1816, and in the 18th and 19th centuries the island was one of the main sources in Scotland. Between 1862 and 1880, some 20,000 ounces of silver are said to have been extracted from the island's mines.

2.4

2.5

Assaying and the Assay Offices

Precious Metals: The Law concerning Standards and Marks

As noted above, gold and silver have to be mixed, or alloyed, with baser metals, to make them practically useful. Silver was normally alloyed with copper, and gold with a mixture of silver and copper. The addition of just 7.5% copper to pure silver results in an alloy with twice the tensile strength and more than twice the hardness and durability of the fine metal.

Unfortunately, unscrupulous craftsmen soon discovered that it is virtually impossible to tell by eye how much of the cheaper metal is present in the silver mixture, and it was an easy way to make money by passing off inferior metal as being of a higher standard than it really was. To prevent this, governments, starting in England but also in other European countries, passed a series of laws that required goldsmiths to have their wares tested or 'assayed' to prove they were of a certain quality of fineness. If they were above the minimum legal standard, they had to be marked with a series of punches to prove this. These marks were originally added in the London Goldsmiths' headquarters or hall, giving the world the term 'hallmarks' as an enduring benchmark of quality. The assaying and hallmarking of precious metals is the earliest recorded form of consumer protection in the world. A fortuitous result of using marks to validate the legal controls is that we can now often tell, centuries later, the identity of the maker, the date, and the place of manufacture.

Methods of assaying, or testing the purity or 'fineness' of precious metals, evolved over the centuries as knowledge and techniques improved. Initially the test could be done by eye with a touchstone: the piece to be tested (whether gold or silver) was rubbed on a piece of fine-grained black stone – the 'touchstone' – leaving a streak the colour of which was compared to that from a piece of known fineness. In the hands of a skilled assayer this could be very accurate. However for most of our historic period, 'cupellation' or 'fire assay' was the most common form of test. This was basically a refining process where a sample was scraped from the item to be tested and accurately weighed. It was then wrapped in lead sheet and put into a bone-ash container or 'cupel' and melted in a furnace. The cupel absorbed all the non-precious metals, leaving an amount of pure silver. (When testing gold, some silver is also left, which has to be dissolved out in nitric acid.) The remaining pure metal is then weighed and the two weights compared to give the percentage purity of the alloy. Early silver vessels often retain the 'assay-scrape' where the sample was taken – possibly to prove that assaying had been performed by the cupellation method and to reinforce the validity of the hallmarks. The 1681 regulations set out by the Privy Council which reinforced the Scottish standard and introduced changing annual date-letters, required 'the deacon of the Goldsmiths of Edinburgh to take assay thereof by the copel-assay and no otherways'.[8] In the 19th century an accurate chemical means of assaying silver – 'titration' – was introduced; and more recently, a non-destructive and highly accurate method known as 'X-ray fluorescence' (XRF) has done away with the need to take physical samples from the tested piece.

Legislation Standards and Mark

The first legislation on hallmarking in Scotland was passed by Parliament on 6 March 1458, in an attempt to protect the King's subjects from certain craftsmen, who had obviously been trying to sell wares made from inferior alloys. The law followed earlier English and Continental practices stating that any craftsman who wished to sell silver or gold wares legally must first 'mark' or stamp it with his own unique mark, so that it could be identified as his work. Further, a deacon or leader of the craft was to be appointed in any town or burgh where there were working goldsmiths. This 'understandande and cunnande man of gude concience' [i.e. a skilful and honest man] was to test all wares made by his fellow craftsmen, and if they were at or above the correct standard of 'fineness' he was to mark the piece with his mark. Thus the earliest Scottish 'hallmarks' consisted of the maker's mark followed by the deacon's mark (as yet there was no mark to indicate in which town the craftsmen were based).

This initial legislation also laid down the standard quality of the metal alloy that was legally allowable. Gold was to be no worse than 20 parts pure gold mixed with four parts alloy (i.e. 20 carat, or 83.3% pure gold[9]), and silver was to be no worse that 11 parts pure silver to one part alloy (i.e. 91.6% pure

silver). This meant that, for the first time in Scotland, goldsmiths' customers were guaranteed that if they bought fully marked items the metal used to make them was of the correct purity, and that both the craftsman and deacon could be prosecuted with the full force of law if they were found to be cheating. Their goods and lives would be forfeit to the king. The law also stated that if there is only one goldsmith working in any given town, and therefore no one to act as deacon, then the head officer of the town was to stamp the second mark, although it does not make clear how this official was to perform the necessary assaying.

Abuses seem to have continued, and a further Act was passed in 1473 which stated that 'through the negligence and avarice of … goldsmiths … the said silver … is mynging with laye and other stuife … so … that the peepil [are] gretly scaithit and dissavit' [i.e. goldsmiths were mixing poor quality alloy to the hurt and deceit of the customers]. Again a warden or deacon was appointed to examine the quality of the metal. No mention is made of the actual standards, so we presume that those of 1458 continued.[10]

The next piece of legislation comes in 1485 and yet again decries the great damage that was being done to the country by goldsmiths selling inferior work. In an attempt to tighten this up it was appointed that a mark, indicating which town the piece was made in, was to be stamped alongside that of the maker and deacon. The standard for silver was set again at 11 penny fine or 91.6%. A gold standard is not mentioned and it is presumed that the 20 carat standard continued.[11] From this date all lawful silver should have borne three marks: the maker's mark; the deacon's mark; and the town mark. Unfortunately almost 75 years were to elapse before an object bearing these marks survived – the St Mary's Mazer [3.5].

Several other Acts of Parliament continued to set minimum standards for the fineness of silver and gold and prescribed the marks to be used. In 1681 the Privy Council insisted on certain reforms, including the introduction of annually-changed date-letters. Scotland had her own Parliament until 1707 and her own Privy Council until 1708. The brief table on pp. 18-19 shows the principal legislation as it applied in Scotland.

* * *

Marks not struck at an assay office are not hallmarks. The only two assay offices that have ever existed in Scotland are those of Edinburgh, which still continues, and Glasgow, which operated from 1819 until 1964. As a general rule, the locally-struck marks in the various burghs of the kingdom are not hallmarks at all. For the most part they were applied in the goldsmiths' workshops and the silver thus marked was not subjected to independent assay. A term such as 'local mark' or 'silver mark' describes such marks more accurately; similarly these marks, excluding the maker's initials, are sometimes referred to as 'accompanying marks', because they accompany the maker's initials. In a sense they are all maker's marks, since the maker and no one else was responsible for them. There are some early instances of non-Edinburgh work having been assayed, as is shown by the presence of an assay-scrape, usually just above the mark, but this usage appears to be confined to certain periods in Aberdeen, Canongate, Dundee and Glasgow. What seems certain is that any accompanying marks struck without the benefit of third-party assay, at least since 1681, are technically illegal, even though they are now accepted in most quarters without question.

Edinburgh Assay Office

As we have seen, assaying in Edinburgh was originally carried out by the deacon of the Goldsmiths' Incorporation, probably in his own shop or booth. In 1701 the Incorporation eventually acquired its own premises, and the assay office was situated within the Goldsmiths' Hall from then until now. The Hall's location has varied over the years, starting out in a building abutting Parliament House in Edinburgh's High Street. It is now in Broughton Street, Edinburgh, and is the only assay office in Scotland.

Glasgow Assay Office

Glasgow Assay Office, and the Glasgow goldsmiths' trade in general, mirrored the changing fortunes of the city. By the early 19th century it was buoyant enough to merit its own assay office. An Act of Parliament in 1819 established the Glasgow Goldsmiths Company as a corporate body with the duty of running an assay office in the city, with jurisdiction over a district comprising the city itself and an area 40 miles to its south and west. The permitted standards of metal were the same as those of Edinburgh, but the Sterling standard was to be shown by use of a lion rampant mark. The town mark was the traditional representation of the City arms: tree, fish and bell.

Glasgow Assay Office flourished throughout the 19th century, but fell into decline after the First World War. It struggled on after the Second World War, but was eventually closed in 1964. Its remaining assets and records were transferred to the care of the Incorporation of Goldsmiths of the City of Edinburgh.

2.7 PIX BOX FOR THE GOLD DIET

Early 20th century
H 12.5 cm; L 45.5 cm; W 15 cm
Lent by the Incorporation of Goldsmiths of the City of Edinburgh

Rectangular mahogany box, with central oval brass slot mouth inscribed 'GOLD PIX BOX / INCORPORATION OF GOLDSMITHS / 9 CARAT'; and four other slots with rectangular brass plaques inscribed '14 CARAT', '9 CARAT', '18 CARAT' and '22 CARAT'; with double locks for the deacon and treasurer.

The assay-master was required by law to keep a small representative sample of each pound of marked gold for each of the legal standards of 9, 14, 18 and 22 carat (set in 1932). This was known as the 'diet' and was placed in the box which could only be opened by the deacon and treasurer together. Each year the contents were independently tested by an officer of the Royal Mint, to ensure that the assay-master was working to the required accuracy.

2.8 BALANCE

Used at Edinburgh Assay Office, 19th century until the 1970s
H 56 cm; W 42 cm; Dp 31 cm
Lent by the Incorporation of Goldsmiths of the City of Edinburgh

Accurate weighing was crucial to the assaying process.

2.9 THE ASSAY-MASTER'S ACCOUNTS

Two volumes, 1681-90 and 1690-1702
Lent by the Incorporation of Goldsmiths of the City of Edinburgh

Two volumes which cover the first 21 years of hallmarking by an assay-master rather than by the deacon of the Incorporation. [See image on p. 19.]

Scottish Hallmarking Legislation

1458

First Act. The deacon of the craft to assay the work. Standards required: for gold, 'xx granys' (20 grains, i.e. 20 carats or 83.333 %); for silver 'xj granys' (11 grains, i.e. 11/12 or 91.6̇ %). Marks required (same for gold and silver): maker's mark and deacon's mark. Where there was only one goldsmith in a town, he was to show his work, marked with his own mark, to the head officers of the town, who were to stamp their own mark on the work.[12]

1473

A warden and deacon to be appointed in each town where goldsmiths work. They are to examine the work and put their marks on it. Note: no mention of standards or of a maker's mark.[13]

1475

Goldsmiths forbidden to melt any coins to make wrought work, because of the scarcity of coinage in circulation.[14]

1485

A deacon and searcher to be appointed in each burgh where goldsmiths work. Standard (silver): 'xjd fyne' (11/12 or 91.6̇ %, same as in 1458). Gold not mentioned. Marks appointed: maker's mark, deacon's mark, town mark.[15]

1490

For silver: Standard is to be the same as 'the new siluer werk of brugess' (the standard of Bruges, at that time equal to the touch of Paris). Unfortunately it is by no means clear exactly what this standard was, but it seems to have been 'Sterling or better'. Silver marks required: maker's mark and deacon's mark. For gold: the work is to be returned to the customer at the same standard as the goldsmith received it from the customer; marks not stated. Note: the standard of Bruges was later divided, there being a high standard for large-work and a lower one for small-work; there is some evidence that Scotland's goldsmiths, at least in Edinburgh, were attempting to comply with these alterations.[16]

1555

For silver: the old Scots standard of 'elleuin penny fyne' (91.6̇ %) is restored. Marks: maker's mark and town mark. (A deacon's mark is not mentioned in the act because the deacons of all crafts were temporarily abolished at the time. Instead the magistrates appointed a goldsmith to be a 'visitar' to inspect and mark the work.)
For gold: no goldsmith is to make or offer for sale any gold under the just fineness of 22 carat (91.6̇ %).
Note: this raising of the standard for gold to 22 carat comes 20 years before the same requirement came into force in England. The standards for silver and gold were the same percentage at 91.6̇ %.[17]

1681

The deacon of goldsmiths in Edinburgh to assay the silver by cupellation and to mark it with 'the date by the A.B.C.' (i.e. an annually changing date-letter). The goldsmiths in other burghs are to mark their work with their own mark and 'with the A.B.C.', and to send in their scrapings annually to be assayed in Edinburgh. Work marked otherwise to be deemed illegal under the act.[18]

1719

This is the first act of a parliament of Great Britain to affect Scottish goldsmiths. It came into force on 1 June 1720. It is a shambolic act, so carelessly worded as to be largely unenforceable in Scotland except for the collection of plate duty. It required Sterling standard (92.5 %) as the minimum standard to be used in Scotland for the first time, but it is clear that this seldom if ever happened until 1758, and then only temporarily. Theoretically Britannia standard (95.8 %) became an optional higher standard for the first time, but there is no evidence of it ever having been actually used in Scotland until the 19th century. The maker's mark was to consist of his initials, as formerly. The provisions in the act with regard to assay-office marks were so ludicrous that they were never enforced in Scotland, and do not deserve to be mentioned.[19]

1784

Duties on silver and gold were imposed in the same way as they were in England. All silver made in the whole of Scotland was to be sent to Edinburgh for assay and marking so that duty could be collected on it. In practice this happened only to a small extent, except in the cases of Canongate and Glasgow. The monarch's head was to be applied as a mark to show that the duty had been paid.[20]

1790-1815

Five short acts of Parliament concerned mostly with alterations (always upwards) of the duty payable on wrought plate.

1819

This act established the Glasgow Goldsmiths' Company and the Glasgow Assay Office. It required Sterling standard to be the minimum and it determined what marks should be used there.[21]

1836

This act restated the requirement to send work from all over Scotland (except from the Glasgow area) to Edinburgh for assay and marking. It worked better than the previous attempt in 1784, but was still not universally observed. Sterling standard was required as the minimum.[22]

1854-84

There were several more short acts relating to gold, to foreign imports and to exemptions from marking.

1890

Duty on wrought gold and silver was abolished. Consequently the monarch's head duty mark (introduced in 1784) was discontinued.

1974

This act established the British Hallmarking Council with effect from 1 January 1974 and came into full effect on 1 January 1975. It repealed the whole of the acts of 1719, 1819 and 1836, and the local acts of 1819 and 1826 in relation to Glasgow. Platinum was included for the first time as a metal which required to be assayed and marked. The Edinburgh Assay Office was obliged to adopt a lion rampant instead of its traditional thistle as the Scottish standard mark, an imposition fiercely resisted at the time, but to no effect.[23]

2.10 EDINBURGH ASSAY OFFICE: KING'S DUTY BOOK

2 December 1799 to 4 October 1805

H 42 cm; W (closed) 29 cm; W (open) c.60 cm

Lent by the Incorporation of Goldsmiths of the City of Edinburgh

This book records all the wares brought to Goldsmiths Hall for assaying each day by individual makers. The weights of items are recorded, as duty was paid on each ounce of wrought silver or gold. A 'duty', or tax, on all silver and gold assayed in Great Britain was introduced in December 1784. It started at eight shillings per ounce for gold and six pence per ounce for silver, but varied over the years. To show that this duty had been paid, the assay offices had to stamp another mark, the sovereign's head, on all wares, and keep proper records. The Duty was repealed in 1890.

2.11 GLASGOW ASSAY OFFICE REGISTRATION PLATES

19th century

Lent by the Incorporation of Goldsmiths of the City of Edinburgh

Silversmiths assaying their wares at Glasgow were required to register their maker's punch with the Assay Office there, and a record impression was kept on copper plates. Impressions of the official standard, town

and date-letter punches were also kept on copper plates. When the office closed in 1964, these registration plates and their records were transferred to the Incorporation of Goldsmiths of the City of Edinburgh.

2.12 CUP AND COVER

Robert Gray & Son, Glasgow, 1821-22

Marks (cover underside): king's head (duty mark); tree, fish, bell, etc. (Glasgow); 'RG/&S' (maker Robert Gray & Son); lion rampant (Glasgow sterling standard mark); 'C' (Glasgow date-letter 1821-22); stamped order no. '152' (underside of foot)

H (overall) 40 cm; D 24.4 cm; W 33.2 cm; Wt (all-in) 145.45 oz

Lent by Glasgow Museums and Art Galleries; purchased at Sotheby's sale, Gleneagles Hotel, 28 August 1975, lot no. 56

Reference: McFarlan (1999), pp. 216-17, pl. 7

Bell-shaped body based on Greek *krater* form, with applied band of cast and chased fruiting vine, two vine stem handles and chased acanthus leaves on lower body and cover. Inscription engraved on bowl: 'PRESENTED / To Kirkman Finlay Esquire. / By the Glasgow Goldsmiths Company. / In grateful acknowledgement of his able & successful exertions / IN THE HOUSE OF COMMONS / Respecting the Act establishing an Assay Office / IN THE CITY OF GLASGOW. / MDCCCXIX'.

Kirkman Finlay, a prosperous and influential Glasgow merchant, was MP for the burgh at this time

2.9 (detail)

19

and was instrumental in guiding the legislation setting up the Glasgow Goldsmiths Company through the House of Commons. This Act gave the Company authorisation to set up and run an assay office to serve the city and a district 40 miles to the south and west.

2.13 FOOTED SALVER

Edward & Sons, Glasgow, 1963-64

Marks: 'E&S' (maker Edward & Sons); tree, fish, bell, etc. (Glasgow); lion rampant; thistle (standard marks); 'R' (date-letter 1963-64)

Lent by Glasgow Museums and Art Galleries

Circular dished salver, on spreading trumpet foot. Upper surface engraved: 'The last piece of silver hallmarked at Glasgow Assay Office before it closed in 1964. Ernest Walker [signature] Assay-master'.

This was produced by the long-established Glasgow firm of Edward & Sons for the Glasgow Assay Office

to mark its official closure on 31 March 1964, and was the last piece ever assayed and hallmarked there. The Glasgow Assay Office had been operating at a loss for a long time before the departmental Committee on Hallmarking in 1959 recommended that it be closed, and all hallmarking in Scotland concentrated in Edinburgh.

'The Lovable Craft'

The Incorporation of Goldsmiths of the City of Edinburgh is the oldest body corporate in Scotland still performing the function for which it was instituted: namely, to administer the assaying and marking of silver and gold, and to regulate the craft itself. In their earliest records they referred to themselves as 'The Lovable [or Lauable] Craft', meaning lawful and legally competent.

It was this body in Edinburgh, and the Incorporations of Hammermen in other towns, that tried to ensure that all goldsmiths not only complied with national laws on assaying and the quality of metal, but also conformed to their own craft regulations. The Incorporation of Hammermen of Perth, to which the goldsmiths of that burgh belonged, was apparently even older, since it had an altar dedicated to its patron saint, St Eloi, in St John's Church by 1431, only seven years after the Act of Parliament which brought the office of deacon into existence in Scotland; however, that Incorporation has long ceased to function as an organisation.

The craft structure under which the different incorporated trades operated was similar in all the burghs where goldsmiths worked. In Edinburgh the goldsmiths were numerous enough to form their own Incorporation of Goldsmiths and had separated from the Hammermen by 1492 at the latest. In most other burghs they formed part of the Incorporation of Hammermen. These Incorporations controlled all aspects of their members' work, particularly admission, and until this medieval system began to disintegrate in the 18th century it was legally impossible to set up as a craftsman without being a member of the appropriate incorporation.

Each incorporation had a system of masters training apprentices, who afterwards usually served for a time as journeymen and were then eligible to

2.12

2.13

2.12   2.13

20

become masters. This was normally on the payment of an appropriate fee, completing a test of skill or 'essay' piece, undertaking an oral exam, and being 'of guid lyfe and conversatioun'! An apprentice usually served for seven years, the master supplying board and lodging but no wage. However, the normal period as a journeyman was between one and three years 'for meat and fee', i.e. board and a reduced wage, reflecting his increasing usefulness to the master in his business. These periods were not set, however, and did change with time. The journeymen, who feature less frequently than the masters in the written record, appear from time to time, often trying to assert their rights to better wages and working conditions. They were particularly important as they formed the backbone of the workforce and considerably outnumbered the freemen masters. In Edinburgh they formed the Journeymen Goldsmiths' Society in 1750; and that body in turn teamed up with the Incorporation of Goldsmiths to march in the Great Reform Jubilee parade in 1832 under the banner of United Goldsmiths [see 4.1].

This training system, where craft skills and techniques were passed on from master to apprentice, lasted from the medieval period up to the 20th century, although it started to break down as early as the 18th century as mechanisation and the factory system began to take hold. It was this local system which attempted to ensure the competence of a goldsmith to make 'weill and sufficient wrocht' wares for their customers, while national legislation guaranteed the quality of the metal they used.

As well as the obvious burghs where we have evidence of goldsmiths with surviving marked work, there are a number of other places, such as Linlithgow and Stirling, where we know goldsmiths worked in early times, but for whom no work or marks are known. Both those burghs were sites of royal palaces and they had their own goldsmiths from time to time, mostly attending upon the monarch and the court. In Linlithgow we find John Speddy (1426-31) and James Amisfield (1472), both mentioned in the Exchequer Rolls. In Stirling we know of at least a dozen goldsmiths who were there before 1600. They included Michael Rynd and his son-in-law, the elder William Stalker, who also feature in Edinburgh. Other burghs where goldsmiths worked before 1600 include Berwick, Dumbarton, Dunfermline, Haddington, Lanark, Roxburgh and St Andrews.

In Haddington, *c.*1505-*c.*1510, we find David Furrous, not a goldsmith but a merchant, who supplied George Brown, Bishop of Dunkeld, with a tabernacle 'out of Flanderis', a pontifical gold cross, and other precious items of altar graith. He should be mentioned because he represents the many entrepreneurs who brought gold and silver, both wrought metal and coinage, into the kingdom from the Continent and were probably also sometimes responsible for exporting it. Scotland did not exist in a vacuum: the German Ocean, which we now call the North Sea, was not a barrier but a busy highway which connected Scots with their European neighbours. Merchants and others could traverse it without the necessity of travelling through unfriendly England. Bruges, and later Campvere, were Scottish staple ports in the middle ages, and huge quantities of merchandise, including foreign coinage and wrought plate, passed through them to be landed at Berwick, Leith and Aberdeen. The fruits of the resulting exposure to foreign ideas and artistic endeavour are well exemplified by the maces of the University of St Andrews [8.1, 8.2], the earlier mace being of foreign origin and the later one clearly Scottish and wrought in imitation of it.

The objects in this section mainly illustrate the life and work of the Incorporation of Goldsmiths in Edinburgh. There is, however, a large amount of available documentation concerning the goldsmiths in all the other burghs of Scotland.

2.14 ACT OF COUNCIL, 1525-26

Act of the Town Council of Edinburgh in favour of the Incorporation of Goldsmiths of Edinburgh, 1525-26

H 17.7 cm; L 40.5 cm

Lent by the Incorporation of Goldsmiths of the City of Edinburgh, deposited in NAS (GD1/482/21)

This document is now the oldest possession of the Incorporation of Goldsmiths of Edinburgh. It is dated 31 January 1525/26. Its survival is fortuitous because no record of its contents has been preserved in the surviving Council Register. Although we are calling it here an Act of Council, it is in effect a subsidiary Seal of Cause, but there are reasons for keeping the distinction. The original Seal of Cause had probably already been granted by about 1490, but was lost in the 16th century. A new one was granted in 1591.

The Act of Council includes the names of Adam Leys, 'dekin and kirkmaster of the said craft at this present tyme', and 15 other masters. The names are in the same order as that in which they stand at the beginning of the Nominal Roll in the Minute Book, and in all probability that part of the Nominal Roll is likely to have been copied from it. The wording makes it tacitly clear that the Town Council acknowledged the Goldsmiths' existing status, and that they recognised Adam Leys as already being the deacon.

The document relates that the Goldsmiths had handed in a supplication stating that they wished to do honour to God and St Eloi in St Giles Church, but that they had no altar assigned to them. They asked to be given the disused altar of the Holy Blood for the purpose, situated 'behind the north kirk dure', and to rededicate it to St Eloi, their patron saint. St Eloi (St Eligius) was the patron saint of blacksmiths, hammermen and goldsmiths throughout Europe, except in England where they had their own St Dunstan.

The Town Council agreed to their request. They appointed the offering day, on which a public collection was to be made for the upkeep of the altar, to be the day following Midsummer's Day, since St Eloi's principal feast day (1 December) was already reserved for the Hammermen's Incorporation, who had had a different altar dedicated to the same patron since at least 1477. Importantly, the Goldsmiths are permitted to make statutes for the advantage and profit of their craft.

The Goldsmiths' new aisle and altar had been vacated by the Merchants in 1518. It was, and still is, a small side-chapel set at right-angles to the nave and parallel to the north transept of St Giles.

2.15 FIRST MINUTE BOOK OF THE INCORPORATION OF GOLDSMITHS OF EDINBURGH, 1525-1738

Closed: H 31 cm; W 20.5 cm; D 80 cm

Open: H 31 cm; W 45.5 cm ; D c.55 cm

Lent by the Incorporation of Goldsmiths of the City of Edinburgh; deposited on loan to NAS (GD1/482/1)

References: Dalgleish and Maxwell (1987), p. 4; first parts transcribed with notes and comprehensive index by Jean Munro and Henry Steuart Fothringham as *EGM* (2006)

Volume I of the Edinburgh Goldsmiths' Minutes (*EGM*) is a treasury of information which tells us a great deal about the working lives of those goldsmiths who became freemen from 1525 until 1738. The Minutes up to the 1630s were recompiled by James Steuart, the Incorporation's clerk at that time. (The physical book probably dates to *c*.1634). The compilation was undertaken to bring together all the laws and other circumstances of the Incorporation, so that an authoritative petition might be made to Charles I asking to have all the Goldsmiths' former privileges ratified. It is now in print as far as 1700.

The volume begins with the Incorporation's Prayer (still used at meetings today), oaths to be taken on admission, etc. (now dispensed with), and the oral examination administered to each aspiring entrant. Then comes the Nominal Roll, in which the freemen's names were entered, but without dates. The body of the text is in three main sections: part A comprises mostly the election of deacons and the admission of freemen; part B covers the booking of apprentices; and part C gives the remaining acts and statutes of the goldsmiths' craft. There are also some miscellaneous items in different parts of the volume which have been gathered together in the printed version as part D.

2.19

The Gold Smiths of Edinburgh Armorial Badge. Motto. God with Us.

Officer Goldsmiths' Incorporation.

2.16 TRAVELLING WRITING SET

Thomas Cleghorne II, Edinburgh, 1674

Mark: 'TC' in monogram only (maker and deacon Thomas Cleghorne II 1673-74)

L 18 cm; D (base) 5.7 cm; Wt 6.29 oz

H.MEQ 1238; given by the Incorporation of Goldsmiths of the City of Edinburgh

References: *EGM* (2006) A331, *et seq.*; Dalgleish and Maxwell (1987), no. 18

Composite piece in five sections which, when screwed together, forms the shape of a hand bell with cylindrical handle. The sections are a candle holder, a sand box, an inkwell, a quill holder, and a seal matrix. The rim of the sand box is engraved: 'Giftit * be * the * Goldsmiths* of * Ed.r. * to * Nicol Sommervell / their Clerk Anno 1674'.

Nicol Somervell, as Clerk of the Incorporation at that time, was undoubtedly heavily involved in the legal work leading up to the granting of the Incorporation's Royal Charter in 1687. This writing set, which was presented at the beginning of Somervell's first term of office, has only the maker's mark for Thomas Cleghorne. Cleghorne was deacon in 1673-74, when he made the writing set. It came into the possession of the Cunningham family of goldsmiths who presented it to the Incorporation in 1819.

2.17 CHAIR OF THE DEACON OF THE INCORPORATION OF GOLDSMITHS OF EDINBURGH

Probably by Francis Braidwood, Edinburgh, *c*.1809

H 112 cm; W 75 cm; D 75 cm

Lent by the Incorporation of Goldsmiths of the City of Edinburgh

Reference: Dalgleish and Maxwell (1987), p. 47, no. 55

Armed chair, mahogany and leather, the back, arms and feet carved with lions' heads and paws. This

chair was probably made by the Edinburgh furniture maker Francis Braidwood as part of the furnishings bought to equip the new Goldsmiths Hall on South Bridge, Edinburgh, in 1809.

2.18 BADGE AND CHAIN OF OFFICE OF THE DEACON OF THE INCORPORATION OF GOLDSMITHS OF EDINBURGH

P. Cunningham & Sons, Edinburgh, 1809-10

Badge: H 9 cm; W 5.8 cm

Lent by the Incorporation of Goldsmiths of the City of Edinburgh

Reference: Dalgleish and Maxwell (1987), p. 47, no. 58

Gold plain oval badge struck with the arms of the Edinburgh Incorporation, suspended from a chain. The badge shows the arms of the Incorporation as they were used up to 1987, when a new coat of arms was matriculated with the Court of the Lord Lyon. The deacon still wears the badge today at ceremonial and official occasions.

2.19 UNIFORM OF THE OFFICER OF THE INCORPORATION OF GOLDSMITHS OF EDINBURGH

Replica, made by David Wilcox, based on the illustration of the Officer, in a collection of watercolour sketches of *Old Edinburgh Characters* by J. C. Howie, *c*.1840

H 195 cm; W 56 cm; Dp 6 cm

Lent by the Incorporation of Goldsmiths of the City of Edinburgh

Reference: Dalgleish and Maxwell (1987), p. 10, col. pl. 3

The Officer was a paid servant of the Incorporation who acted as caretaker for the Hall and performed a variety of official duties to uphold the status and dignity of the Incorporation. The watercolour sketch on page 22 shows him wearing the silver armorial shoulder badge and the bicorn hat, both of which still survive.

2.20 ARMORIAL BADGE OF THE OFFICER OF THE INCORPORATION OF GOLDSMITHS OF EDINBURGH

James Tait, Edinburgh, 1725-26

Marks: 'JT in monogram' (maker James Tait); castle (Edinburgh); 'EP' (assay-master Edward Penman); 'V' (date-letter 1725-26)

H 21 cm; W 17 cm; Wt 12.4 oz

NMS: IL.2003.48; lent by the Incorporation of Goldsmiths of the City of Edinburgh

Reference: Dalgleish and Maxwell (1987), no. 60, pl. 31

2.16 (mark inset)

Oval central panel cast and chased with the arms of the Incorporation, based on the arms of the London Goldsmiths' Company; crest is a diamond ring, with the motto 'GOD WITH US' in a ribbon above. Rim of the badge has 'THE GOLD SMITH'S OF EDINBURGH'S ARMORIAL BADGE' in raised letters, the outer edge pierced with holes for fixing it to a garment.

Goldsmiths, like most other Trade Incorporations, exercised a traditional right to have their own insignia and badges, often decorated with their arms, for display at their official functions and celebrations. This badge is the earliest surviving piece of the Goldsmiths' insignia showing their arms, although only the central section has the maker's mark. It is very similar in shape and construction to several existing 18th-century armorial badges relating to other Edinburgh trades and institutions, such as the wrights and masons and that of the Officer of the Bank of Scotland [see 8.14]. However, it is possible this badge was altered in the early 19th century, as the wording of the outer rim is not consistent with the earlier date. It had certainly achieved its present shape by about 1840 when it is depicted sewn on to the sleeve of the Officer in a watercolour of that date [see p. 22].

2.21 CARVED STONE PANEL, SHOWING A GOLDSMITH'S WORKSHOP (MODERN CAST)

From the frieze in the portico of George Heriot's School, Edinburgh, c.1630

L 69 cm; H 38 cm

Reproduced courtesy of the Governors of George Heriot's Trust

Reference: Dalgleish and Maxwell (1987), no. 17

George Heriot III (see p. 25) died in 1624, leaving c.£23,000 sterling from his fortune to endow a hospital to care for and educate orphan sons of Edinburgh burgesses. His executors took some time to wind up his complicated estate, and work on the building did not start until 1628. Although the architect is unknown, the master mason responsible for the early phase of work was William Wilson. Construction continued under several masons and intermittently until it was finally completed in 1693. The building has been described as the most complete example of Jacobean architecture in Scotland.

This panel shows the earliest surviving depiction of a goldsmith's workshop in Scotland. One of the most remarkable features, however, is just how little such a workshop changed over the centuries. The main elements – bench with semi-circular work positions,

PORTRAIT OF DEACON FRANCIS HOWDEN

Unknown artist, c.1817, oil on canvas in ornate gilt-wood frame

H 268 cm; W 177 cm

Lent by the Incorporation of Goldsmiths of the City of Edinburgh

Reference: Dalgleish and Maxwell (1987), p. 16, no. 54, pl. 4

Francis Howden was a prolific Edinburgh goldsmith and important member of the Incorporation. Admitted as a master in 1781, he went on to become deacon in 1811-13. However, it was his various stints as Treasurer that led to him being captured in oils. He was instrumental in reorganising the Goldsmiths' Widows' Annuity Scheme – which he points to in the painting. This was a very necessary financial safety net for the widows of deceased masters, at a time when there was no state provision for hard times. In 1817 he was presented by the Incorporation with a piece of silver as a mark of gratitude for this work by the Incorporation, and this is presumably the cup shown in the background. He is also shown wearing the deacon's gold badge of office, and is standing by the deacon's chair [2.17 and 2.18].

GEORGE HERIOT III

Oil on canvas, attributed to John Scougall,
copy of a portrait of about 1615

H 151 cm; W 120 cm

Lent by the Governors of George Heriot's Trust

Reference: *The Art of Jewellery in Scotland*, p. 30

George Heriot is perhaps Scotland's best-known goldsmith/ jeweller. However, his fame owes more to the immortality bestowed on him by Sir Walter Scott in *The Fortunes of Nigel* (where the nickname 'Jinglin Geordie' first appears), and to his charitable endowment of the Edinburgh school which bears his name, than it does to his work as a craftsman. No piece of gold or silver work survives with his maker's mark, and only one or two jewels can be confidently ascribed to his workshop. We do know, however, that he made and supplied a large amount of jewellery for the Royal Family, especially for Anne of Denmark, consort of King James VI and I. His vast fortune was principally derived from this Royal patronage, and from his role as money-lender to the King and Queen. In 1609, for example, the Queen owed him £18,000 sterling.

Heriot, like many Edinburgh goldsmiths, came from a family steeped in the craft. His father, also George, was a very prominent Edinburgh goldsmith, and served as deacon for most of the period 1565-1608; he was a member of Edinburgh City Council, 1584-85 and 1586-87; he repre-sented Edinburgh in Parliament; and he received at least one commission from King James VI.

George Heriot was born in 1563. Two younger brothers, David and James, also became goldsmiths, being admitted as freemen on 26 January 1593 and 14 May 1594 respec-tively. George himself, having been apprenticed to his father, was admitted as a freeman on 28 May 1588. Previously, in 1586, he had married the daughter of an Edinburgh trades-man, with whom he had three sons and a daughter. His father gave him £80 to set up a 'booth' on the north side of St Giles. In his small workshop, reputedly just seven feet square, he produced gold and silver work of such quality that in 1597 he was appointed goldsmith to Queen Anne for life. The same year the Incorporation of Goldsmiths of Edinburgh elected him their deacon. In 1601 he was appointed King's jeweller, and probably about this time began to lend both the King and the Queen considerable sums of money. In 1603 he followed the court to London and established himself near the New Exchange in the Strand. He became a leading supplier of jewellery, gold and silver work to the Court, and to members of the aristocracy.

After his first wife died, he married Alison Primrose in 1609. She was daughter of James Primrose of Carrington, clerk to the Scots Privy Council and grandfather of the first Earl of Rosebery. This alliance indicated, and·reinforced, the social status which he had acquired. Royal debts, how-ever, went unpaid, so in 1620 he was awarded a three-year grant of the tax on sugar, doubtless an extremely lucrative arrangement.

By the time of his death in 1624 he owned an estate at Roehampton and a house near St Martin-in-the-Fields. His second wife died childless in 1613 and two of his sons died during their sea passage to London. With his family much reduced, he left almost half of the staggering sum of over £50,000 sterling to endow a charitable institution for the sons of 'decayed burgesses of Edinburgh', along the lines of London's Christ's Hospital. George Heriot's School continues to this day to commemorate his name, his achievement and his philanthropy.

complete with leather bags to catch gold and silver
scrapings, the furnace, anvil, hammers and other tools
– would be quite recognisable to a silversmith today.

2.22 'A PERFECT BOOK OF ARMS'

Illustrations to accompany the *Balfour Armorial*, c.1633

Lent by Lyon Office, Edinburgh

Two intriguing entries in the Register of the Privy
Council in 1630 censured certain goldsmiths for
engraving unauthorised armorials on their work
(9 July and 5 August 1630). The rules and procedures
governing the use of heraldry have always been much
stricter in Scotland than in any other country in the
world. They were, and still are, enforceable by law.
Seventeen named Edinburgh goldsmiths were com-
plained against by their lordships as having been guilty
not only of error but of unwillingness to reform their
malpractices. Part of the prescribed remedy was that
the Lord Lyon was to compile a perfect Book of Arms
and give an exact copy of it to the deacon of the Goldsmiths, to remain with him and his successors, to serve
as an authority to govern the engraving of correct arms
from thenceforth. The deacon's copy is no longer to be
found and in all probability it was lost in the fire at
Goldsmiths' Hall in 1796. However, what is believed
to be the Lord Lyon's copy still exists and is now in
Lyon Office. It relates to the verbal description given
in the manuscript *Balfour Armorial* of about the
same date, now in the National Library of Scotland.

An additional requirement imposed on the Goldsmiths by the Privy Council was that they were forbidden to make silver badges for messengers-at-arms
without a warrant from the Lord Lyon. This was
because some messengers, who had been dismissed
by the new Lord Lyon, and who had had their badges
of office confiscated, were applying covertly to certain
goldsmiths for unauthorised replacements.

All this heraldic activity was due to the zeal of the
newly-installed Lord Lyon King of Arms, Sir James
Balfour of Denmiln and Kinnaird (1600-57). Sir James,
like the proverbial new broom, immediately applied
to the Privy Council to introduce measures to curb
abuses, especially the engraving of unauthorised arms.

2.23 PANEL PAINTED WITH THE ARMS OF THE INCORPORATION OF GOLDSMITHS OF EDINBURGH

Unknown artist, 1832

H 86.5 cm; W 96.5 cm

Lent by the Incorporation of Goldsmiths of the City of Edinburgh

Reference: Dalgleish and Maxwell (1987), no. 62

Wooden panel with gilt wood frame; painted with the
arms of the Incorporation on a shield supported by
the figures of Mercury and Britannia with a circular
shield inscribed 'Reform Jubilee 1832', a scene of the
City of Edinburgh in the background, and their motto
'God With Us' in a ribbon above.

As with other trades and professions across
Scotland, some goldsmiths were active in the political
agitation which resulted in the passing of the Reform
Act in 1832. Before this, political representation within
the burghs had been strictly within the control of the
self-electing Town Council. Although the Incorporation
of Goldsmiths in Edinburgh had some representation
on the Council, through their deacon, individually they
had no vote. The passing of the Reform Act effectively
gave the vote to the growing middle classes: there had

never been any intention on the part of most reformers to grant full democratic rights to the working classes or to women. The changes meant that anyone owning property valued at over £10 per year could now vote for their member of parliament. This removed the in-built domination of the Town Council by the merchants, and prevented the Council's interference in the selection of the Incorporation's deacon.

Before the celebrations on the passing of the Act, the Incorporation was asked, and agreed, to lend their banners and insignia to the Society of Journeymen Goldsmiths who took part in the great Reform Jubilee Trades Procession through the streets of Edinburgh on 11 August 1832. This consisted of representatives of 71 trades, carrying no fewer than 120 flags, 300 banners and about 600 insignia of various kinds, and stretching in a line nearly three miles long, five abreast, moving from Bruntsfield Links down to Leith Walk. The Goldsmiths were number 52 in the procession, and there is a detailed account in *The Scotsman* newspaper of the day of their representatives and insignia. The journalist singled out for praise the young lady playing the part of Britannia (a reference to the higher quality metal then in use) '… bearing aloft her trident and riding in a triumphal car … who … deported herself with great propriety and was hailed with repeated acclamations …'. This panel was no doubt part of the decoration of this 'triumphal car'.

2.24 GONFALON OF THE INCORPORATION OF GOLDSMITHS OF EDINBURGH

*c.*1832 / H 167 cm; W 118 cm

NMS: H.LF 25; given by the Incorporation of Goldsmiths of the City of Edinburgh

Swallow-tailed flag for suspension from pole with crossbar; of blue-green silk painted with a cartouche shaped shield with the arms of the Incorporation of Goldsmiths of Edinburgh, with sprigs of thistles to either side and 'Goldsmiths'/ 'God With Us' in ribbons above and below.

Such flags were for carrying in processions, and this one may well have been painted specifically for the huge civic procession through the streets of Edinburgh to mark the passing of the Great Reform Act in 1832. The Goldsmiths of Edinburgh were particularly prominent in this march [see 2.23]. The gonfalon continued to be used for ceremonial purposes and appears in several late-19th century photographs of the interior of Goldsmiths Hall.

2.25 CUP

John Crichton III, Edinburgh, 1881-82

Marks (on body): queen's head (duty mark); thistle (assay mark); 'J.C' (maker John Crichton); castle (Edinburgh); 'Z' (date-letter 1881-82)

H 18 cm; D (rim) 8.1 cm; D (foot) 7 cm

Lent by the Incorporation of Goldsmiths of the City of Edinburgh

Silver, goblet-shaped cup, on slender baluster stem; the body chased with elaborate strap-work; panels engraved with the arms of the Incorporation of Goldsmiths of Edinburgh and inscriptions. The inscriptions on the cup relate that Crichton, a member of a long-established family of Edinburgh goldsmiths, started his apprenticeship on 18 October 1854 and completed it on 18 October 1861, after the usual seven years' service. He was not admitted as a Master of the Incorporation until 1882 when this cup was presented as his traditional 'essay piece'. The intervening years were passed as a journeyman to some other master. He went on to become deacon in 1889 and treasurer in 1891.

Notes

1 Atkinson (1825), p. 1.
2 Ibid., p. 9.
3 King James VI to Sir Bevis Bulmer.
4 Clayton (1985), p. 200.
5 Quoted in Finlay (1991), p. 49.
6 Atkinson (1825), p. 49.
7 We are indebted to Iain Gordon Brown for this reference from the Lothian Papers (NAS GD 40/XVIII/1/1), quoted in Brown (1987), p. 7.
8 *RPC* (Register of the Privy Council), third series, vol. 7, pp. 103-04 (16 April 1681), para. 7.
9 *APS*, 1457, cap. 8, II, 48.
10 *APS*, 1473, cap. 17, II, 105.
11 *APS*, 1485, cap. 15, II, 172. When measuring the quality of gold, each ounce was traditionally divided into a nominal 24 grains or carats, and alloys were described as a fraction of this – i.e. pure gold is 24 carat, while for example 9 carat gold contains only 37.5% pure gold and 62.5% alloy.
12 *APS*, James II, cap. 8 (6 March 1457/8).
13 *APS*, James III, cap. 17 (23 July 1473).
14 *APS*, James III, cap. 7 (7 December 1475).
15 *APS*, James III, cap. 15 (26 May 1485).
16 *APS*, James IV, cap. 13 (15 February 1489/90).
17 *APS*, Mary, cap. 34 (20 June 1555).
18 *RPC*, Act of the Privy Council (25 February to 9 June 1681).
19 6, George I, cap. 11 (1719).
20 24, George III, sess. 2, cap. 53 (1784).
21 59, George III, cap. xxviii (19 May 1819).
22 6 and 7, William IV, cap. 69 (1 October 1836).
23 Act 21, Elizabeth, cap. 43 (25 July 1973).

Surviving the Melting Pot

3

Introduction

Because of their versatility, silver and gold are arguably the original 'green' materials, endlessly capable of being melted down and recycled into either hard cash or newer, more fashionable pieces. This more than anything has led to the absolute paucity of surviving Scottish marked domestic silver wares from the period before about 1660. Despite a determined attempt, it has still been impossible to find more than about two dozen early examples of hollow ware. Although there are certainly some surviving examples that have not been located, in truth very few actually survived the melting pot. This does not mean, however, that Scotland was always devoid of a rich and varied range of silver and gold wares, as those pieces that do survive present a tantalising glimpse of what must have been a fascinating and much larger corpus of work.

This illusive wealth in the domestic sphere is also hinted at in what survives for ceremonial and ecclesiastical use. A large number of church communion and baptismal vessels survive from the 17th century onwards (although virtually nothing survives from earlier than 1585), and some ceremonial pieces such as the Scottish university maces are absolute glories of the craft. Their survival will be discussed in later chapters, but for the moment we will look at the reasons for the disappearance of so much early silver and gold used in the homes of wealthy Scots.

As noted above, the value of silver and gold vessels was primarily in the weight and quality of the metal; and the need for an owner to liquidate his assets to provide ready cash was simply achieved by literally melting down the family silver. This no doubt accounted for the astonishing dearth of surviving early pieces. In times of national emergency, gold and silver vessels could be, and were, gathered in and converted into cash to prosecute whatever cause was current. During the religious wars of the 1640s, for example, the Covenanting Party set up well-organised war committees to raise cash. These committees had the power to gather in 'all silver worke and gold worke in Scotland' and to melt it down for the common cause.[1] The owners were promised compensation for the value of their plate, but in the meantime this act no doubt spelled the end of many fine examples of domestic silver and gold. It appears that £293,650 worth of silver was handed to the Mint in a single year, equating to 91,750 ounces of plate being melted down and turned into coin.[2] In 1644 an Aberdeen baronet, Sir Thomas Burnett of Leys, handed in nearly 4000 ounces of his family silver, and in 1649 he was still awaiting compensation.[3]

{opposite page}
3.7 THE CRAIGIEVAR MAZER, c.1575-91

The other enemy to the survival of early vessels was simply the vagaries of fashion. By their very nature, expensive gold and silver vessels were luxury goods, sought after by the wealthy, powerful and fashion-conscious élites of society. The ability to display one's good taste as well as wealth by an elaborate display of appropriate vessels in 'the most modern fashion' was a social necessity.

In the late medieval and early modern periods, while it is clear that Scotland commanded less disposable wealth for such luxury goods than her southern neighbour, this poverty was relative. Even a cursory study of the numerous surviving inventories makes it clear that across a wide range of social standings there was a considerable amount of silver being used. Not only the royal household and the great aristocratic families, but the lairds, gentry and growing merchant class also aspired to own 'weill wrought' plate, and listed it accordingly in testaments and household inventories and accounts.

The inventory of Sir Colin Campbell of Glenorchy, dated 1640, gives some indication of the range and quantity of silver vessels deemed appropriate to a Highland chieftain. Among many other items mentioned are twelve silver plates, four great silver chargers, a great silver basin and laver 'partlie overgilt', a dozen silver trenchers and a dozen silver saucers, several great silver cups with covers, 'a silver cuppe partlie overgilt with ane face on the bottome of it', six silver-gilt goblets 'that goes within [each] other', three silver-gilt salt fats, and a 'great maser with ane silver lip quhilk will conteine a quart quhilk also has ane silver foot' (a near perfect contemporary description of a typical Scottish standing mazer). The Glenorchy inventory goes on to enumerate over 50 silver spoons (but no forks or knives are mentioned), and many pieces were engraved with the laird's arms or name.[4] It is likely that not all of this was made by Scottish goldsmiths, as many Highland lairds had extensive social, political and economic contacts with England and the Continent – but much undoubtedly was.

Nor was Colin Campbell of Glenorchy's inventory exceptional. Just a few years before, in 1635, the 3rd Earl of Mar and his mother divided the goods of his recently deceased father and noted that he was to have 'the best Bason and Laver thereto, one dozen of best silver Dishes, one Dozen of silver Trenchers, ane Mazer, the Best Silver Cupe, and little Silver Cups for aquavite, the best Salt, ane Vinegar Stoupe, ane other Silver Stoupe for drink, one Duzon of Spoons, two Silver Chandlers …'.[5] What now survives of such household plate in no way shows this range. With the exception of the remarkable group of mazers, one now searches in vain for Scottish silver plates, trenchers, cups and salts and 'chandlers' (candlesticks).

Even further up the social scale one finds the same problem. The vast stores of silver and gold plate, jewels and other treasure amassed by Stewart monarchs such as James III, IV and V in the heady days of the Scottish renaissance of the 15th and 16th centuries are now largely gone. Again, what does survive suggests that Scottish goldsmiths were capable of supplying the wants of the nation, even if their technical skill was somewhat inferior to that of the best Continental workers. The magnificent Scottish Crown and Sceptre, now part of the Honours of Scotland displayed in the Crown Room of Edinburgh Castle, were refashioned in the 1530s and '40s by the Edinburgh goldsmiths John Mosman and Adam Leys respectively. That Scotland possesses the oldest surviving royal crown in Britain, and indeed one of the oldest in Europe, is sometimes overlooked.

But further down the social scale the picture is repeated, with little now surviving to represent the work of Scotland's early craftsmen. A few years after the remaking of the crown, in 1567, a Kirkcaldy merchant, Robert Wilson, successfully laid claim to the goods of one Marion Williamson, the widow of a merchant. Within a fairly extensive list of household goods and plenishings, there was recorded 'ane silver spone … ane silver drinking piece … [and] … ane maser'.[6]

By the beginning of the early modern period, lairds and merchants were clearly trying to emulate their social superiors in displaying their wealth and taste in increasingly elaborate displays of plate. This desire continued to manifest itself into the 19th century when the possession of a set of six silver teaspoons, or a silver tea-service, ranked alongside the acquisition of a long-case clock as a mark of social respectability. There are many other examples in 16th- and 17th-century inventories of the wide range of silver goods that were made and supplied by Scottish goldsmiths.

However, as can be seen in the catalogue below, virtually nothing survives, and what does presents a curiously distorted picture. The survivals often seem to be 'curiosities' – mounted nautilus shells, coconuts and mazers. It is possible that as these were not made entirely of silver, they were not considered worth melting down. Certainly mounted items form a disproportionate amount of the surviving corpus. One of the major difficulties confronting the researcher is that there are so few surviving marked objects that there is not enough material for corroboration; it is sometimes difficult to identify accurately persons of the same initials at about the same time.

Mazers

In the second half of the 16th century the mazer was a common form of drinking vessel, both for practical use and as an ostentatious ornament. Only nine Scottish mazers still exist, but numerous inventories show that there were many others which have not survived. Nevertheless, there are more mazers than all the other forms of drinking vessels of that period put together.

Of the nine known Scottish mazers featured in this book, the Bute Mazer [3.1] is unique among them for its early date, its wooden bowl with no stem, and its original lid. While the boss, bowl and lid date from c.1320, the rim, straps and foot were added in the 16th century at about the time that standing mazers were the height of fashion.

Mazers were status symbols of their time, often possessed by well-to-do merchants and burgesses and by the landed gentry. Although inventories of noblemen also show the presence of mazers in that class of ownership, none of them has survived. The burgess class could afford them because their money went further if they were paying mostly for a wooden bowl with only comparatively few ounces of silver added to it.

The form of the mazer passed through various stages of evolution during the c.80 years of its greatest popularity (c.1540-c.1620). From as early as 1575 the term 'silver mazer' can be found, which is clearly in contrast with what we think of as the typical form with a wooden bowl. The weight of metal in these so-called silver mazers makes it clear that they were indeed made wholly of silver, and so we need to find a way to distinguish between silver mazers and vessels of similar weight described merely as cups.

The answer lies in the method of manufacture. The Minutes of the Incorporation of Goldsmiths of Edinburgh show that there were different rates chargeable for mazer work and for cup work. In about 1555 the goldsmiths of Edinburgh were allowed to charge 36 pence per ounce for mazer work, while plain work was charged at 32 pence per ounce.[7] This was presumably because of the greater difficulty and ornamentation of the work.

Two examples of silver mazers have survived, each of them unique, both from the early years of the 17th century. They are the objects known as the St Leonard's Mazer [3.8] and the Bell of Cowcaddens Mazer [3.9]. Controversy has hitherto existed as to whether the St Leonard's Mazer originally had a wooden bowl, or was made as we know it today with a silver one. There now seems no doubt the latter is the case and that it is the sole surviving representative of the standing silver mazers, once common in many households. It is transitional in the form and method of manufacture between the traditional wooden-bowled mazer and the all-silver cup. It is different from the latter in that its rim was made separately and then fitted to the silver bowl in the same way as it would have been attached to a wooden one. It also shows how the mazer-shaped communion cup evolved, as discussed on page 143. The Cowcaddens Mazer, though a unique survivor, represents a relatively common type of vessel in its day. A number of inventories refer to silver mazers of roughly comparable weight, sometimes several in one household.

Notes

1 Burns (1892), pp. 144-45.
2 R. B. K Stevenson (1972), p. 90.
3 Act Charles II, 12 June 1649 (APS, vol. VI(ii), pp. 404-05).
4 Breadalbane (Marquess of) (1855), pp. 346-48.
5 NAS: Mar and Kellie Papers (GD 124/3/37).
6 Macbean (1908), pp. 314-15.
7 EGM (2006), C26, p. 213.

3.1 THE BUTE MAZER

Unmarked; bowl, boss and lid c.1320; rim, foot and straps c.1565; possibly by Peter Lymeburner, Glasgow

H 11 cm; D (bowl) 25.7 cm; Wt (all-in) 28.26 oz

Lent from a private collection at Mount Stuart

Provenance: Bannatyne of Kames family; McGregor of McGregor; How of Edinburgh

References: Renwick (1897); J. H. Stevenson (1931), pp. 217-55; How (1934[ii]), pp. 394-96; Finlay and Fothringham (1991), pp. 30-31; Barrow (1998), pp. 122-32 and plates; Glenn (2003), pp. 34-38

3.1

3.1 (details)

Maplewood bowl set on a simple rolled silver foot, joined to a silver rim by six hinged and pinned dentilled straps; the deep rim has a serrated lower edge, then a beaded wire and a panel with the inscription against a cross-hatched ground, finishing with a stamped wire of lozenges and squares. The inside of the bowl is set with a silver gilt and enamel print cast, cased and engraved, with a central lion surrounded by six enamelled shields with the arms of the supporters of Robert Bruce (1314-30).

Dr Glenn, in her recent masterly assessment of the Bute Mazer, puts the print firmly in the period 1314-27 and suggests it was commissioned by the Gilbertson family (ancestors of the Hamiltons). She has no doubt that it is by a Scottish craftsman. The mazer eventually came into the hands of the Bannatyne of Kames family on the Isle of Bute, as is recorded on the inscription. They were probably responsible for having a new foot, rim and straps added, to consolidate what was by then an old and fragile vessel.

The rim being unmarked, there can be no certainty as to its maker, but a small scrap of circumstantial evidence suggests it might have been Peter Lymeburner, goldsmith in Glasgow. The engraving round the rim mentions Robert, son of Ninian Bannatyne of Kames, who conducted business in the house of Peter Lymeburner, goldsmith in Glasgow, on 22 April 1567. From this we know the two men knew each other on a business footing. It is thus reasonable to speculate Lymeburner could have made the mounts for this mazer.

3.2 THE WATSON MAZER

Possibly Adam Leys, Edinburgh, c.1540

Marks: fleur-de-lis in an octagonal punch with concave sides, struck four times (poss. maker's mark of Adam Leys, Edinburgh)

H 15.3 cm; D (bowl) 18.9 cm; Wt (all-in) 24.74 oz

NMS A.1948.132; purchased with help from the National Art-Collections Fund: London Scot Bequest

References: Finlay (1948 [iii]), pp. 101-02; How (1949), pp. 16-17; Finlay and Fothringham (1991), pp. 61-64 and pl. 18

The wooden bowl has a silver-gilt rim engraved with a running motif of foliage issuing from cornucopiæ below a slightly scalloped edge emphasised with engraved feathered lines. Print consists of a roundel engraved with the coat of arms of Watson of Sauchton between the initials 'D V', for David Watson of Sauchton, and is raised on a boss of 16 radiating raised lobes which match the strap-shaped lobes on the foot. The stem, attached to the bowl by a later silver flange and iron screw-thread, is engraved with a band of running foliage against a hatched background. The inscription round the foot reads: 'TYNE * GEIR * TYNE LITIL * TYNE HONOVR TYNE MVCKIL TYNE * HART * TYNE AL *' ['lose possessions, lose little; lose honour, lose much; lose heart, lose all'].

32

The Watson Mazer is evidently the earliest in the sequence of Scottish standing mazers, coming near the end of the reign of James V (1513-42) and roughly contemporary with the Scottish Crown and Sceptre. While stylistically rather unlike the later mazers, the coat of arms on the print and the inscription around the foot show that it is of Scottish origin. Recent spectrographic analysis of the different parts does not bear out earlier findings that purported to show that the silver of the foot was of a different composition from that of the rim and print. On the contrary, it is now believed that the two parts were not married together, as previously thought, but that the mazer is a coherent whole and stands today substantially as it was made. What is also certain, however, is that it was at some remote time seriously damaged and was rather clumsily repaired, hence the anomalies of its present construction. The controversy which once surrounded the mazer seems at last to have been laid to rest.

The new attribution of the Watson Mazer to Adam Leys is only a very tentative speculation. It has to be admitted at once that there is no other example, either known or suspected, of a 16th-century Scottish goldsmith using a rebus of his surname rather than his initials (usually in monogram) as his maker's mark. The nature of such marks as may have been used in Scotland before the Act of 1555 is unknown, since it is reasonably certain that the goldsmiths were not complying with the provisions of the previous acts on the subject. It is clear that there were very many fleur-de-lis punches from different places across Europe, and that not all of them were intended to indicate a town of origin; some were perhaps standard marks and others maker's marks. This usage, so widespread and diverse, is a complex matter of which no complete study has yet been undertaken.

3.2 (detail)

3.2

3.3

3.4

3.3 THE TULLOCH MAZER

James Gray, Canongate, c.1557

H 19.8 cm; D (bowl) 20.3 cm; D (print) 7.6 cm; Wt (all-in) 28.2 oz

Marks (on rim): 'IG' in monogram (maker James Gray); stag lodged (Canongate)

Lent from a private collection at Mount Stuart

Provenance: Tulloch of Tannochy family; How of Edinburgh (1933)

References: Elizabethan Exhibition (1933); RSM (1948), no. 180; How (1934[ii]), pp. 400-01; Finlay and Fothringham (1991), p. 67

The baluster stem is chased and repoussé in three panels of acanthus foliage, a cord of guilloche connecting the stem to the foot, the latter repoussé with 15 oval cabochon lobes; the moulded silver-gilt rim is profusely decorated with scrolling foliage issuing from a green man and a green woman, and with various creatures among the leaves. The print is fixed to the bowl by four pins and is inscribed 'HONORA ◊ DEVM ◊ EX TOTA ◊ ANIMA ◊ TVA', together with the date '1557'. There is a letter 'T' on each side of the coat of arms of Tulloch of Tannochy.

This is the earliest fully-marked definitely ascribed piece of Scottish silver and arguably represents the finest work of any Scottish goldsmith of the 16th century. Its engraved date is only two years after the Act of 1555 which reinstated the Old Scots Standard after the period when the Standard of Bruges had prevailed. The figures of the green man and green woman are unique as designs on Scottish silver of the period.

3.4 THE GALLOWAY MAZER

James Gray, Canongate, engraved date 1569

Marks: on the rim, below engraved initials; stag lodged (Canongate); 'IG' in monogram (maker James Gray)

H 20.7 cm; D (rim) 22.2 cm; D (foot) 14 cm; Wt (all-in) 35.26 oz

NMS H.MEQ 148; purchased with the help of the National Art-Collection Fund, The Pilgrim Trust, and Society of Antiquaries of Scotland

Provenance: by descent to the Earl of Galloway; Sotheby's sale, London, 1954

References: Burns (1892), pp.194-95; How (1934[ii]), pp. 405-08; Finlay and Fothringham (1991), p. 67; RCEWA (1954), R1

Maplewood bowl, with silver gilt rim attached by a band of cut foliage decoration, the rim body engraved with a running band of scrolling foliage, within which are three shields, engraved with the arms of Stewart and Acheson, an 'eagle displayed' (the Acheson crest) and initials 'AS EA'. The bowl is set on a baluster stem chased with acanthus leaves, which in turn is set

3.2

3.2 (detail)

3.2 (detail)

3.3

3.3

3.3 (detail)

3.3

3.4

3.5

on a spreading stepped foot, with egg and nail head moulding. The inside of the bowl has a circular boss engraved with a band of scrolling foliage on a hatched ground, with the initials 'AS.AE' above, and in the centre the inscription 'Proverb. 22 / Ane . good . mane / is . to . be . chosen / above . great . riches / and . loving . favour / is . above . silver and . above / moste . fyne /. Golde. / 1569'.

With the earlier Tulloch Mazer [3.3], these are the finest examples of the type, displaying a very distinctively Scottish interpretation of the Renaissance love of foliate decoration. Its commissioner was clearly a man of considerable taste. Archibald Stewart became Lord Provost of Edinburgh in 1579, and his descendants went on to inherit the Earldom of Galloway. The mazer, which probably passed to the Earls of Galloway in the mid-18th century, was no doubt commissioned to mark Stewart's marriage to Ellen Acheson in 1569, the same year he was admitted as a burgess of Edinburgh.

3.5 ST MARY'S MAZER

Alexander Auchinleck, Edinburgh, c.1556-58 or 1561-62

Marks (on rim): 'A' monogram (maker Alexander Auchinleck); castle (Edinburgh); 'TE' in monogram (deacon Thomas Ewing)

H 16 cm; D (bowl) 22.8 cm; D (foot) 11.3 cm; Wt 20.09 oz

Lent by the University of St Andrews

References: Burns (1892), pp. 192-93; How (1934[ii]), pp. 396-97; Finlay and Fothringham (1991), p. 64-65, pl. 19(i)

Provenance: St Mary's College, University of St Andrews

The wooden bowl is mounted with a narrow simple reeded border which is unengraved. Print is engraved with the date '1567', with a biblical quotation round the border and another in a central escutcheon; around the shield is engraved: 'COLLEGIV * NOVVM * SCTE * ADREE'. The tubular stem flares to a foot.

The Latin biblical inscription round the border of the print reads, in the King James Version: 'For the law was given by Moses, but grace and truth came by Jesus Christ' (John 1:10). The shield in the centre of the print is engraved with the date '1567' and a further inscription which translates as 'Whether therefore ye eat or drink, or whatsoever ye do, do all to the glory of God' (I Corinthians 10:31). Although these words are of a pious nature, they do not have a direct bearing on the sacrament of communion, either in the pre-Reformation Catholic liturgy or the Reformed Kirk; it would therefore be stretching a point to argue that this mazer was originally intended as a communion cup. It seems more likely that it was a communal vessel to be passed round the college table in the manner of a loving cup.

The date of the mazer is still problematic. It seems most unlikely it would have been made before the hallmarking act of 1555. In all probability it dates from either 1556-58 or 1561-62. In either case it is the earliest fully marked piece of Edinburgh silver.

3.6 THE FERGUSSON MAZER

John Mosman II, Edinburgh, c.1576

Marks (on rim, print and stem): 'AC' (acting deacon Adam Craig); castle (Edinburgh); 'JM' in monogram (maker John Mosman II)

H 19.6 cm; D (bowl) 22.4 cm; D (print) 9.7 cm; D (base) 13.7 cm; Wt (all-in) 25.86 oz

Lent from a private collection

Provenance: Fergussons of Kilkerran; How of Edinburgh; Randolph Hearst; S. J. Phillips

References: How (1934[ii]), pp. 398-400; Finlay and Fothringham (1991), p. 65, pl. 19(ii)

The wooden bowl has a deep plain flared silver rim, finished with a double reeding above the hatched decorated edge. The circular print bears the arms of Fergusson impaling Durham and the initials 'DF' above and 'ID' to either side, for David Fergusson of Kilkerran and his wife, Isobel Durham. The border of the print bears the inscription: 'QUID . HABES . QUOD . NON ACCEPISTI . SI . ACCEPISTI . QUID . GLORI-

3.6

3.5

3.6

ARIS . 1 CORIN 4 *' ['What hast thou that thou didst not receive? Now if thou didst receive it, why dost thou glory?' (I Corinthians 4:7)]. The plain trumpet stem flares to a stepped foot decorated with a band of repoussé work below a course of dentilation.

This mazer has for a long period of time been mis-attributed due to the order in which the marks are struck in all three places. If we take the engraved date, 1576, at face value, we find that the deacon in that year was Michael Gilbert II who, being indisposed, refused to serve; however, the Privy Council ordered him to accept office as deacon and appointed Adam Craig to act for him in the matter of assaying and marking the brethren's work, 'to supple and help the said Michaell in the using of the said office at sic tymes as he salbe requirit upoun him'. Thus we should expect to find Adam Craig's mark as acting deacon in that assay-year. Latest research suggests that the maker was probably John Mosman II.

3.7 THE CRAIGIEVAR MAZER

Possibly by James Cok or John Cunningham, Edinburgh, possibly c.1575-91

Marks: 'IC' in monogram (possibly for James Cok or John Cunningham); castle (for Edinburgh); 'GH' in monogram (George Heriot II)

H 21.5 cm; D (bowl) 23 cm; D (foot) 14 cm; Wt (all-in) 32.82 oz

Lent from a private collection at Mount Stuart

Provenance: Forbes Sempill of Craigievar family; How of Edinburgh

References: Dalgleish and Maxwell (1987), no. 3; Jackson (1911), vol. II, p. 632 (a, b); How (1934[ii]), pp. 403-05; Finlay and Fothringham (1991), pp. 67-68, pl. 21(i); RSM (1948), no. 5

The wooden bowl is fitted with a deep rim which is engraved with birds and beasts among scrolling foliage and what appear to be acorns. The grip of the rim is lobed, each chased with a tri-foliate design. The circular print has a wreath of engraved foliage around its border, and the centre bears the arms of Petrie of Portlethen impaled with those of Forbes of Craigievar, for Robert Petrie, Provost of Aberdeen, and Anna, daughter of Sir William Forbes of Craigievar, who were married in 1665. The foliate baluster stem is somewhat similar to those of the Tulloch and Galloway Mazers with the addition of a prominent knop.

There has been, and still is, some difference of opinion as to the maker of this mazer. The maker's mark appears to be 'IC' in monogram, which Jackson ascribed to James Crawford, who was admitted as a freemen of the Incorporation of Goldsmiths on 12 October 1591. However, there are two other possible candidates with the same initials who should be considered: namely James Cok, admitted 15 February 1574, and John Cunningham, admitted 28 May 1588.

Turning to the deacon's mark, there is no doubt about the identity of its owner, George Heriot II, deacon in 1565-67, 1575-76, 1579, 1583-85, 1586-87, 1589-91, 1594-96, 1603-04 and finally 1607-08. This choice of possibilities leaves us very uncertain as to the true maker and date. The one option that can apparently be ruled out is the usually accepted one of James Crawford in 1591, because George Heriot II had ceased to be the deacon in the month preceding that in which James Crawford became a freeman, so they did not overlap on that occasion. If Crawford was indeed the maker, then it would have been during one of the later deaconships of George Heriot II; this seems unlikely, as the form suggests an earlier date. If John Cunningham were the maker, then it could date from 1589 onwards. If James Cok were the maker, it could be as early as 1575, which would place it much closer in date to the other standing mazers and seems stylistically much more probable. Further speculation appears useless without new evidence or insight.

3.8 ST LEONARD'S SILVER MAZER

Unmarked, apparently Scottish, c.1600

H 19.1 cm; D (bowl) 23.8 cm; D (foot) 13.7 cm; Wt 30.54 oz

Lent by the University of St Andrews

References: Burns (1892), pp. 193-94; How 1934[ii]), pp. 408-10; Finlay and Fothringham (1991), p. 79-80, pl. 24(i)

The plain reeded rim is attached to the plain bowl just as if the bowl were made of wood or other material. The stem is likewise riveted to the bowl in mazer-fashion; there is no print. The elegant stem has a central knop and the foot is chased in a manner similar to the Fergusson and Craigievar Mazers.

This is the only surviving Scottish standing mazer with a silver bowl, a type of vessel once quite common. It is clearly the inspiration for the mazer-shaped communion cups which followed some 20 years later.

3.7   3.9

3.9 THE COWCADDENS MAZER

Probably Thomas Cleghorne, Edinburgh, c.1613-15)

Marks (near rim): 'JD' monogram (deacon James Denneistoun); castle (Edinburgh); '?TC' conjoined, much rubbed (maker Thomas Cleghorne); assay-scrape above the marks is aligned with two assay-scrapes on lower part of the bowl and foot plate

H 8.3 cm; D (rim) 20.2 cm; D (foot) 6.8 cm; Wt 17.22 oz

Lent from a private collection

References: *Empire Exhibition* (1938), no. 46; RSM (1948), no. 11 (owner J. M. Sanderson); Finlay and Fothringham (1991), p. 94, pl. 32(ii); W. D. Campbell, *pers. comm.*; C. J. Burnett, Ross Herald, *pers. comm.*

Plain mazer-shaped bowl, with wide rim, soldered onto small shallow raised bowl with moulded foot-rim, join disguised by a moulded wire with 'V' toothed decoration. Inside, central domed disc is engraved with arms for Inglis and Stewart; outer rim engraved with arms for Bell impaling Inglis, and Bell impaling Campbell.

An equally fascinating and perplexing piece, its marks are here reattributed. The arrangement of the marks would normally indicate James Denneistoun as the maker and Thomas Cleghorne the deacon. However, Thomas Cleghorne did not serve as deacon until 1640, apparently far too late for the style of this bowl. As Denneistoun was deacon in 1613-15 and 1619-21, it seems more likely that he was the deacon and Cleghorne, admitted as a freeman in 1606, the maker.

The family descent of the mazer, indicated by the engraved arms, would seem to confirm this. The arms in the centre or boss of the mazer bowl are for James Inglis, a merchant burgess and sometime Provost of Glasgow, and Marion Stewart whom he married in 1615, giving a possible date of manufacture. The arms on the side of the bowl are, first of all, for Patrick Bell of Cowcaddens and Margaret Inglis, who married in 1618. Margaret was a daughter (possibly by an earlier marriage) of James Inglis. Patrick Bell was Provost of Glasgow in 1634-36. The second set of arms is for their son, master Patrick Bell of Cowcaddens, a graduate of Glasgow University, and his wife Mary Campbell whom he married in 1649. The engraving of both of these sets of arms seems to be in the same hand and was possibly completed to mark this later marriage in 1649, although it certainly replicates the style of the earlier arms in the boss.

3.10 THE GLASGOW UNIVERSITY LOVING CUP

James Fairbairn, Edinburgh, 1659

Marks (on rim): 'I.F' (maker James Fairbairn); castle (Edinburgh); 'I.F' (deacon James Fairbairn 1651-53, 1657-59); no assay-scrape above marks, but visible on underside of foot-rim, foot and stem

H 24.5 cm; D (rim) 21.8 cm; D (foot) 15 cm; Wt 35 oz 2 dwt

Lent by the University of Glasgow

References: Williams (1990), no. 2; Reid (1957), pp. 118-23

Deep almost hemispherical bowl, with spool and knop stem set on plain stepped foot. Outer rim of the bowl engraved: 'COLLEGII + GLASGVENS + POCVLVM + I OTH ION' ['The Loving Cup of the College of Glasgow']; the inside is engraved with 'PIE / IVSTE / SOBRIE' within a wreath of stylised foliage.

Long known as the 'University Loving Cup', this impressive drinking vessel is exceptionally important in the history of Scottish silver. Its shape is clearly reminiscent of the many large wide-bowled communion cups that originate in the 1630s (see chapter 7, p. 141). However, extant documents in the university's archive prove this cup is the direct successor to two earlier mazers. The first one appears in an inventory of 1582, as 'ane great sylver maser of 17 unce wicht', and later in an inventory of 1614 which describes it as being engraved with the college's name. This mazer was probably then given to William Stalker to be melted down and turned into a new larger mazer in 1617.

Stalker, author of the Ballochyle Brooch [3.13], was paid £21 15s for this work. Stalker's mazer is again mentioned in an inventory of 1643, but did not enjoy a very much longer life. It was in turn given to James Fairbairn, deacon of the Edinburgh Goldsmiths in 1658, to be 'changed into a new Large Cup weighing tuo pund four ounces'. Fairbairn's detailed account for this work exists in the university's archive. This vessel is therefore unique in documenting not only the continuous process of melting down and refashioning of old vessels, but also in providing direct stylistic evidence of the transition from the mazer shape to the large communion cup shape of the 17th century.

3.13

3.10

3.12

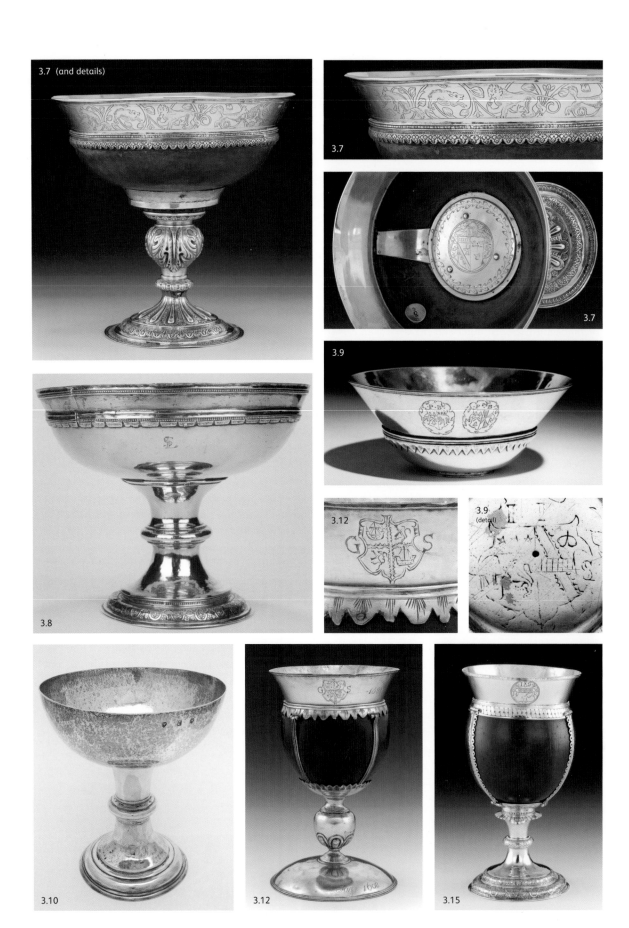

3.7 (and details)

3.7

3.7

3.9

3.8

3.12

3.9 (detail)

3.10

3.12

3.15

3.11 THE SETON-HAMILTON MEDAL

Michael Gilbert II, Edinburgh, 1562

D 3.2 cm

NMS H.1967.436; purchased in 1967

Reference: *Medallic Illustrations* (1885), vol. 1, p. 27

Circular gold medal. The obverse has the initials 'GS' and 'IH' in monogram, for George Seton and his wife Isabella Hamilton; the reverse has a thistle head within three interlinked crescents, and the date 1562.

George Seton was a devoted follower of Mary, Queen of Scots, and became her Master of the Household. In 1550 he married Isabella, daughter of Sir William Hamilton of Sanquhar. It is not known why the Edinburgh goldsmith Michael Gilbert II was commissioned to produce both gold and silver versions of this medal, but he was required in 1563 by the Privy Council to hand over the punches for it to the Warden of the Royal Mint, so that no more could be issued.

3.12 COCONUT CUP

Probably James Hart, Canongate, c.1610

Mark: 'IH' (maker possibly James Hart, Canongate)

H 17.9 cm; D (rim) 11 cm; D (foot) 11.1 cm; Wt 10.84 oz

NMS A.1960.762; given by Major and Mrs C. J. Shaw of Tordarroch

Provenance: Mrs Shaw MacKenzie

References: *Renaissance Decorative Arts* (1959), no. 113; Finlay and Fothringham (1991), pp. 94-95, pl. 21(i)

Bowl is formed from coconut shell mounted with a deep flared rim, having a notched lower edge engraved with chevrons; four hinged reeded straps connect rim to a lower scratch-engraved scalloped rim, set on a short stem with a large round knop with an arcaded design, resting on a broad, slightly domed foot. The rim is engraved with two coats of arms and the initials of George Sinclair of Mey (third son of the 4th Earl of Caithness), his wife Margaret, daughter of the 7th Lord Forbes, and the date 1588. The foot, possibly a later replacement, is engraved 'Forss 1608'.

There has been some doubt about both the date and authorship of this cup. George Sinclair and Margaret Forbes are said to have married before 1583 and he was dead by 1616. As the maker's mark is identical to that on a group of disc-end spoons with the engraved date 1617 [see 3.35], it is fairly certain that the maker was Scottish; and indeed the general style is certainly reminiscent of 'mazer-work' and other late 16th- or early 17th-century pieces. A possible candidate is James Hart in the Canongate.

3.13 THE BALLOCHYLE BROOCH

William Stalker, Glasgow, c.1610

Marks: (on upper edge) 'V S' in monogram twice, one above the other; (on underside) as above, but with crisp assay-scrape above

D 13.8 cm

NMS H.NGB 177; joint ownership conveyed to NMS by A. M. MacIver-Campbell

References: Finlay and Fothringham (1991), pp. 46-47 and pl. 14(ii); *Renaissance Decorative Arts* (1959), no. 108

Central hemisphere of natural rock crystal, mounted in plain silver collar naïvely engraved with inscription 'De Serve and Haif the Hevin Bebif', surrounded by a parcel gilt band of egg and dart decoration adjoining the outer scalloped octagonal body with points terminating in pierced trefoils. The panels are engraved alternately with MacIver/Campbell arms, the initials 'MC' and strap-work.

This magnificent brooch was long in the possession of the MacIver-Campbell family of Ballochyle, Cowal, Argyll, who used it as a talisman against witchcraft and disease. The last in a series of impressive, crystal-mounted brooches from the western Highlands and Islands, the Ballochyle is the only one with a maker's mark. In the past this mark has been interpreted as 'AS' and the maker unidentifiable; however, the positioning of the assay-scrape in the usual place above the mark means that it should in fact be interpreted as 'W S', for William Stalker, goldsmith in Glasgow.

3.14 THE CADBOLL CUP

Unmarked, late 16th century

H 15.3 cm; D (rim) 16.3 cm; D (base) 10.7 cm; Wt 15.89 oz

NMS H.MEQ 958; purchased from S. J. Phillips, London, 1970, with the aid of the National Art-Collections Fund, the NMAS Endowment Fund and a special Treasury Grant

Provenance: Mr D. MacLeod of Cadboll

References: *PSAS* 103 (1970-71), p. 244; *PSAS* 104 (1971-72), pp. 306-15; RCEWA (1970[ii]), R17

Wide, shallow bowl, the outer surface chased and engraved with panels of alternating interlace and foliate decoration of a West Highland character, highlighted by parcel gilding; the baluster stem decorated with strap-work, all set on a stepped trumpet foot, with the rim stamped with interlace decoration.

One of the most important cups in Scotland, this is nevertheless an enigmatic piece. Unmarked, it bears general stylistic similarities to the form of some communion cups of the early 17th century, especially that

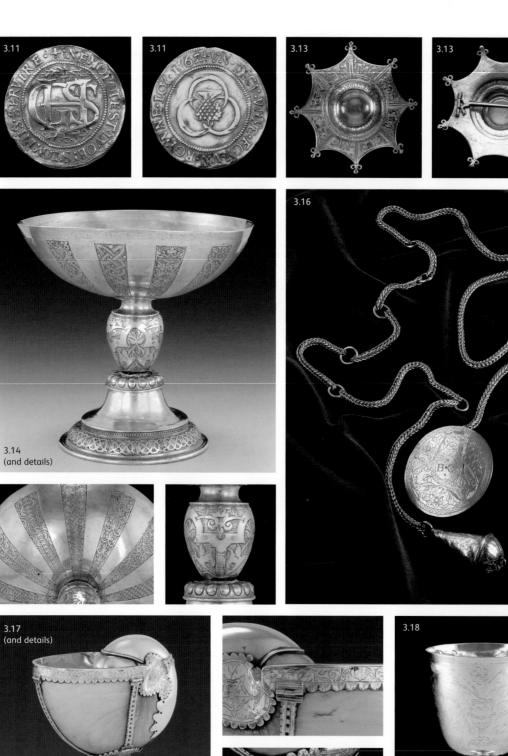

3.11

3.11

3.13

3.13

3.14
(and details)

3.16

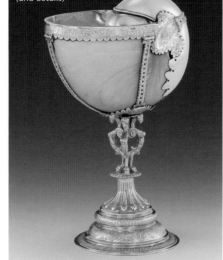

3.17
(and details)

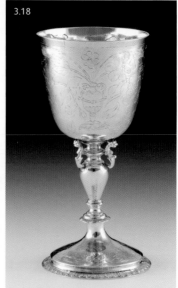

3.18

from Forgue [7.1], while the foot of the cup is very similar in style to the Lossit/Ugadale Brooch. However, the unusual decorative scheme has raised doubts that the cup was in fact assembled from separate parts, including possibly a French wine cup stem. Analysis done in the 1970s of the silver composition of the bowl, stem and foot sought to confirm this theory. Recent XRF analysis undertaken by the National Museums Scotland analytical research team is far less certain about different surface compositions for the sections of the cup, as 'all its components have consistently high silver composition', above the 916 standard. Given the well-documented connections between France and Scotland, it is possible that the cup represents a contemporary fusion of Scottish and French elements.

3.15 COCONUT CUP

Thomas Lindsay I, Dundee, c.1600

Marks: 'TL' (maker Thomas Lindsay I); pot of lilies (Dundee)

H 20.9 cm; D (rim) 11.2 cm; D (foot) 9.8 cm; Wt (all-in) 12.12 oz

Lent from a private collection at Mount Stuart

Reference: RSM (1948), no. 279

On circular stepped foot with two shoulders, the upper one with scrolls and ovolos, the lower one in trefoil foliate scrolls. The plain spool stem has central knop with punched cross scroll decoration. A flat lined and notched flange is above the stem, above which is a vertical band of dentils. Three hinged straps are threaded down the centre with pierced arched edging on either side. The flared rim is above a semi-guilloche design, and the rim has integral reeded moulding above and below.

Engraved in a roundel is a shield of arms, three quartrefoils in chief above a stag's head erased. The letters 'IS' are above, with 'M' at the dexter side and 'R' at the sinister.

3.16 MIDSIDE MAGGIE'S GIRDLE

Adam Wilson, Edinburgh, 1608-10

Marks: 'AV' in monogram (maker Adam Wilson); castle (Edinburgh); 'RD' conjoined (deacon Robert Denneistoun)

L (chain) 140 cm; D (disc) 6.9 cm

NMS H.NA 388; presented in 1897 by Robert Romanes and James Curle junior, descendants of Margaret Hardie, the original owner

References: A. J. S. Brook (1888[ii]), pp. 445-52; J. A. Smith (1873), pp. 321-25; Romanes and Curle (1897-98), pp. 195-204; *Renaissance Decorative Arts* (1959), no. 141; *EGM* (2006), B37, A89

Chain of interwoven silver wire, terminating in a circular disc with fastening hook at one end, and a domed conical pendant at the other; disc is engraved with a band of intertwined foliage and flowers with the initials 'BC' in the centre.

Girdles such as these were worn around the waist to fasten garments. Very few survive, making this one of the earliest examples of hallmarked personal adornment in Scotland. It is traditionally said to have been given by John Maitland, 2nd Earl of Lauderdale, to Maggie Hardie, the wife of one of his tenants, Thomas Hardie, in Midside Farm. This was in gratitude for continuing to pay their rents while the royalist earl was imprisoned in the Tower of London from 1652-55 during Oliver Cromwell's Commonwealth.

3.17 THE HERIOT LOVING CUP

Robert Denneistoun, Edinburgh, 1611-13

Marks (on upper face of foot flange): 'RD' in monogram (maker Robert Denneistoun); castle (Edinburgh); 'DP' monogram (deacon David Palmer); underside of the foot has two aligned assay-scrapes on its constituent parts

H 22 cm; L 14.5 cm; D (base) 9.5 cm; Wt 17.35 oz

Lent by the Governors of George Heriot's Trust

References: Finlay and Fothringham (1991), pp. 93-94, pl. 32(i); Dalgleish and Maxwell (1987), no. 7; RSM (1948), no. 9; *Renaissance Decorative Arts* (1959), no. 142; *Scot. Nat. Mem.* (1890), p. 298

The cup is a nautilus shell with a gilded silver liner (probably later) and strap mounts, fixed by a screw to a parcel gilt cast stem formed from three harpie-like mannerist figures on a lobed and stepped foot (similar to the foot of the Craigievar Mazer).

The mounting of what were at the time rare and exotic objects, such as ostrich eggs, coconuts and nautilus shells, was fashionable throughout Europe in the 16th and 17th centuries. However, with the exception of a number of coconut cups, few Scottish examples have survived, and the Heriot Cup is unique.

It may well have belonged to George Heriot III at some point, as a loving cup is mentioned in one of his inventories, and a small shield on the side of the rim is faintly engraved with initials which could be interpreted as 'GH'. It was for this reason the cup was presented to the governors of the school in 1792 by

3.15

3.16

a Mr John Stewart, a former pupil, and friend of the then chairman of governors and Lord Provost of Edinburgh, Alexander Cunningham. From that date onward, the cup was used at the school's anniversary dinner in June every year to toast the 'Immortal Memory of the Founder'.

3.18 WINE CUP

Thomas Cleghorne I, Edinburgh; deacon Adam Lamb, c.1627-29

Marks (below the rim): 'TC' in monogram (maker Thomas Cleghorne I); castle (Edinburgh); 'AL' conjoined (deacon Adam Lamb); assay-scrapes on baluster and undersides of foot and foot-rim; underside of foot scratch-engraved 'MR/1830' and 'ME'

H 16.8 cm; D (bowl) 8.2 cm; D (foot) 8.1 cm; Wt 7.09 oz

Lent from a private collection at Mount Stuart

References: Finlay and Fothringham (1991), p. 95, pl. 32(ii); RSM (1948), no. 16

Bowl engraved with an urn from which issues twined stems of flowers and foliage, supported on a baluster and spool stem by three debased harpie-like creatures; the stem on spreading trumpet foot with tongue-and-dart rim; the upper part of the foot lightly engraved with entwined flowers including rose, carnation, daffodil and tulip.

This is the earliest surviving Edinburgh-made secular wine cup. It differs significantly in style from the other early wine cups by Robert Gardyne in Dundee [3.24], but the supporting figures bear some resemblance to those on the Heriot Loving Cup [3.17]. The style and the particular castle punch suggest that the cup dates from Adam Lamb's first term as deacon.

3.19 COCONUT CUP

Andrew Denneistoun, Edinburgh, 1637-39

Marks (on rim just below lip): 'AD' conjoined (maker Andrew Denneistoun); castle (Edinburgh); 'IS' monogram (deacon John Scott); all below an assay-scrape; two additional assay-scrapes on underside of flared foot and another on underside of foot-flange

H 20.4 cm; D (lip) 9.4 cm; D (foot) 7.4 cm

Lent from a private collection

Reference: Finlay and Fothringham (1991), p. 95, pl. 33

The coconut is mounted with a silver rim and a silver foot joined by three silver reeded straps. The plain

baluster stem is attached to a silver plate riveted to the nut, the lower end meeting the slightly wasted flared foot, the latter engraved with a stylised tulip with a strap-shaped leaf at each side. The shoulder mount is engraved without any punctuation with three sets of initials: 'EMS' in monogram, 'NB' and 'ES', all in 17th-century hatched capital lettering (so far, the initials have not been identified). Opposite this engraving is a further inscription, 'MAK HIM STAKER ROB GIB', in the same lettering, immediately below the mark. The expressions 'Mak him staker' and 'Rob Gib' refer to Rob Gibb, fool to James VI. The saying 'Rob Gibb's Contract' conveyed expressions of conviviality and pledges of faithfulness.

3.20 WINE FUNNEL

Possibly Adam Lamb, Edinburgh, c.1640

Marks (on rim of body): 'A.L' thrice (maker Adam Lamb)

H 9.3 cm; D 5.9 cm; Wt 0.897 oz

NMS H.MEQ 686; purchased from Gordon Small, Edinburgh, in 1964

References: Finlay and Fothringham (1991), p. 100, pl. 34; EGM (2006), C122

Plain conical body with slightly tapering spout, with suspension ring soldered to rim. This is the only known 17th-century Scottish funnel and it was presumably used for decanting wine, although it is very small for such a task.

Adam Lamb's mark on the funnel differs in size and shape from other recorded examples. Makers may either have changed their punches over the years, or had different sizes of punch available at any given time, as recommended in the Edinburgh Incorporation's Minutes for 1652.

As the funnel carries Adam Lamb's mark struck only three times, it is possible that he may have made it while acting as deacon, striking the second mark in error instead of the castle town mark.

3.21 (detail)

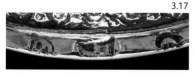

3.17

3.18

3.20

3.22
(and detail)

3.26

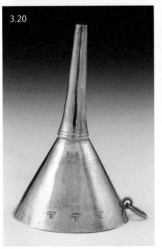

3.20

3.21

3.25

3.23

3.24

3.21 COCONUT CUP

Robert Gardyne II, Dundee, early 17th century

Marks: 'RG' (maker Robert Gardyne II); pot of lilies (Dundee)

H 20.2 cm; D (rim) 12.7 cm; D (foot) 9.8 cm; Wt (all-in) 11.8 oz (Scratch Wt '9 onc 12d')

Lent from a private collection at Mount Stuart

Provenance: How of Edinburgh, 1939; previously owned in Cornwall

References: RSM (1948), no. 279; Finlay and Fothringham (1991), p. 95

Bowl formed from coconut shell mounted with silver flared rim having a notched lower edge engraved with chevrons, the rim engraved '* 1612 * I•F * MG *', probably a marriage inscription. Four hinged reeded straps connect the rim to a baluster stem with knop, stamped with guilloche work, set on a stepped foot, decorated with stamped arcading virtually identical to that on the St Leonard's Mazer.

3.22 TASTER

Thomas Cleghorne I, Edinburgh, probably 1646-48

Marks (below rim with vestigial assay-scrape above): 'TC' in monogram (maker Thomas Cleghorne I); castle (Edinburgh); 'JS' in monogram (deacon John Scott 1637-39 and 1646-48)

H 2.3 cm; L (across handles) 15.7 cm; Wt 1.99 oz

NMS H.MEQ 1567; purchased at Christie's and Edmiston's sale, Shaw of Tordarroch, 29 March 1983, no. 104

References: EGM (2006), A108, B141; Dalgleish and Maxwell (1987), no. 13; Dietert (2007), p. 590

A small, shallow bowl, with slightly inverted base, decorated all over with repoussé flowers and foliage; two applied lug handles engraved with the initials 'M/WG' and 'AG'. This is the earliest surviving Scottish taster, presumably used for wine and is evidence of the Scots' love of imported wines. The castle mark appears to be that associated with Scott's second term as deacon.

3.22 (detail)

3.23 COMMUNION CUPS FROM RAIT AND KILSPINDIE KIRK

Robert Gardyne II, Dundee; engraved date '1634'

Marks (on rim): 'RG' (maker Robert Gardyne II); pot of lilies (Dundee); 'RG' (maker's mark repeated); assay-scrape above marks

(1) H 22.7 cm; D (bowl) 10 cm; D (base) 9 cm; Wt 10.48 oz

(2) H 23.2 cm; D (bowl) 10 cm; D (base) 9 cm; Wt 11.5 oz

Lent by Rait and Kilspindie Parish Church via Perth Museum and Art Gallery

Reference: Burns (1892), p. 383

Narrow-mouthed, deep bowls on slender baluster and knop stems, with trumpet foot with band of stamped ovolo decoration; bowls engraved 'FOR KILSPINDIE AND RAIT 1634' and 'M/DW' for Maister David Williamsone, minister of the parish, 1622-46.

The stems are of a very similar design to those used by several Edinburgh goldsmiths on communion cups from the 1580s to 1630s [e.g. Roseneath cups and Balmaghie cups, 7.2 and 7.4]. The Gardynes of Dundee and Perth are problematic to disentangle. These cups were probably made by Robert Gardyne II in Dundee. They are very similar in design to 3.24 (some 14 years later; see below), emphasising there was no stylistic difference between communion cups and domestic wine cups.

3.24 THE MERCER STEWART MARRIAGE CUPS

Robert Gardyne II, Dundee, c.1648

Marks (on rim): 'RG' (maker Robert Gardyne II); pot of lilies (Dundee); assay-scrape above

(1) H 20.6 cm; D (bowl) 9.9 cm; D (foot) 8.1 cm

(2) H 20.3 cm; D (bowl) 9.9 cm; D (foot) 8.1 cm

Lent by the Mercer-Nairne family

Provenance: by descent from the original owner

Reference: Finlay and Fothringham (1991), p. 115 and pl. 36

Narrow-mouthed, deep bowls on slender baluster and knop stems, with trumpet foot with band of stamped ovolo decoration. Bowls engraved with initials and impaled arms of Sir James Mercer of Aldie and his wife Jean, eldest daughter of Sir Thomas Stewart of Grantully. They were married in 1648, now believed to be the date when the cups were made.

This is the only known pair of Scottish domestic silver cups to have survived from so early a date. In

3.21	3.22	3.23	3.24

form they are extremely like the Kilspindie communion cups by the same maker [see 3.23]. Like Edinburgh-made cups of the period, these have assay-scrapes on the bowl and constituent parts of the foot, suggesting that Robert Gardyne II was well aware of the legal requirements relating to assaying.

3.25 COCONUT CUP

Patrick Gardyne, St Andrews, c.1650

Mark (on rim): 'PG' (maker Patrick Gardyne, St Andrews); there is no visible assay-scrape

H 9.9 cm; D (lip) 10.9 cm; D (foot) 7.4 cm; Wt (all-in) 6.88 oz

Lent from a private collection at Mount Stuart

References: Finlay and Fothringham (1991), p.107; RSM (1948), no. 338

Bowl formed from half a coconut shell mounted with a silver everted rim, having a notched lower edge, with crude chevron vertical lines. Four hinged reeded straps, two with opposing reeded S-scroll strap handles, connect the rim to a plain spreading collet foot, soldered to the projecting flange.

3.26 CAPSTAN SALT

Patrick Gardyne, St Andrews, c.1650

Mark (on stem): 'PG' (maker Patrick Gardyne); saltire in oval (St Andrews); 'PG' repeated; assay-scrape above

Engraved with the hatched initials 'CT'

H 8 cm; D 12.1 cm; Wt (all-in) 12.22 oz
(Scratch Wt '15 ounce 11 drop')

Lent by the University of St Andrews

References: Finlay and Fothringham (1991), p. 107, pl. 40(ii)

Salt is capstan-shaped; two parts of the spool are joined by a central girdle. Bowl has been repaired with a patch. It is engraved below the girdle with the initials 'CT' in hatched lettering; otherwise completely plain.

This is the only known Scottish communal 'salt-fat' to survive from before the era of the trencher salt. It is very plain and simple and is possibly not typical of earlier ones mentioned in inventories, which are often said to be heavier and probably more elaborate.

3.25

3.26

Spoons

A spoon is an essential, practical long-lived tool that has not changed in function since it was introduced, although designs, shapes and sizes have changed, and specialisations have developed. Originally there was no such thing as separate tablespoons, dessert spoons or soup spoons; simply a single implement used for eating and serving out of the common pot.

Spoons were, however, a mark of social position, as evidenced by the continued currency of the old statement of a privileged start to life: 'born with a silver spoon in his mouth.' From the 16th century, household inventories make it clear that many families owned increasing numbers of spoons, presumably to provide for guests, who still brought their own portable knives and later, forks.

No marked Scottish-made spoons survive from before the second half of the 16th century.

There are only five different patterns of spoon in Scotland before the introduction of the trefid after the Restoration: seal-top; disc-end, puritan; slip-top and box-top, there being only a single surviving example of the last two.

The relative positioning and the orientation of maker's, deacon's and town marks on the stem of spoons is crucial in identifying which represents the maker and which the deacon. In several instances the relative proximity of the town mark to a mark would suggest it was that of the deacon, as he would apply both his and the town mark at the same time, whereas the maker applied his mark earlier. Such variations, where they are crucial in identifying the maker, will be noted in the entries below.

Seal-top Spoons

Seal-top spoons are so called because the finial often included an engraved or cut device that could be used as a seal. They were in use in Scotland and in England, but the three surviving Scottish examples, apparently dating from the 1570s, differ considerably in style and construction from English spoons. They have thin rectangular-section stems in contrast to the usual hexagonal stems of the English type, and small oval or rectangular seal-tops. The bowls are all almost circular and have a more or less pronounced 'rat-tail' – all factors that may derive from Continental types.

3.27

3.27 THE CUNNINGHAM SEAL-TOP SPOON

William Cokkie, Edinburgh, *c.*1573

Marks (on upper face of stem, reading from seal-top):
'WC' in monogram (maker William Cokkie); castle (Edinburgh);
'AC' conjoined (deacon Adam Craig 1572-74); assay-scrape on underside of stem near bowl

L 16 cm; Wt 1.22 oz

NMS H.MEQ 139; bequeathed by Mr George Henderson, 1943

References: How and How (1952), p. 324; *Empire Exhibition* (1938), no. 138, pl. 48

Seal-top engraved '1573'; back of bowl engraved 'HC' either side of a heraldic 'shake-fork'. The initials and device engraved on the bowl suggest that this spoon may have belonged to Hugh Cunningham of Watterstoun, the third son of 3rd Earl of Glencairn. [For more early Cunningham family spoons, see 3.30 and 3.40.]

3.28

3.28 FERGUSSON SEAL-TOP SPOON

Robert Gardyne I, Dundee, *c.*1576

Marks (on back of stem): pot of lilies, struck vertically (Dundee); 'RG' struck horizontally nearer the bowl (maker Robert Gardyne I); no visible assay-scrape

L 15.4 cm; Wt 1.03 oz

Lent from a private collection at Mount Stuart

Provenance: Fergussons of Kilkerran; How of Edinburgh (1936)

References: How and How (1952), p. 326, illus. p. 327; Finlay and Fothringham (1991), p. 65

3.29

The sides of the finial are decorated with a band of fleur-de-lis on a matted background; there is a similar band at the junction of stem and bowl. The finial, which has become oval with wear, is engraved with the initials 'DF' for David Fergusson of Kilkerran. The back of the bowl is engraved with the initials 'ID', believed to be for Isobel Durham, David Fergusson's wife. Their marriage is thought to have taken place in 1576 and the spoon may possibly date from that time. Until 1935 the spoon had always been associated with the Fergusson Mazer [3.6], which dates from the same year. However, because of the lack of definite information about the maker, the date of the spoon is somewhat speculative.

3.27

3.28

3.29 THE JACKSON SEAL-TOP SPOON

James Cokkie III, Edinburgh, 1577-79

Marks (reading from seal-top): assay-scrape; 'IC' in monogram (maker probably James Cokkie III); castle (Edinburgh); 'VC' in monogram (deacon William Cokkie 1577-79)

L 16.5 cm

3.29

Private loan on loan to Amgueddfa-cmyru (National Museum Wales)

Provenance: Trustees of the late Sir Charles Jackson

References; How and How (1952), p. 328, pl. 3; *Empire Exhibition* (1938), no. 137, pl. 48

Nothing engraved on seal-top; underside of bowl engraved 'A.B', probably later replacements of earlier lettering.

Disc-end Spoons

Disc-end spoons, although not a unique form to Scotland, do seem to be more common here than elsewhere, and they certainly make up the majority of surviving early Scottish spoons. There is a considerable variation in design, but all have a flat disc terminal, engraved with initials or devices, frequently with a smaller oval 'cushion' below, engraved with guilloche work or a date. The stems often have chevron and leaf devices engraved at the upper and lower joints, while, like the seal-tops, they all have basic 'rat-tails' and mainly circular bowls. The stems of the earliest examples are comparatively slender, but as the sequence progresses the stems tend to broaden considerably, flaring out towards the terminals. This type of spoon may be what was being referred to as 'silver spoones with round knapit endis' in an inventory of 1640 (*Black Book of Taymouth*, p. 348).

3.30 GROUP OF DISC-END SPOONS

George Heriot II, Edinburgh, c.1582

Marks (reading from the terminal): 'GH' in monogram; castle (Edinburgh); 'EH' in monogram (deacon Edward Hairt 1579-81, 1582-83 and 1585)

L 17.3 cm; Wt 1.43 oz

NMS H.MEQ 9-13; presented by the Queen's and Lord Treasurer's Rembrancer as Treasure Trove, 1865

References: How and How (1952), p. 332; *PSAS* 4 (1864-65), p. 88; *PSAS* 59 (1924-50), p. 120-27

Face of disc engraved 'I*B' under a coronet; underside of bowl engraved 'A C' either side of heraldic shake-fork, probably for Alexander Cunningham, son of the 4th Earl of Glencairn, and his wife Jean, daughter of John Blair of that Ilk, who married in 1582. These spoons were originally thought to have been made by Edward Hairt with George Heriot II as deacon, giving a much wider date range as Heriot was deacon many times. However, a close inspection of the marks on all the spoons show that the castle mark and Hairt's mark are always positioned facing the bowl, and with the same spacings relative to one another, suggesting they were applied together. Heriot's mark is the other way up and at a variable distance from the other two, suggesting he was marking as maker before sending them to be assayed. The date of the marriage above would fit in with Hairt's second deaconship.

Originally seven spoons (one fragmentary) were found in a house in the Townhead at Irvine, Ayrshire, in the early 19th century: five (including the bowl fragment) were presented to the National Museum of Antiquities as Treasure Trove, while the other two became part of the Marquess of Bute's collection.

These spoons are possibly the only known pieces of George Heriot II's work to have survived, although his mark as deacon appears on several other items.

3.31 THE CANONGATE DISC-END SPOON

George Cunningham, Canongate, c.1589

Marks (from disc-end); 'GC' (maker George Cunningham); stag lodged (Canongate); 'XI.D' (11 penny fine standard mark)

L 14.6 cm; Wt 1.07 oz

NMS H.MEQ 26; purchased in 1902

Reference: *PSAS* 59 (1924-50), pp. 120-27

The disc is engraved 'D*M / M*D' with '1589' below. This remarkable spoon proves that goldsmiths outside Edinburgh were aware of and attempted to comply with national legislation relating to the quality of silver. The final mark on the spoon 'XI.D' means 'eleven deniers', or the eleven penny fine standard of 11 parts pure silver in every 12 parts of alloy. This standard (916 in the modern millesimal notation) was introduced with the original hallmarking legislation in 1458 and repeated in 1555 (see p. 18). The town mark is that of Canongate as appears on the Tulloch and Galloway Mazers [3.3 and 3.4].

3.32 THE FALKLAND PALACE SPOON

John Lindsay, Edinburgh, 1608-10

Marks (struck horizontally, reading from the bowl): 'I.L' (maker John Lindsay); castle (Edinburgh); 'RD' in monogram (deacon Robert Denneistoun 1608-10). There is an assay scrape to the right of the marks towards the disc

L 16.5 cm; Wt 1.32 oz

Lent from a private collection at Mount Stuart

Reference: How and How (1952), vol. II, p. 342, illus. p. 343

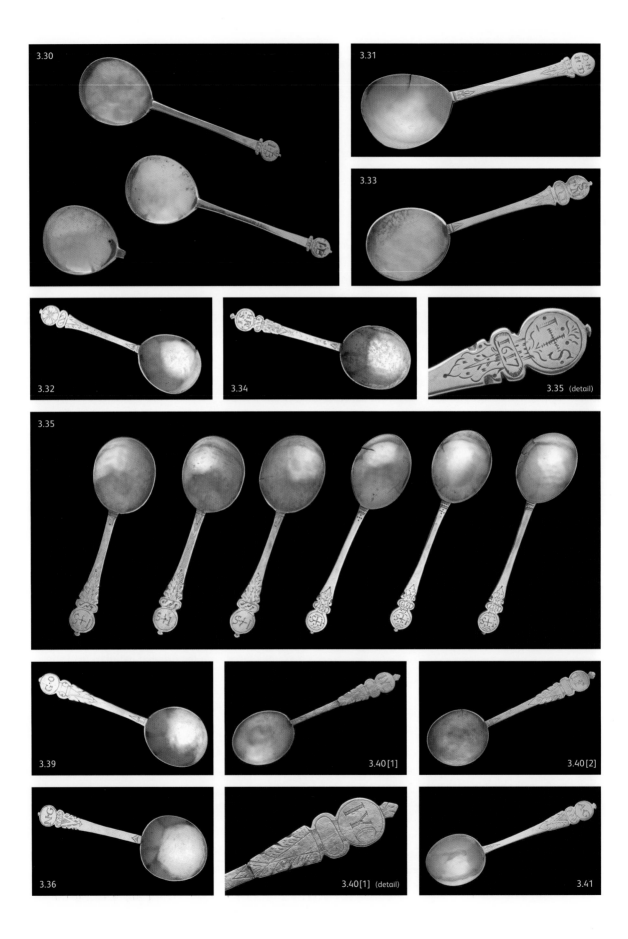

3.30

3.31

3.33

3.32

3.34

3.35 (detail)

3.35

3.39

3.40 [1]

3.40 [2]

3.36

3.40 [1] (detail)

3.41

Disc engraved on the front with a four-petal flower-head, perhaps representing a potentilla (*Potentilla tormentilla*); the back engraved 'IR' above the rat-tail.

3.33 DISC-END SPOON

Gilbert Kirkwood, Edinburgh, 1611-13

Marks (from bowl): 'GK' in monogram; castle (Edinburgh); 'DP' in monogram (deacon David Palmer 1611-13); assay-scrape

L 17.2 cm; Wt 1.3 oz

NMS H.MEQ 140; bequeathed by Mr George Henderson, 1943

Upper face of disc engraved 'S/I.M.'.

3.34 DISC-END SPOON

George Crawford, Edinburgh, c.1611-13

Marks (from bowl): 'GC' in monogram (maker George Crawford); castle (vertical) (Edinburgh); 'DP' in monogram (vertical) (deacon David Palmer 1611-13)

L 17.8 cm; Wt 1.72 oz

Lent from a private collection at Mount Stuart

Reference: How and How (1952), vol. II, p. 346, illus. p. 347

Disc engraved with the initials 'IS/MR' within a circle.

3.35 GROUP OF SIX DISC-END SPOONS

Possibly James Hart, Canongate, c.1617

Mark: 'IH' conjoined (for maker, possibly James Hart, Canongate)

(Group 1) Av. L 18.4 cm; Av. Wt 1.28 oz

(Group 2) Av. L 18 cm; Av. Wt 1.28 oz

NMS H.MEQ 3-8; presented by the Queen's and Lord Treasurer's Rembrancer as Treasure Trove, 1859

Reference: *PSAS* 59 (1924-50), pp. 120-27

All discs engraved with initials 'I+S' and backs of the bowls with 'CM'. Although these spoons clearly all belonged to the same family, they are in fact two groups of three. Three are engraved with the date 1617 in the cushion below the disc, while the other three have 'mantling' style engraving in the same place. Maker's marks are also positioned differently – the first three being towards the terminal of the spoon and much crisper; while the second three are more centrally positioned on the stem and are more poorly struck. It is possible that they represent two batches of spoons acquired by the owner at different times. They were found at the Hill of Culrain, Edderton, Ross-shire.

The maker's mark on these spoons has not been previously identified, but if the engraved date on the first three spoons is to be believed, one goldsmith with the correct initials can be suggested: James Hart in Canongate. The mark on all six spoons is the same as that on the coconut cup engraved with the dates 1588 and 1608 [see 3.12].

3.36 DISC-END SPOON

John Kirkwood, Glasgow, c.1620

Marks (horizontally on back of stem, bowl to left): 'IK' in monogram, three times (maker John Kirkwood, Glasgow); distinctive double assay scrape to the right of the third mark, extending onto the back of the cushion

L 16.95 cm; Wt 1.45 oz

Lent from a private collection at Mount Stuart

Reference: How and How (1952), vol. II, p. 340, illus. p. 341

Front of the disc engraved 'N.G' in a circle, the back of the disc engraved much later with the initials 'AH/KR' in italic script; the back of the bowl engraved 'x C D x' above the date '1600', the initials and date both divided by the rat-tail.

3.30

3.31

3.32

3.33

3.34

3.35

3.36

3.37 THE OLIPHANT SPOON

Robert Ker, Canongate, *c.*1630

Marks: 'R.K' over star (maker Robert Ker); 'XI*D' (eleven penny fine standard mark); stag lodged (Canongate)

Lent from a private collection

Reference: Finlay and Fothringham (1991), p. 116, pl. 36(ii)

Disc, cushion and stem decorated with stamped cinquefoils and roundels. This is the only recorded piece by Robert Ker.

3.38 DISC-END SPOON

Robert Gardyne, Dundee, perhaps *c.*1630s

Marks: 'RG' (maker Robert Gardyne); pot of lilies (Dundee town-mark); no assay scrape; punches look very similar to those on the Fergusson Spoon [3.28]

L (approx.) 14.8 cm

Lent by Strathmore and Kinghorne Estates (Holdings)

Disc engraved with 'L' over 'EL'. It is conjectured 'L/EL' may stand for Lady Elizabeth Lyon, probably born sometime in the late 1630s, only daughter of the 2nd Earl of Kinghorne, and who married the 1st Earl of Aboyne in 1665. If this identification is correct, it was perhaps a christening present to her.

3.39 DISC-END SPOON

George Robertson, Edinburgh, 1640-42

Marks (from the bowl): 'GR' horizontal (maker George Robertson); castle, vertically (Edinburgh); 'JF' vertical (acting deacon, John Fraser); assay-scrape beyond the marks, extending into the back of the cushion

L 17.8 cm; Wt 1.66 oz

Lent from a private collection at Mount Stuart

Reference: How and How (1952), vol. II, p. 346, illus. p. 347

Front of the disc engraved 'G.O' within a circle, back of the disc engraved with the date '1634'; the back of the bowl engraved 'ED' either side of the rat-tail.

3.40 TWO DISC-END SPOONS

John Scott, Edinburgh, 1642-44

Marks (from bowl): 'JS' in monogram (maker Jon Scott); castle (Edinburgh); 'I.F' (acting deacon John Fraser 1642-44); assay-scrape

(1) L 19.2 cm; Wt 1.63 oz / (2) L 18.4 cm; Wt 1.45 oz

NMS H.MEQ 36 and 37; presented by the King's and Lord Treasurer's Rembrancer as Treasure Trove, 1924

Reference: *PSAS* 59 (1924-50), pp. 120-27

One disc is engraved 'IC' with a heraldic shake-fork between, the back of the bowl engraved 'DC'; the other disc is engraved 'I.F' and the bowl 'BC'.

The spoons were found in the foundations for a new building at 172 High Street, Irvine, Ayrshire, in 1923, with a hoard of 351 coins and an unmarked silver cane-top engraved with the arms of Cunningham of Cunninghamehead and 'D/EC', probably for Dame Elizabeth Cunningham. The coins, a mixture of Scottish and English, were thought to have been deposited about 1640.

The initials on the spoons undoubtedly refer to members of the Cunningham family, but it is difficult to identify individuals exactly, although the second spoon may have belonged to James Fullarton of Fullarton and his wife Barbara Cunningham, sister of Dame Elizabeth, who married in 1624. The Cunninghams generally supported the Covenanting Party during the civil wars of the 1640s, and the unsettled nature of the times was no doubt the reason for burying the hoard.

3.41 DISC-END SPOON

Adam Lamb, Edinburgh, *c.*1642-44

Marks (from bowl, all vertical): 'AL' conjoined (maker Adam Lamb): castle (Edinburgh); 'J.F' (acting deacon John Fraser 1640-42)

L 18.8 cm; Wt 1.85 oz / Lent from a private collection

Disc engraved 'A.G', the bowl with 'E G', with rat-tail between.

3.39

3.40

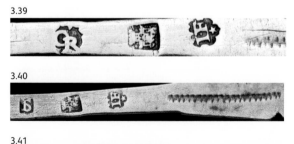

3.41

3.42

3.43

3.45

3.42 CHILD'S DISC-END SPOON

John Scott, Edinburgh, c.1646-48

Mark (on back of stem): 'IS' only (maker John Scott); no assay-scrape

L 13.3 cm; Wt 0.87 oz

Lent from a private collection at Mount Stuart

Reference: How and How (1952), vol. II, p. 346, illustrated p. 347

Disc engraved with a sprouting onion; the back of the bowl engraved 'IS' in broad lettering. This spoon was probably made during one of the terms when John Scott was deacon, 1637-39 or 1646-48; the form of the spoon would suggest latter period.

3.43 DISC-END SPOON

Peter Neilson, Edinburgh, 1648-50 or 1655-57

Marks (vertical, from bowl): 'PN' conjoined (maker Peter Neilson); castle (Edinburgh); 'GC' (deacon George Cleghorne 1648-50, 1655-58); assay scrape

L 18.3 cm; Wt 1.60 oz

Lent from a private collection at Mount Stuart

Provenance: Mrs Maxwell

Reference: Jackson (1905): where the marks on two such spoons are shown, the property of a Mrs Maxwell; this spoon may be one of them or another, perhaps from the same set

The disc engraved 'B.B' above a zig-zag scrape.

3.44 TWO DISC-END SPOONS

Thomas Moncur, Aberdeen, c.1650

Marks: 'TM' conjoined (maker Thomas Moncur, Aberdeen)

L 17.5 cm

Lent by Aberdeen Art Gallery and Museums; from a group of three spoons sold at The Morris Collection sale (1984), the other purchased by NMS

Provenance: Christie's & Edmiston's sale, Glasgow, The Morris Collection, 3 July 1984, lot 91

Reference: James (1981), pp. 32-33

Disc engraved 'L/WE'. The maker's mark on this spoon is the same as that on a small fully-marked Aberdeen wine taster [5.2].

3.45 SLIP-TOP SPOON

Gilbert Kirkwood, Edinburgh, 1608-10

Marks (struck vertically on 'thumb' facet of the stem): 'GK' in monogram (maker Gilbert Kirkwood); castle (Edinburgh); 'RD' in monogram (deacon Robert Denneistoun 1608-10); assay-scrape immediately above marks

L 17.5 cm; Wt 1.70 oz

Lent from a private collection at Mount Stuart

Reference: How and How (1952), vol. II, p. 350, illus. p. 351

Plain square-section stem set at 45 degrees to the horizontal, with vestigial rat-tail to the bowl, the terminal at an abrupt angle, suggesting an intermediate form between a true slip-top and a stump-top. Back of the broad oval bowl is engraved with the initials 'WB/D'. Below are vestiges of further early initials, apparently beginning with 'A'.

3.46 BOX-TOP SPOON

James Symontoun, Edinburgh, 1651-53, 1657-59

Marks (from bowl): 'I.S' (maker James Symontoun); castle (Edinburgh); 'I.F' (deacon James Fairbairn 1651-53, 1657-59)

L 19.1 cm; Wt 1.9 oz

NMS A.1958.43; purchased from Thomas Lumley Ltd, London, 1958

Almost circular bowl with rectangular section stem terminating in box-shaped terminal with knop; no rat-tail; upper face of stem engraved with chevron hatching; the underside of the bowl engraved with ownership initials 'S/GM' over 'D/AS'. This is a unique design with no other parallel in Scotland.

Puritan Spoons

Puritan spoons are so called because this relatively plain design with squared top found favour for a relatively short time during and after the Commonwealth period (1650s and '60s). Rare in Scotland, the design differs from London-made examples. The rectangular section stems flare out to a straight-cut end, occasionally relieved with vestigial notches. The upper faces of the stems are again frequently decorated with stylised chevron and leaf motifs.

3.47 THE BARNCLEUTH PURITAN SPOON

George Cleghorne, Edinburgh, c.1653-55

Marks (from bowl): 'GC' (maker George Cleghorne); castle (Edinburgh); '*AB' (deacon Andrew Burrell 1653-55, 1659-61); assay-scrape

L 19.2 cm; Wt 2.08 oz

Lent from a private collection

Provenance: by descent; Sotheby's sale, Gleneagles, 30 August 1982, lot 483; How of Edinburgh

Back of bowl engraved with ownership initials 'QH/MD'. Said by the original owner to have been found in the garden of Barncleuth House, and thought to have belonged to Quintin Hamilton of Barncleuth and his wife, Marion Denham, married sometime after 1653.

3.48 PURITAN SPOON

George Cleghorne, Edinburgh, 1657-59

Marks (horizontally, from bowl): 'GC' in monogram (maker George Cleghorne); castle (Edinburgh); 'IF' (deacon James Fairbairn 1657-59), accompanied by a long ill-defined assay-scrape

L 19 cm; Wt 1.52 oz

Lent from a private collection at Mount Stuart

Reference: How and How (1952), vol. II, p. 354, illus. p. 355

The terminal has three V-shaped notches, the back of the terminal engraved 'GH'. The back of the bowl is engraved 'IG'.

3.49 PURITAN SPOON

David Boog, Edinburgh, 1665-67

Marks (from bowl): 'D*B' (maker David Boog); castle (Edinburgh); 'I.S' (deacon James Symontoun 1665-67); assay-scrape

NMS H.MEQ 40; presented by the King's and Lord Treasurer's Rembrancer as Treasure Trove, 1924

References: How and How (1952), vol. II, p. 358; PSAS 59 (1924-50), pp. 126-27

Stem engraved with crude foliage, underside of bowl engraved with ownership initials 'R*M'. Found when digging a trench for water pipes in Church Street, Haddington, East Lothian, September 1923.

Maker Boog had a troubled career; he was fined £40 Scots by the Incorporation in September 1663 for working in 'insufficient metal'. He seems to have mended his ways as analysis confirms this spoon to be well above standard.

3.50 PURITAN SPOON

Thomas Lindsay II, Dundee, c.1665

Marks (from bowl): 'TL' (maker Thomas Lindsay II); pot of lilies (Dundee); assay-scrape

L 17.6 cm; Wt 1.32 oz

NMS H.MEQ 1176; purchased from Grantully Castle Antiques, 1976

Stem engraved with stylised foliage and pronounced notches in end, engraved with date '1640'); underside of bowl engraved with ownership initials 'AS/IM' in the centre of bowl; with rat-tail join.

This is a unique spoon in many ways – the notched and shaped end possibly prefigures the later trefid design, while the rat-tail at the bowl/stem join harks back to the earlier disc ends.

Linsday II also made the magnificent Fithie basin [see 7.16] and communion cups for St Vigean's Parish in 1677. He was obviously aware of the legislation regarding the quality of the metal he used, as this spoon has a very distinct assay-scrape.

3.51 PURITAN SPOON

Alexander Reid II, Edinburgh, *c.*1667

Marks (from bowl): 'crown over AR' (maker Alexander Reid); castle (Edinburgh); '.AS.' (deacon Alexander Scott 1667-69)

L18.7 cm; Wt 1.73 oz

NMS H.MEQ 616; presented by Miss Sylvia Steuart, London, 1962

Stem engraved with stylised tulip and 'DF'; back of bowl engraved 'HM/1667'.

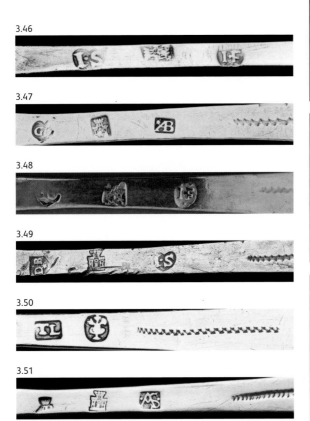

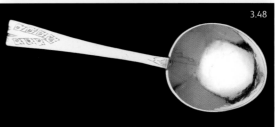

Edinburgh:
The Golden Age

4

Introduction

From the reign of James II, about 1447, Edinburgh was confirmed as the capital of the country, with the Royal Court, Parliament and courts of justice concentrating their activities there. This in turn drew an increasing number of the powerful and wealthy, and the city developed as a commercial and economic centre. Because of this, Edinburgh, for most of our period, was undoubtedly the main centre of the goldsmiths' trade, providing the demand for fashionable and high status goods that they were able to supply.

Most of the earliest references to goldsmiths in Edinburgh, and also in adjacent Canongate, are to their activities in the Mint, either as mint-master, moneyer, die-sinker or engraver. By the 16th century (and doubtless earlier) they were also bankers, money-lenders, pawn-brokers and finance facilitators. Merchants relied on them to evaluate the foreign currency and wrought plate that came into their hands. When the Bank of Scotland was established in 1695, Edinburgh goldsmiths played a role in its early development. Because of their relatively better education and high standing in the community, they often took part in local government. The deacon was usually *ex officio* a town councillor, and others served as trades' councillors; both participated (and the deacon or his representative still does) in the Convenery of Trades of the burgh, a body established to maintain the rights and privileges of the craftsmen against the overbearing might of the merchants' guild. Some represented Edinburgh at the Convention of Royal Burghs or were commissioners to Parliament. Many served (one still serves today) as trustees of the Edinburgh Trades' Maiden Hospital; James Mitchelson, goldsmith, was the hospital's treasurer for 16 years in the middle of the 18th century.

In 1526 there were 16 masters in the Incorporation. However, together with their apprentices and journeymen, they probably numbered about 60 people who, with their families, were entirely dependent on the goldsmiths' craft for their livelihoods. The 18th century saw a gradual increase in the number of freemen masters to about 40, and the craft seldom, if ever, exceeded that number at any one time. By the mid-20th century the numbers had dwindled to scarcely a handful; at the time of writing there are once more 16 freemen members, just as there were in 1526.

Many masters trained two or even three apprentices at once, each at a different stage of his apprenticeship. A few freemen possibly worked alone without an apprentice or journeyman to assist them, but most would take an apprentice soon after they qualified themselves as freemen,

… Edinburgh silver-work of considerable value …

{REGISTER OF THE PRIVY COUNCIL: 1681}

{opposite page}
4.2 THE STRATHMORE SALVER, 1667-69

and most would also have one or more journeyman working under them. The larger workshops in the 18th century must have employed a considerable number of journeymen; this accounts for most of the apprentices who did not go on to become freemen in their turn, because they served instead as journeymen to established masters, either by preference or out of economic necessity.

There were dynasties of goldsmiths for several generations in a family, either father to son or father-in-law to son-in-law; an apprentice was often related to his master or subsequently married his master's daughter, and overall formed a close-knit community. The goldsmiths of Edinburgh came from a variety of backgrounds. There were a few with humble rural origins; there were many sons or sons-in-law of goldsmiths and merchants, some sons of the manse, and a few whose fathers followed other crafts in the burgh. One of the largest groups came from the families of the landed gentry all over Scotland. The occupations of merchant, lawyer, soldier, goldsmith, surgeon and the church were those most favoured by the younger sons of gentry. There are many examples of careers from rags to riches and vice versa. A goldsmith's prosperity was often dependent as much on his family connections as on his skill as a workman. Reputations spread by word of mouth and recommendation, even more so than today. Much of 18th-century Edinburgh trade was dominated by a few workshops that appear to have cornered the market in well-off clients and lucrative commissions. Those without such connections struggled to get enough work to stay in business, even though they may have been exceptionally skilled, like John Clark [see 8.16].

The goldsmiths' quarter was concentrated, at least from the 15th century, at the solar plexus of Edinburgh, in the area immediately around St Giles' Church. This was no accident: the merchants also congregated there to transact their business at the burgh cross and they needed the goldsmiths to be on hand to verify the value of the foreign and native currency in which they dealt. By the end of the 18th century the New Town was being developed and some goldsmiths crossed over the newly-built North Bridge to take up premises, still smelling of fresh paint, in Princes Street or George Street. Many others moved down the hill from St Giles to South Bridge. Goldsmiths' Hall, which had stood next to the church for all of that burgeoning century, was destroyed 'with

all that it contained' by fire in 1796. The new Hall was established first in Hunter's Square opposite the Tron Church and then on the west side of South Bridge. In the early 20th century the Hall moved again to Queen Street. In the 1970s it uprooted once more, to Granton Road on the north side of the city; then, after a short spell in Manor Place, it settled in its present magisterial location in Broughton Street in a converted church.

The business of being a goldsmith could be precarious because it was dependent on external circumstances. Wars, foreign and civil, pestilence, famine, recession, even prolonged severe frost or dirty weather, all caused frequent downturns in the prosperity of the goldsmiths' customers, for these were times when everyone had more important things to think about than commissioning something from their favourite goldsmith. Partly as a defence against unforeseen events and unpreventable circumstances, goldsmiths tended to diversify into whatever activities they could devise to maintain their businesses, themselves and their families. As mentioned elsewhere, many were merchants dealing in a wide range of goods; one sold tea, another lottery tickets, another kept a coffee house; several were also dentists. Some gave up the unequal struggle and turned to other professions, such as apothecary, surgeon or physician. A considerable number emigrated from Edinburgh to London, or to the Caribbean, United States, and later Australia, India and other parts of the British Empire. A number sought work nearer their roots in one of the northern burghs where a modest living might be had by being a moderate-sized fish swimming in a much reduced pond.

With a few exceptions, the quality of workmanship of Edinburgh goldsmiths exceeded that of those working in the other burghs of the kingdom. The greatest amount of expertise was concentrated in Edinburgh and Canongate, and the wealthiest customers tended to patronise the Edinburgh goldsmiths rather than those from the other burghs. The goldsmiths of the capital were in touch with what was going on in London, Bruges, Paris and other centres furth of Scotland; they had mostly spent some time abroad themselves as journeymen after completing their indentures. These conditions did not usually prevail in provincial towns, which looked no further than Edinburgh for enlightenment.

Edinburgh goldsmiths were not far behind those

in London in adopting new styles, fashions, methods of working and indeed prices [see 4.33]. From as early as the 1450s we have evidence of a number of Scottish goldsmiths plying their trade in London. After the Restoration of the monarchy in 1660 there was gradually more interchange of ideas across the border. In the 1680s and '90s a small number of Huguenot goldsmiths made their way to Edinburgh (and at least two settled as far north as Old Aberdeen).

During the course of the 18th century Edinburgh was the centre of that astonishing phenomenon known as the Scottish Enlightenment, which positively sparked with a myriad of ideas, philosophies, new thoughts on education, art, architecture, sculpture, literature, economics, design and cutting-edge technologies. The goldsmiths reaped a rich harvest from those who congregated in the city to discuss all these and every other subject under the sun which overflowed their brains and flooded all the printing presses. Nothing was too rococo, too baroque, too neo-classical, too anything; but the goldsmiths could cope with the requirements of all these neo-Renaissance men who wanted to commission something that would show off their taste, learning and culture. If a customer wanted something, the goldsmiths would make it; if they did not have time to make it themselves, they imported it ready-made from Sheffield, Birmingham or London. Wares had probably always been bought in from the south and this trend increased dramatically in the second half of the 18th century. Not only stock but technologies too: Messrs William and Patrick Cunningham were complimented by the Incorporation of Goldsmiths for having set up the first establishment in Edinburgh for the manufacture of plated goods. Mass-production techniques were gradually introduced as the goldsmiths sought to stay competitive with their southern fellows. All through that century there was a gradual increase in the number of people specialising in specific skills such as engraving, chasing, embossing and casting. The arts of the seal-engraver and lapidary flourished as never before.

The forward momentum of the 18th-century wave of prosperity and progress carried over into the 1800s and 1810s, but then came Waterloo. How strange it was that such a final victory over a long-standing foe should have resulted not in increased prosperity, but in a sudden downturn in the economy, 'a general flatness of trade'. There was a sudden sharp increase in bankruptcies among goldsmiths and customers alike. The next 35 years would witness a slow and painful process of economic regeneration and determined rebuilding of businesses. New fortunes would be made, but only after protracted hard work. However, a good many goldsmiths' businesses survived this turbulence, such as Mackay & Cunningham in Edinburgh or Robert Gray & Son in Glasgow. Others faltered or went to the wall.

A measure of prosperity returned from the middle of the 19th century until the next national catastrophe: the First World War. After 1918 business picked up slowly, but things were never the same. The nature of the trade was changing fast. Mechanisation was replacing the hammer and burin of the skilled journeyman with the machine of the factory-floor operator. More silver was imported from workshops south of the border, and less was home-made or home-designed. Between the wars there was little innovation or artistic merit in much that was made. There were some honourable exceptions to this, however, such as the remarkable output of Brook & Sons [6.18], and the enormous banqueting service made by Tatton & Son for George V's silver jubilee in 1935 [6.21] which is still used at the Palace of Holyroodhouse.

This output of the workshop of Tatton & Son represented a high point in an otherwise uninspired decade. The pattern of the trade was changing again. After the Second World War the lowest ebb of the Incorporation was reached. For a few years in the 1950s there were only three freemen goldsmiths in Edinburgh; it seemed as if the writing was on the wall.

But the Incorporation was not dead; it was only sleeping. Kept going by the tenacity and devotion of its long-time deacon, Henry Roy Tatton, it survived its near-death experience and in 1975 took on a new lease of life. An act of Parliament was procured in its favour and new life was breathed at last into the oldest body corporate in Scotland. By then the amount of silver and gold being assayed in Edinburgh was approximately 0.4% of the total amount passing through the four surviving assay-offices of the United Kingdom. Today the figure is 12%, an increase by a factor of thirty. While much of that throughput now consists of light silver chains, pendants and other trinketry, mostly made outside Scotland, there has been a remarkable renaissance of the craftsman-designer-silversmith.

Never before in Scotland has the current phenomenon, exemplified by the Millennium Collection for Bute House [10.15-22] and the 'Silver of the Stars' project (pp. 214-16), been equalled. A second Scottish Enlightenment in the world of the silversmith has erupted to match the present blossoming in the fields of Scottish literature, sculpture, architecture, painting and the performing arts. Once again there are patrons prepared to commission innovative work, and to take an active interest in its conception and design; as in the 18th century, new money begets new commissions; Scottish goldsmiths are venturing into new waters. The Incorporation in Edinburgh is burgeoning anew, and it has recently established a charitable trust, reaching into its back pocket for the funds, some of which derive from its shrewd investment in the original issue of Bank of Scotland shares made more than 300 years before.

The continuity of the past is, and always has been, the springboard of the present and the seed-bed for the future.

PARLIAMENT CLOSE, EDINBURGH

Attributed to John Kay, David Wilkie, and others
Oil on panel, n.d. / H 59 cm; W 91.1 cm
Lent by City of Edinburgh Museums and Galleries

This painting presents a glimpse of the vibrant social and economic life of Edinburgh about 1790. Centred around Parliament Close was an area populated by goldsmiths. Their Hall, established there in 1700, also housed the Assay Office, and can be seen to the left, abutting on to Parliament House. It had shops below which were at this period leased to the goldsmiths David Downie and James Welsh. It was burned down in a disastrous fire in January 1796: 'The whole tenement, consisting of Goldsmiths Hall, with their records, papers &c., the Assay Office, and shops of Mr. Bowman and Mr. Downie were totally consumed, with every thing that they contained. The loss is very considerable' (*Edinburgh Magazine*, 1796).

Other goldsmiths' shops can be seen nestled around the High Kirk, including those of William Auld, Peter Mathie, Patrick Robertson and Alexander Gardner. These were swept away in the restorations of the exterior of the church in 1829. Until the New Town was well established and drew the fashionable and wealthy classes across the North Bridge, the goldsmiths continued to live and work where their customers were, in the overcrowded, high lands and tenements of the High Street. They particularly favoured the area around St Giles whether, as shown here, to the south side, or in the Luckenbooths on the north side.

4.1 BANNER OF THE UNITED GOLDSMITHS OF EDINBURGH

Unknown artist, 1832

H 160 cm; W 130 cm

NMS H.LF 26; given by the Incorporation of Goldsmiths of the City of Edinburgh

Reference: Dalgleish and Maxwell (1987), no. 61

Green silk banner painted with a cartouche-shaped shield, quartered with the arms of the Incorporation of Goldsmiths, a figure depicting Justice, the castle of Edinburgh, a figure depicting Earl Grey, and the Goldsmiths' motto 'God With Us' below; set within a spray of thistles, shamrocks and roses; in a ribbon above, 'UNITED GOLDSMITHS & RELATIVE PRO-FESSIONS', and in a ribbon below, 'PURGE THE BASE METAL FROM THE GOLD'.

This was painted specifically to be carried by the Society of Journeymen Goldsmiths during the great Reform Jubilee Trades Procession on 11 August 1832, to mark the passing of the Scottish Reform Act of that year [see 2.23 and 2.24 for other examples of Gold-smiths' insignia]. The Journeymen Goldsmiths asked the Incorporation to borrow their existing insignia for the parade, but the subject matter of the banner makes it obvious that it was created specially for the day. The figure of Earl Grey relates to his pivotal role in passing the act, while the figure of Justice no doubt relates to the hope that a more just and equitable franchise would follow. The castle is obviously a direct reference to Edinburgh's town mark.

4.1

4.2 'THE STRATHMORE SALVER'

Alexander Scott, Edinburgh, 1667-69

Marks: 'AS' (maker Alexander Scott); castle (Edinburgh); 'AS' (deacon Alexander Scott, 1667-69)

D 33 cm; Wt 17.22 oz

NMS H.MEQ 799; purchased from Graus Antiques, London, 1965

References: Dalgleish and Maxwell (1987), no. 14; Maxwell (1964), p. 325; Glamis Book of Record (1890), p. 95; Fothringham (2001[iii]), p. 88

Circular plate, wide rim, chased and embossed with acanthus leaves and void ovals; the central print is engraved with the arms of Patrick Lyon, 1st Earl of Strathmore. It originally had a central trumpet foot, and it probably started life as a tazza.

In the 1660s and '70s the Earl of Strathmore set about rebuilding his family's fortunes, which had been grievously damaged during the Covenanting wars. He recorded his success in his *Book of Record*, and noted in 1684 that he had bought a parcel of second-hand silver plate from 'Mr Cockburn the Goldsmith'. This had originally belonged to the Earl of Perth, the Lord Chancellor, who had recently fallen from royal favour and was imprisoned in Stirling Castle. Cockburn agreed to remove Lord Perth's arms from some of the plate and to re-engrave it with Lord Strathmore's. This salver, originally a tazza or fruit dish, as recorded in an inventory of 1695, is one of these re-engraved pieces, made some 20 years before by Alexander Scott.

4.3 *THE GLAMIS BOOK OF RECORD*

Lent by the Earl of Strathmore and Kinghorne

References: *Glamis Book of Record* (1890); Fothringham (2001[iii]), pp. 81-93

Manuscript diary kept by Patrick, 1st Earl of Strath-more, 1684-89, incorporating a record of household and other expenses. This includes a record of his transactions with James Cockburn in 1689 for some £3000 Scots (*c.*£250 sterling). At about the same date the Earl paid the artist Jacob de Wit £5 sterling for a portrait of his wife.

4.2

4.4 PORRINGER AND COVER

Alexander Reid III, Edinburgh, 1682-83

Marks (on base and cover rim): 'AR' (maker Alexander Reid III); castle (Edinburgh); 'JB' in monogram (assay-master John Borthwick); 'b' (date-letter 1682-83)

H 18 cm; L (across handles) 19 cm; Wt 17.46 oz

NMS H.MEQ 1467; purchased in 1981

Provenance: collection of the late Sir John Noble, Bart.

References: *Empire Exhibition* (1938), no. 4, pl. 3; Dalgleish and Maxwell (1987), no. 19; Finlay and Fothringham (1991), p. 121, pl. 60(ii); *EGM* (2006), B151, A261, *et. seq.*

Straight-sided bowl, the lower section formed of repoussé acanthus leaves, set on a fluted cushion foot; two opposed cast S-scroll handles with birds-head terminals; the cushion cover has a protruding cut scalloped rim, is chased with a profusion of leaf work, and has a hollow cast strawberry and leaf finial.

Pieces with this type of extravagant decoration are rare in Scotland and this covered porringer is an exceptional survival. It carries the mark of assay-master John Borthwick (the first to hold the office) and the newly-introduced variable annual date-letter 'b' for 1682-83.

4.5 'THE LION TANKARD'

James Cockburn, Edinburgh, 1685-86

H 18.3 cm; D (rim) 12 cm; D (base) 14.6 cm; Wt 33.68 oz

Marks (under rim): 'IC' in monogram (maker James Cockburn); castle (Edinburgh); 'JB' in monogram (assay-master John Borthwick); 'e' (date-letter 1685-86)

NMS H.MEQ 1597; purchased in 1960, in conjunction with City of Edinburgh Galleries and Museums, from T. Lumley, London, after export licence deferral

References: Finlay and Fothringham (1991), p. 121, pl. 50: RSM (1948), no. 32; Malcolm (1945) (HBOS Archives Original Subscription Ledger Acc. 2002/008)

Plain straight-sided body, with plain cushion lid, rope moulding applied round base, body and lid rim; thumb-piece in the form of a lion resting its forepaws on a ball; C-scroll handle with shield-shaped terminal. The remaining survivor of the only known matched pair of Scottish 17th-century tankards, its companion was stolen from Huntly House Museum, Edinburgh, in 1994. Stylistically this piece is also highly unusual, possibly borrowing from Scandinavian sources.

4.6 TWO SMALL LIGHTHOUSE CASTERS (FROM A SET OF THREE)

Andrew Law, Edinburgh, 1693-94

Marks (on base): 'AL' (maker Andrew Law); castle (Edinburgh); 'JB' in monogram (assay-master John Borthwick); 'n' (date-letter 1693-94)

(1) H 15.8 cm; D (foot) 6.9 cm; Wt 5.858 oz

(2) H 15.8 cm; D (foot) 7 cm; Wt 6.374 oz

Lent by the City of Edinburgh Museums and Galleries; purchased with the aid of the National Fund for Acquisitions

Provenance: Sotheby's sale, 2 December 1965, lot 200; property of Miss J. M. L. Wardlaw; Christie's sale, 24 June 1981, lot 71

Reference: Clayton (1985), pl. 99

Plain cylindrical bodies set on domed feet with moulded rim; domed lift-off covers with wire and hook attachments, with pierced scroll and foliage decoration, the top with applied cut-card scroll-work, knop and ball finial; upper body is engraved with full arms for Sir John Ramsay of Whitehill and his wife Anna, daughter of Sir John Carstairs of Kilconquhar.

These are the two remaining pieces from the earliest complete Scottish set of casters – the largest caster was stolen in 1994. Called lighthouse casters because of their shape, this style was popular until the end of the 17th century. They were used for dispensing sugar and other spices, including dry mustard, at the table.

4.7 THE KINLOCH MONTEITH

Colin McKenzie, Edinburgh, 1698-99

Marks (on base): 'MK' conjoined (maker Colin McKenzie); castle (Edinburgh); 'JP' in monogram (assay-master James Penman); 'S' (date-letter 1698-99)

H 23.5 cm; D (rim) 32.7 cm; D (base) 19.7 cm; Wt 70.26 oz

Lent by the City of Edinburgh Museums and Galleries

References: RSM (1948), no. 45; Finlay and Fothringham (1991), p. 122, pl. 57; Lee (1978), no. 85

The bowl is in eight lobed panels on a stippled background, the rim with cast and applied foliate and scroll edge; on circular gadrooned stepped foot, with two opposed ring and knop drop handles each issuing from a grotesque mask. One panel is engraved with a shield of arms of Kinloch impaling Rocheid for Sir Francis Kinloch of Gilmerton, 3rd Baronet, and his

4.4

4.5

4.2

4.4 (and detail)

4.6

4.7 (and detail)

4.5

4.8

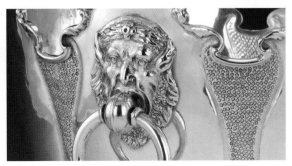

wife Mary, sister and co-heiress of Sir James Rocheid of Inverleith, 1st Baronet, and daughter of Sir James Rocheid of Inverleith.

This is the joint earliest surviving Scottish monteith [see 1.5]. It has the same arms as the tankard by John Seatoun of the same year [4.8], and was possibly commissioned to mark the marriage of Sir Francis Kinloch to Mary Rocheid, heiress of the Inverleith estate to the north of Edinburgh.

4.8 THE KINLOCH TANKARD

John Seatoun, Edinburgh, 1698-99

Marks: 'IS' in monogram, with mullets to either side, in a circle (maker John Seatoun); castle (Edinburgh); 'JP' monogram (assay-master James Penman); 'S' (date-letter 1698-99)

H 20.5 cm; D (lip) 12 cm; D (base) 16 cm; Wt 42.04 oz (base engraved 'G' and Scratch Wt '44u 8d')

Lent from a private collection at Mount Stuart

References: RSM (1948), no. 44, attributed to James Sympsone; Finlay and Fothringham (1991), p. 121

Tapering cylindrical body on spreading gadrooned foot, with applied reeded mouldings; stepped domed lid with gadrooned rim, spool and half-knop finial; elaborate cast thumb-piece with hinge; C-scroll handle with shield terminal and foliate bead and spool rat-tail. Engraved arms of Kinloch impaling Rocheid [cf. 4.7]. Their marriage is said to have taken place in c.1705, but it could have been earlier, possibly the date of the making of the monteith and tankard. The Kinloch and Rocheid families were both prominent and very successful Edinburgh merchant dynasties.

4.9 LAVER OR JUG

Thomas Ker, Edinburgh, 1701-02

Marks (on base): 'T.K' (maker Thomas Ker); castle (Edinburgh); 'JP' in monogram' (assay-master James Penman); 'W' (date-letter 1701-02)

H 22.4 cm; D (foot) 8.3 cm; Wt 26.40 oz

Lent from a private collection at Mount Stuart

Reference: RSM (1948), no. 50

The lower part of the body consists of a compressed sphere, the upper part is tapering-cylindrical with a narrow bombe section below the reeded rim, all standing on a gadrooned foot with reeded rim; the covered spout has a hinged heart-shaped flap covering the pouring-hole; the stepped domed lid has a gadrooned rim and urn finial, the foliate-scroll thumb-piece with a beaded rat-tail, the S-scroll handle with a pointed terminal and applied foliate beaded rat-tail.

Although there is no evidence this jug was ever used for baptism and, as such, is the earliest secular example of its type, the construction of the spout is similar to a few baptismal lavers. The maker Thomas Ker was also responsible for the very elegant toilet ewer made for Charles, 1st Earl of Hopetoun, in 1706-07 [see 4.32], and this laver may have originally accompanied a wash basin of some sort.

4.10 THE KEIR TOILET SERVICE

Colin McKenzie, Edinburgh, 1703-04

Marks: 'MK' conjoined (maker Colin McKenzie); castle (Edinburgh); 'JP' in monogram (assay-master James Penman); 'y' (date-letter 1703-04)

Casket: L 27.5 cm; H 11 cm; Wt 72.71 oz

Large covered boxes: D 13.5 cm; H 8.4 cm; Wt 17.1 oz

Small covered boxes: D 8.8 cm; H 6 cm; Wt 7.75 oz

Pomade pots: H 5 cm; D 4.7 cm; Wt 2.49 oz

Candlesticks: H 15.3 cm; Wt 11.98 oz

Hair brushes: L 14.5 cm; W 7.5 cm; Wt (all-in) 7.38 oz

Whisks: L 22 cm; Wt 3 oz

Two-handled bowls: D c.14.5 cm; Wt 9.56 oz

Pin cushion: L 18 cm

Mirror: H 49.5 cm

Wt (in total excluding mirror and brush backs): 198 oz

Lent anonymously

Provenance: The Hon. Marion Stewart, daughter of Alexander, 5th Lord Blantyre, on her marriage to James Stirling of Keir; by descent until sold by the family at Christie's sale, London, Wednesday 24 March 1982, lot 79, A Royal Collection 1982-99

References: Oman 103 (1939), pp. 70-75, no. 937; Finlay and Fothringham (1991), pp. 123-24, pl. 62

4.6	4.7	4.8 (above), 4.10 (below)	4.9

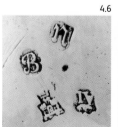
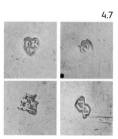
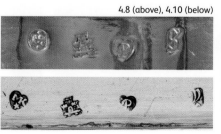
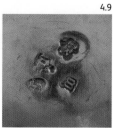

Consisting of a mirror, comb box, a pair of large circular covered boxes, a pair of smaller circular covered boxes, a pair of two-handled covered bowls, a pair of octagonal small covered pots, a pair of cast candlesticks, a pair of oval brushes, a pair of whisks, and a rectangular pin cushion. All of stepped form with simple mouldings, and all engraved with a cipher for the Honourable Marion Stewart, within an elaborate baroque cartouche with coronet above.

This is the only known complete Scottish-made toilet service in existence. It was probably commissioned for the wedding of Marion Stewart to James Stirling of Keir in February 1704. Marion was the daughter of Alexander, 5th Lord Blantyre. Her brother Walter was served heir to Frances Teresa Stuart, the Duchess of Richmond and Lennox. Frances bequeathed her fortune, including her own magnificent Lennoxlove Toilet Service, made in Paris, to Walter in 1702. This was probably the inspiration for Marion to acquire a Scottish-made example for her new home at Keir. James Stirling, Marion's husband, was in the opposite political camp to the Blantyres, being a staunch Jacobite. He was imprisoned several times for his involvement in the failed Jacobite Rebellions of 1708, 1715 and 1745, and had his estates forfeited in 1715. This does not seem to have put a strain on his marriage, as he and Marion went on to have 22 children.

4.11 CHOCOLATE POT

Robert Bruce, Edinburgh, 1708-09

Marks (on body rim): 'RB' (maker Robert Bruce); castle (Edinburgh); 'EP' (assay-master Edward Penman); 'D' (date-letter 1708-09).

H 26.5 cm; D (base) 11.7 cm; L (spout to back) 16.5 cm; Wt 25.20 oz

Lent by Dundee City Council (McManus Galleries and Museum)

References: Deitert (2007), p. 167, wrongly dated c.1720; EGM B213, A411, A 413

Tapering, straight-sided body on plain moulded foot, with cast faceted S-scroll spout and S-scroll wooden handle at right angles to spout, the handle sockets with cut-card leaf decoration. Hinged, domed lid with applied cut-card work leaves and a hinged baluster finial allowing for a stirring implement.

Scottish chocolate pots are extremely rare; this is the earliest example by many years [see 9.12]. Chocolate pots can be identified by their hinged or sliding finials to allow a stick, or molinet, to be used to stir up the chocolate sediment in the bottom of the pot. Chocolate drinking was introduced to England in the 1650s, and no doubt reached Scotland soon after, although early documentary references are rare.

4.12 CASTER

Colin McKenzie, Edinburgh, 1708-09

Marks: 'MK' conjoined (maker Colin McKenzie); castle (Edinburgh); 'EP' (assay-master Edward Penman); 'D' (date-letter 1708-09)

H 21 cm; D (foot) 8.7 cm; Wt 14.36 oz

Lent from a private collection at Mount Stuart

Reference: RSM (1948), no. 58

Tapering-cylindrical body on simple domed foot with simple moulded girdle which conceals the slip-on cover and long inner sleeve, the upper part of the cover pierced with quatrefoils, its reeded domed top with acorn finial; engraved with a crest – crossed swords on a wreath, with motto above: 'PARATUS • AD • ARMA'.

A very unusual style for Scotland, it may have been influenced by Irish casters. The crest and motto are for Johnston of Johnston and Hiltown. The original owner was said to be Sir John Johnston, a merchant in Glasgow who joined the Jacobite army during the 1715 Rebellion and fought at the battle of Sheriffmuir.

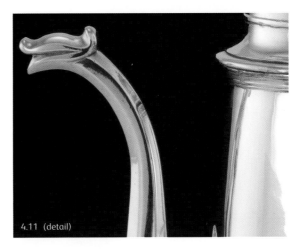

4.11 (detail)

4.11

4.12

4.10 (and details)

4.10

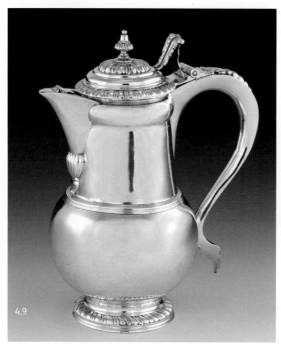

4.9

4.10

4.10

4.11

4.12

Lady Grisell Baillie's Silver

Lady Grisell Baillie (1665-1746), daughter of Patrick Hume, 1st Earl of Marchmont, was a remarkable woman. A member of a staunch Presbyterian family, she was revered as a heroine for hiding and protecting her father during the 'Killing Times' of the 1680s, when Presbyterians and Covenanters were being harried by Royalist Government forces. She is said to have hid him in the vault under the parish church and fed him with food secretly taken from her own plate, lest the servants become suspicious and inform on them. The family managed to escape to exile in The Netherlands, where the young Grisell showed great skill in managing a large household and business interests. This was to serve her in good stead when they returned to Scotland after King James was deposed and the Protestant William of Orange was installed as king.

In 1691 she married George Baillie of Jerviswood, a member of another strongly Presbyterian family, and a rising political star. They had a long and happy marriage. During his prolonged absence on political business in Edinburgh and London (he was a great supporter of the Union of 1707), Baillie left her in absolute charge of the estates and household. How she performed these duties is recorded in fascinating detail in her Household Account books. These give a wonderful, human glimpse into the functioning of a successful landed family, detailing everything from medicines bought for the children to annual yields of the farms. They provide a particular insight into the development of social and domestic fashions, and record the purchase of silver and other necessities for the tea and dinner tables – even detailing recipes and the order of serving meals.

Lady Grisell died in 1746 'full of years and good works'. A few pieces of her silver remained in the family and can be identified today.

4.13 TWO-HANDLED CUP AND COVER

John Seatoun, Edinburgh, 1709-10

Marks: 'IS' in monogram (maker John Seatoun); castle (Edinburgh); 'EP' (assay-master Edward Penman); 'E' (date-letter 1709-10)

H 26.9 cm; L (across handles) 31.8 cm; D (foot) 14.6 cm

Wt 59.46 oz

NMS H.1991.20; purchased from Partridge Fine Arts, London, 1991

Provenance: by descent to the Earl of Haddington; Sotheby's sale, London, 30 November 1967, lot 109; John Noble Esq.; Christie's sale, 2 December 1981, lot 114

References: Finlay and Fothringham (1991), p. 132 and 140, pl. 66(ii); E. A. Jones (1936[ii]), pp. 118-25.

Plain, slightly flaring U-shaped body set on a stepped foot, with two opposed cast S-scroll handles surmounted by button knops; the stepped domed cover with an acorn finial. The body is engraved with the arms of George Baillie of Jerviswood and Mellerstain.

Somewhat unusually, this covered cup does not seem to appear in Lady Grisell's otherwise highly detailed and precise household accounts, unlike her careful entry for the coffee pot and milk jug below [4.14]. It is a particularly large and handsome example of this type of cup and was certainly appropriate to emphasise the improving fortunes and status of the Baillie family. The maker's mark used to be ascribed to James Sympsone, but Fothringham has argued convincingly that it should be reattributed to John Seatoun. From an analysis of the extant assay-masters' accounts, it is clear that Sympsone made very little silver, and then only between the years 1686 and 1697. Besides, he was buried in Edinburgh's Greyfriars churchyard on 30 January 1700. Seatoun, on the other hand, sent a prodigious amount of silver to be assayed from 1688 (the date he was admitted to the Incorporation) to 1702 (the date the account books cease).

4.14 COFFEE POT AND HOT MILK JUG

Colin McKenzie, Edinburgh, 1713-14

Marks: 'MK' conjoined (maker Colin McKenzie); castle (Edinburgh); 'EP' (assay-master Edward Penman); 'I' (date-letter 1713-14)

Coffee pot: H 24 cm; L 21 cm; Wt 35.73 oz

Milk jug: H 18 cm; L 16 cm; Wt 15.11 oz

NMS H.MEQ 899 and 900; purchased from How of Edinburgh in 1968, with the aid of the National Art-Collection Fund, The Pilgrim Trust, and Society of Antiquaries of Scotland

Provenance: by descent to the Earl of Haddington; sold at Sotheby's sale, 30 November 1967, lots 110 and 111

4.13 (above) and 4.14 (below)

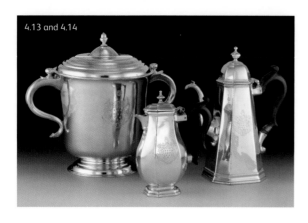

4.13 and 4.14

References: Dalgleish and Maxwell (1987), no. 29; RSM (1948), nos 68 and 69; Maxwell (1967), pp. 199-200; Finlay and Fothringham (1991), pp. 136-37, 143, pl. 73(i)

The pot has a tapering octagonal body, with simple base moulding, S-scroll spout, a hinged domed lid with baluster finial and a wooden scroll handle. The jug has an octagonal flattened baluster shaped body set on a stepped foot, with stepped hinged lid with baluster finial. Both are engraved with arms for George Baillie of Jerviswood and Mellerstain.

These are the earliest examples of a Scottish coffee pot and hot milk jug, although there is no doubt that wealthy and fashionable Scots were certainly drinking the beverage long before this date. There are about 30 known contemporary accounts of the maker Colin McKenzie's work still extant, including the one for this coffee pot and milk jug. Dated January 1714, it reads: ' … to workmanship of the silver Coffee pot and Milk pot at 2s. 2d. per ounce, and there was some odds in the weight of plate I gave him to make them off; They weigh 50 ounce and 12 drop; and three handles cost 17s. Total £6. 8s. 3d.' Again this illustrates the practice of having old silver melted down to make new more fashionable pieces, while it is also interesting that the canny Lady Grisell bought spare handles for the pots.

A Tea-table Miscellany

Providing silver vessels for the increasingly popular and highly fashionable social custom of tea-drinking became a lucrative business for Scottish goldsmiths in the 18th century. The first surviving Edinburgh-made teapot dates to 1714. However, it is worth discounting here, once and for all, the notion that the lack of any earlier tea wares in Scotland somehow proves that tea arrived in this country many decades after it arrived in England. Documentary references make it clear that tea came to Scotland at roughly the same time as England in the mid-17th century, and its initial expense likewise made it the preserve of the wealthy gentry.[1]

It is also probable that the first teapots used in Scotland in the 1680s were of imported Chinese porcelain or stoneware, but it is equally clear from documents that silver teapots were in use long before the first surviving Scottish-made one. The Countess of Caithness paid Thomas Ker, in Edinburgh, for the repair of a silver teapot in 1695.[2] The reason for the relatively late date of the first surviving Scottish teapot is probably the same as for the paucity of early domestic silver in general. Such items were of exceptionally high value and social status and were therefore governed by the dictates of the taste of their fashion-conscious owners. Old pots would have been handed over to the goldsmith as scrap for reworking into the most current style. (For example, the Earl of Breadalbane bought a new 'cadelpot' from Colin McKenzie in 1710, but recovered part of the total cost by handing over an older, smaller caudle pot to be melted down as scrap.[3]

After this stuttering start the survival rate for tea wares improves throughout the 18th century, possibly correlating to the reduction in cost of the tea itself. Several Scottish goldsmiths made a speciality of this branch of work: George Cooper in Aberdeen made some very elegant teapots and some of the earliest surviving Scottish tea caddies; meanwhile in Edinburgh, William Aytoun made a wide range of

'A SQUABBLE AT A TEA PARTY'

Unknown artist, c.1745, Penicuik Drawings

The only known contemporary illustration of a Scottish 18th-century tea-party, showing many of the pieces used in a normally sedate and fashionable event: a silver bullet-shaped teapot, a silver tea kettle, and a china teacup and saucer. What caused the 'squabble' is not known.

[Reproduced courtesy of Sir Robert Clerk of Penicuik]

teapots, tea kettles, caddies, milk jugs and more. However, the undoubted master of this area was James Ker, who made so many surpassingly elegant teapots that the late Ian Finlay referred to him, somewhat lyrically, as 'the Prince of Teapot Makers'.

Notes

1   Young (2002): *Elegant Dining*, pp. 108-09 (Victorian and Albert Museum, 2002).
2   NAS: Breadalbane Papers [GD 112/15/60].
3   NAS: Breadalbane Papers [GD 112/15/230/7]. I am grateful to Miss Tawney Paul for many of the Breadalbane references used in this book.

4.15 TEAPOT

Colin McKenzie, Edinburgh, 1715-16

Marks (on base): 'MK' conjoined (maker Colin McKenzie); castle (Edinburgh); 'EP' (assay-master Edward Penman); 'L' (date-letter 1715-16)

H 10.8 cm; L 23.5 cm; Wt 17.06 oz

NMS K.2004.209; purchased, 2004, from Nicholas Shaw Antiques

Plain apple-shaped body, with straight tapering spout and wooden C-scroll handle, the pull-off cover with simple wooden knop finial. This is one of the earliest surviving Scottish teapots.

4.16 TEAPOT STAND

Colin McKenzie, Edinburgh, 1718-19

Marks (on base): 'MK' conjoined (maker Colin McKenzie); castle (Edinburgh); 'EP' (assay-master Edward Penman); 'O' (date-letter 1718-19)

D 10.7 cm; Wt 2.78 oz / Lent from a private collection

Provenance: collection of James Ivory

Reference: RSM (1948), no. 79

Plain circular shallow dish set on a simple collet foot. This is the earliest surviving example of a Scottish teapot stand. They were used to protect the polished surfaces of wooden tea tables from hot bases of teapots.

4.17 CREAM JUG

Mungo Yorstoun, Edinburgh, 1714-15

Marks: 'MY' (maker Mungo Yorstoun); castle (Edinburgh); 'EP' (assay-master Edward Penman); 'K' (date-letter for 1714-15)

H 11.5 cm; L (across handle) 11 cm; D (foot) 5.3 cm; Wt 7.8 oz

NMS H.MEQ 1294; purchased at Sotheby's sale, Hopetoun House, 13 November 1978, lot 77

Reference: Dietert (2007), p. 170

Baluster body on cushion foot, with arched faceted pouring lip, and prominent double curve cast handle with scroll ends.

A particularly robust and bulbous jug, this is reminiscent of the shape of much larger beer jugs of the period. It is the oldest example of a Scottish cream jug. It is not at all clear whether such jugs were used for milk or cream to be added to tea or coffee, or for cream to go with dessert dishes. Given the Scots' penchant for 'multi-use' vessels, it may well have served all three.

4.18 TEA CADDY SET

William Aytoun, Edinburgh, 1728-29; James Clark, Edinburgh, 1767-68

Marks (on base of caddies): 'WA' (maker William Aytoun); castle (Edinburgh); 'EP' (assay-master Edward Penman); 'Y' (date-letter 1728-29)

Marks (on base of sugar box): 'CLARK' (maker John Clark); castle (Edinburgh); thistle (standard mark); 'N' gothic (date-letter 1767-68)

Tea caddies: H 10 cm; W 7.7 cm; Dp 4.8 cm; Wt 9.05 oz
Sugar box: H 10.5 cm; W 7.9 cm; D 7.9 cm; Wt 13.41 oz
Outer box: H 12 cm; L 21.5 cm; D 10.8 cm

NMS H.MEQ 1255-7; purchased from How of Edinburgh, 1978

Provenance: Christie's sale, London, 23 March 1978, lot 98

Comprising two tea caddies with later matching sugar box, in a shagreen covered wooden box mounted in silver. Caddies and sugar box of plain rectangular form with simple moulded bases, and stepped domed hinged lids; caddies engraved with crest and motto for Stewart.

4.15

4.16

4.17

This is the earliest known set of Edinburgh-made tea caddies. The two smaller boxes would have been for green and black tea, while the larger box would have been for sugar. The lockable, fitted case emphasises the high cost of tea and the need to secure it from pilfering. Scottish tea caddies are in general rare before about 1750, and most of those that do survive were made in Aberdeen or Glasgow. The maker of the caddies, William Aytoun, seems to have specialised in tea and coffee wares.

4.19 TEA KETTLE, STAND, LAMP AND SALVER

James Mitchelson, Edinburgh, 1736-37

Marks: 'IM' (James Mitchelson); castle (Edinburgh); 'AU' (assay-master Archibald Ure); 'G' script (date-letter 1736-37)

Kettle and stand: H (max.) 44 cm; Wt (all-in) 95.16 oz (Scratch Wts [kettle] '57 o 8 dr'; [stand] '26 o 10 dr'; [burner] '8 o 9 dr')

Salver: D 23 cm; Wt 48.76 oz (Scratch Wt '49 o 3 dr')

NMS H.MEQ 638.A-C and 639; purchased from How of Edinburgh in 1963

Kettle with compressed spherical body, flush hinged lid, S-curved spout and swing-curved loop handle (the foot locates into the stand by a pin and hinge arrangement); stand on three cabriole legs and shell feet with wooden insulators, with a band of cast openwork scroll and medallion decoration; separate burner sits in a ring attached to the legs. The flat circular salver has a moulded shaped border, set on four scroll and shell feet; a threaded socket in the centre of the underside was presumably designed to locate a silver tripod tea-table. Both kettle and salver flat-chased with bands of matching elaborate rococo foliage, scrolls, shells and diaper work. Body of the kettle engraved with contemporary arms for Alexander Garden of Troup, and Jean, daughter of Sir Francis Grant of Cullen.

This impressive kettle and salver is a *tour de force* of the maker's art, displaying raising, casting, engraving and particularly chasing of the highest order. The set was probably at one time complemented by a silver tripod stand which would screw in to the underside of the salver. No such Scottish-made tripod survives, but they were certainly used in Scotland, as the Earl of Strathmore had one by Simon Pantin of London, dated 1724.

4.20 POSSET POT AND COVER

Charles Blair, Edinburgh, 1724-25

Marks: 'CB' (maker Charles Blair); castle (Edinburgh); 'EP' (assay-master Edward Penman); 'u' (date-letter 1724-25)

H 25 cm; W (across handles) 30 cm; D (lip) 17.8 cm; Wt 55.5 oz

Lent from a private collection at Mount Stuart

The bucket-shaped body is on a simple stepped foot, with scroll handles with dog-nose terminals. Upright spout with straight central section and pierced strainer; stepped domed cover with acorn finial. Engraved with contemporary arms for George Innes, writer in Edinburgh (although Innes did not record these arms in the Lyon Register until 15 August 1733).

This is the second of only two surviving large covered spout cups, the other being that by Walter Scott, won as the Edinburgh town prize at Leith Races in 1707 [see 9.15]. They seem to have been known as posset pots or posset dishes with covers in the 18th century, and the Leith Races Prize example was certainly referred to as such in late 18th-century Hopetoun House inventories. Posset was an alcoholic drink of ale mixed with milk.

4.21 CASTER

Charles Blair, Edinburgh, 1724-25

Marks (on base and cover): 'CB' in a heart (maker Charles Blair); castle (Edinburgh); 'EP' (assay-master Edward Penman); 'U' (date-letter 1724-25)

H 16 cm; D (max.) 10.5 cm; D (base) 6 cm; Wt 10.6 oz

Lent from a private collection at Mount Stuart

The plain bowl-shaped body is on simple domed foot, the bell-shaped cover pierced with open scrollwork with acorn-and-knop finial. This form is quite unlike anything found in Scottish or English silver of the period. It was probably used for sugar.

4.22 THE ANNANDALE BOWL AND STAND

William Aytoun, Edinburgh, 1725-26

Marks (on bases): 'WA' (maker William Aytoun); castle (Edinburgh); 'EP' (assay-master Edward Penman); 'V' (date-letter 1725-26);

Bowl: L 20.5 cm; W 12.2 cm; Wt 12.94 oz (Scratch Wt [base of bowl] '13 – 7')

<table>
<tr><td align="center">4.19</td><td align="center">4.20</td><td align="center">4.21</td></tr>
</table>

4.15

4.16

4.18

4.19

4.18 (detail)

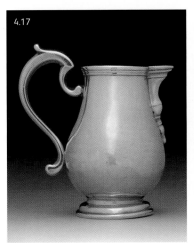

4.17

4.20

4.21

Stand: L 22.7 cm; W 19.5 cm; Wt 12.39 oz

Lent from a private collection at Mount Stuart

Reference: RSM (1948), no. 93

Oval bowl with plain heavy oval collet foot, wavy rim with applied moulded wire; two opposing S-scroll cast handles; matching shaped oval stand with similar wavy border, on plain substantial collet foot. Bowl and stand are engraved with crest 'a winged spur' and motto 'NUNQUAM NON PARATUS' and Marquess's coronet for James Johnstone, 2nd Marquess of Annandale (succeeded 1721, died 1730). This bowl and stand has no obvious surviving parallel. It may have fulfilled a variety of uses at the table or on the sideboard.

4.23 EIGHTEEN DINNER PLATES

Harry Beathune, Edinburgh, 1722-23

Marks (underside of rim): 'HB' (maker Harry Beathune); castle (Edinburgh); 'EP' (assay-master Edward Penman); 'S' (date-letter 1722-23)

D (each approx.) 25 cm; Wt (each approx.) 20 oz

Lent by The Huntington Library, Art Collections and Botanical Gardens; gift of Mrs James R. Page

Provenance: Earl of Abercorn; Mr and Mrs James Page; acquired through 1966 bequest of Mrs James R. Page

Reference: Deitert (2007), p. 193

Circular plates with wide border and heavily gadrooned rim; borders engraved (possibly later) with arms of Meaux or Meux quartering three others.

Surviving Scottish 18th-century dinner plates are extremely rare, yet contemporary accounts and inventories make it clear they were made and used in considerable quantities. Engraved numbering sequences on the backs of these 18 plates show that they were once part of a much larger set of at least 60.

4.24 PLATE OR DISH

Dougal Ged, Edinburgh, 1741-42

Marks (inside bottom of bowl): 'GED' (maker Dougal Ged); castle (Edinburgh); 'GED' (acting assay-master Dougal Ged); 'M' (date-letter 1741-42)

D 18.5 cm: H 0.31 cm: Wt 9.07 oz

Lent from a private collection

Circular dish with deep body, everted rim superbly deep-chased and repoussé with cherubs, grapes and vine foliage. This is probably a fruit or dessert plate, and as such is exceptionally rare.

4.25 CAKE OR SEAFOOD BASKET

William Dempster, Edinburgh, 1747-48

Marks: 'WD' (maker William Dempster); castle (Edinburgh); 'HG' (assay-master Hugh Gordon); 'S' (date-letter 1747-48)

L 37.5 cm; H 24 cm; W 35 cm; Wt 58 oz

NMS A.1963.34; purchased at Sotheby's sale, 21 March 1963, lot 161, with a contribution from the Railton Fund

Provenance: Michael Tennant Esq.

References: Finlay and Fothringham (1991), p. 145, pl. 81(i); Finlay (1963), pp. 443-44

Body in form of a scallop shell, set on three dolphin legs, with a handle in the form of a sea-horse; the cast rim is decorated with sea shells. This basket illustrates some Scottish makers' love of zoomorphic decoration [see ovoid coffee urns, 4.40-47]. It has been described in the past as a cake or bread basket, but the subject matter of the decoration suggests that it is likely it was used to serve seafood at the table, possibly in conjunction with small silver scallop shell dishes occasionally mentioned in contemporary inventories. Unique in Scotland, there are other similar London-made examples of the same and later date.

4.26 TEA URN

Patrick Robertson, Edinburgh, 1778-79

Marks: 'PR' (maker Patrick Robertson); castle (Edinburgh); thistle (Edinburgh standard mark); 'H' (date-letter 1778-79)

H 45 cm; W 25.5 cm; D 28.5; Wt 116.87 oz

NMS A.1898.391; purchased in 1898

References: Finlay and Fothringham (1991), pp. 160, 166, pl. 96; Baker (1973), pp. 89-94

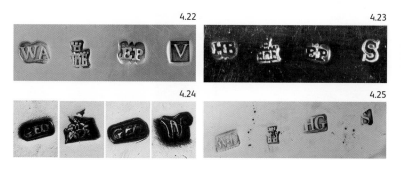

4.22   4.23   4.23 (detail)

4.24   4.25

Large ovoid body with shallow fluting, enlivened by husks; set on incurved base with guilloche decoration and a fluted stem; two elongated beaded strap handles; a gadrooned domed cover, chased with acanthus leaves; fitted internally with a holder for a hot iron. Engraved with full arms for Sir Thomas Miller of Glennlee, Lord Justice Clerk, and his wife Anne, daughter of John Lockhart of Castle Hill.

This elaborately neo-classical design is based on a pattern produced by the Birmingham firm of Bolton & Fothergill. However, it is not identical and illustrates the maker Robertson adapting a fashionable English design, rather than buying a piece in and retailing it on.

4.27 SAUCE BOAT

David Downie, Edinburgh, 1783-84

Marks (either side of spout): 'DD' (maker David Downie); castle (Edinburgh); thistle (Edinburgh standard mark); 'D' (date-letter 1783-84)

H 12 cm; L 18.2 cm; Wt 6.72 oz

MS K.2004.206; purchased in 2004

Oval body set on a stepped pedestal foot, with shaped everted rim and cast double C-scroll handle; body engraved with crest and motto for the Earl of Stanhope.

4.28 TRAY

McHattie & Fenwick, Edinburgh, 1804-05

Marks: 'M&F' (makers McHattie & Fenwick); castle (Edinburgh); thistle (Edinburgh standard mark); 'king's head' (duty mark); 'Y' (date-letter 1804-05)

L 59 cm; W 36.3 cm; Wt 96 oz

NMS H.1992.1830; purchased in 1992

Rectangular tray, with gadrooned rim and loop handles, engraved Greek key border; set on four scroll feet; the centre later engraved with an elaborate broad band of flowers foliage and butterflies, signed 'Rt Jeffrey, Edin, May 52' (in mirror script). This is a good example of an earlier piece of plate being later

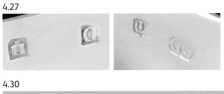
4.27

4.30

engraved to render it more fashionable. It is, however, extremely unusual for this to be documented with the engraver's signature, albeit reversed out. Robert Jeffrey is recorded as an engraver in the High Street, Edinburgh, from at least 1824, and then as an engraver and printer at 116 Rose Street, Edinburgh, 1856-63.

4.29 PAIR OF CANDLESTICKS

George Fenwick II, Tobago/Edinburgh, 1814-15

Marks (on bases): 'G F. TOBAGO'; 'GF' (maker George Fenwick II); castle (Edinburgh); thistle (Edinburgh standard mark); 'I' (date-letter 1814-15); 'king's head' in two-lobed punch (duty mark)

(1) H 23.3 cm; D (base) 11.4 cm; Scratch Wt '19 oz'

(2) H 23.6 cm; D (base) 11.3 cm; Scratch Wt '20 oz 1dr'

NMS K.2003.25/26; purchased from C. & L. Burman, London, 2004

Plain columnar form set on circular domed bases, with capitals formed of three cast boars' heads, with inset nozzles and drip-trays with integral rising prickets; the bases are engraved with the arms, motto and crest of Ferguson of Pitfour.

Made for George Ferguson of Pitfour (1749-20), an Edinburgh advocate who became a judge as Lord Pitfour. He also served as Lieutenant Governor of the island colony of Tobago in the Caribbean where his family owned substantial sugar plantations at Castara. The maker George Fenwick II also had a strong connection with Tobago, as his mark shows, and presumably with the Fergusons, as he died at Castara in September 1821.

As the drip-trays are engraved with the numbers '6' and '7', it is clear that they are from a very substantial set of sticks.

4.30 PUNCH BOWL

Charles Bendy/Richard Haxton, Edinburgh, 1825-26

Marks (on rim): 'CB' (maker Charles Bendy); 'king's head' (duty mark); thistle (Edinburgh standard mark); castle (Edinburgh); 't' (date-letter 1825-26); 'RH' (engraver Richard Haxton)

D (rim) 24.9 cm; H 14.2 cm; D (foot) 15 cm; Wt 41.86 oz

NMS H.MEQ 1593; purchased at Christie's sale, Gleneagles, 26 August 1985

Plain, deep hemispherical bowl, set on stepped domed foot; the interior engraved with the royal arms with a label of three points for the Prince of Wales.

A perplexing piece in several ways, this imposing bowl has apparently two makers' marks. The first is for Charles Bendy, recorded as a working silversmith from at least 1820. He sent a variety of wares to Edinburgh Assay Office and was certainly capable of

4.22

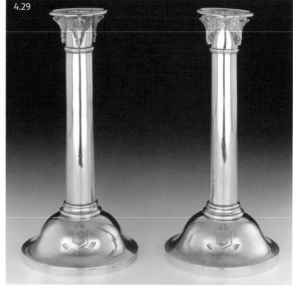

4.29

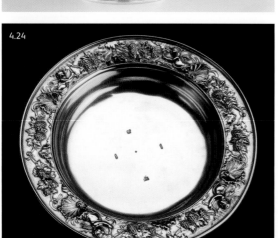

4.24

4.23

4.26

4.25

4.25
(detail)

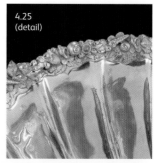

4.25
(detail)

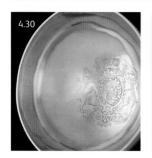

4.30

4.27

4.28

making this bowl. The second mark is for Richard Haxton, recorded as a jeweller between 1799 and 1840, who seems to have been a specialist box-maker, many of which were engraved. It is possible he was responsible for the high quality engraving on the bowl. The arms are clearly those for the Hanoverian Monarchy from 1801 to 1837 and for a Prince of Wales. However, after the accession of George IV to the throne in 1820, there was no Prince of Wales until Victoria's son Edward.

Family Affairs

Patrons and Patronage: The Earls of Hopetoun and their Goldsmiths, *c.1698-c.1760*

Goldsmiths, more than any other craftsmen, were heavily dependent on the complex relationship that existed between patron and supplier. This was the case whether the patron, and therefore the fount of commissions and business, was a large organisation such as the church, state or university, or whether it was an individual. In Scotland, particularly in the 17th and 18th centuries, there is growing evidence of detailed webs of interlinked family connections – spheres of social, cultural and political influence.

The surviving silver acquired by the first two Earls of Hopetoun from a succession of Edinburgh goldsmiths illustrates these webs of relationships beautifully. Charles Hope, 1st Earl (1681-1742), and John, 2nd Earl (1704-81), successively bought or commissioned silver from, among others, James Penman, Thomas Ker, Harry Beathune, James Ker and William Dempster. That a successful and powerful landed family would patronise the leading and most fashionable craftsmen of the city is not surprising, but perhaps the extent of the links between the craftsmen themselves is. Thomas Ker and Harry Beathune were both apprenticed to James Penman in 1685 and 1694 respectively. Penman was one of the most influential craftsmen of his day, who trained more prominent early 18th-century Edinburgh goldsmiths than anyone else. James Ker, perhaps the single most influential Edinburgh goldsmith, was both Thomas's son and apprentice. William Dempster, although originally apprenticed to Charles Dick-

son, transferred to James Ker's tutelage in 1739. There he prospered, not only going into partnership with Ker, but also marrying his daughter Violet in 1751.

Here we can see a craft 'dynasty' of apprentice following master, running parallel with, and providing high-status wares for, successive generations of a landed dynasty over a period of 60 years. Although we know little of the political allegiances of most of these goldsmiths, it is clear that James Ker at least was a committed whig and unionist, and therefore an appropriate choice of craftsman for a man like Charles, the 1st Earl of Hopetoun, whose political and probably financial success was firmly linked with the pro-unionist Hanoverian monarchy. It is simplistic and probably wrong to suggest that political leanings were a dominant factor in a patron's choice of craftsmen. However, there is no doubt that most of the factions dominated by great men of Scotland's political élites used their influence and patronage to create spheres of influence that permeated most levels of Scottish society.

The Hopes of Hopetoun were descended from 16th-century Edinburgh merchant burgesses, who doubtless had links and professional dealings with the goldsmiths of the day. In the 17th century the family prospered. Sir James Hope became Master of the Mint and acquired the valuable lead and silver-bearing lands of Leadhills in Lanarkshire from his wife, Anne Foulis, daughter of an important Edinburgh goldsmith. A talented mineralogist, he also acquired lead and silver mines in the Bathgate area. The family also acquired the lands of Abercorn near Queensferry and renamed the estate Hopetoun after their original property in Leadhills. Charles Hope's mother was the influential and fashionable Lady Margaret Hamilton, daughter of the 4th Earl of Haddington. She was instrumental in commissioning the architect Sir William Bruce to start work on a new house at Hopetoun, to mark her son's marriage to another notable heiress, Henrietta, daughter of the Marquess of Annandale in September 1699.

Charles and his son, James, 2nd Earl of Hopetoun, developed Hopetoun House into one of the great houses of state, utilising the talents of William Bruce, then William, James and Robert Adam. These patrons also succeeded in amassing an extensive collection of Scottish and English silver to complement the architecture of the house, the changes in architectural style being reflected in the silver. Fashionable architecture and changing tastes dictated no

CHARLES HOPE, 1ST EARL OF HOPETOUN (1681-1742)

Oil on canvas, by David Allan, painted sometime after
the Earl's death in 1742, with ongoing building work
on Hopetoun House in the background.

[Reproduced courtesy of Hopetoun Preservation Trust]

less up-to-the-minute fashion in the contents of the
house. Hence the development in what was deemed
appropriate for public show, to those who were
granted audience at the Earl's 'court', or perhaps more
accurately, the Countess's. The lady's toilet, very much
part of a public spectacle, gave way to the demands
of the tea and coffee ceremonies, again presided over
by the lady of the house. Having entertainments in the
elegant dining rooms at Hopetoun also demanded
an increase in appropriate silver vessels to both serve
and eat from. The extensive archive still preserved
at Hopetoun House details the advancing fortunes
of the family and their acquisition of more and more
silver. This reaches a crescendo in 1833 when the
house's entire collection of silver was enumerated
in a privately printed book, *The Hopetoun Plate, a
descriptive list, with dates and weights of each
article*. This list runs to over 70 densely printed pages
and amounts to many thousands of individual
pieces, ranging in size and scale from the huge wine
cooler and cistern by William Lukin, now in the
Victoria and Albert Museum, to an individual fruit
spoon, weighing two ounces.

Most of this vast collection remained at Hopetoun House until a series of major sales in 1953 and
1977 dispersed much of it. National Museums Scotland were fortunate to acquire, over the intervening
years, some major pieces from this wonderful collection.

4.31 PAIR OF WALL SCONCES

James Penman, Edinburgh, 1698-99

Marks (on reflectors and drip-pans): 'JP' in monogram (maker
James Penman); castle (Edinburgh); 'JP' (assay-master James
Penman); 'S' (date-letter 1698-99)

(1) H 25 cm; W 18 cm

(2) H 25 cm; W 18.3 cm

NMS K.2006.198.1 and 2; purchased with assistance of Heritage
Lottery Fund, The Art Fund, and the Cecil & Mary Gibson Bequest

Provenance: purchased at Sotheby's sale, London, 1 June 2006,
Important Silver and Gold Boxes, lot 130; Sotheby's sale, London,
25 June 1953, Property of Hopetoun Estates Company, lot 153,
acquired by S. J. Phillips

References: exhibited at Royal Scottish Museum, Edinburgh
(1922); loan exhibition of Old Silver in aid of Queen Charlotte's
Hospital, Seaford House, London (1929); RSM (1948), no. 43;
E. A. Jones (1933), pp. 153-61; Clayton (1985), p. 333; Finlay and
Fothringham (1991), p. 124

Thin-gauge silver oval backplates with plain reflectors
flanked by embossed and chased, trumpet-playing
putti, surmounted by baskets overflowing with fruit;
below, elaborately chased scrolling foliage issues from
grotesque masks which also contain the sockets into
which fit the detachable scrolling branches with plain
reeded drip-pans and sockets. Mounted on (later)
velvet-covered wooden boards.

The Hopetoun Sconces are unique in the corpus
of Scottish historic silver, no other examples of such
Scottish-made wall sconces having survived. Commissioned in the same year as work started on Hopetoun
House, there seems little doubt they were intended as
part of the interior decoration of Sir William Bruce's
baroque masterpiece. In subject matter and style, they
complement the set of decorative paintings by Peter
Tideman, representing the rewards of learning and the
patronage of music. Equally, they are in perfect stylistic harmony with Alexander Eizat's carved wooden
garlands of fruit and foliage in the central staircase.

James Penman (*c.*1649-1733), son of an Edinburgh
merchant, was a prolific maker. In 1698-99 (the year in
which the sconces were made) 1172 ounces of silver
from his workshop was sent to the Edinburgh Assay
Office; while for the period 1681-1702 (when the
Assay Master's Accounts survive) he sent a total of
45,365 ounces for assaying and marking.

4.32

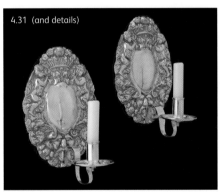

4.31 (and details)

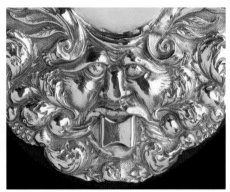

Unfortunately comparatively little of Penman's output has survived. What has includes 14 pairs of communion cups, candlesticks, thistle cups, quaichs, a mirror and a two-handled cup and cover. All his work exhibits a restrained, well-proportioned and well-made elegance.

The Hopetoun Sconces are by far Penman's most exuberantly decorated work, but are well within his artistic and technical abilities. Penman trained at least 13 apprentices, seven of whom went on to become significant masters in their own right. No other Scottish goldsmith succeeded in training as many first-rate goldsmiths as James Penman; as a result his importance goes far beyond his own work and life, laying the foundations of much of the excellent work that was to show itself in the first half of the 18th century.

Penman was therefore an obvious choice for the young and fashionable Charles Hope and his new bride when he wanted a craftsman to produce silver to complement the interiors of his newly-building Hopetoun House.

4.32 EWER, BASIN AND COMB BOX (PART OF A TOILET SERVICE)

Thomas Ker, Edinburgh, 1706-07

Marks (rim of ewer, base of basin, marker's mark only on base of box): 'T.K' (maker Thomas Ker); castle (Edinburgh); 'JP' in monogram (assay-master James Penman); 'B' (date-letter 1706-07)

Ewer: H (max.) 21.4 cm; D (rim) 10.5 cm; D (base) 10 cm; Wt. 22.75 oz (Scratch Wt '23u : 3d')

Basin: H 13.4 cm; D (rim) 25.9 cm; D (base) 12 cm;

4.31

4.32

Wt 26.80 oz (Scratch Wt '27u : 7d')

Box: H 9.5 cm; L 26.4 cm; W 20 cm; Wt 37.33 oz

NMS H.MEQ 1512, 1513 and 1566; ewer and basin purchased in a private treaty sale from Lord Hopetoun, *per.* Messrs Christie's, 1982; box purchased at Christie's & Edmiston's sale, Glasgow, 29 March 1983, Shaw of Tordarroch, lot 103

References: Hopetoun Archives, NRAS 888, bundles 2781, 2787, vols 300, 302 and 305; E. A. Jones (1933); Dalgleish and Maxwell (1987), no. 46

Helmet-shaped ewer, on domed stepped foot, with scroll handle and beak spout; the basin plain with simple wire moulded rim, set on a stepped foot; the box rectangular with stepped base set on four simple bun feet, with stepped hinged lid; all engraved with 'LH' in monogram, surmounted by an earl's coronet, within a foliate wreath, for Charles Hope, 1st Earl of Hopetoun.

These seem to be the sole surviving pieces of a much more extensive toilet set ordered from Thomas Ker for Henrietta, Countess of Hopetoun, possibly emulating her mother-in-law Margaret who owned a spectacular service by Anthony Nelme, dated 1691. Original accounts in the Hopetoun archives, unfortunately undated and difficult to interpret accurately, list 'a comb box, 2 powder boxes, 2 patch boxes, 2 little cups, 2 pomade boxes, 2 servers, 2 bottles, 1 pin-cushion, 2 candlesticks, 1 glass frame and 2 brushes', in all costing £79 14s 6d sterling. The basin and ewer were presumably added slightly later.

This service, both as recorded and represented by these wonderfully restrained and elegant pieces, bears a striking resemblance in style and composition to both the Nelme Service and the Keir Service by Colin McKenzie 1703-04 [4.10]. Henrietta's service survived more or less intact until the early 19th century when it appears in inventories of 1820 and 1833. However, by 1883 only the ewer and basin are mentioned in the privately printed house inventory. These pieces appear to have been of special significance to the family, possibly due to the fact that George IV used the basin to wash his hands during his brief sojourn at Hopetoun during the momentous Royal Visit to Scotland in August 1822. The box survived by being incorporated, possibly by mistake, into the 1691 Nelme Service and sold together in 1953.

An Expensive Tea Service

4.33 PART TEA AND COFFEE SERVICE

James Ker, Edinburgh, 1734-35

Marks: 'IK' (maker James Ker); castle (Edinburgh); 'AU' (assay-master Archibald Ure); 'E' script (date-letter 1734-35)

Kettle: H 44 cm; W (max.) 30 cm; Wt 111.25 oz

Milk jug: H 14.7 cm; L 19 cm; Wt 17.17 oz (Scratch Wt '17 oz 10 dr')

Sugar basin: H 7.8 cm; L 15.4 cm; Wt 12.93 oz (Scratch Wt '13 oz 9 dr')

Spoon tray: L 20.5 cm; W 10 cm; Wt 6.82 oz (Scratch Wt '7 oz')

Salver: L 23.8 cm; W 23.8 cm; Wt 18.1 oz (Scratch Wt '19 oz 5 dr')

NMS H.MEQ 1208-11: purchased at Christie's sale, London, 15 June 1977, Property of the Marquess of Linlithgow and the Hopetoun Preservation Trust, lot 121

References: Hopetoun Archives, NRAS 888, bundle 3032; Dalgleish and Maxwell (1987), no. 47; Clayton (1985), pl. 650

Comprising spherical tea kettle with stand and lamp, bullet-shaped hot milk jug, oval sugar basin, spoon tray and shaped salver all chased with shells, scrolls and trellis work, all engraved with crest and motto for Charles, 1st Earl of Hopetoun.

This is all that remains of a much larger tea and coffee ensemble, ordered by the 1st Earl from James Ker and detailed in an account dated February 1735. These surviving pieces were originally accompanied by: 'a coffe pott weights 66 oz 12dr' (undoubtedly a large ovoid urn, as discussed on p. 81); two small 'flatts' or salvers (which remained at Hopetoun until sold in the 1953 sale, lot 115); a large teapot weighing a massive 37 ounces; and a set of twelve teaspoons and matching pair of tongs.

In all Ker charged the Earl £135 17s 4d for the set. He did not, however, receive this amount. In a wonderfully illuminating postscript to the account, the canny Earl queried the amount Ker was charging for workmanship, given as three shillings per ounce. To back up his argument with the goldsmith, Hopetoun quotes current London prices for 'Tea Plate' as being 'Plain per ounce – 1 shilling, Engraven – 1s 3d, Carved or Chased – 1s 6d, Fluted – 2s'. Ker was obviously charging twice the current London rate for chased work, and accordingly his bill was annotated 'Deduct

4.33 4.34

JAMES KER OF BUGHTRIGG (1700-68)

Allan Ramsay, 1754 [detail]

Oil on canvas / H 74.9 cm; W 62.2 cm

Lent by the National Gallery of Scotland (NG 1886)

Provenance: by family descent to Mrs F. G. Ker; presented to National Gallery of Scotland in 1937

References: Smart (1999), no. 296; Dalgleish and Maxwell (1987), pp. 14-15, no. 53, illus. 3A

James Ker was without doubt one of the most talented and important goldsmiths in 18th-century Edinburgh, and dominated the craft both technically and politically throughout the middle years of the century. This rather gloomy depiction of him by Ramsay captures him just as he was about to lose his seat in the House of Commons, but that he was a member of parliament at all is remarkable. In fact he was the only craftsman in the 18th century to represent Edinburgh at Westminster – a task usually reserved for members of the city's merchant élite.

As we have noted, Ker was the son of Thomas Ker the Edinburgh goldsmith, born to him and his wife Margaret on 14 September 1700. The family was related to the aristocratic house of Ker Marquesses of Lothian, and shows another example of younger sons of gentry going into the socially acceptable trade of the goldsmith. James was apprenticed to his father at the unusually young age of 8 on 12 July 1709, the same year his father was elected deacon of the Incorporation. The normal age for the son of a goldsmith to be apprenticed was between 11 and 14, while the sons of other tradesmen could be even older, up to 17 or 18. Doubtless Thomas was an influential master and his son clearly inherited his talent and business sense. Unfortunately Thomas did not live to see his son prosper,

dying in 1714 'of a decay'. James's apprenticeship was transferred to another unknown master, and he disappears from the record until 1723 when, after completing an essay of 'a diamond ring and a gold seall', he was admitted as a master of the Incorporation. In 1742 Ker married Elizabeth, daughter of Lord Charles Kerr, brother of the 2nd Marquess of Lothian, cementing his relationship with that noble house. In all, James seems to have had 21 children, only one of whom, William, followed his father into the goldsmiths' craft.

James prospered in his craft, as can be seen by the sheer number of items that survive bearing his mark. It is impossible that all were made by Ker personally, who most likely had a well-manned workshop, with apprentices, journeymen and servants to keep his business functioning at a highly productive level. Certainly he was successful enough to be able to buy himself into the land-owning classes. In 1736 he bought the estate of Bughtrigg near Jedburgh in the Borders for £1500.

He was also prominent in the affairs of the Incorporation and the city, serving as deacon and town councillor on numerous occasions. Politically he was a Whig. In the chaos that surrounded the aftermath of the 1745 Jacobite Rebellion, the members of the Town Council, who elected the city's single Westminster member of parliament, chose Ker to be their MP. He was a staunch supporter of the Duke of Argyll, despite the fact that Argyll seems to have mistrusted him: 'I am told he is weak and whimsical, though his professions of zeal for the present administration are strong enough.' However, Ker's hold on the office could not last, and at the next elections in 1754 the Edinburgh merchants closed ranks and he was defeated. During his tenure as MP, he entered into a business partnership with his erstwhile apprentice, William Dempster. Dempster went on to marry Ker's daughter Violet in 1751. Between them Ker and Dempster produced some of the finest examples of Edinburgh silver and gold of the period. They were responsible for three of the four surviving gold King's Prizes for Leith Races [see nos 9.16-9.19]. Curiously, Ker never referred to himself as a goldsmith or silversmith, preferring the title 'jeweller' which seems to have had even more cachet than 'goldsmith'. Unfortunately there are no surviving examples of his jewellery. He retired from his lucrative business in 1763, having supplied customers such as the Duke of Gordon, the Earl of Breadalbane, Lady Grisell Baillie, the Marquess of Lothian and, of course, several generations of the Hopetoun family. He died on 24 January 1768 in his house at Drumsheugh, just outside Edinburgh.

one half the workmanship it having been refer'd to the London Price'. What Ker thought of this is not recorded, but a final terse little addendum to the account perhaps indicates that the patron-craftsman relationship was not without stresses: 'NB the weight is taken upon Mr Ker's word.'

4.34 SUGAR BOWL

James Ker, Edinburgh, 1745-46

Marks (on base): 'IK' rubbed (maker James Ker); castle (Edinburgh); 'HG' (assay-master Hugh Gordon); 'L' script (date-letter 1745-46)

H 5.8 cm; D 13.1 cm; Wt 7.73 oz

NMS Q.L.1983.26; ex-Miller Collection accepted by HM Government in lieu of Inheritance Tax and allocated to NMS

Circular body, with shaped everted rim chased with foliage and scrolls, set on three legs with spreading paw feet. The plain body is engraved with a monogram 'LH' under an earl's coronet for James, 2nd Earl of Hopetoun. Despite his earlier contretemps with the 1st Earl, James Ker continued to provide silver for the new 2nd Earl, who inherited from his father in February 1742.

Fine Dining at Hopetoun House

4.35 SUGAR CASTER

James Ker, Edinburgh, 1738-39

Marks (on base around centre): 'IK' (maker James Ker); 'AU' (assay-master Archibald Ure); castle (Edinburgh); 'I' (date-letter 1737-38)

H 18.2 cm; D (base) 6.1; Wt 7.78 oz

Lent from a private collection

Bulbous vase-shaped body, with fluted skirt, set on stepped foot; domed lift-off panelled cover, with alternating pierced panels of diaper and scrolls, with vase finial; engraved to front with crest of 'a broken globe' with motto in ribbon above, 'at spes non fracta' for Hope of Hopetoun. This is a particularly unusual and innovative design, unlike most casters of the period.

4.35

4.33

4.36 CAKE OR BREAD BASKET

James Ker, Edinburgh, 1745-46

Marks (on base in line): 'IK' (maker James Ker); castle (Edinburgh); 'HG' (assay-master Hugh Gordon); 'Q' (date-letter 1745-46)

W (across handle) 32.5 cm; H 20 cm; L 33.2 cm; Wt 61.22 oz

Lent by City of Edinburgh Museums and Galleries

Provenance: Christie's & Edmiston's sale, Shaw of Tordarroch Collection, 29 March 1983, lot 80; Christie's sale, London, 4 March 1992, lot 193

Oval body on skirt foot, all pierced with scroll-work; cast rim decoration of scrolls shells and masks; swing handle with caryatid-like figures on scroll supports; flattened handle thickens in middle to contain an engraved circular foliate cartouche with monogram 'LH' with earl's coronet above; the base of the basket is engraved with a circular foliate cartouche with the arms of Hope.

Scottish bread baskets are scarce, yet Hopetoun House had three examples in the mid-18th century. They were used to bring bread or cake to the table.

4.37 MONTEITH

James Ker, Edinburgh, 1746-47

Marks: 'IK' (maker James Ker); castle (Edinburgh); 'HG' (assay-master Hugh Gordon); 'R' (date-letter 1746-47)

H 24.6 cm; D 30.7 cm; Wt 74 oz

Lent by Aberdeen Art Gallery and Museums Collections

Provenance: sold by How of Edinburgh to Major I. Shaw of Tordarroch in 1966; purchased by Aberdeen Art Gallery and Museums at Christie's sale, London, Shaw Collection of Important Scottish Silver and Pistols, 29 March 1983, lot 89

References: Lee (1978), no. 310; Hopetoun Archives, NRAS 888, bundle 313

Plain circular body with applied reeded rim, on domed spreading foot; detachable notched rim with applied simple moulding; engraved with monogram 'LH' and earl's coronet, within a circular foliate cartouche, for James, 2nd Earl of Hopetoun.

Hopetoun House in the 18th century possessed no less than three monteiths: one that was won as a prize at Leith Races [see 9.15]; a massive fluted example by Harry Beathune weighing some 175 ounces; and this more modest but still impressive example. The detachable rim meant that it could be used either to cool wine glasses before they were brought to the table, or as a punch bowl, and it is recorded in an inventory of 1773 as 'a large plain Monteith with a coler [collar]'.

4.38 PAIR OF SAUCE BOATS

Ker & Dempster, Edinburgh, 1748-49

Marks (on base): 'K&D' in engrailed punch (maker Ker & Dempster); castle (Edinburgh); 'HG' (assay-master Hugh Gordon); 'T' (date-letter 1748-49)

(1) L 20.2 cm; H 11.5 cm; Wt 13.72 oz (Scratch Wt '16 = 8')
(2) L 20.3 cm; H 11.7 cm; Wt 13.97 oz (Scratch Wt '16 = 12')

Lent from a private collection

Wide bodies with shaped everted rims and wide pouring lips, set on four scroll and hoof feet, with tri-form terminals; double C-scroll handle with acanthus leaf moulding; engraved with a crest of 'a broken globe' with motto below, 'at spes infracta', and earl's coronet above, for the Earl of Hopetoun.

4.39 CAKE OR BREAD BASKET

William Dempster, Edinburgh, 1757-58

Marks (on base): 'WD' (maker William Dempster); castle (Edinburgh); 'HG' (assay-master Hugh Gordon); 'C' (date-letter 1757-58)

L 39.8 cm; H (max.) 28 cm; W 31.5 cm; Wt 65.66 oz (Vestigial Scratch Wt '67 = 12' for 67 oz 12 drop)

NMS H.MEQ 1204; purchased at Christie's sale, London, 15 June 1977, Property of the Marquess of Linlithgow and the Hopetoun Preservation Trust, lot 115

Reference: E. A. Jones (1933), pp. 156-57

Oval body on four scroll feet, the sides pierced with panels of scrolls and quatrefoils, and the rim with applied shell and scroll moulding; cast swing handle enriched with chased foliage and fruit; the centre of the body engraved with 'H' monogram with an earl's coronet above.

Made some twelve years after Ker's basket [4.36], it provides an interesting illustration of changing styles. It was one of the numerous pieces of historic family silver taken by the 2nd Marquess of Linlithgow to India where he served as Viceroy and Governor General from 1936-43.

4.36

4.38

4.39

4.35

4.35
(detail)

4.39 (detail below)

4.37

4.38

4.36 and below
(details)

4.36

Uniquely Scottish: Egg-shaped Coffee Pots

One of the most unusual, and not a little bizarre, survivals in the corpus of Scottish domestic silver is the group of ovoid-bodied urns that have no direct parallel elsewhere in England or the rest of Europe. They are in fact uniquely Scottish, and the surviving 16 or so examples all share the same basic design and construction. They comprise a variation of an ovoid or egg-shaped main body, with a spout and spigot for drawing off liquid a little above the body base. All are set on three equally-spaced cabriole legs, which have a variety of feet designs. One of their most distinctive features is the use of two opposed loop handles in the form of writhing serpents with dolphin-like heads. A love of such zoomorphic experiment seems to have been a feature of some Scottish goldsmiths' work. (Robert Gordon in Edinburgh made a wonderful sauce boat with a dolphin handle in 1746, while the spectacular clam-shell shaped basket by William Dempster in 1747-48 boasts a superb sea-horse handle.) To date, no example by a Scottish maker from outside Edinburgh has been found.

Despite being well known to previous scholars, no one has yet managed to offer a convincing point of origin for their highly idiosyncratic design. Carl Hernmark suggested that the idea originated in The Netherlands: given the long-term trading and cultural links between the two nations, this is entirely possible. However, their developed form seems to be entirely Scottish. The basic shape may derive from the much earlier practice of mounting ostrich eggs in silver, but no direct reference for this has yet been found. Indeed, there is still even a considerable debate as to their very function. They have been referred to as either coffee, tea or hot water urns in turn. Ian Finlay described them as coffee urns, while Timothy Schroder considered that they should be regarded as hot water urns and suggested they served the same function as the kettle 'and seem to have replaced the latter earlier in Scotland than in England'.

It can be argued, however, that they are more likely to be coffee urns. From a practical point of view they are well suited to dispensing coffee. The situation of the spouts, some way up the body, allowed coffee grounds to settle in the base, while the liquid could be drawn off without disturbing the sediment. Many of the extant urns seem to have had provision for a spirit heater, either attached, suspended from chains, or in the form of a separate burner pan. Virtually all of them are marked around the point of the base and most marks display a higher degree of wear than in other objects. This is entirely consistent with the need to polish the area most discoloured by the use of a spirit burner. The need for such heaters can be explained by the early preference for drinking both tea and coffee as hot as one could bear it.

The most convincing argument for their use in dispensing coffee, however, comes from several contemporary documents where they are, somewhat confusingly, referred to as 'coffee pots'. John Rollo referred to the large and handsome urn now in the National Museums Scotland collection as a 'coffe poot' [see 4.44], while the extensive tea and coffee set commissioned from James Ker by Lord Hopetoun in 1735 contained a 'coffe pott', now sadly lost. Weighing in at over 62 and 66 ounces respectively, there is no doubt that these vessels were not conventional singled-handled pouring coffee pots, which generally weighed between 25 and 35 ounces. The Breadalbane Papers contain an account, again from James Ker, which leaves no doubt as to the function of the urn in question. In 1741 he supplied Lord Glenorchy with a 'Silver egg Coffe Pott', a relatively modest example weighing in at only 38 ounces, but complete with chased decoration and a wooden spigot handle.

Of the 16 urns recorded, dating to between 1719 and 1768, eleven occur during the period 1719-40. During the same time only five 'standard' coffee pots can be traced. Is it possible that these ovoid urns were the preferred mode of serving coffee in Scotland in the early part of the 18th century? It is highly likely that there were originally many more in existence, now disguised in contemporary accounts and documents as 'coffee pots'. At this time coffee, like tea, was a highly fashionable drink within élite Scottish circles, and much care and money was lavished on buying and serving it in elaborate rituals. These distinctive urns would have certainly been a talking point at any such gathering.

4.44 (left)

4.40

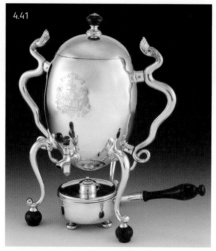

4.41

4.46

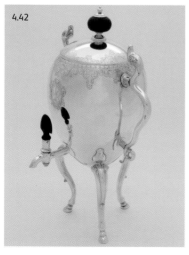

4.42

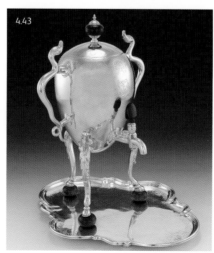

4.43

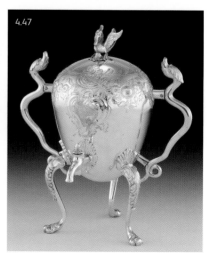

4.47

4.40 URN

William Aytoun, Edinburgh, 1719-20 or 1723-24

Marks (on base): 'WA' (maker William Aytoun); 'P' (1719-20) or 'T' (1723-24); illegible (presumably 'EP' for assay-master Edward Penman); castle (Edinburgh)

H 31 cm; L (across handles) 26.3 cm; Wt 46.84 oz

NMS Q.L.1983.13: ex-Miller Collection; accepted by HM Government in lieu of inheritance tax and allocated to NMS

Reference: Deitert (2007), p. 577

Plain egg-shaped body, on three scroll legs, with clamshell feet; two opposed handles shaped as mythical serpents; domed flush-fitting cover, with simple ivory bun finial, the 'mouth' join between the body and cover flat chased with bands of alternating scrolls, fruit, foliage and shells; spout with scroll T-shaped spigot; three suspension loops below leg joints for a missing suspended burner.

This is the earliest recorded example of this type of urn (although as the date-letter is rubbed, there is a slight possibility that it could be read as 'T' for 1723-24). The presence of suspension loops indicates that it originally had a spirit burner. Maker William Aytoun made at least one other egg-shaped urn almost 20 years later in 1736-37, now in the John Hyman Collection at Colonial Williamsburg; it is considerably more sophisticated in its detailing and decoration.

4.41 URN WITH SPIRIT BURNER

James Mitchelson, Edinburgh, 1724-25

Marks: 'I.M' in a shaped punch (maker now ascribed to James Mitchelson; formerly pertained to John Main); castle (Edinburgh); 'EP' (assay-master Edward Penman); 'u' (date-letter 1724-25)

Urn: H 30.7 cm; W (across handles) 24.7 cm; Wt 65.90 oz

Burner: L (over handle) 22.7 cm; D 9.3 cm; H 7.2 cm; Wt (all-in) 118 oz

Lent from a private collection at Mount Stuart

References: RSM (1948), p. 899; Finlay (1948[iv]), pp. 88-93; Dietert (2007), p. 577

The urn is a plain egg-shaped body on three scroll legs with scroll and socket feet terminating in original turned wood bun feet; spigot to the short spout has a shaped small wooden handle; two opposed silver handles are shaped as mythical serpents, cast with multiple-layered mouths. Domed flush-fitting cover

has a wooden bun finial and spool neck. Engraved back and front with full arms of Craig of Riccarton.

The burner is shaped as a brandy pan on three simple bun feet, the detachable cover with a hinged lid over the wick-sleeve, with turned wooden handle. The body and cover are each engraved with the crest, with motto above, of Craig of Riccarton

The urn is *en suite* with the spirit-burner of the same date and maker. It is the only one in the group to have this arrangement for heating the contents. It may have had a dual purpose: two small locating plooks and the joint of the handle would allow the burner to be fitted to a suitably-constructed dish-ring.

4.42 URN

Probably by James Ker, Edinburgh, 1733-34

Marks (on base): partial maker's mark, possibly 'IK' for James Ker; castle (Edinburgh); 'AU' (assay-master Archibald Ure); 'D' script (date-letter 1733-34)

H (max.) 34.5 cm; D (rim) 11.8 cm; Wt (all-in) 55.98 oz

Lent by Glasgow Museums and Art Galleries; Stirling Maxwell Collection; gifted in 1966 by Mrs Anne Maxwell Macdonald and family in memory of Sir John Stirling Maxwell; part of gift of Pollok House and Estate to the City of Glasgow

Plain egg-shaped body set on three cabriole legs with hoof feet, two opposed handles shaped as mythical serpents; the lift-off domed cover with wooden knop, the spigot with inverted shield-shaped handle; 'mouth' chasing with bands of shell, scroll and foliage; front-chased and engraved with a crest, 'a stags head erased' with a motto 'I AM READY' in a ribbon above (for Maxwell), all in a circular shield surrounded by an elaborate scroll.

Although the marker's mark is partially obscured, the similarity in the decoration around the mouth to the urn from the National Museums Scotland collection [4.43] makes it virtually certain that James Ker was the maker.

4.43 URN WITH TRAY

James Ker, Edinburgh, 1735-36

Marks (on base of urn and tray): 'IK' (maker James Ker); castle (Edinburgh); 'AU (assay-master Archibald Ure); 'F' (date-letter 1735-36)

4.40

4.41

4.42

Urn: H 37 cm; W (across handles) 27.5 cm; Wt 60.85 oz

Tray: L 37 cm; W 30.5 cm; Wt 36 oz

NMS H.MEQ 1573 and 4; purchased from How of Edinburgh, 1984

References: (for urn) *Scottish Art Review* (1984), vol. XVI, How of Edinburgh; (tray) Phillips, Edinburgh, 22 July 1983, lot 245, How of Edinburgh (tray later reunited with urn); Dalgleish and Maxwell (1987), p. 45, no. 48; Deitert (2007), p. 577

Urn with plain egg-shaped body on three leaf-capped cabriole legs with hoof feet and wooden bun finials; two opposed handles shaped as mythical serpents; domed flush-fitting cover with wooden bun finial, the mouth join flat-chased with bands of alternating shells and scroll foliage; spigot with wooden spade-shaped tap; body front engraved with a crest, an anchor within a shield and motto, 'Spero Meliora', in a ribbon below. Tray with shaped moulded rim and four button feet, the edge flat-chased to match the urn.

This is the only surviving example of an urn with matching tray, designed to accommodate the urn at one end and a coffee cup at the other. Reminiscent of the much more usual tea kettle and salver combination, this is a typically elegant creation of James Ker.

4.44 URN

John Rollo, Edinburgh, 1735-36

Marks (on base): 'IR', boar's head (maker John Rollo); 'F' (date-letter 1735-36); 'AU' (assay-master Archibald Ure); castle (Edinburgh)

H 32.4 cm; L (across handles) 27 cm; Wt 61.11 oz

NMS Q.L.1983.14; ex-Miller Collection; accepted by HM Government in lieu of inheritance tax and allocated to NMS

Plain egg-shaped body, on three leaf-capped cabriole legs with hoof feet; two opposed handles shaped as mythical serpents; domed flush-fitting cover with wooden bun finial, the mouth join flat-chased with bands of alternating shells and scroll foliage; spout with bone leaf-shaped tap.

The original owner of this urn can be identified from John Rollo's Account Ledger [see 4.45] as 'The Honble Andrew Wauchope of Niddrie Esq', who paid '£23. 5. 8.' in 1735 for 'one Coffe Poot 62 ozn 2dr

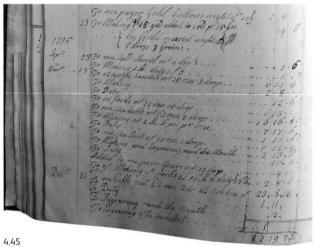

4.45

at 7sh 6pe pr'. He paid £1 11s Duty and £12 for 'Ingraving rund the mouth'.

There is no mention of any armorials being engraved, and curiously the bands of beautiful, light flat chasing around the join between the body and cover are referred to as an 'Ingraving rund the mouth'.

This reference is one of several which prove that at least some of these urns were for serving coffee. It is possible that references to other urns exist in family papers, where they too have been disguised as coffee 'pots'. There is no doubt, however, that the weights

4.44   4.47

4.43

84

match up with these much more substantial urns.

The discrepancy between the actual weight of the urn today and the weight in the bill can be accounted for by the normal loss of silver to centuries of polishing, which in items of this weight normally amounted to about one ounce.

4.45 ACCOUNT LEDGER OF JOHN ROLLO, GOLDSMITH IN EDINBURGH, 1731-37

Dimensions (closed): H 38.5 cm; W 26 cm; D 4.5 cm; (open) H 38.5 cm; W 53.5 cm; H c.6.5 cm

Lent by City of Edinburgh Council, Libraries and Information Services – Central Library; given to Edinburgh Central Library by Messrs John Grant, Booksellers, Edinburgh, 1947

Full leather bound account book, pages hand lined, fly page inscribed 'John Rollo Gold = Smith in Edinbr. / his Ledger No A'; alphabetical index of customers to front.

This exceptionally rare document provides a unique insight into the practical financial and working arrangements of an important Edinburgh goldsmith. The ledger lists the accounts of some 126 customers, ranging from the Dukes of Queensberry, Athol and Perth to vintners, merchants and other goldsmiths. The majority of Rollo's customers were minor landowners, lairds, merchants and professionals. His main turnover was undoubtedly in jewellery and small wares (buckles and spoons appear frequently), whereas the larger, more impressive pieces figure much more rarely. Tea wares, however, were something of a speciality. His most lucrative customers were not necessarily the dukes and earls – James (later Lord) Ruthven, Rollo's brother-in-law, bought £392 19s 10ds worth of goods from him, while the Good Toun of Edinburgh spent over £160 in 1737 alone, including £95 17s for a gold cup for the King's Prize for Leith Races. Andrew Wauchope of Niddrie spent a total of £153 17s with him for a wide range of goods, besides the coffee urn [4.44], including a child's whistle, a large tea kettle, a set of three casters and cruet stand, and many knives, spoons and forks.

4.46 URN

Unidentifiable maker, c.1744-59

Marks (on base, very rubbed): maker's mark indecipherable; castle (Edinburgh); 'HG' (assay-master Hugh Gordon, 1744-59); no date-letter

H 28.5 cm; W (across handles) 26.5 cm; Wt 55.14 oz

Lent from a private collection

Compressed egg-shaped body, on three leaf-capped cabriole legs with shell and paw feet; two opposed handles shaped as mythical serpents; mouth and upper body heavily chased with flowers, foliage and masks; domed hinged lid with wooden bun finial.

This urn is much more elaborately finished than the earlier examples: the scales of the serpent handles, the 'feathering' on the backs of the cabriole legs, and the depth of chasing, suggest a maker like Ebenezer Oliphant. Unfortunately the marks are completely illegible.

4.47 URN

Alexander Aitchison, Edinburgh, 1767-68

Marks (on base): 'AIT' (maker Alexander Aitchison); 'N' (date-letter 1767-68); castle (Edinburgh); thistle (Edinburgh standard mark)

H 28.8 cm; W (across handles) 26.5 cm; Wt 44.59 oz

Lent by Dundee City Council (McManus Galleries and Museum)

References: J. Bell (1964); Dietert (2007), p. 578

Compressed egg-shaped body, on three cabriole legs with paw feet; two opposed handles shaped as mythical serpents; the upper body heavily chased with foliage and flowers; hinged domed lid with cast pelican finial; engraved with a contemporary coat of arms for McLauchlan in a fine rococo cartouche.

This would appear to be the latest in the sequence of ovoid coffee urns. The chased decoration is heavier and much more obviously rococo in character. The marks are unusually crisp and unworn, suggesting that it was not used with a burner and thus did not need the same amount of cleaning to the base.

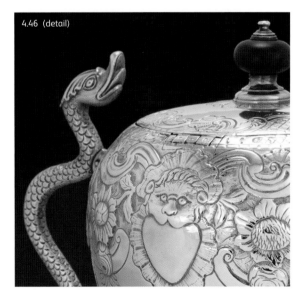

4.46 (detail)

Making their Mark: Burgh Silver

with Colin T. Fraser

Introduction

The evolution of the goldsmiths' craft in the other Royal burghs of Scotland broadly follows that outlined in Edinburgh (pp. 55-58). Many of the earliest goldsmiths and mint-workers came from the Low Countries. One has only to look at their names – Alebode, Copyn, Derind, Folpolt, Meinard, Pagan and others – to see what a dominant position they occupied in these trades in medieval Scotland. Among the first of these was Raul Derling, mint-worker and goldsmith in Dunfermline 1186-1205, who is thought to have made the Reliquary Shrine of St Margaret (now lost). We also find John Cokin in Perth in the 1190s, Henry Bald in the same town in *c.*1219, Eugenius in Dumbarton in 1271, and Martin in Aberdeen in 1281. These few are mentioned to show that there was a wide spread of goldsmith activity across the country from a relatively early date.

In Dundee the Hammermen received their Seal of Cause in 1483, and Ranald McGreig became a burgess as goldsmith there in 1517. Angus McGrubbing, goldsmith, is recorded as owning land in Glasgow in 1560. The large number of pieces mentioned in early royal, ecclesiastical and private inventories suggests a healthy local trade. Some of the few surviving examples may have been the work of these early burgh craftsmen, but as they are unmarked we cannot confidently ascribe them to any individual.

In the 17th century Thomas Wallace became a burgess of Dumfries in 1625, having been apprenticed to Robert Thomson in Edinburgh; George Steill was known in Brechin from 1649 to 1666. Then, from the later 17th century, one sees a burgeoning of goldsmiths in different towns. With the exception of some earlier communion cups and a few domestic pieces, it is principally from the 1680s onwards that we start to find their surviving work and marks in any quantity.

Silversmithing was primarily an urban craft, partly because of the number of customers and accumulation of wealth that towns generated. In order to be allowed to operate within the confines of a burgh, and thus benefit from its economic trading privileges, craftsmen were obliged, from the mid-15th to early 19th centuries, to belong to the trade incorporations that were an integral part of town governance. In the case of goldsmiths in all Scotland's burghs except Edinburgh, this usually meant belonging to the local Incorporation of Hammermen (see chapter 2, pp. 20-21).

With few exceptions, it is not until the mid-17th century that we can marry surviving marked pieces to individual goldsmiths in specific towns.

All uther goldsmithes of this kingdome ...

{DRAFT LETTER TO BURGH GOLDSMITHS, *c.*1689}

{opposite page}
5.26 THE TROTTER TANKARD, *c.*1765

Craftsmen in each burgh used local 'town marks' which help to identify where items were made, no doubt in an attempt to comply with national hall-marking legislation (see p. 18-19). Generally these marks were based on some element of the town's coat of arms. Some are rather unusual: Inverness goldsmiths used a camel, while Glasgow was represented by its famous 'tree, fish and bell'. Others used simple contractions of the town name: for example 'ABDN' for Aberdeen, sometimes with a contraction mark over the letters. From the 17th to the 20th century some 30 towns and burghs had silversmiths whose wares and marks survive.

In 1681 the Privy Council sought to control the goldsmiths' activities by insisting on proper assaying. The goldsmiths of Edinburgh were instructed not only to manage their own affairs, but also to have responsibility for the quality of wrought silver and gold made throughout the kingdom. In 1689 John Borthwick, both deacon and assay-master at the time, drafted a letter to be sent to all the goldsmiths known or thought to be working in the other burghs, with instructions on how to proceed. The draft was kept within the Incorporation's First Minute book. It is particularly interesting as on the reverse is a list of 13 goldsmiths in seven burghs, presumably the masters to which fair copies were sent. Those who are mentioned are Robert Brock, James Stirling, Thomas Cumming, George Luke and James Cumming (brother of Thomas), all in Glasgow; Matthew Colquhoun in Ayr; Robert Gardyne in Perth (or St Johnstoun as noted in the list); David Auchterlonie in Montrose; William Scott, Alexander Galloway and George Walker in Aberdeen; William Scott in Banff; and Robert Elphinstone in Inverness. While it is not a complete list of goldsmiths working in Scotland at the time, it gives a fascinating insight into the distribution and numbers of the senior masters of the craft. This book contains examples of work by 11 of these 13.

Even before then there had been some moves to control the output of goldsmiths working in Canongate, Glasgow, Dundee and Aberdeen, and perhaps in other towns also. The presence of an assay-scrape, often immediately above the marks, shows that somebody, presumably an independent third party and not the goldsmith himself, had assayed the work.

Canongate goldsmiths complied, more or less, with the national regulations from at least the 1580s onwards [see 3.31, Canongate Spoon], though the earliest known Canongate work [3.3 and 3.4, Tulloch and Galloway Mazers] carries only a maker's mark and town mark, but shows no standard mark or assay-scrape. The town mark however is apparently struck with the same punch from the 1550s until about 1630 and possibly later. From the time of George Cunningham [3.31, Canongate Spoon] to Robert Ker [3.37, Oliphant Spoon], a standard mark, 'XID', was also used, signifying 11 pennyweights fine, or 91.6 %.

The earliest-known Glasgow silver bears only a maker's mark and an assay-scrape [see 3.13, 3.36, Ballochlyle Brooch and Disc-end Spoon]. In 1681 Glasgow goldsmiths started to use a cycle of date-letters synchronous with those in Edinburgh. However, their 'town' marks are mostly different from one goldsmith to another, showing that they used their own punches, and also that, despite the presence of an assay-scrape on some items, these may not have been applied by a central authority. It has still to be determined exactly how, and for how long, these systems operated in the different burghs, but the documentary evidence is hard to come by.

Dundee silver from the middle years of the 17th century sometimes bears an assay-scrape [see 3.24, Mercer Stewart Cups] and sometimes not [7.16, Fithie Basin]. There seems to be no documentary evidence for why this should be so.

In the case of Aberdeen goldsmiths, we know that in 1649 William Anderson was appointed 'tryar' of all silver work wrought in the town. His mark and assay-scrape may be found on several pieces of Aberdeen-made silver for a number of years after that date. In this publication, the neighbouring burghs of Aberdeen and Old Aberdeen are treated together.

During the 18th century we find the local marks of many more goldsmiths in the more prosperous burghs. The general pattern of maker's mark and town mark continued, but other marks were often added to these. Random letters of the alphabet were sometimes added. These may sometimes be pseudo date-letters, either indicating a particular year or in imitation of that system. In the latter case they are not a safe guide as to the date of manufacture, as with the 'D' mark used by William Scott, younger, in Elgin [5.37, 5.38]. Other letters appear to be of a different character, such as the 'S' in mid-century Glasgow, which appears on the work of most goldsmiths of the period. This appears to signify something other than date, possibly the standard of the metal.

At no time was there ever an assay office in any place in Scotland except in Edinburgh and for a time in Glasgow, so marks struck locally in the various burghs round Scotland were not 'hallmarks'.

In 1784 the Act of Parliament which introduced duty on wrought plate required all goldsmiths in Scotland to send their work to the Edinburgh Assay Office to be assayed and marked and have the duty collected on it. Many goldsmiths, notably those in Glasgow and Canongate, complied with this requirement, and this is why 'local' marks in those places cease at that time. However, the majority of goldsmiths in other burghs continued to mark their work locally for themselves without the benefit of independent assay, in defiance of the new regulations. Some goldsmiths, such as William Hannay in Paisley and Robert Keay in Perth, sent a token amount to Edinburgh for assay, but continued to mark much of their outputs locally.

The Incorporation of Goldsmiths in Edinburgh was powerless to enforce the law throughout the country and made several pleas to the tax authorities for assistance in the matter, but without much result. One or two prosecutions followed, but not enough action was taken to stamp out the practice of marking work locally. The Assay Office had an altercation with Alexander Cameron from Dundee, who had been marking his work for himself; it turned out to be well below the required standard. Cameron then started sending his work by ship to Newcastle for marking because of his falling out with the authorities in Edinburgh.

One result of the 1784 Act was that the goldsmiths of Glasgow felt hard-done-by. They resented having to send their work by coach or canal to Edinburgh and they wanted an assay office of their own. It took 35 years of agitation and lobbying before they got their wish. From 1819 to 1964 an Assay Office operated in Glasgow.

Elsewhere in the country the situation arising from the 1784 Act remained unaltered until 1836, when a further Act of Parliament came into force. This sought to bring together all the existing legislation on the subject and to accommodate the provisions of the Glasgow act of 1819. From that date many more provincial goldsmiths found themselves obliged to comply with the law, and the number of locally-struck marks reduced considerably. Even so, some locally-marked work continued to be made and sold illegally right through the 19th century.

Some goldsmiths complied with the requirement of sending their work to Edinburgh or Glasgow to be marked and then added marks of their own afterwards. This practice continued into the 20th century, one or two even registering a place mark as well as their maker's mark with the assay office of their choice. A handful habitually sent their work for assay to one or other of the English assay offices.

In addition to all the marks struck by known goldsmiths in identifiable burghs, there are over 150 sets of marks which appear, in all probability, to be Scottish, but which cannot be ascribed satisfactorily to any individual or location. Some of them are one-off marks, without any apparent 'relations'. Others fall into any one of eight groups or 'families' of marks which may be identified by sharing one or more marks in common. Most of these families of marks appear to date from the period 1790-1840, the time when the greatest proliferation of goldsmiths in Scotland's burghs was taking place. One can hazard a guess at some of their identities, but others are still altogether baffling.

Other factors came into play in the first half of the 19th century which helped to bring most local marks to an end. The improvement of roads and the coming of the railways made it easier for potential customers to travel to Edinburgh or Glasgow. There they could buy their teapots and salvers, instead of relying on their local silversmiths who, with few exceptions, were only capable of making flatware and a few other simple items when called for.

The exclusive privileges of all the incorporated trades had been unenforceable for decades and were finally abolished in 1846. This weakened the incorporations fatally; the majority either went to the wall or turned themselves into self-help societies, providing pensions for their surviving members and their families. The goldsmiths who continued to work had to struggle against the industrialisation of their craft. It was now more easy and economic to import ready-made goods from factories in England than to make their own work. The trade had changed forever.

The early 20th century saw a low ebb in silver made in the various burghs outside the two main centres, and this continued until after 1945. Then a gradual revival began to take place. However, the phoenix which arose from the ashes of the Second World War was a different bird from the one which had preceded it. The surviving businesses in the big towns had become high-street jewellers who did a little silver work on the side or bought it in from the south. Alongside them a new breed of craftsmen and craftswomen was arising, trained not in a master's workshop but in the art colleges in Edinburgh, Glasgow, Aberdeen and Dundee (see chapter 10).

5.3

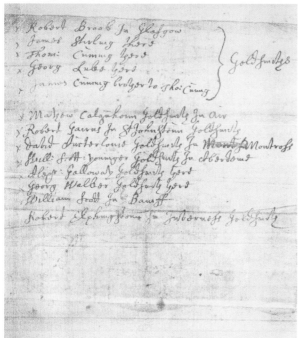

DRAFT LETTER FROM THE INCORPORATION OF GOLDSMITHS OF EDINBURGH

Paper, *c.*1689; 16.8 cm x 21.5 cm
Lent by the Incorporation of Goldsmiths of Edinburgh via the National Archives of Scotland

Aberdeen and Old Aberdeen

5.1 COMMUNION CUP OF FINTRAY

Hew Anderson, Aberdeen, *c.*1633

Marks (on rim): tower incuse (Aberdeen); 'HA' in monogram (maker Hew Anderson)

H 20.3 cm; D (bowl) 13.3 cm; D (foot) 9.8 cm

Lent by the kirk session of Fintry, Kinellan and Keithhall Church

Reference: Burns (1892), p. 264

Wide bowl on slender baluster stem, with spreading stepped foot, the rim with a band of stamped ovolo decoration. Bowl is inscribed: 'FOR . THE . HOLIE . COMMVNIOVN . AT . FINTRAY . Mr ADAM . BARCLAY . MINISTER . 1633'.

This cup appears to be the oldest surviving piece of marked Aberdeen silver. Burns wrongly suggested the marks were for Alexander Reid in Edinburgh. However, the maker's mark is clearly 'HA' in monogram, while the only other mark, an incuse single towered castle, in no way resembles any of the Edinburgh town marks. The minister who commissioned the cup, Adam Barclay, was a graduate of King's College in Aberdeen and went on to be Professor of Divinity there in 1642. The cup is known locally as St Meddan's Cup. Traditionally it is said to have been made of silver from a reliquary of that saint which, before the Reformation, was 'wont to be carried about the parish in procession for the purpose of bringing down the rain or clearing up the weather …'. If this is true, it is evidence of one reason for the disappearance of pre-Reformation church silver (see chapter 7, p. 141).

5.2 TASTER

Thomas Moncur, Aberdeen, *c.*1650

Marks (below rim): 'WA' in monogram ('tryer' or assayer William Anderson); 'ABD' (Aberdeen); 'TM' conjoined (maker Thomas Moncur); assay-scrape above

W (over handles) 10 cm; Wt 2.25 oz

Lent from a private collection

Plain circular bowl, with raised central boss, engraved 'G MG / C MK' (the lower initials are unclear and may have been erased and over-written); with two opposed shaped handles, upper faces engraved with simple scrolls. This little vessel was presumably a wine taster, but may also have served as a sweet-meat dish. Its wonderfully clear marks illustrate the attempts of Aberdeen's goldsmiths and burgh authorities to comply with national legislation controlling the quality of metal and assaying. It is as fully marked as any Edinburgh silver of the period, with maker's mark, that of the 'tryer' William Anderson (fulfilling the same task as the Edinburgh deacon), a town mark, and the assay-scrape to show it had been properly sampled. The Act of the Town Council of 1649 required all wares to be 'sufficient and markit with the prob', i.e. marked with a probe, meaning the burin which was used to remove a small sample of metal.

5.3 QUAICH

William Scott I, Aberdeen, c.1681-82

Marks (below rim): 'VS' conjoined (William Scott I); 'ABC' (misunderstood attempt at a date-letter – see below)

D (rim) 7.4 cm; W (over lugs) 11.8 cm; H 2.1 cm; Wt 1.38 oz

Lent from a private collection

Traditional shallow-bodied shape, with two opposing lugs with down-turned ends, set on a simple ring and flange foot; the body engraved with stave and withie lines, the resultant segments engraved internally and externally with alternate stemmed flowers, foliage and birds; lugs engraved with foliage and shaded border.

This elaborately engraved quaich is probably the work of William Scott elder, when resident in Aberdeen, c.1681-82. There has been much discussion in the past about the origin of the 'ABC' mark on this and other pieces by Scott, it being suggested that he also worked in Aberchirder and this was a 'town' mark for that place. There is no evidence for this; more likely, Scott either failed to understand fully the order of the Privy Council of 1681, which insisted all makers throughout Scotland work up to standard and apply date-letters to their wares, or he simply chose to interpret its wording literally. The act actually states in two places that 'new made work bear the date by the A B C' and that 'goldsmiths in other burghs of the kingdom shall set their name upon his work marked with the ABC' – literally what appears on this quaich.

5.4 COCONUT CUP

William Scott I, c.1680

Marks (on rim): 'VS' conjoined (William Scott I)

H 18.9 cm; D (rim) 10.2 cm; D (base) 9.6 cm

Lent by Aberdeen Art Gallery and Museums

References: James (1981), p. 40; *Applied Art Through the Alphabet* (Aberdeen Art Gallery and Museum); *North East Silver* (Peterhead Museum, 1988)

This cup is formed from a polished coconut shell, mounted with scalloped rim engraved 'IB / MI 1650', with four hinged and pinned straps attaching the rim to base mounts. The mounts are engraved with all-over floral and geometric pattern. The stem has an inverted tear-shaped knop with fluted section, over spreading embossed foot and rim with stamped ovolo decoration.

Dating this cup is problematic. William Scott elder, whose mark appears on the rim only, seems to have been working in Aberdeen from 1666 until about 1690 when he moved to Banff, and the engraving on the rim mount is similar to that on the above quaich [5.3] dated to c.1681. However, the style and construction of the stem and foot seem to be earlier, and indeed are reminiscent of such pieces as the Craigievar Mazer and the Heriot Loving Cup [see 3.7 and 3.17]. It is possible that the cup as it stands is a composite piece, reconstructed by Scott from an earlier cup to celebrate an anniversary of the marriage of 'IB' to 'MI' in 1650. This is, however, speculation.

5.5 PAIR OF THISTLE CUPS

George Walker, Aberdeen, c.1690

Marks (on base): 'GW' (maker George Walker); gothic 'a' (pseudo date-letter); 'ABD' with dash (Aberdeen); 'U'

H 8.9 cm; D (rim) 8.6 cm; D (foot) 5.1 cm; Wt 5.71 oz

Lent by Aberdeen Art Gallery and Museums

References: *Applied Art through the Alphabet* (Aberdeen Art Gallery and Museum)

5.3

5.6

5.2

5.4

Simple bell-shaped bodies with applied pricked dot-decorated girdle two-thirds from base, with applied double-lobed calyx, resting on a simple foot-rim with 'wavy' band of decoration, the C-scroll strap handles with raised thumb-piece and 'rope' moulding; bodies with engraved initials 'I.S/M.M.'

5.6 TEAPOT

Robert Cruickshank, Old Aberdeen, c.1710-20

Marks: 'RC' (maker Robert Cruickshank); gothic 'b'? (pseudo date-letter); 'AB' (Aberdeen)

L (spout to handle) 22 cm; H 12.8 cm; D (rim) 7.7 cm; D (foot) 7.7 cm; Wt 15.46 oz 9 (Scratch Wt '17 o 11 d')

Lent by Boston Museum of Fine Art, gift of Mrs John Lowell, 1991

Plain barrel-shaped body, with simple foot-rim, straight tapering spout, wooden C-scroll handle, and simple upstanding rim mouth. The hinged flat lid has an external shaped hinge and wooden bun finial. Body engraved (at later dates) with names indicating unbroken family descent from Elspeth Burnet and her husband Alexander Middleton, through their son Alexander Middleton junior, who moved from Aberdeenshire to Boston around 1735, to the donor who presented it to Boston Museum of Fine Art in 1991.

The town mark and gothic letter on this well-provenanced teapot are similar to the marks on a tankard by Cruickshank in King's College, Aberdeen University.

5.7 TWO TABLESPOONS

(1) Samuel Le Reivier, Old Aberdeen, c.1700

Marks: 'SR' with star below in heater-shaped shield (maker Samuel Le Reivier); three fleur-de-lis with French-style crown; 'AB' over a star in a shield matching that of the maker's mark (Old Aberdeen)

L 19.5 cm; Wt 1.8 oz

(2) George Robertson, Aberdeen, c.1710

Marks: 'GR' (maker George Robertson); three castles arranged two over one (Aberdeen); 'GR' repeated; gothic 'e' (pseudo date-letter)

L 19.7 cm; Wt 1.79 oz

Lent from a private collection at Mount Stuart

Reference: James (1981), pp. 50-51

From a set of six made in two lots of three, virtually identical to one another and engraved *en suite*, with oval bowls and longish rat-tails. Wavy-end terminals engraved 'A/I' all beside 'S' in an unusual arrangement. Maker Robertson was presumably commissioned a few years after Le Reivier to make additional spoons for a set.

5.8 PAIR OF BEER MUGS

John Walker, Aberdeen, c.1720

Marks (on base): 'IWR', the W and R conjoined (maker John Walker); three castles twice (Aberdeen)

H 9.2 cm; D (rim) 6.8 cm; D (foot) 4.6 cm; Wts 6.79 oz and 6.64 oz; Wt (total) 13.43 oz

Lent from a private collection at Mount Stuart

Straight-sided bell-shaped bodies have everted rims, with central broad reeded girdles and scroll handles with pronounced scroll terminals; they are engraved opposite the handles above the girdles with initials 'RS/AG'. The foot-rim of one mug has a scratch weight '13 o 14 d'.

5.9 TEAPOT

George Robertson, Aberdeen, c.1725

Marks: 'GR' twice (maker George Robertson); three towers (Aberdeen); gothic 'e' (pseudo date-letter)

H 15.3 cm; D (base) 9 cm; L (spout to handle) 27.4 cm

Lent by Aberdeen Art Gallery and Museums; purchased in 1969 with the assistance of the National Art-Collection Fund and Webster Bequest

Provenance: Sotheby's sale, 21 December 1967, lot 230

References: James (1981), p. 61, pl. 6; Dietert (2007), p. 509

Teapot is on a stepped pedestal foot; with straight spout and leaf-capped S-scroll handle; with applied scalloped hinge and scalloped boss beneath wooden finial. Body is engraved with arms for John Urquhart (1688-1726), 20th Laird of Meldrum, Aberdeenshire, with the initials 'JC' on the opposing side. This pot was possibly commissioned as a marriage or anniversary piece; the initials are for John Urquhart's wife, Jean Campbell, and both their family mottoes are engraved on the body. Urquhart was a member of the last Scottish Parliament before the Union in 1707.

5.8

5.7 (1 and 2)

5.9

5.4

5.2

5.5

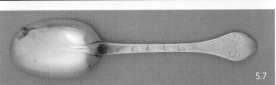

5.7

5.8

5.9

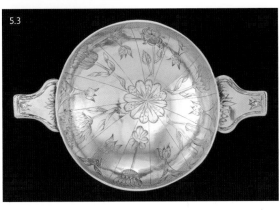

5.3

5.6 (detail)

Elspeth Burnet   m 1705
Alexander Middleton Jr
Mary Middleton
Mary Lovell
Mary Lovell Pickard
Ann Bent Ware
Mary Pickard Winsor
Mary Pickard Winsor 2nd

5.10 THE KIRKHILL TEA SERVICE

George Cooper, Aberdeen, c.1730

Marks: 'GC' (maker George Cooper); three towers (Aberdeen); gothic 'e' (pseudo date-letter)

Teapot: H 11.5 cm; L (max.) 22.5 cm

Tea caddies: H 12.7 cm; L 8.7 cm; W 6 cm

Sugar bowl: H 8.9 cm; D (rim) 12 cm

Cream jug: H 9.5 cm; D (rim) 4.9 cm

Lent by Aberdeen Art Gallery and Museums; purchased at Sotheby's sale, 20 November 1986, lot 108, with the aid of grants from the Friends of Aberdeen Museums, Incorporation of Goldsmiths of the City of Edinburgh, and the Local Museums Purchase Fund

Provenance: by descent to the Earl and Countess of Southesk to the 1950s

References: Exhibition of Scottish Art, Royal Academy of Arts London (1939), nos 959, 960; *Connoisseur* 135 (1955), p. 90, How of Edinburgh, advertisement; James (1981), pp. 63-65; Dalgleish and Maxwell (1987), no. 67; Finlay and Fothringham (1991), p. 188, pl. 108; Dietert (2007), p. 564

Comprising teapot, sugar bowl and cover, cream jug and pair of tea caddies. The teapot is of tapered form with straight spout and S-scroll silver handle; the lid has an applied hinge and reeded border; the finial is on a silver support with oval wooden knop. The circular sugar bowl is on a spreading foot, with a combined cover and teapot stand. The cream jug has a baluster body and sparrow-beak spout. The pair of octagonal tea caddies have stepped shoulders, and domed pull-off covers. The sugar bowl, cream jug and tea caddies are all engraved with the crest of a boar's head erased with the motto 'BYD BEE' ['wait and see'] and the initial 'B'.

This tea set was said to have been acquired by the Burnett of Kirkhill family, then passed to the Bannerman family in 1737 when Margaret Burnett, eldest daughter of Thomas Burnett, married Alexander Bannerman. It then descended to the Earls of Southesk on the marriage of Ethel, daughter of Sir Alexander Bannerman, to Charles, 10th Earl of Southesk.

This unique tea service illustrates why George Cooper is recognised as one of Scotland's top teaware makers of the early to mid-18th century. In quality and output Cooper rivalled the best Edinburgh goldsmiths.

5.11 LARGE SALVER OR TEA TABLE

George Cooper, Aberdeen, c.1735

Marks: 'GC' three times (maker George Cooper); three towers (Aberdeen); gothic 'e' (pseudo date-letter)

D 52 cm; Wt 110 oz

Lent by Aberdeen Art Gallery and Museums; purchased in 1975 with assistance from the Local Museums Purchase Fund and the Jaffray Bequest

Provenance: John Bell of Aberdeen (Mr W. S. Bell's private collection)

References: Finlay and Fothringham (1991), p. 188; John Bell of Aberdeen (advert), in *Scottish Art Review* VI (1956), no. 1, p. 41

Of shaped circular form with straight and crescent section raised border, the well with a chased border of flower head and scroll design. Raised on six shell feet it also has a threaded socket to centre of underside, possibly for attaching to a tripod. The centre is engraved with arms and motto probably for Adam Duff, Provost of Aberdeen 1774-75, who succeeded his father in 1731.

This is one of the largest surviving Scottish 18th-century salvers, and was probably intended to be used either as a salver or alternatively the top of a tripod tea table, like the one by James Mitchellson of 1736-37 [see 4.19].

5.12 TEAPOT

Alexander Forbes, Aberdeen, c.1735

Marks (on base): 'AF' (maker Alexander Forbes); three towers (Aberdeen); unidentified shield mark

H 16.5 cm; L 25 cm; D (base) 8 cm; Wt 21.92 oz

Lent from a private collection

Reference: How (1941), p. 22

Spherical body is on a stepped pedestal foot, with S-scroll silver handle and semi-fluted scroll spout, shaped hinge and knop finial to lid; round the mouth is deeply chased with scalloped band of fruit, flowers and foliage. The body is engraved with arms, crest and motto 'Vincenti Dabitur', in a ribbon below.

This is one of the finest surviving Aberdeen-made teapots, displaying excellent chasing.

5.10

5.12

5.10

5.11

5.12

5.13
(detail below)

5.15

5.16

GINGER

NUTMEG

CINNAMON

5.13

5.13 PAIR OF CANDLESTICKS

Colin Allan, Aberdeen, *c*.1750

Marks: 'CA' (maker or retailer Colin Allan); three towers twice (Aberdeen); anchor

H 17.5 cm; D (base) 11.2 cm

Lent by Aberdeen Art Gallery and Museums; purchased at Christie's & Edmiston's sale, The Morris Collection, 3 July 1984, lot 118

Provenance: Christie's sale, London, 16 April 1947, lot 93; Noble Collection

References: RSM (1948), no. 252; Finlay and Fothringham (1991), p. 90; James (1981), pp. 72-75, pl. 9

Deep baluster sockets have pull-out circular nozzles, above knopped baluster stem on stepped domed bases with scalloped foot-rim, chased with floral and trellis-work borders. Engraved with a crest, a hand clasping a shell, and the motto 'Virtute et opera' for Duff.

These highly unusual candlesticks bear the marks of Colin Allan, one of Aberdeen's most talented gold-smiths. However, it is possible that these sticks could have been imported from the Continent and merely chased, engraved and retailed by Allan.

5.14 PART TEA SERVICE

John Leslie, Aberdeen, 1798-99

Marks: 'IL' (maker John Leslie); 'ABD' (Aberdeen); castle (Edinburgh); thistle (standard mark); 'S' (date-letter 1798-99); king's head (duty mark)

Teapot: H 14.2 cm; L 27.3 cm; Wt 17.06 oz

Teapot stand: L 16.7 cm; W 13 cm; Wt 5.43 oz

Sugar basket: H (max.) 17 cm; L 15.5 cm; Wt 7.19 oz

Lent by the Clan Leslie Charitable Trust

Provenance: (teapot and stand) unknown; (sugar basket) V. J. Cumming Collection; Lyon & Turnbull sale, The Murray Collection, 20 August 2003, lot 223

References: Loan Exhibition of Scottish Art and Antiquities (1931), no. 110; *Empire Exhibition* (1938), no. 136, pl. 31 (V. J. Cumming Collection); James (1981), pp. 83-85, pl. 12; Leslie (2004), p. 19

Part-service of teapot, stand and sugar basket, the oval bodies with reeded rims, bright cut borders and cartouches, all with engraved initials 'IMD' within a bright cut oval. The Clan Leslie Charitable Trust reunited the pieces of this part-service, after they had become separated sometime before 1938.

5.15 TEAPOT AND STAND

James Erskine, Aberdeen, *c*.1800

Marks (on base of teapot and stand): 'IE' (maker James Erskine); 'ABD' (Aberdeen)

Teapot: H 16.3 cm; W 27.4 cm; D 10 cm; Wt 17.665 oz

Stand: W 20 cm; D 14 cm; Wt 5.074 oz

Lent from a private collection

References: John Bell of Aberdeen Collection (1961), no. 32; Dietert (2007), p. 553

The teapot is formed as twelve concave panels, with straight spout and curved fruit-wood handle. Domed cover has a flush hinge and oval outline fruitwood finial. The body and lid is engraved with foliate scroll and hoop and dot borders with two vacant cartouches on opposing sides. The stand is of identical outline, with similar engraved details and borders, with vacant central cartouche, on four claw and ball feet.

5.16 SPICE BOX

William Jamieson, Aberdeen, *c*.1810

Marks: 'WJ' three times (maker William Jamieson); 'ABD' (Aberdeen)

H 10.1 cm; D 6.9 cm

Lent by Aberdeen Art Gallery and Museums

Reference: James (1981), p. 122, fig. 35

Cylindrical form, with three pull-off compartments simply inscribed respectively 'GINGER', 'NUTMEG' and 'CINNAMON', each with a moulded reeded rim, the slightly domed cover with integral pierced steel grater. The lid is engraved with a crest, a boar, beneath the motto 'Vires Animat Virtus' in a scroll.

Personal use of spices and herbs was popular in Britain. As with snuff-boxes and vinaigrettes, it became a fashionable sign of one's social position to bring out a personal grater. This started with very simple small cylindrical examples and slowly moved to more decorative types. This unusually large example, presumably made for the table rather than the pocket, having three compartments, is a comparative rarity.

5.16

5.13   5.14   5.15   5.17

Arbroath

5.17 PENKNIFE

Andrew Davidson, Arbroath, c.1825

Marks (on blade): 'AD' (maker Andrew Davidson); crowned head (maker's accompanying mark); portcullis (Arbroath)

L 13.9 cm; W 1.2 cm; L (handle) 7.5 cm; Wt. 1.86 oz

Lent by Arbroath Museum

Handle is of rounded rectangular form with simple prick-dot border, the centre chased with floral and scroll decoration, the tapered silver blade engraved in script 'Ann Goodall'.

5.18 GOBLET

Andrew Davidson, Arbroath, c.1836

Marks (under rim, very rubbed): 'AD' (maker Andrew Davidson); portcullis (Arbroath); crowned head (maker's accompanying mark)

H 18.6 cm; D (rim) 12.5 cm; Wt 14.24 oz

Lent by Arbroath Museum

Plain slightly tapered bowl with engraved inscription, 'Presented / To / William Stratton Esq. / By The People Employed In His Mill / As A Token Of Gratitude. / For his Kind and Benevolent Conduct / Toward them / Arbroath January 1836', above a baluster section with alternate decoration of acanthus and laurel leaf; on a knopped stem and domed spreading foot-rim with embossed flower head and foliate border.

Ayr

5.19 QUAICH

Matthew Colquhoun, Ayr, c.1685

Marks (four times): 'MC' conjoined (maker Matthew Colquhoun)

D 15 cm; W (over lugs) 22.8 cm; H 6 cm; Wt 8.18 oz

NMS K.2005.345; purchased at Christie's sale, London, Important Silver, Tuesday 5 July 2005, lot 45, with help from the Dr Cecil and Mary Gibson Bequest Fund

Provenance: Sotheby's sale, London, 28 February 1974, lot 117

References: Glasgow International Exhibition (1888); noted by A. J. S. Brook, in Burns (1892), p. 576

Circular body on collet foot with two hollow down-turned lugs; the body is engraved with stave and withie lines, with alternate panels filled with engraved tulips and roses; the handles are engraved with foliate borders and the initials 'M * F / I * C'.

The fact that this quaich has only the maker's mark may be an indication that it was made before the date of the Incorporation's letter of 1689 (see p. 88). Colquhoun was probably in business in Ayr by about 1683; the style of the quaich is perfectly in keeping with this suggested dating of c.1683-c.89.

Banff

5.20 COCONUT CUP

William Scott I, Banff, c.1690

Marks: 'VS' in monogram twice (maker William Scott I); fish (Banff); gothic 'd' (pseudo date-letter)

H 15.4 cm; D (rim) 8.7 cm; D (foot) 8.9 cm; Wt 7.39 oz

Lent from a private collection at Mount Stuart

Reference: RSM (1948), no. 291

Coconut bowl with plain silver everted rim fixed to stem by four hinged and pinned reeded straps; with rounded baluster stem, disc flange and plain stepped foot. The foot is engraved with the initials 'IO' and 'HD' within winged feather mantling.

It is thought that this combination of marks relates to the elder William Scott's time in Banff, c.1690-1701.

5.21 TEAPOT

Unknown maker, Banff, c.1715-20

Marks (on base, either side of centre point): 'BANF' (Banff); possibly 'IS' or 'SI' in rubbed punch

H 11.2 cm; D (foot) 7.3 cm; L 23.5 cm; Wt 14.351 oz

Lent by Aberdeenshire Heritage, Banff Museum; purchased in 1981 with the aid of the National Fund for Acquisitions and local donations

References: Bertie (2001), p. 3; Pickford (1989) (for Jackson), p. 592; MacDougal (1991), quoted in Finlay and Fothringham, pp. 203-04

5.18  5.19   5.20  5.21

Body on moulded foot-rim; straight tapering spout with diamond-shaped panel soldered to lower base of spout; simple C-scroll light fruitwood handle pinned to simple silver sockets. Mouth of body and lid chased with bands of diamond and stylised foliage decoration, and the body engraved with a crest, an oak tree with a stag lodged below (possibly for Pennycuik [*sic*.]).

There is considerable speculation about the maker of this exceptionally fine, important teapot. While the town mark is sharp and unambiguous, the maker's mark is far from clear. It has stylistic similarities to the earliest recorded dateable Scottish teapot by Colin Campbell, Edinburgh, 1714-15 (sold at Sotheby's, London, Nov. 1972; current whereabouts unknown).

5.22 SUGAR BOWL AND CREAM JUG

Patrick Gordon, Banff, *c.*1735

Marks (on bases of both): 'PG' twice (maker Patrick Gordon); 'BANF' (Banff); 'B' (date-letter)

Jug: H 11.3 cm; L 9.5 cm; D (base) 5.3 cm; Wt 5.716 oz (Scratch Wt '6 ou 1 dr')

Bowl: H 7.2 cm; D 13.4 cm; Wt 6.11 oz (Scratch Wt '7 oun 7 dr')

NMS K.2004.208.1 and 2; purchased from Nicholas Shaw Antiques

Provenance: The Late Sir John S. B. Noble Collection

References: Finlay and Fothringham (1991), pp. 212-13, pl. 120(i); RSM (1948), no. 294; *Empire Exhibition* (1938), nos 91, 93, pl. 39

This bowl is of plain hemispherical form with shaped moulded rim, set on spreading circular foot; the jug is of sparrow-beak form on a spreading circular stepped foot, the S-scroll handle engraved 'JD'. Each engraved with a crest, a stag's head erased, and motto 'Virtute et Opera' for Duff. The crest and motto of 'William Duff of Bracco', Banffshire, were matriculated thus with the Lord Lyon on 19 July 1723.

These beautiful tewares are concrete proof that some silversmiths working in the smaller burghs were perfectly capable of producing elegant and well-made pieces in the highest fashion. This jug and bowl, along with a bullet teapot (whereabouts currently unknown), are the only known pieces of Patrick Gordon's work. They show that he was an accomplished craftsman, comparable with his contemporary Colin Allan in Aberdeen. They were stolen from the Noble Collection many years ago, but were later recovered.

5.23 CUP AND COVER

William Byres, Banff, *c.*1790

Marks (below rim): 'WB' (maker William Byres); 'BANF' (Banff); gothic 'Q' rubbed

H 30.8 cm; W 25.5 cm; D (foot) 11.2 cm; Wt 29.02 oz

NMS H.MEQ 957; purchased from Grantully Castle Antiques, 1969

Provenance: John Bell of Aberdeen

Reference: Finlay and Fothringham (1991), p. 213, pl. 118(i)

The vase-shaped body is on a simple spreading foot, with beaded rim and foot; two opposed beaded high loop handles; domed cover with writhen knop finial; the body is engraved with swags and husk and two shields, inscribed 'AID' and 'The Gift of / Miss Abernethie / to her Niece / Mrs Duff'.

This is another example of an accomplished piece in the prevailing neo-classical fashion of the day by a 'country' goldsmith. Generally known for his flatware, this cup is the largest piece by William Byres known to have survived. From its slightly off-beat proportions it is clear that it was made by Byres and not bought in from Edinburgh or elsewhere.

Canongate

5.24 THISTLE CUP

Walter Graham, Canongate, *c.*1695

Marks (on the base): 'WG' with fleur-de-lis below (maker Walter Graham); stag's head with cross between antlers (Canongate); 'O' (date-letter, probably 1694-95)

H 8 cm; D (rim) 8.4 cm; D (foot) 4.1 cm; Wt 5.29 oz

Lent from a private collection at Mount Stuart

Reference: RSM (1948), no. 181

This cup has a bell-shaped body with an everted rim on a simple concave collet foot, the lower part of the body applied with ten alternate applied lobes and ten cut-card darts below a central simple reeded girdle, applied with a reeded scroll-strap handle. Engraved opposite the handle, above the girdle, with the initials 'ID/MH' in hatched lettering.

5.22   5.24

5.23

5.18

5.14

5.19

5.17

5.21

5.20

5.22

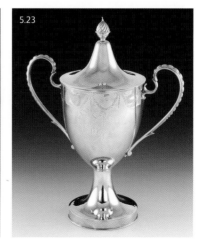

5.23

5.25 LOCHIEL'S SWORD

Hilt by Colin Mitchell, Canongate, *c*.1740s

Marks (rear quillon and knuckle-guard): 'CM' three times (maker Colin Mitchell); 'L' (pseudo date-letter); stag's head erased (Canongate); 'WA/S' (stamped underside of quillon, for Walter Allan, Stirling)

L (max.) 99 cm; L (hilt) 18 cm; W (hilt) 13 cm

Lent by Donald Cameron of Lochiel

References: Maxwell (1981), pp. 408-18; The Swords and the Sorrows (1996) (exhibition), no. 1:22

Backsword with silver pommel and basket hilt of conventional form, circular section bars, with panels pierced with quatrefoils and stars. Blade is of 17th-century type. Known as 'Lochiel's sword' and long associated with Donald Cameron of Lochiel, 19th Chief, who led his Clan 'out' in the 1745-46 Jacobite Rebellion. Colin Mitchell was active as a goldsmith in the Canongate from 1727 to 1753 when he died in debt. His papers were impounded by the Edinburgh Commissary Court, and they show that he produced several silver hilts and scabbard-mounts for Walter Allan, the well-known Stirling-based swordsmith. Their customers included MacDonald of Clanranald, Stewart of Glenbuckie and Lord Glenorchy.

5.26 THE TROTTER TANKARD

William Craw, Canongate, *c*.1765

Marks (on base): 'WC' twice (maker William Craw)

H (max.) 22.1 cm; D (base) 14.2 cm; D (rim) 9 cm; W (across handle) *c*.21 cm; Wt 43.83 oz (Scratch Wt '43=13')

Lent by the City of Edinburgh Museums and Galleries; purchased at Christie's sale, David Morris Collection, 3 July 1984

References: Finlay and Fothringham (1991), pp. 177-78; Dietert (2007), p. 484

The baluster form body is divided into four panels by flutes, set on plain moulded foot-rim, the hinged lid mirroring the body shape; S-scroll handle with stepped ball terminal with upright solid thumb-piece. Front of the body is engraved with a coat of arms in foliate oval cartouche for Trotter of Mortonhall, quartering Trotter of Charterhall; it is engraved 'AB' in mono-gram on upper part of thumb-piece; cover engraved with the Trotter crest, a horse led by its dismounted rider, with motto 'IN PROMPTU' in ribbon above.

5.27 PAIR OF CANDLESTICKS

Michael Forrest, Canongate, hallmarked Edinburgh, 1770-71

Marks (spaced equally around inner part of underside of base, corresponding to base lobes): 'MF' twice (maker Michael Forrest); stag's head (Canongate); castle (Edinburgh); thistle (Edinburgh assay-mark); gothic 'E' (Edinburgh date-letter 1770-71)

(1) H 22.5 cm; D (base) 13 cm; Wt 18.17 oz
(2) H 22.3 cm; D (base) 13.1 cm; Wt 16.972 oz

Lent by City of Edinburgh Museums and Galleries

Reference: Finlay and Fothringham (1991), p. 178

On lobed stepped bases, with sunken centres; baluster and vase stems; the spool sockets with detachable lobed drip-pans. Lower part of the stems engraved with a crest, a phoenix surrounded by a belt with the motto 'VIVE UT POSTEA VIVAS'. As Michael Forrest did not become a freeman in the Canongate until 16 August 1770, these sticks represent some of his earliest work.

5.28 SUGAR BOWL

John Robertson, Canongate, *c*.1765

Marks (on base in a line): 'I.R' (maker James Robertson); stag's head (Canongate)

H (max.) 14.7 cm; L 14.2 cm; W 10.3 cm; L (foot) 8.5 cm; W (foot) 6.5 cm; Wt 7.85 oz

Lent from a private collection

Reference: Finlay and Fothringham (1991), p. 178, pl. 120(ii)

Oval inverted-pear-shaped body on stepped foot, with gadrooned rim; upper part of body chased with swags of foliage and flowers between vacant ovals, with a gadrooned rim; the hinged twisted-wire handle with void cartouche in the centre. This lovely basket shows that Robertson was a goldsmith of taste and skill.

5.26 (detail)

5.25

5.26

5.27

5.28

Cupar

5.29 WINE FUNNEL

Robert Robertson, Cupar, *c.*1825

Marks: 'RR' twice (maker Robert Robertson); fleur-de-lis in octagonal punch (Cupar)

H 12.5 cm; D 8.7 cm; Wt 3.06 oz / Lent from a private collection

The deep-bellied circular bowl has an everted rim, the interior pierced with a simple pattern. The pull-off spout section has a simple incised reeded border and tapered spout.

Dumfries

5.30 BREAD BASKET

Joseph Pearson, Dumfries, *c.*1800

Marks: fouled anchor (Dumfries); 'IP' (maker Joseph Pearson); stag's head (Dumfries); 'e' (pseudo date-letter)

L 29.8 cm; W (rim) 22.7 cm; H 23.5 cm

Lent by Dumfries Museum

The plain rectangular basket has a reeded moulded edge, with simple spreading foot. The swing handle is formed from three wires with central square cartouche. The cartouche is engraved with a crest and a stag's head, and the motto 'Si Je Puis'.

5.31 CHRISTENING MUG

David Gray, Dumfries, *c.*1830

Marks: 'DG' (maker David Gray); unicorn (Dumfries); wreathed anchor (Dumfries); 'G' (pseudo date-letter)

H 7.1 cm; D 6 cm

Lent by Dumfries Museum; purchased Christie's sale, Glasgow, May 1981, with the aid of the National Fund for Acquisitions

Reference: Finlay and Fothringham (1991), p. 200

The plain can-shaped body has a reeded rim and foot and simple scroll strap handle. The body is engraved in script: 'From his / Godmother / MHD / to / CW'.

Dundee

5.32 QUAICH

Thomas Lindsay II, Dundee, *c.*1680

Marks (below rim): 'TL' (maker Thomas Lindsay II); pot of lilies (Dundee, very rubbed)

D (bowl) 10 cm; W (over lugs) 15.8 cm; H 4.5 cm; Wt 4.52 oz

Lent from a private collection at Mount Stuart

Deep bowl is engraved internally with twelve stave-lines, but is plain on the outside; set on a simple collet and rim foot. The hollow-section shaped lugs are engraved with 'I / C*H' and 'G / I*W' respectively.

Note that the maker of this quaich was not Thomas Lumsden, Montrose, as has sometimes been suggested. Lindsay II's working dates, so far as known, are *c.*1662 to *c.*1688, giving a bracket of 26 years during which the quaich might have been made; we suppose it to be from the latter half of that period.

5.33 TEAPOT AND STAND

Alexander Johnston, Dundee, *c.*1740

Marks: 'IA' in shaped punch twice (maker Alexander Johnston); pot of lilies (Dundee); 'T' or 'L' in script (probably the former because it would then be the same way up as the other punches) (pseudo date-letter)

Teapot: H 14.5 cm; D (foot) 8.2 cm; Wt 24.02 oz

Stand: D 19 cm; H 3 cm; Wt 7.95 oz

Lent from a private collection at Mount Stuart

References: RSM (1948), no. 282; Finlay and Fothringham (1991), p. 193

Teapot is of compressed spherical form on circular domed foot; moulded acanthus-capped curved spout; the S-scroll silver handle with strong volute moulding and thumb-piece; hinged lid with riveted silver bun finial; the body and lid flat-chased round the mouth with bands of scrolling foliage, shells, flowers and

5.29

5.30

5.31

5.32

5.33

5.24

5.27

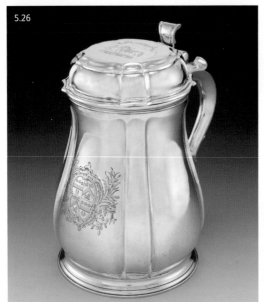

5.26

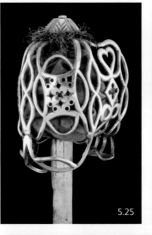

5.25

5.31

5.29

5.28

5.30

fruits, and two small opposing void cartouches; engraved under the foot: 'EX DONO R : F : AD M : M'. The shaped circular stand has 16 lobes in the manner of a strawberry dish, on three hoof feet possibly a later addition; chased with a deep band of foliage, scrolls, flowers, fruit and shells, engraved on the underside in script 'Ex Dono R : F : ad M : M :', above a large script letter 'F'.

5.34 TABLE BELL

John Steven, Dundee, c.1760

Marks (inside crown): 'IS' (maker John Steven); pot of lilies (Dundee)

H 13.2 cm; D 9 cm; Wt (all in) 10.18 oz

Lent by Dundee City Council (McManus Galleries and Museum)

This bell is unusually large and of circular section, opening to a wide lip, with reeded moulding wires at the shoulder and sound-bow. Engraved at a slightly later date with initials 'JL', but otherwise plain; the baluster handle is of dark-stained fruitwood or laburnum with a silver finial rising to a ribbed ball with small button. The silver clapper is shaped as a hand-seal with domed cap, attached by a chain of three double links, all original.

Larger hand bells such as this are very rare and are usually associated with the dining table, where they were used to summon a servant. Smaller bells were usually part of a writing desk's furnishings in conjunction with an ink stand, again used to summon a servant to take a letter to the post carrier.

5.35 CAKE BASKET

William Scott, Dundee, c.1790

Marks (on upper side of rim): 'WS' inverted (maker William Scott); pot of lilies (Dundee); 'W' (pseudo date-letter); 'WS' inverted (maker's mark repeated); pot of lilies repeated on underside of strap handle

L 33 cm; W 26.1 cm; H (rim) 9 cm; H (handle) 26.8 cm; Wt 23.43 oz

Lent by Dundee City Council (McManus Galleries and Museum)

Reference: Finlay and Fothringham (1991), p. 183, pl. 112(i)

Oval, with beaded edge, the conventional piercing is relieved by urn medallions alternating with bowed knots, separated by swags of foliage, the pierced strap handle with simple two-leaf hinges; the oval gallery foot with matching simple piercing and beaded rim. There are no arms or inscription.

There has been some debate as to whether the basket was made by William Scott, or merely bought in and retailed by him. However, as the area where the marks are stamped has been deliberately left unpierced to accommodate them, this would seem conclusive evidence that it was made and marked in Scott's own workshop.

5.36 PAIR OF CANDLESTICKS

Alexander Cameron, Dundee, c.1820

Marks (on upper side of the foot-flange, struck together in a single punch): (no maker's mark); 'DUN/DEE' (personal punch associated with the work of Alexander Cameron); 'C' (pseudo date-letter); thistle (pseudo assay-mark); pot of lilies (Dundee)

(1) H 16.4 cm; W (base) 10.7 cm; Wt 8.613 oz
(2) H 16.4 cm; W (base) 10.7 cm; Wt 8.893 oz

Lent by Dundee City Council (McManus Galleries and Museum)

Reference: Finlay and Fothringham (1991), p. 194, pl. 112(ii)

Each stick is of square outline with shaped curved corners, the base stepped, with circular well and flat flange rim, the octagonal-section knopped, with the tapered stem rising through an octagonal cushion to a circular capstan spool nozzle with central girdle. There is no engraving.

Elgin

5.37 THISTLE TOT CUP

William Scott II, Elgin, c.1710

Marks (on base): 'VS' conjoined (maker William Scott II); 'D' (pseudo date-letter)

H 4.3 cm; D (rim) 4.4 cm; D (foot) 2.5 cm; Wt 1.24 oz

Lent from a private collection

This cup has a flared everted lip and slightly tapered body, applied with a simple moulded girdle, engraved above the girdle 'A.C / M.C', below the girdle applied

5.34

5.35

5.36

5.37

with ten lobed and beaded calyx. With simple S-scroll strap handle and collet foot.

If the 'D' letter-punch on this cup corresponds to the Edinburgh date-letter for 1708-09, the maker must be William Scott younger. However, the letter is common on Scott's work and most other letters are lacking, so it may be no guide at all as to date. His father, also William, died in 1701, just after both had moved to Elgin from Banff and had been admitted to the Elgin Hammermen. Both seem to have used the same maker's punch, and it is difficult to identify clearly who made what and in which town.

5.38 THE HUNTLY SPORRAN

William Scott II, Elgin, *c.*1706-*c.*16

Marks (on rear of mount): 'VS' in monogram (maker William Scott II); 'ELGIN' (Ɲ reversed) (Elgin); 'D' (pseudo date-letter)

W (cantle) 20.6 cm; D (rim closed) 1.6 cm;

Wt (all-in) 14.441 oz

Lent from a private collection

References: Clayton (1971), p. 383, pl. 565; Moss (1994), p. 17

Shaped silver cantle with moulded and reeded top rim, hinged face-plate secured by two bun-hinge pins at the side and fastened with lockable bun and button finial. Back-plate with two strap-staples, soldered. With early or original soft leather purse, with four decorative tassels, the inside fitted with three compartments, with silver wire frame dividers matching outline of cantle. The front of the cantle engraved with the arms and coronet of Alexander, Marquess of Huntly, and his wife, Lady Henrietta Mordaunt.

This is the earliest known silver-mounted sporran. The arms are for Alexander, Marquess of Huntly, who married Lady Henrietta Mordaunt in 1706. As he succeeded to the dukedom of Gordon in 1716, the arms on the sporran must date to 1706-16. It may have been made for the 1706 marriage.

Family tradition states it was worn by the Marquess at the battle of Sheriffmuir on 13 November 1716. Thus it may be associated with the magnificent silver-mounted Huntly Targe (now in the collections of National Museums Scotland), also traditionally linked to that battle.

5.39 WINE FUNNEL STAND

Thomas Stewart, Elgin, *c.*1825

Marks: 'TS' (maker Thomas Stewart); 'ELN' (Elgin)

D 10.6 cm

Lent by Aberdeen Art Gallery and Museum

Of simple circular outline with moulded rim, the centre slightly domed. Used to hold a wine funnel when not in use, and to prevent drips touching the table. Thomas Stewart, who also worked in Inverness, was operational in Elgin, 1813-*c.*34.

5.40 PRESENTATION SNUFF BOX

William Ferguson, Elgin, *c.*1833

Marks: 'WF' (maker William Ferguson); 'ELGIN' (Elgin)

L 7.5 cm; W 5 cm; D 2.3 cm

Lent by Elgin Museum

Reference: Moss (1994), pp. 88-89

Of rectangular form with applied floral borders around the edges, with a skull and cross bone motif on the thumb-piece. The lid is engraved with a scene of the ruined west door of Elgin Cathedral. The base of the box is inscribed: 'From the Inhabitants of Elgin / AS A REWARD TO / JOHN SHANKS / Keeper of the Cathedral. / For his attention and care of it generally / and in particular / for discovering on the 23rd September 1833 / four Steps in front of the / GRAND ENTRANCE / Which had been hid by rubbish for Centuries / and have now restored this noble / part of the building to its / JUST PROPORTION'.

John Shanks was a well known local character within the Elgin area. He looked after and cared for the ruins of Elgin Cathedral. His discovery and restoration of the steps to the front of the Cathedral gives an idea of the general state of the building at the time. William Ferguson also worked in Peterhead.

5.38

5.38

5.32

5.36

5.34

5.38

5.35 (and detail)

5.37

5.41

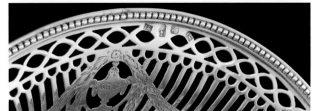

5.42

5.44

5.33

Fochabers

5.41 PRESERVE SPOON OR SUGAR SHOVEL

John McIver, Fochabers, c.1830

Marks: 'JMcI' (maker John McIver); 'FOCHRS' (Fochabers)

L 15 cm; D (bowl) 3 cm; Wt 0.599 oz

Lent from a private collection

Fiddle pattern faceted stem with rounded square shovel bowl; end with engraved script initials 'AH/L'.

Glasgow

5.42 TUMBLER CUP

Thomas Moncur, Glasgow, c.1680

Marks: 'TM' (maker Thomas Moncur, Glasgow)

H 6.7 cm; D 10.2 cm; Wt 5.65 oz

Lent by Glasgow Museums and Art Galleries; purchased in 2005 with help from the National Fund for Acquisitions

Provenance: Christie's sale, London, 26 March 1958, lot 162; ex-John Noble Collection

Reference: Dietert (2007), p. 199; Nicholas Shaw (2004), p. 93

Plain, slightly tapering body with rounded base; engraved with shield of arms and initials 'C/WM' within plumed mantling. Tumbler cups are so called because they were made with rounded bottoms, and they 'tumble' back into an upright position if knocked.

5.43 QUAICH

John Luke I, Glasgow, 1687-88

Marks (underneath, round the centre point): 'IL' (maker John Luke I); tree, fish, bell, etc. (Glasgow); 'G' (date-letter 1687-88); in addition, the underside of each lug is struck with the maker's mark; there is no visible assay-scrape

D (rim) 18.5 cm; W (over lugs) 27.7 cm; D (foot) 10.3 cm; H 7.4 cm; Wt 18.11 oz (Scratch Wt '18 u: 13d')

Lent from a private collection at Mount Stuart

Reference: RSM (1948), no. 193

The bowl is engraved with stave-lines inside and out, those on the inside being very faint. Each side of the bowl is engraved above the withie-lines with three foliated flower-heads (the stalks do not descend below the withies); instead there are plain disembodied chevrons in the corresponding lower compartments. Both lugs are initialled 'B', apparently later, within an unusual decorated border with three leaves at each corner and a serrated design running all the way round. The foot is a concave collet with turned out rim. The maker's mark and date-letter are not known on any other object.

5.44 PATCH BOX AND COVER

William Clerk, Glasgow, c.1695

Marks: 'WC' overstruck twice; 'WC' mis-struck (maker William Clerk)

H (overall) 1.8 cm; D 3.9 cm; Wt 1.05 oz

Lent by Glasgow Museums and Art Galleries; purchased at Christie's sale, London, 24 June 1981, lot 76, with a grant from the Local Museums Purchase Fund

Provenance: ex-John Noble Collection

References: Finlay and Fothringham (1991), p. 109, pl. 45(i); RSM (1948), no. 196

Circular box with lift-off cover, fashioned from delicate wire-work filigree scrolls. Patch boxes were used by ladies to hold cosmetic 'beauty spots' that were popular in the late 17th and early 18th century. Clerk's beautifully delicate filigree box is unique in Scotland, and may perhaps have been part of a toilet service.

5.43

5.44

5.41

5.45

5.42

5.46

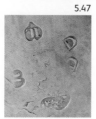

5.47

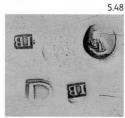

5.48

5.45 SMALL-SWORD WITH SILVER HILT AND SILVER-MOUNTED LEATHER SCABBARD

William Clerk, Glasgow, 1698-99

Marks (on knuckle-guard): 'WC' twice (maker William Clerk); tree, fish, bell, etc. (Glasgow); 'S' (Glasgow date-letter 1698-99); 'WC' on scabbard mount (maker William Clerk)

L 94.5 cm; H (hilt) 7 cm; D (knuckle-guard) 6.5 cm

NMS H.LA 101; acquired from the Whitelaw Collection in 1927

Hilt with globular pommel, knuckle-guard, arms of the hilt and two shell guards. Silver-hilted swords were highly fashionable items in the 17th and early 18th centuries, and several Scottish goldsmiths made fine examples [see Lochiel's Sword, 5.25]. Small silver mounts for scabbards and other accoutrements, probably formed a considerable part of many goldsmiths' businesses. John Rollo's Account Book has many entries for hilts and mounts in the period 1731-37 [see 4.45], while Colin Mitchell in the Canongate also had a considerable trade in these wares. Although we have no record of William Clerk's admission essay, curiously the other Glasgow goldsmith admitted in the same year, James Luke, was set 'ane silver hilt to ane sword' as part of his test of skill.

5.46 TANKARD

Thomas Cumming, Glasgow, 1699-1700

Marks (on underside of lid and base): tree, fish, bell, etc. (Glasgow); 'TC' twice (maker Thomas Cumming); gothic 't' (Glasgow date-letter 1699-1700)

H 20.1 cm; D 14.8 cm; W 22.5 cm; Wt 30.85 oz

Lent by Glasgow Museums and Art Galleries; purchased in 1982 from How of Edinburgh, with a grant from the Local Museums Purchase Fund

Provenance: sold at Sotheby's sale, London, 28 January 1971, lot 100, to Gaskell & Milne's

Tapering cylindrical body on gadrooned foot; domed lid with double knop finial and gadrooned border; scroll handle with beaded spine and scrolled thumb-piece; the body engraved with arms and mottoes for Graham-Dunlop of Douglastown. Engraved under the base: 'This tankard was bequeathed by / William Dunlop of Gairbraid in Canada / TO HIS NEPHEW ALEXANDER GRAHAM DUNLOP YR. / OF GAIR-BRAID IN SCOTLAND / having been left to W.D. / by will of his Aunt Lilas Graham / daughter of Robert Graham / OF KILMANAN GAIRN = BRAID AND LAMBHILL / TO WHOM IT HAD DESCENDED THRO' / HIS MOTHER ALSO A GRAHAM / FROM HER KINSMAN GRAHAM BISHOP OF THE ISLES /

hence it has been called in the family / the Bishop's jug / A. G. D. 1856'.

The Bishop referred to may be Archibald Graham, Bishop of the Isles from 1680 until the abolition of Episcopacy in 1689. He died in Edinburgh 'of fever' on 28 June 1703.

5.47 TANKARD

John Luke II, Glasgow, c.1709-10

Marks (on base): 'IL' in a heart (maker John Luke II); 'D' (pseudo date-letter); tree, fish, bell, etc. (Glasgow)

H 20.6 cm; D (rim) 10.1 cm; D (foot) 14.3 cm; Wt 32.68 oz

Lent from a private collection at Mount Stuart

Tapering cylindrical body, on a plain stepped foot, above which is a reeded moulded band, with simple moulded girdle and reeded rim-band. The stepped domed lid with plain overhanging peaked rim and acorn-and-button finial. Lobed thumb-piece with scroll top; S-scroll handle with dog-nosed terminal, and with lobed and rounded rat-tail ending in a tear-drop. The body is engraved opposite the handle with the initials 'S / RM'.

This would appear to be the mark of John Luke II, who was admitted to the Glasgow Hammermen in 1699. However, there may still be some confusion over the marks ascribed to the two John Lukes and the two James Lukes, who all worked in Glasgow between the 1680s and 1730s.

5.48 TOILET BOX OR TEA CADDY, WITH COVER

James Boyd, Glasgow, c.1709-10

Marks (on base and on cover): 'IB' (maker James Boyd); tree, fish, bell, etc. (Glasgow); 'IB' repeated; 'D' (Glasgow pseudo date-letter 1709-10)

H 11.8 cm; W 8.2 cm; Dp 6 cm; Wt 7.83 oz

Lent by Glasgow Museums and Art Galleries; purchased at Christie's & Edmiston's sale, Glasgow, 30 March 1983, lot 51, with a grant from the Local Museums Purchase Fund

Provenance: Major Shaw of Tordarroch Collection

Rectangular outline, the flat top is engraved round the edge with a running band of chevrons, the corners are filled with stylised leafy chevrons, with cylindrical sleeve for the removable stepped-domed cover. The body is engraved with an elaborate cartouche which contains a shield of arms for Ferrier impaling Galbraith.

If this is indeed a tea caddy, then it is the earliest surviving example in Scotland. It is possible, however, that it is part of a toilet service, which included such canister boxes for holding perfume or cosmetics.

There has been in the past discussion about the identity of its maker, Johan Gotleiff Bilsinds usually being suggested. If the date-letter is to be believed as that for 1709-10 this cannot be the case: Bilsinds was not admitted to the Hammermen's Incorporation until 1717, while James Boyd was admitted in 1707. There is some doubt about the letter 'D', however, as it seems to be the final one used in the regular sequence of date-letters. As it appears on a large number of pieces which seem to come from slightly different dates, it may not be so closely tied to the year 1709-10.

5.49 MINIATURE TANKARD

James Boyd, Glasgow, c.1710

Marks: 'IB' maker's mark only, struck twice (maker probably James Boyd)

H 5.6 cm; D (lip) 2.9 cm; D (base) 3.2 cm; Wt 1.44 oz

Lent from a private collection at Mount Stuart

Similar in outline to the large tankard by John Luke II [5.47], with tapering cylindrical body; lid appears to be cast in a single piece; the tankard is engraved opposite the handle with two intertwining dragons.

There is some possible doubt as to the identity of the maker. The late Mrs How (of How of Edinburgh) favoured James Boyd over Johan Gotleiff Bilsinds on the grounds that Boyd became a freeman of the Incorporation of Hammermen of Glasgow on 8 August 1707 and Bilsinds did not do so until 20 July 1717. The latter date seems rather too late for this tankard and therefore the earlier goldsmith would seem to be the logical ascription. If this interpretation is correct, then it has implications for several other pieces marked by the same maker, currently supposed to be by Bilsinds, which would require them to be reattributed to Boyd. The marks of the two men have never been satisfactorily compared and distinguished from one another.

5.50 BIBLE WITH SILVER MOUNTS

Johan Gotleiff Bilsinds, Glasgow, c.1720

Marks (on heart-shaped mounts): 'IB' (maker Johan Gotleiff Bilsinds); tree, bell, fish, etc. (Glasgow)

H 23.2 cm; W 18.5 cm; Dp 5 cm

NMS H.1996.264; purchased in 1996

Provenance: Christie's sale, Edinburgh, 24 October 1995, lot 478

Leather-bound bible printed by John Hays, Cambridge, 1675, bound with the Psalms of David, printed by Andrew Anderson, Edinburgh, 1676; fastened with two silver hasps with faceted edges, plain ball fasteners and four heart-shaped corner-mounts.

Scottish silver book mounts are exceptionally rare, but do show the range of uses silver was put to in decorating and beautifying domestic objects.

Bilsinds made a range of wares, including communion cups for several parishes in the west. He had obviously stopped working by 1754, when Glasgow Town Council voted him 20 shillings, 'he being old and infirm and reduced to great straits'.

5.51 TANKARD

Robert Luke, Glasgow, c.1735-40

Marks (on base around centre point): 'RL' (maker Robert Luke); 'S' in an oval; tree, fish, bell, etc. (Glasgow)

H 24.8 cm; D (lip) 12.7 cm; D (foot) 13.7 cm; Wt 43.42 oz

Lent from a private collection at Mount Stuart

Baluster-shaped body tucked in on a plain stepped foot, with slightly everted caulked rim, lightly engraved or flat-chased below the rim with a deep band of shell and scroll-work. The stepped domed lid with slightly overlapping peaked rim and acorn-and-button finial. Cast foliate thumb-piece has a scroll top. The S-scroll handle has a dog-nosed terminal and lobed and rounded rat-tail ending in a tear-drop.

5.52 PAIR OF TWO-LIGHT CANDELABRA

Milne & Campbell, Glasgow, c.1760

Marks (on bases): 'M&C' (makers Milne & Campbell); tree, fish, bell, etc. (Glasgow); 'O'

(1) H 32.2 cm; W (across branches) 33.5 cm; W (base) 11.1 cm x 11.1 cm; Wt 30.26 oz
(2) H 32 cm; W (across branches) 33.4 cm; W (base) 11.1 cm x 11.1 cm; Wt 29.86 oz

NMS H.1999.264; purchased in 1999

5.51   5.49   5.50

5.52

5.43

5.52

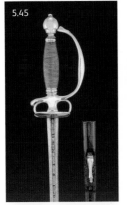

5.45

5.50

5.52 (detail)

5.48 (and detail)

5.49

5.51

5.46

5.48

5.58

5.60

5.47

5.56

5.64

5.54

The candlesticks have shaped-square stepped bases cast with acanthus leaves at the angles, knopped and fluted stems and vase-shaped sockets; each with detachable two-light branches which have central torch finials and S-shaped arms terminating in dolphin heads; spool-shaped sockets with shaped drip-pans following the bases. The bases of the sticks and the sleeves of the branches are engraved 'J.M/H.C'.

Scottish candlesticks with branches are exceptionally rare; only one other set is known, by Colin McKenzie of Edinburgh, 1710-11. They were originally in the Marquess of Linlithgow's collection. The present sticks are a slightly less accomplished attempt at fashionable London sticks, possibly taken directly from a London pattern or via an Edinburgh intermediary. The branches, however, are of a distinctively Scottish form. Around the middle of the 18th century Scottish goldsmiths seem to have been influenced by zoomorphic forms to a degree uncommon in England, as shown, for example, on ovoid coffee urns [4.40-4.47] and the seafood basket by William Dempster, 1747-48 [4.25].

5.53 TWO TWO-HANDLED CUPS

(1) Adam Graham, Glasgow, c.1769

(2) James McEwan, Glasgow, c.1783

Marks: (1) 'AG' (maker Adam Graham); tree, fish, bell, etc. (Glasgow); (2) 'JMc' twice (maker James McEwan); tree, fish, bell, etc. (Glasgow); 'S'

(1) H 19.8 cm; D (rim) 15.8 cm; W 28.1 cm; Wt 41.5 oz

(2) H 19.4 cm; D (rim) 16.1 cm; W 28.2 cm; Wt 39.5 oz

Lent by Glasgow Museum and Art Galleries; purchased from Alexander, Ernest & Sons, Glasgow, 9 February 1965

Campana-shaped body with everted slightly-caulked rim, with two opposing acanthus-capped scroll handles; silver-gilt inside and out, the gilding on the outside having perhaps been renewed at some time. The Graham cup is engraved '1769' on the underside of the foot; the McEwan cup is engraved '1783' on the underside of the foot.

Unusually, these two magnificent cups were not made as a pair, being some 14 years apart in date if the scratch dates on the bases are to be believed.

5.54 BRANDY PAN AND COVER

Robert Gray & Son, Glasgow, 1845-46

Marks: 'RG&S' (makers Robert Gray & Son); tree, fish, bell, etc. (Glasgow); lion rampant (Glasgow sterling standard mark); queen's head (duty mark); 'A' (Glasgow date-letter 1845-46)

L 24.4 cm; D 11.6 cm; H (max.) 9 cm; Wt (all-in) 40.06 oz

Lent by Glasgow Museum and Art Galleries; purchased with a grant from the Local Museums Purchase Fund

Provenance: His Grace The Duke of Hamilton

Reference: McFarlan (1999), pp. 211-22, pl. 8

Plain cylindrical body, with shaped handle stamped with the order number '1523', the spade-shaped terminal engraved with the initials 'CHB' for Châtelherault Hamilton Brandon; the body is engraved with the full arms within a garter of the Order of the Garter, with ducal coronet above, for Alexander Douglas Hamilton, the 10th Duke of Hamilton and 7th Duke of Brandon, the circular flat detachable cover engraved with the same arms. A smaller version of this pan, stamped '1517' under the handle, was sold on 28 August 1988 at Sotheby's, Gleneagles, lot 474.

Greenock

5.55 TABLESPOON

William Clark, Greenock, c.1810

Marks: 'WC' (maker William Clark); wreathed anchor, three-masted ship, oak tree, 'C' (all Greenock marks); 'Breadalbane' (collection stamp)

L 24.5 cm; Wt 2.42 oz

NMS H.MEQ 48; presented by Miss J. C. C. MacDonald of Ballintuim

Provenance: The Marquess of Breadalbane

Old English pattern with pointed oval bowl, stem engraved 'F'. This was once part of the extensive collection of antique Scottish silver amassed by Gavin Marquess of Breadalbane (b.1851-d.1922). Much of his collection, often marked with his distinctive script 'Breadalbane' private mark, was sold at a large sale of over 460 lots at Dowell's in Edinburgh in May 1935.

5.53

5.54

5.55

Inverness

5.56 QUAICH, STAVE-BUILT WITH SILVER MOUNTS

Possibly Alexander Fraser, Inverness, c.1680

Marks (on rim of boss, four times): 'AF' (maker possibly Alexander Fraser, Inverness)

D (bowl) 23.5 cm; W (max. across lugs) 28.5 cm; H 9.6 cm

NMS K.2006.434; purchased in 2006, Nicholas Shaw Antiques

Provenance: Mr Lumsden, who inherited it from his father, whose father in turn is said to have bought it in Inverness early in the 20th century

The walnut body is of feathered staved construction, with 13 staves; the body is bound with split withies and withie foot-rim binding; the upper part of the lugs are mounted with silver, chased with acanthus leaf decoration within a rope border; the centre has a raised silver boss, chased with a band of foliate and shell decoration, and an outer rim engraved with a band of stylised leaf decoration; the centre is engraved with the initials 'I I G'.

This is the largest and most elaborate Scottish three-lugged quaich in existence. Until very recently it has been in private hands, descending through one family at least from the early 20th century, when it was acquired privately in Inverness. This provenance is very important in linking it with its possible maker, Alexander Fraser, goldsmith in Inverness. Fraser is a shadowy character, in terms of his output at least. He is recorded as a goldsmith burgess and guild brother in 1676, and presumably continued working until the turn of the century. He is not mentioned in the revised 'sett' or regulations of the Inverness Incorporation of Hammermen in 1709. This quaich is therefore potentially the only extant marked piece of his work and is of exceptional rarity.

5.57 QUAICH

Robert Elphinstone, Inverness, c.1690s

Mark: 'RE' (maker Robert Elphinstone)

D 5.5 cm; W (over lugs) 9.2 cm; D (foot) 3.2 cm; Wt 0.79 oz

Lent from a private collection at Mount Stuart

The bowl has 16 stave-lines engraved within and without. The collet foot terminates in a flange. The two lugs carry the original engraved initials, 'MB' conjoined and 'IR' respectively. The decoration round them consists of very simple hatched lines in small groups.

5.58 THISTLE CUP

Simon McKenzie, Inverness, c.1706-07

Marks: 'MK' conjoined (maker Simon McKenzie); 'INS' (Inverness); 'B' (pseudo date-letter possibly 1706-07)

H 4 cm; D (rim) 5.2 cm; D (foot) 3 cm; Wt 1.62 oz

Lent from a private collection at Mount Stuart

Reference: RSM (1948), no. 329

Tot-size, wide bell-shaped body with flared rim on reeded flanged foot, the lower part of the body applied with twelve small lobes below the simple moulded girdle, applied with a cast S-scroll handle; engraved opposite the handle above the girdle with 'Suddie'.

5.59 COCONUT CUP

William McLean, Inverness, c.1705

Marks: 'ML' conjoined, pellet below (maker William McLean); 'INS' (Inverness); 'A' (pseudo date-letter, cf. Edinburgh date-letter for 1705-06)

H 17.1 cm; D (rim) 9.5 cm; D (foot) 10 cm; Wt (all-in) 9.19 oz

NMS A.1952.48; purchased at Sotheby's sale, Olympia, 1952

References: Finlay and Fothringham (1991), pp. 204-05, pl. 115; Dietert (2007), p. 198

Bowl formed from coconut shell mounted with silver flared everted rim having a notched lower edge. Three hinged and pinned reeded straps connect the rim to a baluster stem with knop, set on a plain, stepped trumpet foot. The foot is engraved: 'Gift Provost Duff to L MT [conjoined] / AD'.

5.60 THISTLE CUP

Robert Innes, Inverness, c.1720

Marks: 'RI' (maker Robert Innes); 'INS' (Inverness)

H 4.5 cm; W 7 cm; D 5 cm; Wt 1.45 oz

Lent by Inverness Museum and Art Gallery; purchased at Sotheby's sale, 30 June 1981, lot 172, with the aid of the Local Museums Purchase Fund

5.56 5.57 5.59  5.60 5.58

Bell-shaped body with applied simple girdle and lobed calyx, set on a simple rim foot, with reeded strap handle. Engraved above and below girdle 'M / S MK' / 'K MK', the first set of initials probably relating to a minister.

5.61 HOT MILK JUG

John Baillie, Inverness, *c.*1740

Marks: 'IB' twice (maker John Baillie); 'INS' (Inverness); 'H' (pseudo date-letter possibly 1737-38)

H 13.5 cm; L (max.) 13 cm

Lent by Aberdeen Art Gallery and Museum; purchased at Christie's & Edmiston's sale, Glasgow, David Morris Collection, 3 July 1984, lot 163

References: Christie's (1983), lot 41, illus.; Dietert (2007), p. 175

The plain ovoid body is set on three hoof feet, flush-hinged domed cover, with button finial, the 'mouth' engraved with bands of stylised foliage and rope work; simple spout and S-scroll silver handle.

This is a very rare form of hot-milk jug (so defined because of the hinged lid), and is reminiscent of the uniquely Scottish ovoid coffee urns [4.40-4.47], also set on three legs. In England similar jugs were associated with early tea services.

5.62 CREAM JUG

Robert Anderson, Inverness, *c.*1780

Marks (under lip): 'RA' (maker Robert Anderson); camel (Inverness); 'B' (pseudo date-letter)

H 14 cm; L (across handle) 13 cm; D (base) 6.3 cm; Wt 8.9 oz

NMS H.MEQ 1591; purchased at Phillip's sale, Edinburgh, 18 October 1985, lot 98

Reference: Finlay and Fothringham (1991), pl. 116(iii)

Plain everted rim with scroll border on a panelled, ovoid body; set on a spreading panelled foot; with cast scroll snake-form handle. The body has an engraved crest and motto: 'Touch not the Cat but a glove' for MacIntosh. The snake handle on this unique little jug illustrates some Scottish goldsmiths' interest in zoomorphic imagery. Robert Anderson is the first Inverness goldsmith to use a camel as his town mark, it being the dexter supporter of the burgh arms.

5.63 CREAM PAIL

Charles Jameson & Robert Naughten, Inverness, *c.*1815

Marks (on handle): 'J&N' (makers Jameson & Naughten); 'INs.' (Inverness); cornucopia (Inverness)

H 15.6 cm; D 10.2 cm; Wt *c.*9.75 oz

Lent by Inverness Art Gallery and Museum; purchased in 1988 with the aid of a grant from the Local Museums Purchase Fund

Body of slightly tapered cylindrical form with moulded rim; the body with two sections of five reeded bands resembling coopering. Simple handle rising from the rim, with engraved crest of a bird and 'HMF'. A cornucopia, as used in the mark, is the crest of the burgh.

5.64 EGG CUP

Donald Fraser, Inverness, *c.*1810

Marks (on foot-rim): 'DF' (maker Donald Fraser); 'INS' (Inverness)

H 6.4 cm; D (rim) 4.5 cm; D (foot) 4.1 cm; Wt 0.97 oz

NMS K.2005.526; purchased at Lyon & Turnbull sale, Edinburgh, 7 December 2005, lot 358

Of typical form with bell-shaped bowl with engraved initial 'R' in gothic script within a garter, the wide stem and flared base on simple foot-rim. This is the only recorded provincial silver egg cup.

5.65 TABLE BELL

Robert Naughten, Inverness, *c.*1825

Marks (on sound bow): 'INS' (Inverness); 'RN' (maker Robert Naughten)

H 12.8 cm; D 6.9 cm

Lent by Inverness Art Gallery and Museum; purchased in 1994 with the aid of the National Fund for Acquisitions

The slender tapered handle has an acanthus-leaf detail running a third of its length. The angular sound-bow is heavily chased with detailed acanthus leaf and flower head decoration; the lower part of the bow is engraved with the initials 'MM' with a coronet above.

| 5.62 | 5.63 | 5.64 | 5.65 |

5.57

5.59

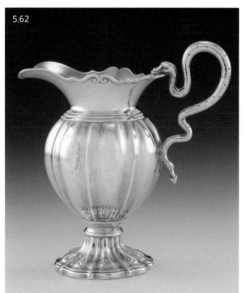

5.62

5.61

5.55

5.65

5.73

5.81

5.63

5.72

5.68

5.77

Leith

5.66 BREAKFAST DISH

George McHattie, Edinburgh, 1820-21, retailed in Leith

Marks: 'HAY' (retailer John Hay); 'LEITH' (retailer); 'GMH' (maker George McHattie); king's head (duty mark); thistle (standard mark); castle (Edinburgh); 'O' (date-letter 1820-21)

D 23.2 cm; Wt 49.23 oz

NMS A.1969.406; purchased from John Bell of Aberdeen, 1962

This circular dish has a reeded border and plain domed pull-off cover with foliate finial. It rests on a stand with reeded border and elegant reeded strap supports to claw feet, mounted centrally with a spirit burner in a circular reeded collet frame.

Montrose

5.67 PISTOL

William Lindsay I, Montrose, c.1680

Mark (on lockplate): 'WL' and crowned hammer (William Lindsay)

L 34.6 cm (bore) 1.5 cm

NMS H.1994.14; purchased in 1994, one of a pair; the other purchased by Montrose Museum and Art Gallery

Heart butt pistol, with dog lock; the iron stock inlaid with silver, finely engraved with foliage and flower heads. The form of the lock mechanism, known as a 'dog lock' because of an external dog-catch, dates the pistol to about 1680, and suggests therefore it was the work of William Lindsay senior. He is first recorded as a goldsmith burgess of Montrose in 1665 at the

baptism of a son, probably William, who also went on to become a Montrose goldsmith. As William junior would have been about 15 when this pistol was made, it seems reasonable to suggest this is Lindsay senior's mark. William senior died in 1683, but unfortunately William junior went on using his father's mark and possibly another simpler one as well. This makes mark-identification not as certain as it could be.

Many burgh craftsmen combined two separate crafts, and as members of the single unified Hammermen Incorporations, this may have been easier than in Edinburgh. Certainly, several goldsmiths/gunsmith combinations are recorded.

5.68 WINE FUNNEL

William Mill, Montrose, c.1810

Marks (on rim and bowl): rose (Montrose); 'WM' (maker William Mill); rose repeated

H 10 cm; Dp 7.2 cm; W 13 cm; Wt 3.05 oz

Lent by Montrose Museum and Art Gallery

Plain oval bowl, with simple pierced interior strainer, detachable cylindrical funnel, and simple rim clip.

Nairn

5.69 HEART OR LUCKENBOOTH BROOCH

Daniel Ferguson, Nairn, c.1850

Marks: 'NAIRN' (Nairn); 'DF' (maker Daniel Ferguson)

L 7.5 cm; W 5 cm; Wt 0.57 oz

NMS H.NGB 70; donated by Miss Begg in 1958

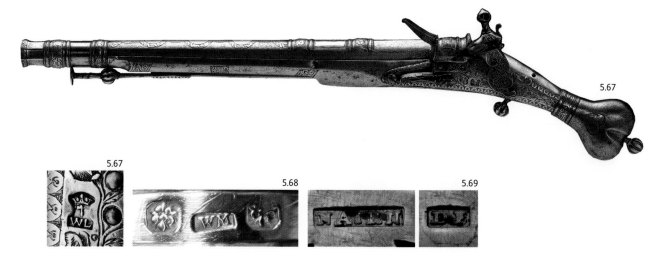

5.67

5.67

5.68

5.69

Of open scroll form with Inverness-type 'spectacles' above surmounted with foliate spray, and scroll terminal. Engraved all over with scroll designs.

The few extant examples of Ferguson's work are all 'luckenbooth' brooches. The term 'luckenbooth', used to describe Scottish heart-shaped brooches, first appears in advertisements in the second half of the 19th century. Before this date they were generally referred to simply as heart brooches.

Paisley

5.70 TEASPOON

William Hannay, Paisley, c.1810

Marks: 'WH' in serrated punch (maker William Hannay); rat or mouse on ear of corn (significance unknown); 'WH' repeated

L 14.2 cm; Wt 0.42 oz

NMS K.2006.194; purchased privately

Old English pattern stem, pointed oval bowl; terminal engraved 'AM/S'.

Perth

5.71 TUMBLER CUP

Robert Gardyne, Perth, c.1680

Marks (on base): 'RG' (maker Robert Gardyne); lamb and flag (Perth); gothic 'a' (pseudo date-letter)

H 6.6 cm; D 8.6 cm; Wt 5.5 oz

Lent by Perth Museum and Art Gallery; purchased at Christie's sale, Glasgow, 3 July 1984, lot 190, with the aid of the Local Museums Purchase Fund

Reference: Rodger and Slattery (2001), p. 21

Plain bucket-shaped body, engraved with initials 'IW' over 'MA'.

5.72 PAIR OF TREFID SPOONS

Robert Gardyne, Perth, c.1680

Marks: 'RG' (maker Robert Gardyne); lamb and flag (Perth); gothic 'a' (pseudo date-letter)

(1) L 18.5 cm; Wt 1.66 oz / (2) L 18.5 cm; Wt 1.61 oz

NMS H.MEQ 142 and 143; bequeathed in 1943 by Mr George Henderson

Reference: *Empire Exhibition* (1938), no. 140, pl. 49, George Henderson Collection

Trefid terminals, rounded oval bowls and rat-tails; the terminals engraved with initials 'KC'. The gothic letter 'a' may be an attempt to replicate the first Edinburgh date-letter for 1681, but the mark was evidently in use for some years.

5.73 TWO TABLESPOONS

James Brown, Perth, c.1725

Marks: 'IB' (maker James Brown); shield of arms; 'FB'

(1) L 20.3 cm; Wt. 1.969 oz / (2) L 20.6 cm; Wt 1.948 oz

Provenance: How of Edinburgh

Lent from a private collection

Hanoverian pattern ridged stems, egg-shaped bowls, with elaborate fleur-de-lis double-drop and rat-tail join, enhanced with engraved scrolls; the terminals engraved 'WF/SG'.

The marks, which have been variously ascribed in the past, are here ascribed with some certainty to James Brown, who was 'licensed to work as formerly' in Perth in 1724. The same maker's punch has been seen on tablespoons bearing the mark 'PERTH', which would seem to put the matter beyond doubt. The coat-of-arms mark is a version of the arms of the burgh of Fraserburgh. We note that Brown's wife was the daughter of the harbour-master in that town, but can offer no further explanation for its presence as a mark. It seems possible that the goldsmith of that name in Elgin a few years later was the same man. The 'FB' punch has not been satisfactorily explained, although the late Mrs How thought the initials referred to Brown's son, Francis. While the identity of the maker of these spoons is not in doubt, one could make a case for saying that he might not have been working in Perth at the time he made them.

5.70

5.71

5.72

5.73

5.74 DIRK AND SCABBARD, WITH KNIFE AND FORK

William Ritchie, Perth, *c.*1800

Marks (on blade): 'W. RITCHIE JEWELLER PERTH'

L 48.6 cm

Lent by Perth Art Gallery and Museum

The baluster wooden handle is carved with basket-weave decoration and studded with silver nails, with circular pommel. The leather-covered scabbard is set with *en suite* knife and two-pronged fork. Applied mounts are punched and chased with foliate and cross-hatched decoration; the knife and fork mounts are similarly decorated.

Provincially-marked dirks and *sgian dubhs* of this period are rare. As the maker's name is on the blade only, William Ritchie may have been the retailer for a specialised dirk maker. This is an early example of the type of elaborate dirk set that was associated with full 'Highland dress' and was beginning to become popular in the late 18th and early 19th centuries. King George IV's visit to Scotland in 1822 gave a spectacular boost to this version of 'national costume'.

5.75 TEAPOT STAND OR CARD TRAY

Robert Dickson II, Perth, *c.*1810

Marks (on base): 'RD' twice (maker Robert Dickson II); double-headed eagle with shield, twice (Perth)

H 3.7 cm; L 15.4 cm; W 13.5 cm; Wt 10.95 oz

Lent by Perth Art Gallery and Museum; purchased in 1966 from John Bell of Aberdeen with the aid of the Local Museums Purchase Fund

Reference: Rodger and Slattery (2001), p. 20

Of rounded rectangular outline with gadrooned edge, raised on four slender cabriole bracket feet. A very unusual form of stand with high feet; while possibly for a square-based teapot, the proportions seem to indicate otherwise. Alternatively it may have been used as a card tray or stand for a dish with a square base.

5.76 VINAIGRETTE

John Scott, Perth, *c.*1840

Marks (inside lid): 'IS' (maker John Scott); double-headed eagle (Perth); eagle, possibly damaged (Perth); 'b' (pseudo date-letter)

L 3.3 cm; W 2.2 cm; H 7 mm; Wt 0.58 oz

Lent by Perth Museum and Art Gallery; purchased from Christie's sale, The Morris Collection, 3 July 1984, with the aid of the Local Museums Purchase Fund

Of rounded rectangular form with reeded borders, the lid engraved with foliate decoration and initials 'IG'. The gilt interior with a hinged grill, pierced and chased with foliate scrolls.

While vinaigrettes, for smelling salts, were a mass-produced mainstay of many English makers, Scottish provincial examples are rare. This is probably because the cheaper English examples cornered the market.

5.77 CURLING MEDAL

Magdalene MacGregor, Perth, hallmarked Edinburgh, 1854-55

Marks: queen's head (duty mark); thistle (standard mark); 'RMcG' (maker's mark of Robert MacGregor, used by Magdalene MacGregor); castle (Edinburgh); 'X' (date-letter 1854-55)

H *c.*12 cm; W 8.5 cm

Lent by Perth Museum and Art Gallery; purchased in 1977 with the aid of the Local Museums Purchase Fund

Reference: Roger and Slattery (2001), p. 3

In the form of a medal, of shaped oval outline with heavily-cast thistle border and integral suspension loop. The obverse has a border reading 'Presented by Gilbert Heathcote Esq.'; centre applied with crossed curling brooms with curling stones and a jack in the angles. Reverse has a border reading 'To the Drummond Castle Curling Club 1854' and is engraved in the centre with the names of winners between 1855 and 1867.

The sport of curling, though not entirely confined to Scotland, has been a characteristic of Scottish rural and town life since at least the 18th century. Many trophies were commissioned, including silver kettles in the shape of curling stones. The present medal is a fine example of a more modest trophy.

5.74   5.75   5.76   5.77

5.71

5.69

5.76

5.74

5.75

5.78

5.74

5.80

5.85

5.80 (from side)

5.83

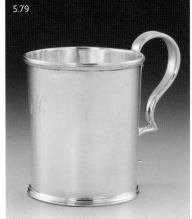

5.79

Peterhead

5.78 CRUET FRAME

William Ferguson, Peterhead, c.1825

Marks (on base, frame and handle): 'W.F' (maker William Ferguson); 'PHd' (Peterhead); 'W.F' repeated, all in shaped punches; on central column securing nut 'W.F' (maker William Ferguson); 'PHD' in plain rectangular punches (town mark)

H (to top of loop) 20.7 cm; L 15.3 cm; W 12 cm; Wt 17.66 oz

Lent by Aberdeenshire Heritage; purchased with the aid of the National Fund for Acquisitions

Reference: Moss (1994), pp. 67-78

Four-bottle cruet frame, with plain plinth-type rectangular base with rounded corners, set on four ball feet; the central tapering cylindrical column terminates in a loop handle and is secured to the base by a square nut. Complete with four (possibly original) cut and faceted glass condiment bottles.

William Ferguson worked in Edinburgh after serving his apprenticeship with Charles Fowler in Elgin, before setting up business in Peterhead. The fact that each separate piece is fully marked suggests that 'WF' was indeed the maker rather than a retailer who bought it in. The construction is robust rather than elegant and is certainly well within the abilities of a good local silversmith. The shape of Ferguson's maker and town marks are reminiscent of the shaped punches used by several Edinburgh craftsmen in the 1820s.

5.79 MUG

William Ferguson, Peterhead, c.1825

Marks (on base around centre point): 'WF' twice (maker William Ferguson); 'PHD' twice (Peterhead); all marks struck in rectangular punches

H (body) 7.9 cm; H (max.) 9.8 cm; D 7.2 cm; Wt 5.053 oz

Lent from a private collection

Provenance: Christie's sale, 26 May 1998, lot 70

Reference: Moss (1994), pp. 67-78

Can-shaped body has a simple moulded foot and rim, the body engraved with foliate script with the initials 'AM'; with moulded S-scroll handle.

This mug shows similar manufacturing characteristics to the cruet [5.78]. During his period in Peterhead, 1825-28, Ferguson seems to have used both shaped and rectangular maker's and town punches.

Stirling

5.80 SNUFF BOX

John Duff, Stirling, hallmarked Edinburgh, 1837-38

Marks (inside box and lid): king's head (duty mark); thistle (standard mark); 'DUFF' (maker J. Duff); castle (Edinburgh); 'F' (date-letter 1837-38)

L 9.6 cm; Dp 7 cm; H 3.1 cm; Wt 6.12 oz

Lent from a private collection

Provenance: J. H. Bourdon-Smith

Rectangular box with cushion body and hinged lid; sides and lid cast and chased with sprays of thistles and roses; the base with machined hatching; interior gilt; a plain panel on the lid is engraved: 'Presented / to / Mr Andrew Miller / By a few of his Friends / In Tullycoultry / As a Mark of their esteem / Decr. 21st. / 1838'.

There has to be a suspicion that this box was bought in, perhaps from Birmingham, as it closely resembles the general pattern of the period and does not betray any typically 'local' characteristics. Duff sent very small quantities of silver for assay.

Stonehaven

5.81 TEASPOON

Alexander Glennie, Stonehaven, c.1840

Marks: 'A.G' (maker Alexander Glennie); 'S T O N H N' in separate punches (Stonehaven)

L 14.3 cm; Wt 0.54 oz

Lent from a private collection

Fiddle pattern stem, the end engraved 'JMF'.

5.78   5.79   5.80   5.81

Tain

5.82 TOT CUP

Hugh Ross I, Tain, c.1710

Mark (on base): 'HR' conjoined (maker Hugh Ross)

H 3.9 cm; D (rim) 5.2 cm; Wt 1.74 oz

Lent by Tain and District Museum Trust; purchased with the aid of the National Art-Collection Fund and the National Fund for Acquisitions

Reference: Quick (2007), p. 7

Squat plain bell-shaped body has an applied reeded girdle, on reeded foot-rim, with simple S-scroll strap handle. The body is engraved 'D.M/H'. These initials may refer to Dame Margaret Haliburton, daughter of James Haliburton of Pitcur, who married first Sir George Mackenzie of Rosehaugh in 1670, and second Roderick Mackenzie of Prestonhall in 1692. She died in 1713.

It is probable there were two, if not three, goldsmiths in Tain with the name Hugh Ross. Despite determined research, it is still difficult to disentangle which is which. If indeed this cup belonged to Dame Margaret Haliburton, the maker was probably Hugh Ross I, who seems to have been working c.1700-30.

5.83 QUAICH

Hugh Ross II, c.1740

Marks (on base): 'HR' conjoined, twice (maker Hugh Ross II); 'SD' with figure of St Duthac between (Tain)

W 12.9 cm; D 8.3 cm; H 3.8 cm; Wt 3.09 oz

Lent from a private collection at Mount Stuart

Reference: RSM (1948), no. 340

Plain, shallow body, with simple collet and flange foot; the unusual lugs broaden out considerably from the bowl, both upwards and downwards, and are engraved with a running motif round the edge; the lugs are engraved with initials 'D MK [conjoined]' and 'A MK [conjoined]'.

This plain but well-made quaich is possibly by Hugh Ross II, who seems to have been in operation in Tain from c.1740-60.

5.84 PEPPER POT

Hugh Ross II, Tain, c.1750

Mark (underneath): 'HR' conjoined (maker Hugh Ross II); 'SD' with figure of St Duthac between (Tain)

H 6 cm; D 4.5 cm; Wt 1.8 oz

Lent by Tain and District Museum Trust

References: Quick (2007), p. 7; Quick (1997), p. 15

Straight-sided cylindrical body has a simple reeded foot, moulded rim and strap-work S-scroll handle; the domed pull-off cover has a similarly decorated rim; the central pierced domed section with engraved border.

Sometimes known as 'Kitchen Peppers', small shakers like these could also be used for fine sand to dry writing ink. The marks on this pepper are very similar to those on the above quaich, and presumably relate to Hugh Ross II.

5.85 COWRIE SHELL SNUFF BOX

Retailed by William McKenzie, Tain, c.1850

Mark: 'Wm McKENZIE' overstriking another maker's mark (retailer William McKenzie)

L 6 cm; H 3.3 cm; W 3.4 cm; Wt 1.05 oz

Lent from a private collection

The shell body is simply mounted with flush-hinged three-quarter opening lid with simple cross-hatched and bright-cut decoration. This type of shell-mounted snuff box is generically termed 'cowrie shell', but they can be made from various species of shell.

Little is known about William McKenzie in Tain. Although he did send silver to Edinburgh Assay Office in 1858-59, it is more likely that he was the retailer. Certainly his mark appears to be superimposed over another two-letter punch, possibly for the maker.

5.82

5.84

5.82

5.83

5.84

5.85

5.86 'TAIN' TOWN-MARK PUNCH

Used by Richard Maxwell Wilkie, *c.*1820

L 6.2 cm

Lent by Tain and District Museum Trust

Reference: Quick (2007), p. 38

Steel, with chamfered edges and tapering face deeply engraved 'TAIN' in reverse. This is a rare survival of an original town-mark punch used by a 19th-century burgh silversmith. Comparisons with marked pieces suggest it was the punch used by Richard Maxwell Wilkie. As most town marks were not centrally applied by a town official, each local maker held his own version along with any other punches he applied to his work. Given the large number of such punches which existed at one time, it is curious how few have survived.

Wick

5.87 WINE FUNNEL

John Sellar, Wick, *c.*1825

Marks: 'JS' (maker John Sellar); 'WICK' (Wick)

L 13 cm; D (bowl) 9 cm

Lent by Inverness Art Gallery and Museum

Deep circular bowl, with gadrooned rim and shell clip; the interior is pierced. Pull-off tapered spout has a reeded border to rim, with three 'staves' running a third of the length.

{opposite page}

5.25 LOCHIEL'S SWORD, *c.*1740s

5.35

Fashioned in Silver

with Colin T. Fraser

Introduction

The century spanning 1840 to 1950 saw enormous social, political and economic changes in Britain and the world: the rise and fall of Empire; surging economy to post-war austerity; growth of the middle and working classes; consumerism and the emergence of the mass market. Obviously, in its own small way, the luxury trade of the bespoke goldsmith, silversmith and jeweller reflected this. In this period of accelerating change, the art of the goldsmith seems generally to have exhibited a conservative reaction, exemplified by an increased demand for 'revivalist' or 'historicist' styles. Structurally, however, the trade had to adapt to the changing economic circumstances; those within it who did not, went to the wall.

At the start of the period the 1836 Hallmarking Act more rigorously enforced the supervisory role of the Incorporation of Goldsmiths of Edinburgh over assaying and marking gold and silver throughout Scotland (with the exception of the area policed by the Glasgow Assay Office). This meant that all local goldsmiths and silversmiths were obliged to send their wares to either Edinburgh or Glasgow for testing and marking. While this did not, as has been suggested before, immediately sound the death-knell of all local craftsmen, it did eventually curtail the proliferation of local marks alone. However, the changing nature of the trade, combined with the increasing mechanisation, dictated by the economies of scale, saw the growth of fewer, larger firms in the major cities, and the move towards retailing and occasionally specialisation in souvenir wares amongst the smaller local firms.

Trade grew in the 19th century, when the high watermark of Victorian society with vast aristocratic households meant lavish entertainments required huge amounts of the most fashionable silver. Changing fashions in 'polite' society led to increased specialisation where, for example, particular knives, forks or spoons were required for ever-increasing numbers of courses. The 1841 Census recorded 641 people engaged in the goldsmiths, silversmiths and jewellery trade in Scotland, with just over half working in Edinburgh.[1] By 1869 this figure had risen to just under 2000, again with the majority concentrated in Edinburgh. Larger firms were beginning to dominate the market, such as D. C. Rait's and Sorley's and Edward's in Glasgow, while Mackay Cunningham & Co. and Marshall & Co. operated in Edinburgh. David Bremner, an Edinburgh journalist, summed up the situation in Edinburgh, if a little jingoistically: 'For a number of years past the silversmith and jeweller trades have been expanding in

6

... a wide field for the exercise of artistic taste

{BREMNER: *INDUSTRIES OF SCOTLAND*, 1869}

{opposite page}
6.26 THE BREADALBANE CASKET, 1894

123

Edinburgh and there are indications that they will increase still further. There are upwards of thirty master jewellers in the city, who employ from half a dozen to thirty men each. All the work done is of a superior kind, no attempt being made to vie with Birmingham in the production of cheap and showy articles, the beauty of which is as transient as that of a flower.'[2]

Equally, the growing middle classes aspired to ape their social superiors and also acquire large canteens of plate, but much of this was mass-produced in the factories of Birmingham and Sheffield. Here Bremner was not quite so upbeat and sounded a note of warning: 'The making of spoons and forks was at one time an extensive branch of the silversmiths trade in Edinburgh, but now there are only two workshops in which these articles are produced. It appears that the profits on spoons and forks are small, and hence there is no inducement to enter into competition with the manufacturers in London, who have extensive establishments in which machinery is applied to most parts of the work.'[3]

The First World War dealt a blow to this social system which, although perhaps obscured for many years, was none the less fatal. Demand for the highly-specialised luxury trade of the bespoke goldsmith dwindled in the pre- and post-Second World War period, and many Scottish goldsmith firms did not survive the social upheavals of the immediate post-war period.

Stylistically the Georgians' love of elegant neo-classicism gave way to a growing demand in the 1820s-40s for 'rococo revival' forms and decoration. In Scotland the realisation of this particular revival is fairly heavy and mechanical, and is relatively easy to distinguish from the original. By the 1840s inspiration was being sought even further back in the mists of time, with the masters of Mannerist, Renaissance, and even 'Gothic' art, being turned to for models. Nowhere is this more obvious than in Mackay & Cunningham's spectacularly eclectic candelabra [6.3], or their model of the 'gothic skyrocket' that is Sir Walter Scott's Monument [6.4]. David Ramsay Hay's elegantly 'modernist' tea and coffee pot [6.1] stand out amidst this tidal wave of revivalism, even though the artist himself saw the principle of his design as being firmly grounded in ancient Greek art.[4]

The earlier growth of interest in a revived, and partly reinvented, Scottish tradition, stemming from the 'Romantic' movement of the late 18th century, also affected the precious metal trades. A particularly important focus for this was the development of a 'national costume' evolving from the Highland military dress of tartan and kilt, which continued to be allowed in the army after its suppression within the populace by the Disarming Act of 1747. This Act was repealed in 1782, and with the encouragement of numerous important individuals and groups like the Highland Society of London, Highland Dress (and with it all the necessary jewellery and accoutrements) became not only tolerated but highly fashionable. However, although traditional models were used, decorative inspiration was as much British as Scottish or Highland, and the resultant profusion of thistles, in association with St Andrew's crosses and roses and shamrocks (after the Union with Ireland in 1801) elicited some distaste among certain Scots, who saw it as an imposition of an invented 'tradition'.[5]

There were numerous 'peaks' in this process of the popularisation of all things traditionally 'Scottish' and 'Highland', the first being the tartan jamboree organised by Sir Walter Scott for the Royal Visit of King George IV to Scotland in 1822. Many Scottish jewellers and goldsmiths went into overdrive to produce all the brooches, buckles, dirks, swords and other dress accessories that were now considered *de rigeur*.

The Royal Family continued to have an effect on such matters of taste, especially after Queen Victoria's first visit to her northern kingdom in 1842. This 'love affair' with Scotland by Victoria and her family and descendants, particularly after Albert acquired the permanent royal retreat at Balmoral in 1852, had a profound affect on Scottish art in general. The development of that particular brand of distilled Scottish tradition known somewhat pejoratively as 'Balmorality', undoubtedly provided a boost not only to local craftsmen and artists, but also to the goldsmiths and jewellers of Edinburgh and Glasgow.

Royal and aristocratic patronage attracted high quality craftsmen, and not necessarily all of them based in the main centres of the trade. The excellent engraving of David MacGregor in Perth (page 135) earned him the Royal Warrant from Queen Victoria and the patronage of local-based Royal courtier, the Marquess of Breadalbane. MacGregor's commissions illustrate the increasing commercial complexity of the trade. While responsible for the complete design of the 'garniture' of casket and two vases produced to mark Breadalbane's Knighthood of the Garter, he sent to Glasgow for the manufacture of the casket, and to London for the vases, presumably finishing off the engraving when they returned to Perth. This sort of part-working could only be accomplished economically and efficiently when the railway system had developed sufficiently to enable reliable communication.

Yet another 'revivalist' trend had an impact on the production of Scottish craftsmen. The middle of the 19th century saw the beginnings of an upsurge in the vogue for 'Celtic' ornamentation, on both jewellery and hollow ware. This was to be a long-lived revival; indeed many firms, not always Scottish, make a living from it today. It developed from the growth of antiquarian and historical interest in the art of Scotland's early peoples. Major 19th-century archaeological finds of important metalwork both in Scotland and Ireland, such as the Hunterston and Tara brooches, inspired many Scottish artists to revive and reinterpret original multi-period decorative motifs, such as intertwined knotwork and fabulous beasts, under the catch-all phrases 'Celtic Revival' or 'Highland' decoration. This was promoted by the publication of accurate representations of Celtic metalwork in various authoritative publications such as those of the Society of Antiquaries of Scotland.

There was also a reaction to the homogenous nature of much mass-produced silverware emanating from large-scale manufactories of London and Birmingham. We begin to see small-scale growth of art-school trained designer/craftsmen, and women, from fairly early in this period. David Bremner, for example, noted in 1869 that Edinburgh had a particularly good School of Design: 'No city in Britain possesses a better School of Design and it is gratifying to know it is largely taken advantage of. Workmen trained in Edinburgh are highly valued by the London manufacturers of plate and jewellery and some of the best work done in the metropolis is by their hands.'[6] Glasgow School of Art was also instrumental in developing that town's own highly distinctive style, and various artists produced excellent pieces of silver. The exponents of the Arts and Crafts Movement of course also looked to hand-crafted silver wares, but again often sought inspiration in the glories of Renaissance and earlier metalwork.

As the 20th century progressed, the traditional apprenticeship model of craft training, supervised by the old incorporations, became less and less relevant. Curiously, one of the last apprenticeships 'booked' by the Edinburgh Incorporation was that of Mr Harry Tatton, immediate past deacon of the Incorporation. He was apprenticed to his father's firm of H. Tatton & Son to help with the production of the massive order for the Jubilee Banqueting Service for Holyroodhouse in 1935 [6.21]. The design of this spectacular service again looked to the craft's history, based as it was on late 17th to early 18th-century trefid and Queen Anne patterns.

Notes

1 Bremner (1869), p. 131.
2 Ibid., p. 125.
3. Ibid., p. 125.
4 Gow (1989), pp. 353-55.
5 Marshall and Dalgleish (1991), p. 57.
6 Bremner (1869), p. 131.

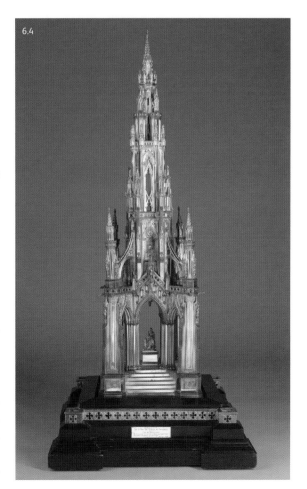

6.4

6.1 TEAPOT AND COFFEE POT

Designer David Ramsay Hay; maker J. & W. Marshall, Edinburgh 1847-48

Marks: 'J&WM' (makers J. & W. Marshall); castle (Edinburgh); 'Q' (date-letter 1847-48); thistle (standard mark); queen's head (duty mark)

Teapot: H 15.5 cm; L 22 cm; D (base) 7.4 cm; Wt 16.53 oz

Coffee pot: H 23.7 cm; L 12.5 cm; D (base) 8.2 cm; Wt 15.62 oz

NMS A.1986.150 and 1; donated by Mrs Helena Rouse, great grand-daughter of the designer

Reference: Gow (1989), p. 353-55

The teapot has a plain body of ovoid form, set on stepped circular foot, scroll spout and C-scroll handle; spherical knop finial to hinged lid. The coffee pot has a plain pear-shaped body with C-scroll handle, domed hinged lid and beak-spout, on circular stepped foot.

David Ramsay Hay, a fashionable Edinburgh designer and decorator, exhibited this tea and coffee pot at a meeting of the Royal Scottish Society of Arts in Edinburgh on 13 March 1848. They were described as being 'manufactured in Edinburgh according to his principles of Symmetrical Beauty'. Hay was an innovator in the practice and teaching of art, and attempted through numerous publications to advance scientific theories of design and colour. The teapot and coffee pot exhibit his interest in the application of geometrical principle to artefact design, especially his fascination with the oval and its 'perfect' form. The result is a timelessly elegant shape that pre-dates the work of Georg Jensen by over 50 years. It stands out in a period when 'revivalist' styles were dominant in silver design.

6.2 BROOCH

John Riddler MacKay, Elgin, c.1860

Marks: 'J.R.MACKAY' (maker John Riddler MacKay); 'ELGIN' (Elgin)

D 6.8 cm; Wt 1.21 oz

Lent from a private collection

Reference: Moss (1994), p. 81

Circular pierced silver brooch, the centre with a brilliant-cut, foil-backed quartz in a claw setting.

Such elaborate 'plaid brooches' were a 19th-century development of the earlier and simpler ring brooches once common in the Highlands, Islands and north-east of Scotland. They became an accepted part of Highland dress, worn at the shoulder with a fly plaid. Originally ring brooches were worn by women to pin together their shawls.

6.3 PAIR OF FOUR-LIGHT CANDELABRA

Mackay Cunningham & Co., Edinburgh, 1871-72

Marks: 'MC&Co' (maker Mackay Cunningham & Co.); queen's head (duty mark); thistle (sterling standard mark); castle (Edinburgh); 'P' (date-letter for 1871-72)

H 57.8 cm; W (across branches) 30.5 cm; D (base) 17.4 cm; Wt 81.88

Lent by the City of Edinburgh Museums and Galleries

Parcel gilt, pierced body with three branches and central holder, elaborately applied with figures of musicians, animals, etc., on a domed circular foot chased with rococo foliage, plaques and applied cast insects and animals.

These candlesticks are an exuberant and highly eclectic mix of styles, combining rococo revival, Gothic and early mannerist work, so beloved of the Victorians. The makers, Mackay & Cunningham, a firm founded by James Mackay and David Cunningham in the early years of the 19th century, became the acknowledged masters of this 'High Victorian' style and produced a large range of monumental pieces.

6.4 MODEL OF THE SCOTT MONUMENT

Mackay Cunningham & Co., Edinburgh, 1876-77

Marks: 'Mackay / Cunningham & Co / Edinburgh'; queen's head (duty mark); thistle (sterling standard mark); castle (Edinburgh); 'u' (date-letter for 1876-77)

H (max.) 110 cm; W (base) 52.5 cm; D 52.5 cm; Wt 446 oz

Lent by the City of Edinburgh Council

A model of the monument in four sections, with a model of the statue of Sir Walter Scott in centre. On black ebonised wooden base with silver fence surround; silver plaque fixed to front of base, inscribed: 'Bequeathed by / The Rt Hon the 5th Earl of Rosebery / to the / City of Edinburgh / "To remind them of one

6.1

6.2

6.3

who was a Loyal and / Devoted Burgess of the City / 4th July 1929".'

This spectacular model represents the 'gothic rocket' designed by George Meikle Kemp, built by public subscription in East Princes Street Gardens, between 1840 and 1844, to commemorate the novelist Sir Walter Scott. The marble statue of Scott in the centre was by Sir James Steell. The model was sent for assay by Mackay Cunningham & Co. on 20 July 1877, when it was described as the Sir Walter Scott Trophy, weighing some 446 ounces. This suggests it may have been originally commissioned as a sporting or racing trophy, and it may well have been won by or presented to the 5th Earl of Rosebery, a great lover of horse racing. Unfortunately there seems to be no record of this in the Rosebery archives, and its history before it was bequeathed to the City of Edinburgh in 1929 remains conjecture.

6.5 RAMSHEAD SNUFFMULL AND CIGAR HOLDER

R. & H. B. Kirkwood, Edinburgh, 1883-84

Marks (on inner rim of snuff holder): queen's head (duty mark); thistle (standard mark); 'R&HB KIRKWOOD / 66&68 THISTLE ST. / EDIR.' (maker R. & H. B. Kirkwood); castle (Edinburgh); 'b' (date-letter for 1813-14)

H 35 cm; W 55 cm; Dp 57 cm

NMS H.NQ 502; presented by the Incorporation of Goldsmiths of the City of Edinburgh

Fashioned from a ram's head, set on three casters; the horns are finished with silver ferrules pierced to enclose pieces of quartz; the top is inset with a domed, hinged container for snuff and cigars, all topped with a faceted, smoky quartz stone; all the silver mounts chased, pierced and engraved with bands of 'Celtic' interlace.

This spectacular example of the Victorian taste for 'Celtic Revival' was used as a communal snuff mull and cigar dispenser on the table of the Edinburgh Goldsmiths Incorporation. Such ramshead snuffmulls were very popular at the time, particularly in officers' messes and with other corporate bodies such as trade incorporations.

6.6 WORKBOX SET WITH AGATES

Possibly Michael Crichton, Edinburgh, c.1885

Marks: 'MC' only (maker possibly Michael Crichton)

H 8.5 cm; L 19.8 cm; W 16.8 cm

NMS H.RL 5; purchased in 1979

Rectangular box, set on gilt silver scroll-work base with four feet, the hinged lid stepped and set with a central faceted citrine; the rest of the body set with cut and polished agates and hardstones. The interior is fitted with sewing and writing implements, all of gilt metal set with cut and polished agates.

Scotland has many rich sources of fine agates, bloodstones, jaspers, 'cairngorms' and granites, which could be cut and polished to make very attractive jewellery. So popular was this class of jewellery that it became known as 'Scotch pebble', despite the fact it was made in many other places such as Birmingham and Germany. Many Scottish lapidaries flourished, particularly in Edinburgh, in the second half of the 19th century, and several prominent firms advertised themselves as producers of Scotch Pebble jewellery, although larger and more elaborate wares such as this work box were rarer.

6.7 'CELTIC' CASKET

Ferguson & MacBean, Inverness; hallmarked Edinburgh, 1889-90

Marks: 'F & M' (makers Ferguson & MacBean); camel (Inverness); 'INVS' (Inverness); thistle (standard mark); castle (Edinburgh); 'h' (date-letter for 1889-90)

H 7 cm; W 9.2 cm; Dp 9.2 cm; Wt 7.04 oz

Lent from a private collection

Reference: Moss and Roe (1999), pp. 103-06

Square casket form, with hinged hipped lid; cast and chased with alternating panels and roundels of 'Celtic' knotwork and 'gripping beasts'; set on four pierced 'gripping beast' feet. This is an intricate example of the vogue for 'Celtic Revival' ornamentation.

6.4

6.5

6.7

6.5

6.3

6.6

6.2

6.7

6.1

6.8 (detail above)

6.9

6.10

6.8 'THISTLE' TEA SERVICE

R. & W. Sorley, Glasgow, 1892-93

Marks (on rim): 'RS/WS' (makers R. & W. Sorley); tree, fish, bell, etc. (Glasgow); lion rampant (Glasgow standard mark); 'V' (Glasgow date-letter for 1892-93); on base 'SORLEY / SILVERSMITHS / GLASGOW'

Teapot: H 14 cm; L 20.5 cm; Wt 17 oz

Hot water jug: H 17.5 cm; L 14 cm; Wt 15.6 oz

Sugar bowl: H 9.9 cm; L 14.6 cm; Wt 6.54 oz

Milk jug: H 8.8 cm; 9.4 cm; Wt 3.71 oz

NMS H.MEQ 1607; purchased from J. H. Bourdon-Smith, London, 1988

Four-piece, matched tea-set of teapot, hot water jug, sugar bowl and milk jug; bodies raised to represent thistle heads, chased with foliage; C-scroll handles; the lids of the teapot and hot water jug have applied cast thistle head and leaf finials.

This pattern was very popular in the second half of the 19th century and several Scottish silversmiths made variants. Indeed tea-sets of this and other much less exciting designs were the 'bread-and-butter' work of many firms, as upwardly mobile Victorians sought to cement social respectability with the acquisition of a silver tea-set and the necessary teaspoons.

6.9 MENU HOLDER

William Robb, Kincardine O'Neil; hallmarked Edinburgh, 1894-95

Marks: thistle (standard mark); 'ROBB' (maker William Robb); castle (Edinburgh); 'K'ON' (Kincardine O'Neil); 'n' (date-letter for 1894-95)

H 2 cm; W 6 cm; Dp 5 cm; Wt 1.88 oz

Lent from a private collection

Plain rectangular base set with sprung holder formed from pierced 'Gothic' monogram of initials 'MIA'.

6.10 SGIAN DUBH

Ferguson & McBean, Inverness; hallmarked Edinburgh, 1898-99

Marks: 'F & M' (makers Ferguson & MacBean); camel (Inverness); 'INVS' (Inverness); thistle (standard mark); castle (Edinburgh); 'r' (date-letter for 1898-99)

L 18.3 cm; W 3.3 cm

Lent from a private collection

Reference: Moss and Roe (1999), pp. 103-06

Full silver handle set with oval cut citrine set, fully chased and engraved with 'Highland' decoration; the leather covered wooden scabbard has a top mount and chape of cast intertwined Celtic beasts. The blade is engraved: 'Ferguson & MacBean / Highland Jewellers / Inverness'. *Sgian dubhs* (from the Gaelic for 'black knife') became common as part of the accoutrements of full Highland dress in the late 19th century. This is an unusually high quality example, with a full silver handle.

6.11 'QUAICH'

James Ramsay, Dundee; hallmarked London, 1900-01

Marks (on rim): 'JR' in diamond (maker James Ramsay, Dundee); lion passant (London standard mark); leopard's head (London); 'e' (date-letter for 1900-01); engraved on base 'RAMSAY/DUNDEE'

L 23.8 cm; D (body) 13.2 cm; H 5.4 cm; Wt 10.1 oz

Lent by Dundee City Council (McManus Galleries and Museum); purchased in 2004 with the aid of the National Fund for Acquisitions

Raised octagonal panelled body, on simple applied circular foot-rim; cast and pierced handles/lugs, depicting two figures representing the Sun and Moon, designed by John Duncan RSA.

The Dundee artist and illustrator John Duncan was a protégé of Patrick Geddes, and was influential in the 'Celtic Revival' movement, teaching design in both Dundee and Edinburgh in the 1890s.

6.12 BROOCH

John Lyle, Ayr, *c*.1900

Marks: 'J.LYLE' (maker John Lyle); 'AYR'

L 5.5 cm; H 3.5 cm

NMS K.2005.525; purchased in Lyon & Turnbull's sale, Edinburgh, 7 December 2005, lot 343

Souvenir badge of gold and oak; pointed oval piece of oak carved with thistles, set in a gold frame with cannetille style mounts with spring pin to rear; the oak centre applied with circular gold plaque, engraved with a depiction of the old bridge and town of Ayr and 'OAK OF THE / AULD BRIG O'AYR / 1252'.

Souvenir items, such as jewellery and especially

6.8

6.9

6.10

snuff boxes, made either entirely or partly from 'celebrity' woods, were very popular in the latter part of the 19th century. Wood from timbers from famous warships, buildings such as Glasgow Cathedral, and famous trees such as the Wallace oak, were all used to make souvenirs.

6.13 BALMORAL HIGHLANDER'S UNIFORM

Kilt and jacket, with accoutrements by William Robb, Ballater, 1903

Marks: thistle (standard mark); 'ROBB / BALLATER' in triangle; castle (Edinburgh); 'w' (date-letter for 1902-03)

NMS A.1988.182; purchased at Phillip's sale, Edinburgh, 20 May 1988, lot 39

Consisting of a Royal Stewart tartan kilt, black wool kilt jacket, black wool Glengarry, and a pair of black leather brogues. The silver-mounted accoutrements are: a horsehair sporran; a kilt belt with buckle; kilt pin; bonnet cap badge; dirk and scabbard, with small knife and spoon; *sgian dubh*; two pairs of shoe buckles; plaid brooch – each piece engraved with 'Celtic' decoration and the royal cipher 'ERI / 1903' (for Edward Rex Imperator).

The Balmoral Highlanders were established by Queen Victoria and consisted mainly of workers from the royal estate. Uniform was worn while on official or ceremonial duties on the estate, or while representing the estate at local events (such as the Braemar Highland Games). Twenty-five new uniforms were commissioned for King Edward VI, and William Robb in Ballater was asked to provide the accoutrements. When the Highlanders were disbanded in 1936, prior to the abdication of Edward VIII, individual members were given permission to retain their 'uniforms and ornaments ... as a memento of their service'.

6.14 RECEIPTED ACCOUNT

For 'Balmoral Highlanders' uniform accoutrements

Paper; H 22.2 cm; W 21.2 cm

Lent by Her Majesty the Queen/The Royal Collection

Dated August 1903, this bill from William Robb in Ballater to His Majesty King Edward VII is for 25 'complete sets of Highland Dress ornaments' for the King's servants at Balmoral. Each set comprised 'bonnet and shoulder brooches, belt buckle, sporran and skindhue [*sic*, i.e. *sgian dubh*], two pairs of shoe buckles and kilt pin', all in sterling silver with 'engraved Celtic ornament', costing £15 per set. The Royal Household paid Mr Robb expeditiously, as the bill is marked 'Paid, with thanks / 13 Sept 1903'.

6.15 INKWELL

Enamels by Lady Gibson Carmichael

Hamilton & Inches, Edinburgh, 1903

Marks: 'H&I' (maker Hamilton & Inches); thistle (standard mark); castle (Edinburgh); 'r' (date-letter for 1898-99)

H 26 cm; W 16 cm; Dp 16 cm; Wt 98.04 oz

NMS H.MEQ 808; purchased in 1965 from L. Lyons, Glasgow

Lent by W. Strang-Steel of Philliphaugh

Reference: Scottish Royal Academy Exhibition (1904), no. 480

In the form of an architectural casket, with lift-off stepped cover with cast lion's head crest finial; the body sides have Ionic columns, behind which are set enamelled panels, all on a gadrooned cushioned base; the interior contains an inset glass inkwell. Three of the four enamelled panels depict female figures with peacocks and elephants; the fourth represents the armorial shield, motto and crest of Sir William Strang-Steel of Philiphaugh and the date '1903'.

The enamels on this casket are by Lady Gibson Carmichael, *née* Mary Helen Elizabeth Nugent, a talented artist who taught enamelling to Phoebe Traquair. William Strang-Steel was a keen art collector and a friend of both Lord and Lady Gibson Carmichael.

6.11

6.15

6.11 (detail)

6.11

6.17
(detail below)

6.18

6.20 (detail above)

6.15

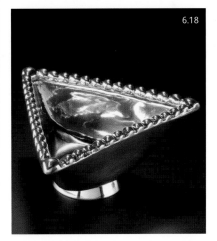

6.18

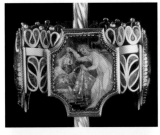

6.16 (detail above)

6.21

6.16 'CUPID AND PSYCHE' CUP

Enamels by Phoebe Anna Traquair

Stand designed by Ramsay Traquair; made by J. M. Talbot, Edinburgh, 1905-06

Marks: 'JMT' (maker J. M. Talbot); castle (Edinburgh); thistle (standard mark); 'Z' (date-letter for 1905-06); enamels signed in monogram on back, 'PAT' (for Phoebe Anna Traquair)

H 34.1 cm; W 17.2 cm; Dp 12.2 cm

NMS A.1989.178; purchased privately in 1989

Provenance: by descent from the family

Reference: Cumming (1993), C102, p. 42

Paua shell mounted on silver stand, stem applied with enamelled plaques and suspended drops in the form of butterflies. Design of the cup was a collaboration between Phoebe and her son Ramsay Traquair, inspired by Renaissance metalwork. Phoebe Traquair, a talented multi-disciplinary artist of the Arts and Crafts Movement, was trained in enamelling techniques by her friend and mentor Lady Gibson Carmichael, who in turn had studied with Alexander Fisher. These enamels are inspired by the story of Cupid and Psyche, a theme to which she returned on several occasions. Traquair used a variety of Edinburgh goldsmiths to produce the silver settings for her enamels.

Little is known about J. M. Talbot, who had a shop at 51 Hanover Street.

6.17 WRITING CASKET

Enamels by Phoebe Anna Traquair

Brook & Son, Edinburgh, 1927-28

Marks: 'B&S'; thistle (standard mark); castle (Edinburgh); 'W' (date-letter for 1927-28); base engraved 'Designed by P A Traquair / Manufactured by Brook & Son Edin.'

H 9.2 cm; L 15.3 cm; Dp 8.2 cm

NMS A.1989.190; purchased privately in 1989

Provenance: by descent from the family

Reference: Cumming (1993), C147

Rectangular casket with hinged lid, set with seven enamelled panels, within a background of angular mouldings, on six square stepped feet; the enamels are all different and depict children, angels, and Cupid and Psyche, in a style typical of Traquair's earlier work.

Presumably this casket was made and set with 'spare' enamels long after they were created. By the mid-1920s Phoebe's eyesight was deteriorating and she did very little work after 1925.

6.18 TRAPRAIN TREASURE REPRODUCTIONS

Brook & Sons, Edinburgh: (triangular dish) 1920-21; (bowl) 1921-22

Marks: 'Brook & Son/87 George St/Edinburgh' (maker's mark); castle (Edinburgh); thistle (standard mark); 'P' on triangular dish (date-letter for 1920-21); 'Q' on bowl (date-letter for 1921-22)

Bowl: H 7.6 cm; D 27 cm

Triangular dish: L 11.5 cm; Dp 10.5 cm; H 5 cm

Lent by Mrs G. Bruce, Edinburgh, descendant of the commissioner

Circular bowl recreated from fragments including a central boss with the head of Hercules and a frieze of wild animals; plain triangular dish, with beaded rim and circular foot-rim.

The spectacular hoard of 4th-century Roman silver, discovered on Traprain Law in East Lothian in 1919, captured both the popular and academic imaginations at the time. The silver, thought to represent payment to a client tribe by the Romans, was in poor condition when found, many of the vessels being cut up for bullion. The Edinburgh goldsmith Brook & Son was commissioned to 'restore' the treasure, and to refashion many of the damaged pieces. They were also commissioned by Mr John Bruce, a Helensburgh businessman and keen amateur archaeologist who helped fund the original excavation, to make a replica set of the Treasure for display in Kelvingrove Museum, Glasgow. The pieces shown here are two of these original replicas.

Brooks also saw a commercial opportunity in making replicas for sale to the general public, and the company was granted permission by the Society of Antiquaries to make copies of a variety of the original pieces. These were very popular throughout the 1920s, '30s and '40s, and many hundreds were sold, particularly the triangular dishes which were produced in several sizes and marketed as 'salts'. These remain popular and the successors to Brook & Son's premises in George Street, Edinburgh – Hamilton & Inches – still make replicas of the salts to this day.

6.18

6.19 PRIZE MEDAL

Thomas Lumsden Brown, Cupar; hallmarked Edinburgh, 1933

Marks: 'TLB' (maker Thomas Lumsden Brown); thistle (standard mark); castle (Edinburgh); 'C' (date-letter for 1933-34)

H 9 cm; W 4.9 cm; Wt. 2.3 oz

Lent from a private collection

Oval medal with cast husk border and elaborate suspension loop; obverse engraved 'Montrose Academy / English / John Hebenton / 1934'; reverse engraved 'Education / Authority / of / Angus'. Despite being made in the 1930s, this design of medal was common from the 1850s onwards.

6.20 PORRIDGE PAN

Brook & Son, Edinburgh, 1935-36

Marks: 'B&S' (maker Brook & Son); thistle (standard mark); castle (Edinburgh); 'E' (date-letter for 1935-36); sovereign's head (1935 Jubilee mark)

D 21 cm; H 18.8 cm; Wt (without handle) 89.16 oz; Wt (with handle) 96.3 oz

Lent from a private collection

Cylindrical body with a frieze of cut-card fleur-de-lis below the rim, with two opposing rail handles of ivory mounted in silver; the detachable cover with a band of cut-card engrailing immediately inside the rim, with hinged flap to accommodate a ladle and with ivory finial, the cover engraved with the Robert Burns grace: 'Some hae meat and canna eat [etc.] ...'. The body is engraved with the arms of McGregor within a bordure argent, between two stylised plumes; with additional detachable silver-mounted ivory baluster handle.

This robust pan, used for keeping porridge warm on the breakfast sideboard, is deliberately 'historicist' in design; the cut-card decoration and the engraving of the arms hark back to the style of the late 17th century.

6.21 PLACE SETTING AND OTHER ITEMS FROM THE JUBILEE BANQUETING SERVICE FOR HOLYROODHOUSE

Henry Tatton & Son, Edinburgh, 1935

Marks: 'HT' with crowned thistle between (maker Henry Tatton & Son); thistle (standard mark); castle (Edinburgh); 'E' (date-letter for 1935-36); king's and queen's heads conjoined (Silver Jubilee mark)

Lent by Her Majesty the Queen/The Royal Collection

Reference: Dalgleish and Maxwell (1987), no. 44

Design of cutlery based on early 18th-century 'trefid' pattern and other items on Queen Anne originals. Each item is engraved either with the Royal Arms as used in Scotland, or with the Scottish Royal Crest.

This spectacular gift by Sir Alexander Grant, to mark the Silver Jubilee of King George V and Queen Mary in 1935, included silver, linen, glass, china and kitchen equipment. The Silver Banqueting Service for 96 guests comprises over 3000 individual pieces and weighs about 18,000 ounces. Designed by J. Wilson Patterson with Henry Tatton and John Cartwright, it was made over a period of 18 months at the Rose Street workshops of Henry Tatton & Son, with George Kerr as master craftsman and John Lawson as chief engraver. Five other goldsmiths and engravers were employed in creating the service and the past deacon of the Incorporation of Goldsmiths, Mr H. R. Tatton, Henry Tatton's son, was taken on as an apprentice by the firm specifically because of this massive order. The bullion silver used to make the service contains a large proportion of Scottish silver, mined at Leadhills.

The entire service, including linen manufactured in Dunfermline by Hay & Robertson, and glass made by the Edinburgh & Leith Flint Glass Works, Norton Park, is still used regularly today.

6.22 NAPKIN RING

William Walter Randell, Braemar; hallmarked Edinburgh, 1937-38

Marks: 'W.W.R' (maker William Walter Randell); 'B.M.R' (Braemar); thistle (standard mark); castle (Edinburgh); 'G' (date-letter for 1937-38)

H 3.6 cm; W 4 cm; L 5.5 cm; Wt 1.42 oz

Lent from a private collection

6.19

6.20

6.21

6.22

Simple oval band with collet set brilliant-cut citrine. William Walter Randall, with William Robb, were the only two silversmiths to work in Braemar and use a Braemar town punch. Randal married one of Robb's daughters, and continued to run the business after his father-in-law's death.

6.23 IONA NUNNERY SPOON

Alexander Ritchie, Iona; hallmarked Birmingham, 1939-40

With original spoon, 13th century

Marks (underside of stem): 'AR/IONA' (maker Alexander Ritchie); anchor (Birmingham); lion passant (standard mark); 'P' (date-letter 1939-40); 'ICA' (Iona Celtic Art)

L 20.2 cm

NMS K.2006.436; purchased privately in 2006

Reference: MacArthur (2003), p. 50

The bowl is of pointed leaf shape, the lower stem rectangular in section cast with interlace, the upper section circular in section, terminating in a leaf and pint finial.

The original 'Iona Spoons', dating to the 13th century, were discovered during some conservation work at the nunnery in 1923-24, and were given to the National Museum of Antiquities of Scotland as Treasure Trove. It is unknown exactly when Alexander Ritchie had the opportunity to handle or copy the spoons, but by local repute the finds from the Abbey were left with him for safekeeping while the work continued and he was allowed to make copies. These copies were immediately popular and became a mainstay of his work.

Ritchie was born on Mull in 1856. After taking courses at Glasgow School of Art, where he developed his love of 'Celtic' arts, he and his wife began designing and making metalwork. They established a shop near the gates to the nunnery, and continued to sell souvenir wares, in copper and silver, until their deaths in 1941. Although he often had his silver pieces manufactured and assayed in London, Chester or Birmingham, Ritchie always had them stamped with his own initials, or 'ICA' for Iona Celtic Arts.

6.24 BROOCH OF LORNE REPLICA

W. Dunningham & Co., Aberdeen; hallmarked Edinburgh, 1950-51

Marks: 'W.D&Co' (maker William Dunningham & Company); thistle (sterling standard mark); castle (Edinburgh); 'U' (date-letter for 1950-51)

Lent by Aberdeen Museum and Art Gallery

Circular brooch, with central lobed chamber set with a hemispherical crystal, surrounded by eight pillars set with pearls, all enriched with wirework.

The Brooch of Lorne is one of a series of great turreted reliquary brooches from Scotland which date to the late medieval period. These historic pieces of metalwork, along with others such as the Hunterston and Tara brooches, captured the imagination of the public in the late 19th and 20th centuries, and numerous goldsmiths throughout the country produced 'replicas' of varying accuracy and scale. William Dunningham & Company, based in Aberdeen, were prolific makers of souvenir items for the booming north-east tourist trade from about 1900 until the 1950s.

6.22

6.23 (spoon)

6.23

Breadalbane Silver
by David MacGregor, Perth

In 1894 the Perth silversmith and designer, David MacGregor, produced what was one of the most remarkable unified groups of Victorian silver in Scotland, combining the era's love of elaborate decoration and historical allusion in a spectacular way. MacGregor was commissioned by 'The Tenantry on the Breadalbane Estates' to design and produce a gift of suitable magnificence to mark the granting of the Knighthood of the Garter to Gavin, 1st Marquess and 7th Earl of Breadalbane. What he eventually delivered was a 'garniture' comprising a silver casket containing an address on an illuminated parchment, an illuminated album, and two large silver covered cups, or vases, set on granite pedestals. An inscription on the casket itself actually refers to this grouping: 'Presented (Containing an Address) to the Most Honourable Gavin Marquess of Breadalbane K.G. along with Pair [sic] Silver Vases and an Illuminated Album.' Close inspection reveals that these pieces were no mere standard 'off-the-shelf' presentation trophy, but an elaborate and highly original creation intimately connected with the recipient. Astonishingly, a significant part of this group survives: one of the large cups or vases, the casket with its illuminated parchment, and most remarkably of all a fully worked-up pencil design drawing, are all now in the National Museums Scotland collections.

Gavin, 7th Earl of Breadalbane, was born in 1851 and succeeded in 1871, on the death of his father John, 6th Earl, to the vast Breadalbane estates in Perthshire and Argyll. These amounted to over 450,000 acres, stretching from Aberfeldy to the Atlantic Ocean. The 7th Earl was created a Marquess in 1885, the original peerage honours having died out in the direct line with John, 5th Earl and Marquess (1796-1862). Gavin lived in the style of a grandee at Taymouth Castle on Loch Tay. He re-established his family's traditional support for the Liberal Party and was a staunch adherent of the established Church of Scotland. Amongst his many other antiquarian interests, he formed a particularly fine collection of historic Scottish and English silver. Gavin died without issue in 1922, having first had to dispose of the eastern portion of the estates, including Taymouth Castle. A series of sales in the 1920s and 1930s finally disposed of much of the large Taymouth collections of furnishings and antiques. Unfortunately no record of the sale of the vases and casket has emerged.

The designer of the presentation ensemble, David MacGregor of George Street, Perth, was one of the most talented, successful and important provincial craftsmen in Scotland. He was active from 1860, and although a working silversmith, sending many items for marking to the Edinburgh Assay Office between at least 1876 and 1889, it was as an 'art engraver and jeweller' that he achieved prominence. He was skilled enough to enjoy royal patronage, although it is not known when he started to use the title 'Jeweller to the Queen'. Perth Museums and Art Gallery own several of his best examples of engraved plaques along with his shop sign [see 6.29] and some fittings from his shop. All his surviving work shows that he

THE BREADALBANE VASE
Design drawing by David MacGregor Perth, 1893
(NMS H.OD 85)

Surviving silver designs are exceptionally rare for Scottish silver. This must have been a final life-size design drawing for the commission of the Breadalbane vases, and is inscribed 'Designed and Drawn by David MacGregor, / Jeweller to the Queen'. Unfortunately it has no secure provenance and was bought from an Edinburgh antique shop in 1991.

was an artist of exceptional talent. Although he does not seem to have fabricated the silver items in the Breadalbane presentation himself, preferring to send them to large manufacturing silversmiths in London and Glasgow respectively, he was undoubtedly the artist behind their final realisation. Almost uniquely for a piece of Scottish historic silver, there still survives a fully worked-up design drawing in MacGregor's own hand, which he presumably sent, with others, to the London firm of Wakely & Wheeler. The inscription above the marks on the surviving vase states that it was both 'designed and wrought' by MacGregor. Presumably this refers to him doing the final chasing and definitely the engraving of the topographical panels, once the main body of the vases had been fabricated. This is presumably the case with the casket made by Edwards, although its basic shape seems to have been a standard with the company. (A similar casket, without the high quality engraving, was sold at Bonham's Scottish sale, on Wednesday 22 August 2000, lot 110.)

Unusually the production and presentation of the vases are well documented. The *Magazine of Art* for 1895 published a photograph of one of the vases with the following commentary: 'We reproduce on this page one of a pair of silver vases which have been presented to the Marquis [*sic*] of Breadalbane by his tenantry on the occasion of his investiture with the Order of the Garter. They were designed by Mr DAVID MACGREGOR, of Perth, and executed by Messrs Wakely and Wheeler, of London. Each stands 25 inches in height, and is mounted on a granite pedestal. They are richly engraved with bands of oak leaves and acorns, and have four panels representing "Taymouth Castle", "the Royal Flotilla on Loch Tay in 1842", "Kilchurn Castle" and "Loch Tulla House", and are good specimens of modern silversmiths' work'.

Although the *Magazine* gives an accurate description of the vases, it failed to mention one of the most significant elements of the vases' decoration; nor did it convey the symbolic importance of the entire carefully thought-out decorative scheme to the House of Breadalbane. On prominent positions on the cover of the vase are highly detailed engravings of a stag hunt and a boar hunt. The stag hunt refers to the use by the Campbells of Breadalbane of stags as their heraldic supporters. The boar hunt also has heraldic significance as the crest of the Campbells is a boar's head. This, however, has far deeper significance as a depiction of the central motif in the Ossianic 'Lay of Dermid', where the near-invincible hero, a nephew of Fionn, kills a gigantic boar, but is tricked in an act of vengeance to his death by being pricked in his vulnerable heel by the boars' poisoned bristles. The scene undoubtedly represents the Campbell (or Clan Diarmaid) descent from their eponymous ancestor Diarmaid O'Duinn. Interest in this probably mythical origin and line of descent was revived in the 19th century, first with the enormous popularity of William Macpherson's *Ossian,* and second with the publication, under Campbell auspices, of versions of the legend recorded directly from Gaelic oral tradition on the Campbell estates.

The prominence of this illustration was probably intended to establish the Marquess of Breadalbane's credentials as rival to the Duke of Argyll for headship of Clan Diarmaid. This seems particularly significant as Gavin, 1st Marquess, was descended not from the main line of Breadalbane chiefs, but from a cadet branch, the Campbells of Glenfalloch. His father, the 6th Earl, had inherited in 1867 after a five-year legal dispute – the Breadalbane Case – over the succession to the titles.

This rivalry and the importance of the 'new' line in establishing their credentials and continuity with the glories of the past, is also evident in the other engraved scenes. Taymouth Castle occupies a central position as the 'caput' of the vast Breadalbane estates. It was initially built in 1806-11 by the architects Archibald and James Elliot, on the site of the old Campbell Castle of Balloch, probably in a conscious attempt to upstage the Duke of Argyll's Castle of Inveraray. Taymouth was comprehensively remodelled and extended by James Gillespie Graham (with contributions by Pugin) between 1838 and 1842, in time to play host to Queen Victoria's famous first visit to Scotland.

Taymouth had become one of the grandest 'Gothic' houses in the country, and was a fitting setting for John, 2nd Marquess of Breadalbane's elaborate entertainment of Queen Victoria and Prince Albert, when they visited him, 7th to 10th September 1842. The visit ended with a grand 'flotilla' of barges rowing down Loch Tay to take the Queen on the next leg of her journey. The royal barge had been specially built for the purpose and was attended by four others, carrying some of the aristocratic entourage of two dukes, three duchesses, three marquesses, two marchionesses, five earls and three countesses who had been present at the visit to Taymouth. This remarkable scene forms another of the main panels on the vase and the spectacle cases [6.27], and was no doubt intended to signify the continuity of royal favour to the House of Breadalbane. The vases and casket of course commemorate the investiture of Breadalbane with the Knighthood of the Garter, but he was already an important royal courtier, having been Treasurer to the Royal Household 1880-85, Privy Councillor 1880, Lord Steward of the Household 1892-95, and Lord High Commissioner to the General Assembly of the Church of Scotland 1883-85. This intimate connection between him and the Royal Family while in Scotland probably played some part in the Royal Goldsmith/Jeweller MacGregor being chosen for the commission, over and above his obvious skill.

A final allusion to the Campbell of Breadalbane's antiquity, and to the vast extent of their estates, is the engraving of Kilchurn Castle, situated on an island at the north end of Loch Awe, with Ben Cruachan rising behind. This castle had been the seat of the Campbells of Glenorchy, the direct ancestors of the Breadalbane peerage.

The resultant pieces form perhaps one of the most interesting collaborations between patron and artist in 19th-century Scotland, and provide a fascinating insight into the commissioning process.

6.25 THE BREADALBANE VASE

Designed and finished by David MacGregor, Perth; made by Wakely & Wheeler, London, 1894

Marks (under rim): 'JW/FCW' (makers James Wakely and Frank Clarke Wheeler); lion passant; leopard's head (London); 'T' (date-letter for 1894); engraved above marks: 'DESIGNED & WROUGHT BY DAVID MACGREGOR, / JEWELLER TO THE QUEEN, PERTH.'

H 66 cm; W (across handles) 50 cm; D (base) 22.5 cm; Wt 190 oz

NMS K.1998.1262; purchased in 1998 from M. Rix

Provenance: private collection in 1989; sold at Christie's sale, London, The Property of a Trust, 26 May 1998, lot 94

Vase-shaped cup on circular stepped foot, chased and embossed with bands of acanthus leaves and four cast boars' heads; fluted stem girt with a marquess's coronet. The body is lobed below a band of acanthus and flowers, the upper body chased and embossed with bands of acorns, thistles and roses, into which are set oval panels engraved with topographical scenes of Taymouth Castle, the Royal Flotilla on Loch Tay 1842, Kilchurn Castle and Loch Tulla House; central to the front and rear are the Arms of Campbell of Breadalbane, surrounded by the collar and George of the Order of the Garter, and an inscription surrounded by the garter belt and motto.

6.26 THE BREADALBANE CASKET

Designed and engraved by David MacGregor, Perth; made by Edwards & Sons, Glasgow, 1893-94

Marks (on base): 'Edward & Sons, / Silversmiths, Glasgow' (engraved); lion rampant (standard mark); tree, fish, bell, etc. (Glasgow); 'W' (date-letter for 1893-94); 'DE/GE' (makers David and George Edward)

L 34.2 cm; H 27.5 cm; W 24.4 cm

NMS H.MEQ 1618; purchased from Mr M. Rix in 1990

Provenance: Sotheby's sale, Gleneagles Hotel, 28-29 August 1989, lot 308

Rectangular box, with hinged, stepped cushion lid; the angles of the box applied with cylindrical 'turrets', each capped with a cast female figure representing countryside pursuits; the four faces of the box have chased and engraved panels depicting Taymouth Castle, Kilchurn Castle, Loch Tay and Kenmore, and a ruined tower house, possibly the original Balloch Castle; the lid has panels of chased intertwined 'Celtic' beasts, separating panels depicting other buildings and views of the Breadalbane estates; the front panel has an engraved inscription: 'Presented / (Containing an Address) / To The Most Honourable / Gavin Marquess of Breadalbane K.G. / Along with a pair Silver Vases and an Illuminated Album / BY THE TENANTRY ON THE BREADALBANE ESTATES / IN THE COUNTIES OF PERTH AND ARGYLL / on the occasion of his having the distinguished honour / CONFERRED UPON HIM / OF THE MOST NOBLE ORDER OF THE GARTER / 1894'. The top of the lid is surmounted by an enamelled shield with the Campbell of Breadalbane Arms, with stag supporters.

The manufacturers were one of the biggest

6.25

6.26

6.25 (details below)

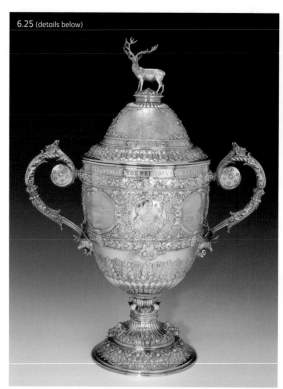

6.26 (details below)

6.27

6.28

6.29

Glasgow concerns in the late 19th and early 20th century. Started by George Edward senior in 1838, by the time they made the casket they were owned by George's sons David and George junior. They opened a London branch in Cheapside in 1874, and became a limited company in 1925, and eventually sold out to Mappin & Webb in the 1960s.

6.27 PAIR OF MATCHING SILVER SPECTACLE CASES

Designed and engraved by David MacGregor, Perth; made by Deakin & Francis, hallmarked Birmingham

Marks: 'D&F' (makers Deakin & Francis); anchor (Birmingham); lion (standard mark); 'x' (date-letter 1897-98)

(1) L 16.5 cm / (2) L 16.5 cm

NMS K.2005.520.1 and 2; purchased from J. H. Bourdon-Smith Ltd, London

(1) A lady's case, with attached chain and chatelaine hook, engraved to front with a portrait of Gavin, Marquess of Breadalbane, with a view of Taymouth Castle below and a marquess's coronet, the Campbell crest (a boar's head), and the motto 'Follow Me' above, all within foliate scroll-work panels. Engraved to rear with the Campbell of Breadalbane arms, with '1872-1897' below; a view of the 'Royal Flotilla 1842' on Loch Tay below, and a view of Kilchurn Castle above, all within foliate scrollwork panels.

(2) A gentleman's case, engraved to front with a portrait of Alma, Marchioness of Breadalbane, with a view of Taymouth Castle below and a marquess's coronet, the Campbell crest (a boar's head), and the motto 'Follow Me' above, all within foliate scroll-work panels. Engraved to rear with the Campbell of Breadlabane arms and '1872-1897' below a view of the 'Royal Flotilla 1842' on Loch Tay, and a view of Kilchurn Castle above, all within foliate scroll-work panels.

These exquisitely engraved matching 'his and hers' spectacle cases were commissioned to commemorate the Silver Wedding of Gavin, 1st Marquess of Breadalbane, and his wife Alma, younger daughter of the 4th Duke of Montrose. They are evidence of the ongoing connection between the Marquess and the designer David MacGregor. The engraved portraits also relate to MacGregor's other work, such as the portrait of

Princess Alexandra [6.28], and his engraved plaque after Holman Hunt's painting of 'Christ Light of the World', now in Perth Museum.

6.28 ENGRAVED PLAQUE

David MacGregor, Perth, 1886

H 31 cm; W (open) 41 cm

Lent by the Worshipful Company of Goldsmiths of London

Gold plaque engraved with the bust of Her Royal Highness Princess Alexandra, wife of Edward, Prince of Wales, later King Edward VII. This is further evidence of MacGregor's royal favour. Princess Alexandra visited Scotland on numerous occasions, staying at Balmoral Castle and Holyroodhouse when the Royal Family was in residence

6.29 SHOP SIGN

From David MacGregor's shop, Perth

H 63.5 cm; W 60.7 cm

Lent by Perth Museum and Art Gallery

Carved wood, painted and gilded. In the form of a rayed star, with crowned central oval, with profile of Queen Victoria, surrounded by a belt with 'Patronised by Her Majesty the Queen'; the rays inscribed 'Silversmith / Engraver / Designer / Goldsmith / Jeweller / Medallist'.

6.25 (detail)

6.27

Kirk Silver

Introduction

The medieval Scottish Church possessed a rich heritage of silver and gold plate; surviving inventories of various religious establishments make this clear. Holyrood Abbey, Glasgow Cathedral and St Andrews Cathedral, for example, all owned hoards of sacramental vessels, reliquaries and books mounted with precious stones. Holyrood in particular had an impressive collection, itemised in an inventory of 1493,[1] including a silver cross weighing 180 ounces and a silver arm of St Augustine weighing 84 ounces. Much of this plate was no doubt imported from Continental centres such as Paris, but some would have been made by Scottish craftsmen. The Reformation of 1560 changed all this. The iconoclastic zeal of the Reformers is often blamed for sweeping away an ancient and rich heritage. Certainly the riots in Perth inspired by John Knox destroyed a great deal of the decoration of St John's Kirk in that town. However, it was not in the interests of the Reformers to alienate from their new Church the wealth that was tied up in the old plate. Much of it had been cannily removed by members of the old Church, or by the lords who appropriated a great deal of its lands, leading to the initial impoverishment of the new Church and its resultant lack of necessary sacramental silver.

The reformed Church of Scotland is seldom given any credit in the popular mind for its patronage of the arts, and John Knox is still falsely castigated for creating a gloomy, stern and unforgiving Presbyterian Church. Knox was not, of course, the architect of the Presbyterian system and was indeed said to have enjoyed music and dancing. Equally, the Reformed Church does have an artistic heritage, albeit a very different one from that of the preceding regime, and this is seen nowhere better than in the Kirk's sacramental silver. Indeed, as discussed above (chapter 3, p. 29), if it were not for the heritage of Scottish church silver we would be left with just a handful of Scottish secular domestic silver for the 16th and most of the 17th centuries. Thus it can be argued that for this period, Scottish church silver is one of the great glories of Scottish metalwork.

From its foundation, the Reformed Church placed enormous importance on the celebration of its two Sacraments: the Lord's Supper (or communion), and baptism. The Kirk's earliest ordinances made it clear that both were to be public occasions 'in the Face of the Congregation', or as the *Form of Worship* published in 1565 states: 'Sacraments are not ordained of God to be used in private corners as charmers and sorceries but left to the Congregation.'[2] This of course was a swipe at the old Roman Catholic practices of private Mass and baptism. However it does empha-

7

Anent the ... ministratioun of ye Sacraments

{ACT OF PARLIAMENT, 1617}

size the establishment of a continuous tradition in the Church of Scotland of the public and communal nature of the sacraments, and this undoubtedly influenced the types of vessels required for them. The *First Book of Discipline* stipulated that every church should have 'a basin for baptism and table for the ministration of the Lord's Supper'.[3] While there is no reference to cups or bread plates, and certainly none to the form they should take, the need for such items is clearly envisaged.

The lack of resources within the new Kirk meant that communion, in particular, was not celebrated as regularly as Knox and his colleagues had intended. Knox wanted it to be celebrated four times annually, but it was often held only once or perhaps twice a year. One of the problems was the lack of necessary vessels because of the Church's extreme poverty. The new Kirk's austerity owed as much to the plundering by the aristocracy and gentry as to the iconoclasm of the reformers. The absolute paucity of surviving 16th-century Kirk plate reflects this. Only four silver vessels made before 1600 survive in the Church. Two – the Forgue Cup, which was made in 1563 [7.1], and David Gilbert's magnificent Rosewater Dish of 1593 [7.14], were not actually given over for sacramental use until the 1630s. Only two communion cups made in the 16th century specifically for church use survive – the Roseneath Cup of 1585-86 [7.2], and the Currie Cup [7.3], which could be as early as 1598.

The situation began to improve in the early 17th century: for the period 1600 to 1617 some 18 cups survive from ten parishes. In 1617 the passing of the most important piece of legislation regarding the provision of church vessels ('The Act anent the furnesing of Necessaris for Ministratioun of ye Sacraments') changed this. An Act of the Scottish Parliament itself, not simply a piece of Church law, it was part of James VI's drive to bring the Scottish Church into line with that of England, and the first piece of legislation designed to spell out precisely what kirks were required to have: 'All the paroche kirkis within this kingdome to be provydit of basins and lavouis for the ministration of the Sacrament of Baptism, and of coupes, tabils and tabilclothes for the ministration of Holie communion.'[4]

From this we should be in no doubt that the provision and use of sacramental plate are an absolutely fundamental part of the Kirk's history and should be viewed as being every bit as important to its heritage as more widely-recognised features, such as historic buildings, furnishings or stained glass. In fact, occasionally the earliest surviving artefacts relating to a congregation are their communion cups. Crucially, the Act also provided the means for acquiring vessels – by imposing a mechanism so that each parish could be taxed to raise the necessary funds.

The sacraments were treated with great solemnity within the Reformed Church. The main feature of baptism was its performance before the normal sermon, hence the positioning of fonts at the front of the church and the use of so many baptismal basin mounts on pulpits. Early baptismal silver is exceptionally rare, and much that does survive shows evidence of having been extensively repaired or even totally renewed [see Trinity College Kirk Baptismal Laver, 7.8]. This no doubt reflects the much more regular and frequent use of baptismal vessels and consequent wear and tear. In densely populated parishes, baptisms must have been carried out virtually every week.

The main feature of communion was that it was not to resemble the Mass of the Catholic Church. The reformers were determined to root the celebration of the sacraments in Calvinist theology. This emphasised the replacement of the Mass by the celebration of the Lord's Supper as a 'common meal', where all participated equally, the model being the family meal, served at tables not altars, using domestic utensils (albeit beautiful ones) not sacerdotal chalices. Instead of a single chalice associated with an exclusive priesthood, communal drinking cups and bread plates were to be used, emphasising the priesthood of all believers. These very powerful messages were at the heart of the Scottish Church throughout the 16th and 17th centuries, and indeed later.

One can see this right away in the earliest surviving cups, which are identical in shape to secular wine cups. The Roseneath Cup [7.2] is basically a domestic wine cup derived from designs then current in London. Ironically however, as there are no surviving secular Scottish wine cups, our knowledge of their form and design comes retrospectively from remaining church cups. This determination to use secular vessels is alluded to by one of the reformer's bitterest foes. In 1563 Ninian Winzet denounced 'Calvinian precherouris' in Scotland for using table basins and tavern cups for dispensing the sacraments.[5]

Although there were no doctrinal reasons for either the shape of cup used or for the numbers acquired by a church, the size might have been influenced by the observance of the custom to take more than a sip from the communal cup. In early regulations for communion services, participants were ordered 'tae sit weel back and tak a deep draught'.[6] Certainly large quantities of wine, normally claret, were consumed at communion services, and cups were filled many times from large flagons such as those from Trinity Kirk [7.6]. In 1609 Patrick Home of Polwarth gave cash to buy three Scots gallons of wine (i.e. *c*.48 imperial pints) for communion services at Logie Kirk.

In the years immediately following the 1617 Act there was an explosion in the production of cups and other vessels, many of which survive to this day.

Of course while production increased, many items must also have disappeared, particularly as the 17th century was beset with long periods of religious war which were responsible for the destruction of much domestic silver. It has already been noted that the Covenanters' war committees, set up to finance armed opposition to the King, specifically demanded that that all silver be handed in for the cause. This makes it all the more surprising that so much church silver from the 1640s and '60s has survived. Exemptions from the war committees' demands must have been possible. But equally important is the fact that church plate was not affected to the same degree by the dictates of fashion that saw the 'recycling' of so much domestic silver into newer, more up-to-date pieces. For many decades, indeed centuries, a communion cup could and did fulfil the same function for which it was originally intended, without need of remodelling, although this happened from time to time. In fact there are references in kirk session records to cups being replaced by pieces in the 'most modern fashion'. More commonly, however, they were replaced, renewed or repaired simply because of damage through long years of hard wear [e.g. the Bolton Cup, 7.22].

There was no stipulation as to the shape or form of the cups and other vessels to be used, and there is considerable variation in the surviving examples. This probably relates to taste and wealth; the larger, more populous parishes of the south-east acquired large 'mazer-shaped' cups, such as those of Trinity and Greyfriars below [7.5, 7.9]. The poorer, smaller parishes of the west and south-west seem to have favoured the smaller, slender yet supremely elegant, 'champagne' type cup [see Balmaghie Cup, 7.4].

The increased demand caused by the 1617 Act must have made the fortune of many goldsmiths, especially those in Edinburgh. One in particular, Gilbert Kirkwood, probably made more church silver at this time than any other goldsmith. He made cups for over 20 parishes and probably many more which have not survived. He certainly amassed a sufficient fortune to set up as a laird, acquiring the estate of Pilrig in 1623.

Yet not all Scottish church silver was made in Edinburgh, or indeed was necessarily specially made as church silver in the first place. A good example of the latter is the fascinating group of plate from St John's Kirk in Perth [7.13, 14], which includes some extremely fine and highly important individual pieces. The magnificent 'Basin' [7.14] by David Gilbert, Edinburgh (1592-93), undoubtedly started life as a secular rosewater dish. It is the only surviving example of this type of 16th-century Scottish dish and was probably used as a baptismal basin or bread plate in the church. This is not the only time a secular rosewater dish and ewer were pressed into use at baptism. A beautiful rosewater dish and ewer made in London in 1602 were later purchased by the kirk session of the Old Kirk in St Giles, Edinburgh, for use at baptisms in 1728. The rest of the Perth group are equally fascinating; two London-made steeple cups of 1610 and 1611 and two cups made in Nuremberg in the 16th century, including the so-called Mary Cup [7.13], have inscriptions that make it clear they came into St John's possession only in the 1630s and '40s. However, the major historical significance of this material is as a group of 16th- and 17th-century secular and domestic plate, later given to the church for sacramental use in the 1640s – a period of civil war which grew out of religious conflict between the Crown and Kirk – a sort of second Reformation.

The 1617 Act made no stipulations about design of vessels or the use of second-hand plate, the Kirk apparently having been concerned only to ensure that any vessels used did not smack of Catholic chalices. Hence secular cups and other vessels could be, and were, reused for communion and baptism. A recent study of kirk session records makes a very convincing case that churches deliberately based sacramental vessels on secular ones.[7] This was part of the conscious effort to emphasise the 'inclusive communality of the faithful', with no intercession by the priest necessary. As one contemporary account stated: 'The minister cometh down from the pulpit and sitteth at the table, every man and woman likewise taking their place … no man acted as priest … each took his communion bread with his own hand out of the basin and gave the cup to otheres sitting at the table.' The St John's Perth group [7.13-7.14] is very important in this respect, as they are demonstrably secular vessels used as church plate.

The large cups acquired by Trinity College Kirk in Edinburgh in 1632 are the earliest examples of what was to become a common type in Scotland (despite being made in London [see 7.5]). It seems clear these were based on earlier mazers, the communal domestic cups *par excellence*, and this was probably no coincidence. In 1629 Zacharie Boyd, an influential Presbyterian divine, when discussing the sacrament of communion in his book *The Last Battell of the Soule*, makes this connection obvious when he enjoined communicants to 'take now the cup of salvation, the great Mazer of His mercy, and call upon the name of the Lord'. Thus, surviving kirk silver forms clear and material evidence of the tensions between King James VI's desire to 'beautify' and 'anglicise' the Church, and the Reformers' determination to root the celebration of the sacraments in Calvinist theology.

The Scottish Church's natural tendency to internal schism led in the 18th and 19th centuries to major rifts and the emergence of numerous rival sects. Starting with the Secession of 1733 and culminating with the Disruption of 1843, many new congregations were formed out of these splits, all requiring adequate provision of communion and baptismal vessels. As many of the rival factions in the 18th century were relatively poor, they often turned to the pewterers rather than the goldsmiths for their needs. However, the increased demand was sufficient to give good business to many goldsmiths throughout the country.

Very little Roman Catholic plate survives from their period of persecution and suppression, from the 16th to the 19th century. The 'old' religion did hold on in certain areas, but the survival of the Holyrood Altar Plate (p. 153) and the Forsyth Chalice and Paten is [7.20] little short of a miracle, and they serve to remind us of the very different forms and styles.

Sacramental silver used by the Episcopal Church in Scotland was to all intents and purposes the same as Presbyterian silver, until the high church Oxford Movement inspired changes in the late 19th century.

Notes

1   Quoted in Burns (1892), pp. 128-29.
2   John Knox (1565), p. 62.
3   John Knox, quoted in Donaldson (1970), p. 127.
4   *APS* (1617), Act 6, vol. iv, p. 534.
5   Quoted in Burns (1892), pp. 195-96.
6   Ibid., p. 17.
7   Todd (2002), p. 101.

7.7 (detail)

7.1 COMMUNION CUP
FROM FORGUE PARISH KIRK, ABERDEENSHIRE

Bowl: Henry Thompsone, Edinburgh, 1563-65

Marks (on rim and upper foot): 'HT' in monogram (maker Henry Thompsone); castle (Edinburgh); 'IC' (deacon James Cokkie, 1563-65)

H 17.7 cm; D (bowl) 18.5 cm; D (foot) 11.9 cm; Wt 16.95 oz

Lent by the kirk session of Auchaber: United Church of Scotland

References: Burns (1892), pp. 205-06; Finlay and Fothringham (1991), pp. 78-79, pl. 23(i); RSM (1948), no. 2

Plain, shallow bowl, set on baluster stem and circular stepped foot with stamped foliate decoration; rim of bowl engraved: 'GIFTIT . TO . GOD . AND . TO . HIS . CHVRCH . BE . IAMES . CREIGHTOVN . OF . FRENDRAVEHT . TO . THE . KIRK . OF . FORRIG . / 1633'.

Although this is known as the earliest surviving cup in the Church of Scotland, it is unlikely that it actually came into church use as early as its date of manufacture. As both the foot and bowl are marked, these are clearly original, but the baluster stem and plain shoulder of the foot look like replacement. A document within the later fitted chest indicates that the silver given to the Church by Frendraught was 'repaired and restored' in 1872. It is possible that the stem dates to this time.

This is the only known piece by Henry Thompsone, who was admitted to the Incorporation of Goldsmiths in May 1561. The circumstances of the donation are fascinating. James Crichton, the Laird of Frendraught, fell under suspicion of murder when his house burned down in 1630, killing Viscount Melgum and the Laird of Rothiemay. Frendraught was never charged with any crime, and made vigorous attempts to clear his name. An old disgruntled servant was convicted and executed for the murder in 1633. It is likely that Frendraught presented the cups to the kirk as a pious offering of thanks to God for his exoneration. He later presented plate to Forgue and other churches.

7.2 COMMUNION CUP
FROM ROSENEATH KIRK, DUNBARTONSHIRE

John Mosman, Edinburgh, 1585-86

Marks (beneath rim of bowl): 'JM' conjoined (maker John Mosman); castle (Edinburgh); 'JM' conjoined (deacon John Mosman)

H 23.2 cm; D (bowl) 9.8 cm; D (foot) 9.2 cm; Wt 9.23 oz

NMS H.KJ 253; purchased from the kirk session of Roseneath: St Modan's Parish Church, Dunbartonshire

References: Dalgleish and Maxwell (1987), no. 2; Burns (1892), p. 269; Finlay and Fothringham (1991), p. 80, pl. 23(ii)

Narrow-mouthed, bucket-shaped bowl with slender baluster and spool stem set on spreading, stepped foot, the outer rim with a band of punched tongue and dart decoration. Originally one of two, the other was owned by the City of Edinburgh Museums and Galleries.

This delicate and elegant cup has essentially the same form as a domestic wine cup, and follows fashionable London styles of the time. It is the earliest surviving cup originally made specifically for church use. The maker Mosman's punch appears twice on the cup as he was both maker and deacon at the time. It was considered acceptable for the deacon, who was always a working goldsmith, to continue to produce and mark his own work during his period of office.

7.3 COMMUNION CUP
FROM CURRIE KIRK, EDINBURGH

Hugh Lindsay, Edinburgh, 1598-1600

Marks (on rim): 'HL.' conjoined (maker Hugh Lindsay); castle (Edinburgh); 'DH' in monogram (deacon David Heriot, 1598-1602, 1604-06); assay-scrape above marks

H 16 cm; D (bowl) 16.6 cm; D (base) 10.2 cm; Wt 10.95 oz

On loan to NMS from the kirk session of Currie Parish Church

References: Burns (1892), p. 209; Finlay and Fothringham (1991), p. 81, pl. 24(i); RSM (1948), no. 7

Wide, deep bowl set on baluster and knop stem, with stepped trumpet foot stamped with trefoil foliate and ovolo decoration. The inside of the bowl is engraved with 'M/ML' within a shaped shield for Maister Matthew Lichtoune, minister of Currie from 1591-1631. The foot is engraved (later) with 'FOR THE KIRK OF CURRIE 1657'. Many Scottish communion cups are engraved with the incumbent minister's initials, preceded by the letter 'M' for 'Maister' or 'Magister', denoting a master or university graduate, which all Scottish ministers were.

7.1

7.2

7.3

7.4 COMMUNION CUP
FROM BALMAGHIE PARISH, KIRKCUDBRIGHTSHIRE

Gilbert Kirkwood, Edinburgh, 1617-19

Marks (on rim): 'GK' in monogram (maker Gilbert Kirkwood); castle (Edinburgh); 'I.L.' (deacon John Lindsay, 1617-19); assay-scrape above marks, on stem and underside of foot

H 19.5 cm; D (bowl) 12 cm; D (base) 8 cm; Wt 8.12 oz

On loan to NMS from the kirk session of Balmaghie Parish Church

References: Burns (1892), p. 265; Finlay and Fothringham (1991), p. 84, pl. 28(i); RSM (1948), no. 14

Delicate V-shaped bowl on slender baluster and spool stem, trumpet foot with stamped ovolo decoration. The bowl is engraved 'P/K B MG' for 'Parish Kirk BalMaGhie' and 'M/HM' for Maister Hugh Mac-Ghie, minister of the parish 1615-38. MacGhie was a member of an important Galloway family which held the right of patronage to the parish.

Communion and Baptismal Plate from Trinity College Church, 1633

Trinity College Church in Edinburgh was originally founded as a collegiate church and hospital in *c.*1460 by Mary of Guelders, widow of King James II. After the Reformation it became the North East Parish Church of the city. The church building was never completed to its original designs and ultimately only the choir and side aisles were built: nevertheless it was still one of the finest examples of gothic architecture in Scotland until it was demolished to make way for the North British Railway in 1848. Between August 1632 and August 1633, the minister of the church organised the acquisition of a remarkable group of sacramental silver, comprising two large communion cups, two large communion wine flagons, two large bread plate basins or plates, and a baptismal laver and basin. Given that the minister, Thomas Sydserf, was a staunch follower of King Charles I's anglicizing church policies, it is probably no coincidence that this silver was acquired in time for Charles's much heralded Scottish coronation in June 1633. The silver was acquired by a combination of pious benefaction and purchase, with funds raised from the congregation.

7.4

7.5 COMMUNION CUP

FT, London, 1632-33

Marks: 'FT' (maker, possibly F. Terry); leopard's head crowned (London); lion passant (standard mark); 'P' (date-letter 1632-33)

H 20.5 cm; D (bowl) 21.1 cm; D (foot) 15.5 cm; Wt 37.10 oz (Scratch Wt on foot '37 oz')

NMS K.2001.466.1; purchased from the kirk session of Holy Trinity Church, Edinburgh with the aid of the Heritage Lottery Fund and the National Art-Collections Fund

References: Burns (1892), pp. 223-24; Finlay and Fothringham (1991), p. 87; Dalgleish and Maxwell (1987), no. 10

Large, almost hemispherical bowl set on a simple circular spool-shaped stem with central knop and a spreading stepped foot with a band of stamped ovolo decoration. The bowl is engraved with a scroll and foliate decoration and the inscription, 'For the North East Parishe', while the centre is engraved with a three-towered castle and 'NE'.

This is one of two cups given to the church on 29 August 1632 by James Roughead and John Edgar, prominent Edinburgh merchants. The session expressed their thanks for this 'maist liberall and charitabill offering'. The most extraordinary feature of these cups is that they were made in London, although they are probably the earliest extant examples of a style that was to become popular in Scotland, clearly being derived from the standing mazers of a few decades earlier. It is possible to argue that the prototype of this type of cup was the St Leonard's Mazer from St Andrew's University [3.8]. Why a London maker was commissioned to make them and the following flagons is unknown, but it may have had something to do with the wanderings of the maker of the other Trinity items, Thomas Kirkwood [see 7.6].

7.6 FLAGON

Unknown maker, London, 1632-33

Marks: escallop (unknown maker's mark); leopard's head crowned (London); lion passant (standard mark); 'P' (date-letter 1632-33)

H 40.5 cm; D (foot) 21.2 cm; Wt 85.88 oz

NMS K.2001.466.1; purchased from the kirk session of Holy Trinity Church, Edinburgh with the aid of the Heritage Lottery Fund and the National Art-Collections Fund

References: Burns (1892), pp. 223-24; Finlay and Fothringham (1991), pp. 87

Body with straight sides, moulded feet and 'cushion'-hinged lids with pierced, shaped thumb-pieces and S-scroll handles, with shaped shield terminals. Body engraved: 'IN THAT DAY THERE SHALL BE A FOVN-TAINE / OPENED TO THE HOVSE OF DAVID FOR

7.2

7.3

7.4

7.5, 6 and 7
(details below)

7.4 (detail)

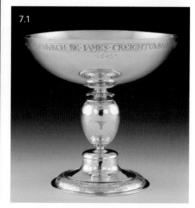

7.1

For the North East Parishe

7.8

SINNE AND FOR VNCLEANNESSE'. Engraved around top of spreading foot: 'GIFTED TO THE NORTHEAST PARISH OF EDINBVRGH BY THE CHARITIE OF SOME HONEST INDWELLERS OF THE SAME ANNO 1633'.

Another London-made piece, this is one of two flagons paid for by a subscription raised among the parishioners of Trinity College Kirk.

The maker of other elements of the Trinity silver, Thomas Kirkwood, had been apprenticed to that other great maker of church silver, Gilbert Kirkwood. A rare document, concerning a financial dispute between the two in 1636, suggests that Thomas, before he was admitted to the Incorporation in 1632, may have travelled to London to perfect his craft. It is possible that he made professional connections while there and called upon them to help him fulfil this large and urgent commission for Trinity.

7.7 BREAD BASIN

Thomas Kirkwood, Edinburgh, 1633

Marks (on upper face of rim): 'TK' conjoined (maker Thomas Kirkwood); castle (Edinburgh); 'GC' in monogram (deacon George Craufuird, 1633-35)

D 50.7 cm; H 5.5 cm; Wt 69.35 oz

NMS K.2001.466.1; purchased from the kirk session of Holy Trinity Church, Edinburgh with the aid of the Heritage Lottery Fund and the National Art-Collections Fund

Plate with wide, plain rims, simple edge mouldings, and shallow bowl, in the centre of which is a raised boss. This boss is engraved with a scene depicting a communion table set with a bread plate, two cups and two flagons, all of the same design as the actual Trinity plate; before the table kneels a praying figure with a star-shaped aura, or glory, around his head (probably representing Christ). Inside of the bowl is engraved: '. WHO . SO . EATETH . MY . FLESH . AND . DRINKETH . MY . BLOOD . HATH . ETERNAL . LIFE . AND . I . WIL . RAISE . HIM . UP . AT . THE . LAST . DAY . IOHN . 6.54 .'

Around the underside of the rim is engraved: '[flower] + THIS + BASONE + WAS + MADE + FOR + THE + NORTHEAST + PARICHE + OF + EDENBRVGH + AND + THAT + AT + THE + CHARGES + AND + BY + THE + CHARITIE + OF + SOME + HONEST + INDVELERS + OF + THE + SAME + ANNO 1633'.

This is one of two of the most remarkable pieces of Scottish church silver ever created. The central bosses are engraved with the only known representation of a Scottish communion in the 17th century, and show a table set with the elements, depicting the actual Trinity College Kirk silver set upon it – a plate with loaves of bread, two large cups, and two large flagons for the wine.

Most astonishingly, however, is the figure to the right who is kneeling to receive communion. This relates directly to an Act of Parliament held at Perth in 1618 in which James VI attempted to bring the Scottish Church more into line with the practices of the English Church, including the requirement for people to kneel to take communion. This was very unpopular with most Scottish people, as it harked back to the ways of the old Roman Catholic Mass. James's son Charles I tried to enforce it, fuelling an upsurge of resentment which led to the signing of the National Covenant in 1638 and the outbreak of civil war, which eventually resulted in the King's execution. This piece of silver is concrete evidence of those momentous historical events.

7.8 BAPTISMAL LAVER AND BASIN

Thomas Kirkwood, Edinburgh, 1633; laver remade by Walter Scott, Edinburgh 1696

Marks (basin): 'TK' conjoined (maker Thomas Kirkwood); castle (Edinburgh); 'GC' in monogram (deacon George Craufuird, 1633-35)

Marks (laver): 'WS' (maker Walter Scott); castle (Edinburgh); 'JP' in monogram (assay-master James Penman); 'X' double struck (date-letter 1702-03)

Basin: D 40 cm; H 7.5 cm; Wt 51.15

NMS K.2001.466.9 and 10; purchased from the kirk session of Holy Trinity Church, Edinburgh, with the aid of the Heritage Lottery Fund and the National Art-Collections Fund

Basin has wide rim, deep lobed bowl with elaborate central raised part-gilt boss. This boss has a plain inset top, which may be a replacement or alternation. A collar around the boss is engraved: 'I ◊ INDEED ◊ HAVE ◊ BAPTIZED ◊ YOV ◊ WITH ◊ WATER ◊ BVT ◊ HE ◊ SHALL ◊ BAPTIZE ◊ YOV ◊ [flower] / ◊ WITH ◊ THE ◊ HOLY ◊ GHOST ◊. MARKE 1 ◊ 8 ◊'. The underside of the base is engraved: 'GIFTED . TO . THE . NORTH . EAST . PARISHE . OF EDENBROVH . BY . IOHN . TROTTER . ELDER . Anno. 1633'.

7.7	7.8 (basin)	7.8 (laver)

The laver body is divided into two sets of lobed panels divided by a plain central band on which is engraved: 'GALATIANS = 3.27 = FOR = AS = MANY = OF = YOU = AS = HAVE = BEEN = BAPTIZED = INTO = CHRIST = HAVE = PUT = ON = CHRIST'. It has a hinged lobed and stepped domed cover with lobed finial; the stepped foot has a raised 'collet', possibly for locating over the boss basin; the covered spout has a heart-shaped pierced pouring hole; the S-scroll handle has a shield-shaped terminal and a scroll and beaded thumb-piece.

Although hallmarked 1702-03, the lobed design and basic style of the laver suggest it was originally made as a partner to this basin, and was extensively repaired or remade by Walter Scott at the later date.

7.9 COMMUNION CUP
FROM GREYFRIARS KIRK, EDINBURGH

Thomas Cleghorne, Edinburgh, 1633

Marks: 'TC' in monogram (maker Thomas Cleghorne); castle (Edinburgh); 'GC' (deacon George Craufuird, 1615-17, 1621-23, 1633-35)

H 22.2 cm; D (rim) 21 cm; D (base) 14.3 cm; Wt 30.42 oz

On loan to NMS from the kirk session of Greyfriars Parish Church

References: Burns (1892), pp. 222-23; Finlay and Fothringham (1991), p. 86; Dalgleish and Maxwell (1987), no. 11

Deep, almost hemispherical bowl; interior engraved with a three-towered castle from the city arms and 'FOR THE CHURCH OF THE SVTH VEST PARICH OF EDINBVRGH / + ANNO + 1633 +'; set on a tubular stem with central knop, on stepped trumpet-shaped foot, stamped with a band of ovolo decoration. One of two cups made by Thomas Cleghorne for the South West, or Greyfriars, parish in Edinburgh. The engraved date suggests they were made in the last deaconship of George Craufuird, which started in September 1633.

Stylistically they borrow directly from the Trinity College Kirk Cups [7.5], and as they were made in

the year after those cups they are probably the first Scottish examples of the large number of this type of wide-bowled mazer-like cups that predominated in the south-east of the country. The reasons for using the mazer shape are discussed above, but the sheer scale of these cups must also relate to the size and wealth of the congregations for which they were made.

7.10 TWO COMMUNION BEAKERS
FROM ELLON KIRK, ABERDEENSHIRE

Abraham van der Hoeven, Amsterdam, 1633

Walter Melville, Aberdeen, c.1642

(1) Marks: bee-hive (maker Abraham van der Hoeven, 1627-77); three 'X's crowned (Amsterdam); 'B' (date-letter 1633); assay-scrape above marks

(2) Marks: 'ABD', but badly struck (Aberdeen); 'WM' in monogram twice (maker Walter Melville); 'WA' in monogram ('tryer' William Anderson); assay-scrape above marks

(1) H 18 cm; D (rim) 11.3 cm; D (foot) 8.4 cm; Wt 10.4 oz

(2) H 18 cm; D (rim) 11.5 cm; D (foot) 8.3 cm; Wt 11.25 oz

On loan to NMS from the kirk session of Ellon Parish Church

Reference: Burns (1892), pp. 427-28

Flared cylindrical bodies, with everted rims, set on simple wire feet, with band of stamped hatched decoration above; the bodies are engraved with symmetrical bands of strap-work, foliage, flowers and swags. The decoration on the Aberdeen beaker is more naïve and less assured in execution. The engraved inscription on the Dutch beaker has 'This Coup is dedicat for the Seruic of God and communion teabell in the church of ellean by John kenedie of keairmock and his spous Janet forbes' above their arms and initials; the base is engraved 'coft from Alexander Hayus'. On the Aberdeen beaker is the inscription: 'Giuen to the kirk of Ellen be Johne Mideltowne burges and baxter in abd. Anno. 1642'.

This beaker form of communion cup was generally confined to the north-east of Scotland, and the Ellon beakers provide an absolutely cast-iron indication of where the form originated. The close economic, cultural and social links between Scotland and the Low Countries are well documented, but these beakers provide first-hand evidence of direct cultural transference from The Netherlands to Scotland.

The earlier beaker was given to the church in 1634 by a local laird, John Kennedy of Kermuck, who bought (or 'coft' in Scots) it from Alexander Hay. Hay seems to have been a mercenary in a Scots regiment that served in the Swedish army during the Thirty Years War. He saw service in The Netherlands,

7.10 (1)

7.9

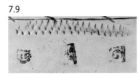

7.10 (2)

7.9

7.13

7.10

7.11

7.12

7.15

7.14

7.16

where presumably he acquired the beaker before returning to Aberdeenshire. This beaker shape was used frequently in the Low Countries as both ordinary drinking cups and as communion cups.

Just under ten year later another local parishioner, John Middleton, a baker and burgess in Aberdeen, presented the church with a second beaker. It is virtually identical in design to the Dutch beaker, but this time it was made in Aberdeen itself by the goldsmith Walter Melville, presumably copying the style directly from the existing Dutch beaker.

7.11 COMMUNION BEAKER
FROM NIGG PARISH KIRK, KINCARDINESHIRE

George Walker, Aberdeen, c.1703

H 15.7 cm; D (base) 7.5 cm; D (rim) 10.3 cm

Marks: 'GW' (maker George Walker); 'ABD' (Aberdeen); 'D' (pseudo date-letter)

Lent by Aberdeen Art Gallery and Museums Collections; purchased in 1974 with help from the Local Museums Purchase Fund

References: Burns (1892), pp. 305-06; James (1981), p. 46

Plain, flaring cylindrical body with everted rim, set on simple wire foot; band of wavy decoration (cf. Walker's thistle cups [5.5]. Engraved inscription round body: 'THIS . CUP . WITH . ITS . FELLOW . WARE . AQUYRED . OUT . OF . THE . EXTRAORDINARIE . COLLECTIONS . GOT . AT . EASTER . IN THE . CHURCH . OF . NIGG . UNDER . THE . MINISTRIE . OF . MASTER . RICHARD . MAITLAND . ANNO . 1703'. Maitland was minister of the Parish of Nigg, 1674-1716. Jacobite in his sympathies, he was deposed from his charge for praying for Prince James Edward Stuart during the 1715-16 Jacobite Rebellion. The inscription also indicates how money was raised to buy new cups when required.

The maker George Walker is recorded as having made cups for over nine local parishes.

7.12 COMMUNION BEAKER FROM
BOYNDIE PARISH KIRK, BANFFSHIRE

Patrick Scott, Banff, c.1720

Marks (on base): 'P.S' (maker Patrick Scott); crowned heart; 'P.S' (maker's mark repeated); 'BANF' (Banff)

H 14.6 cm; D (rim) 11.1 cm: D (foot) 7.2 cm; Wt 11.98 oz

Lent by Aberdeenshire Heritage; purchased by Aberdeenshire Heritage from the Parish of Whitehills, Aberdeenshire, in 2004, with the aid of grants from the National Fund for Acquisitions, Scottish Goldsmiths Trust, Banff Common Good Fund, and the Museums Association's Beecroft Bequest; a second beaker from Boyndie, by Scott of the same date, was sold at Bonham's, Edinburgh, The Scottish Sale, 21 August 2003, lot 131

Plain raised beaker body, with everted, flared rim, set on simple foot-rim of composite moulded wires; engraved (in a single line) around body: 'Dedicated to the Church of Boyndie be Iames Ogilvie of Culphin / 1720'. One of a pair commissioned by James Ogilvie of Culphin, an elder of Boyndie Parish Kirk since 1677.

7.13 THE MARY CUP FROM ST JOHN'S KIRK, PERTH

Foot, stem and lower body: Christoph I. Lindenberger, Nuremburg, c.1555-60

Cover: Robert Gardyne, Dundee, c.1640

Marks (cover): 'RG' (maker Robert Gardyne); pot of lilies (Dundee); 'RG'

H (max.) 41 cm; D (base) 11.8 cm; Wt 30.90 oz

Lent by Perth Museum and Art Gallery; purchased from the kirk session of St John's Kirk, Perth, 2003, with support from the National Art-Collections Fund, and the Heritage Lottery Fund

A composite cup, the vase-shaped lower body, stem and hexagonal foot is chased and cast in the high Renaissance manner, by Christoph Lindenberger of Nuremburg. The two-stage upper body and rim, chased and engraved with strap-work, probably dates to the late 19th century. The stepped and domed cover has a lower rim and stage stamped with foliate decoration and cast masks, surmounted by a band of ovolo stamping; the two-stage dome is engraved with flowers, birds and animals.

This is another good example of an originally secular wine cup being later pressed into service as a communion cup. Although traditionally known as 'The Mary Cup' and said to have been given to St John's before the Reformation by Mary Queen of

7.11

7.12

7.13

Scots, there is no absolute documentary evidence to support this. It is far more likely the cup belonged to a wealthy parishioner who presented it to the church in the 1630s or '40s when the church was gifted other secular plate for sacramental use.

7.14 ROSEWATER DISH OR BASIN FROM ST JOHN'S KIRK, PERTH

David Gilbert, Edinburgh, 1591-93

Marks (on rim): 'DG' conjoined (maker David Gilbert); castle (Edinburgh); 'VC' conjoined (deacon William Cokkie, 1592-93); assay-scrape above

D 46.5 cm; Wt 89.49 oz

Lent by Perth Museum and Art Gallery; purchased from the kirk session of St John's Kirk, Perth, 2003, with support from the National Art-Collections Fund, and the Heritage Lottery Fund

References: Burns (1892), p. 531; Fiona Slattery, *pers. com.*

This circular deep dished basin has a wide rim with two bands of parcel gilt stamped ovolo and foliate decoration; the raised centre has parcel gilt stepped; the domed boss has chased and stamped foliate decoration and an engraved central shield now void, but with traces of earlier arms; the rim is engraved: 'FOR THE KIRK OF PERTH ANNO 1649'.

This is one of the most important pieces of surviving Scottish silver. Originally made as a rosewater dish, presumably for a noble household, it gives some sense of the now lost heritage of early Scottish domestic silver. Over 50 years old and out of fashion by 1649, this no doubt contributed to its pious owner's decision to present it for sacramental use to the church. Although traditionally used as a baptismal basin (the last time being during the church's 750th anniversary in 1992), the term 'basin' does not necessarily mean for use with water, as the Trinity bread basins show [7.7].

7.15 COMMUNION BASIN FROM FORGUE KIRK, ABERDEENSHIRE

Nicholas Jorgensen, Canongate, *c.*1640

Marks; 'NI' in monogram; stag lodged (Canongate)

D 33 cm; Wt 26.17 oz

Lent by the kirk session of Auchaber: United Church of Scotland

Reference: Burns (1892), p. 531

Circular basin, with deep bowl, central raised boss and wide rim; the boss is engraved with the arms of Crichton of Frendraught; the rim has the inscription: 'GIFTIT . TO . GOD . AND . HIS . CHURCH . OF . FORGUE . BY . JAMES . VISCOUNT . OF FREN-DRAVGHT . LORD . CRICHTONE'.

For many years this basin was thought to be of Continental origin; Burns called it 'of foreign manu-facture'. However, the marks make it quite clear that it was made in the Canongate by Nicholas Jorgensen.

This basin is the only extant piece of Jorgensen's work and is recorded in the Turriff Presbytery records as having been given sometime before November 1643 by Lord Frendraught 'to serve the communion tables'.

James Crichton was the son of the donor of the communion cups of Forgue in 1633, and was created Viscount Frendraught in 1643.

7.16 THE FITHIE BASIN, DUNDEE

Thomas Lindsay II, Dundee, *c.*1665

Marks (on rim): 'TL' (maker Thomas Lindsay II); pot of lilies (Dundee); maker's mark repeated

D 48 cm; D (boss) 16.5 cm; H 4.5 cm; W (rim) 7.2 cm; Wt 61.47 oz

Lent by Dundee City Council (McManus Galleries and Museum)

Reference: Finlay and Fothringham (1991), p. 116, pl. 37(i)

Circular basin, with plain rim engraved with arcading and trifid corbels; raised central boss engraved with inscription: '◊ IOHANES ◊ FITHEVS ◊ IN ◊ AMORIS ◊ TESSERAM ◊ ECCLESIÆ ◊ TAODVNENSI ◊ AD ◊ SACRAM // CÆNAM ◊ CELEBRANDAM ◊ VAS ◊ HOC ◊ ARGENTVM ◊ DONO ◊ DEDIT ◊ 1665'. This sur-rounds a contemporary coat of arms presumably for John Fithie, a merchant burgess of Dundee.

This magnificent communion basin, or bread plate, has led something of a charmed life. It was given to the Burgh Church of Dundee 'for the use of the Com-munion Table' on 28 March 1665 by John Fithie, a merchant in the town. In January 1841, along with other communion silver, it was saved from a fire which destroyed the church.

This is an important dated piece of the work of a talented maker, Thomas Lindsay II.

7.14

7.15

7.16

7.17

7.17 COMMUNION CUP
FROM INCHBRAYOCK KIRK, FORFARSHIRE

William Lindsay I, Montrose, *c*.1682

Marks (below inscription): rose (Montrose); 'WL', with crowned hammer above (maker William Lindsay I); rose (Montrose repeated)

H 16.5 cm; D (bowl) 13.2 cm; D (foot) 12.3 cm; Wt 13.2 oz

Lent by Montrose Museum and Art Gallery

Provenance: purchased from the kirk session of Inchbrayock in 1991, one of two cups, the other purchased by a private individual at Sotheby's sale, London, 17 November 1988, lot 57

Reference: Burns (1892), p. 397

Wide, flaring bowl, with baluster and knop stem on spreading foot; the rim is chased with winged cherub heads and flowers; the bowl is expertly engraved with arms and crest for Turnbull, set within extravagant, plumed mantling and the inscription: 'DONUM PETRI TURNBULL DE STRACATHRO, IN VSVM SACRAE COENAE ET POPVLI DE INCH-BREAK'.

The donor of this very fine cup, Peter Turnbull of Stracathro, was a bailie of the Burgh of Montrose and an elder of the parish church there.

Maker William Lindsay I's distinctive mark, with the crowned hammer, is also found on a fine silver-mounted pistol [see 5.67], and on the cups from Forfar and Bervie.

7.17

The Holyrood Altar Plate

Roman Catholic sacramental silver from before the 19th century in Scotland is exceptionally rare. Remarkably, a group of altar vessels commissioned for King James VII's chapel at Holyrood in Edinburgh survives, and among it are items by Scottish makers.

In 1687 James VII created a Chapel Royal for Catholic worship in the palace of Holyroodhouse. The furnishing of it was the responsibility of his fellow Catholic, the Earl of Perth. Perth had a full suite of silver altar plate made in London and sent up via Leith to Holyrood in December 1686. Once in Edinburgh, it was deemed necessary to add a locally-made sanctus bell and incense spoon to the London-made pieces, which included a monstrance for displaying the host, a thurible or incense burner, a ciborium for containing the Host, and a chalice and paten.

James VII's Roman Catholicism was immensely unpopular with most Scots and ultimately led to his deposition and replacement by the Protestant William of Orange and his wife Queen Mary in 1688-89. James's Chapel Royal did not survive this religious and dynastic regime change, and was ransacked by the Edinburgh mob in December 1688. However, some of the silver altar plate did survive, having been rescued by one of the resident chaplains, David Burnett, who escaped with it to Banffshire where he was sheltered by the Duke of Gordon. The altar plate remained hidden in the area at Presholme, and in 1702 was donated to the Scottish Catholic Mission by James VII's widow. The plate remained in the north-east until 1802, when the monstrance, thurible and incense boat were sent down for use by the exiled French Royal family who were lodging in Holyroodhouse. These pieces remained in Edinburgh, ending up in 1834 in the newly-founded St Margaret's Convent. The pieces that remained in the north-east eventually came under the care of the Scottish Roman Catholic hierarchy in Aberdeen. Both of these bodies agreed to reunite the Holyrood Altar Plate in 1967, when both groups were placed on long-term loan in what became the National Museums Scotland.

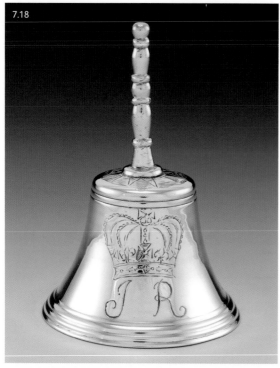

7.18 SANCTUS BELL

Zacharius Mellinus, Edinburgh, 1686-87

Marks (on sound bow): 'ZM' (maker Zacharius Mellinus); castle (Edinburgh); 'IB' in monogram (assay-master John Borthwick); 'f' (date-letter 1686-87)

H 12 cm; D (sound bow) 7.9 cm; Wt 6.32 oz

NMS IL.2003.47.8; on loan to NMS from the Scottish Roman Catholic Hierarchy

References: Dalgleish and Maxwell (1987), no. 21; MacRoberts and Oman (1968), pp. 285-95

Of traditional hand-bell shape, with moulding wires and spool and baluster handles; the body is engraved with a crowned 'IR' for King James VII.

7.19 INCENSE SPOON

Walter Scott, Edinburgh, c.1686-87

Marks: 'WS' (maker Walter Scott)

L 10.2 cm; Wt 0.30 oz

NMS IL.2003.47.4; on loan to NMS from St Margaret's Convent, Edinburgh

Reference: MacRoberts and Oman (1968), pp. 285-95

Small trifid-end spoon, with vestigial rat-trail drop, end engraved with an earl's coronet, presumably for James Drummond, Earl of Perth, who commissioned the Holyrood Altar Plate at the behest of James VII.

7.20 THE FORSYTH CHALICE AND PATEN

Zacharius Mellinus, Edinburgh, c.1688

Mark (on chalice foot): 'ZM' (maker Zacharius Mellinus)

Chalice: H 19.7 cm; D (rim) 7.5 cm; D (base) 11.6 cm; Wt 10.39 oz

Paten: D 11.6 cm; Wt 1.85 oz

NMS IL.2003.47.9 and 10; on loan to NMS from the Scottish Roman Catholic Hierarchy

Reference: MacRoberts and Oman (1968), pp. 285-95

Chalice has a small deep bowl on baluster stem with trumpet and cushion foot; stem and foot chased with acanthus leaves. The paten of circular dished form; the centre engraved 'IHS' with cross and scratched 'S.H. IMP. ORA PRO BENEF. VIV. ET. DEFUNCTIS 24 JUNII. A.D. 1688. H.F.S.I' around the rim.

Made in 1688 for Father Henry Forsyth, a Gaelic-speaking Jesuit missionary priest, who used them in ministering to the Catholic community around Braemar and Balmoral until his death in 1708. They seem to have been preserved at Presholme along with the Holyrood Altar Plate.

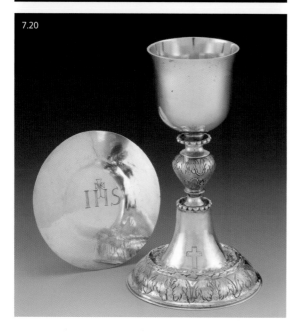

7.21 BAPTISMAL LAVER AND BASIN FROM MEIGLE

James Cockburn, Edinburgh, 1693-94

Marks (on laver, below rim, to right of handle; and on rim of basin): 'IC' in monogram (maker James Cockburn); castle (Edinburgh); 'IB' in monogram (assay-master John Borthwick); 'N' (date-letter 1693-94)

Laver: H 20.5 cm; D (lip) 12.8 cm; D (foot) 9.8 cm; L (over lip and handle) 22.3 cm; Wt 22.33 oz

Basin: D 39.4 cm; H 5.6 cm; W (rim) 5.6 cm; Wt 40.74 oz

Lent from a private collection at Mount Stuart

Provenance: private collection until sold to present collection, 1931

Reference: Exhibition at Hammond Museum (1969)

Laver is on plain domed foot with gadrooned flange, the lower part of the helmet-shaped body applied with a broad band of foliate cut-card work, with applied girdle above the inscription. Plain everted and caulked rim, with shaped open spout, S-scroll handle of angular section with headed rat-tails top and bottom and applied cut-card work highlighting the joins; with cushion and button thumb-piece. Inscription reads: 'HONORABILIS DOMINUS, DOMINUS DAVID KINLOCH DE / EODEM, EqES ET BARONET HOC GUTTURNIUM / ECCLESIAE DE MEGIL DONO DEDIT IN USUM ET / EXEMPLUM 22 DIE NOVEMBRIS MDCXCIII ◊.' The donor was Sir David Kinloch of Kinloch, 1st Baronet, created by James VII in 1685. He was one of the principal heritors of the parish.

The basin is of deep dish form, the plain rim with wide simple moulding; inscription around rim reads: 'VIR GENEROSUS ANDREAS GRAY HOC LAVACRVM ECCLESIAE DE MEGIL IN USUM ET EXEMPLUM DONO DEDIT 22 DIE NOVEMBRIS MDCXCIII'. The identity of the donor, Andrew Gray, has not yet been established, but he is assumed to have been a heritor of the parish.

The inscriptions on both vessels are remarkable for their initial letters, 'H' and 'V', each of which is elaborately engraved in a square cartouche surrounded by foliage, much in the manner of a wood-cut block. This is a rare treatment which we have not seen elsewhere on Scottish silver of this date.

7.22 COMMUNION CUP FROM BOLTON PARISH KIRK, EAST LOTHIAN

George Ziegler, Canongate, c.1696

Marks (on rim): stag's head twice (Canongate); 'G.Z' twice (maker George Ziegler)

H 17.5 cm; D (rim) 16.7 cm; D (base) 12.7 cm; Wt 14.27 oz (Scratch Wt on foot '14 on 11 dr')

NMS H.KJ 318; purchased from the kirk session of Bolton and Saltoun Church, 1985 (one of two cups, the other purchased by City of Edinburgh Museums and Galleries)

References: Burns (1892), p. 367; Finlay and Fothringham (1991), p. 115, pl. 35(i)

Wide shallow bowl on slender baluster and spool stem, with plain spreading, stepped foot; outside of bowl engraved 'FOR THE CHURCH OF BOLTON'; underside of foot engraved with initials 'M/IS' (Maister John Sinclair, minister of the parish) and 'GB:PB:IB: AY:DS:WS:WS:DG: DF:WS' for members of the kirk session of the time.

These cups seem to be replacements for, or remade from, two cups originally acquired by the kirk in 1670. The session minutes give an interesting insight into the acquisition and status of church plate in general. The money for the original cups was taken from the surplus in the Poor Fund with the injunction that 'if the extream necessities of the poor did call for it, they should be sold again for their use'. The cups were clearly not seen as being in any way inviolably sacred and, like domestic plate, could be converted into cash as and when required. These early cups were indeed melted down and George Ziegler was paid £29 10s 6d Scots for 'casting the communion cup of new'. The term 'casting' here is not strictly accurate in the technical sense, as the cups are both hammered and cast.

7.23 COMMUNION CUP FROM WEST LINTON PARISH KIRK, MIDLOTHIAN

David Dunlop, Canongate, 1702

Marks (inside bowl, around centre point): 'DD' twice (maker David Dunlop); 'S' gothic (cf. Edinburgh date-letter 1698-99); stag's head (Canongate)

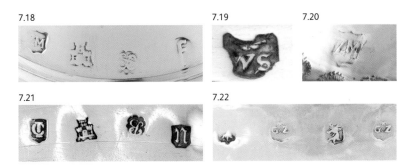

7.18   7.19   7.20

7.21   7.22

H 16.7 cm; D (bowl) 16.2 cm; D (foot) 9.4 cm; Wt 10 oz

Lent by the kirk session of St Andrew's Parish Church, West Linton

Reference: Burns (1892), pp. 368-69, erroneously attributed to George Ziegler

Wide shallow bowl on baluster stem, stepped plain trumpet foot; rim of bowl engraved: 'In Ecclesiam Lintonensem 1702'. One of two cups made by David Dunlop in the Canongate for West Linton Kirk. Dunlop first makes an appearance in the Hammermen's records there in 1701 (admitted as burgess on 18 September in same year). It is not know to whom he was apprenticed, but he was probably working before he first appears in the records, as the West Linton Cups also have a pseudo date-letter indicating they were possibly made in 1698-99.

Another example of goldsmiths in burghs outside the capital trying to follow national legislation regarding date-letters (p. 88). The marks are of interest in the understanding of the mechanism of how churches acquired plate. In many cases cups were undoubtedly made to commission. However this might not be the case with the West Linton Cups. The stamped date-letter suggests they were made in 1698-99, while the engraved date on the bowl suggests they were acquired by the church three years later in 1702. The year of acquisition is confirmed by session records, which state that on 2 April 1702 'the session now having money in our hands it was proper to buy therewith two silver cups for the communion'.

Unfortunately there is no record as to why or how David Dunlop in the Canongate was chosen, but the goldsmith may have already had them 'in stock' in 1702 and simply sold them to the minister.

7.24 COMMUNION CUP
FROM STOW PARISH KIRK, MIDLOTHIAN

John Rollo, Edinburgh, 1733

Marks (on rim): 'IR' (maker John Rollo); castle (Edinburgh); 'AU' (assay-master Archibald Ure); 'F' (date-letter 1736)

H 25.5 cm; D (bowl) 12.3 cm; D (foot) 11.1 cm; Wt 12.29 oz

NMS H.1994.715; purchased from the kirk session of Stow St Mary of Wedale and Heriot Parish Church

Reference: Burns (1892), pp. 254-55

Deep, bell-shaped bowl set on knopped tubular stem and plain spreading stepped foot; inscribed 'These

two Sacramental Cups were Gifted to the / Parioch of Stow by the Revd. Mr. James Douglas / Minister of the Gospell there from Anno. 1693 when / he was admitted till Anno. 1732 when he deceased, and / presented to the Kirk Session by Jean Allan his Relict 1736'.

John Rollo's Account Book records payment for these cups on 18 June 1736, from a 'Mrs Douglas Relick of Mr Douglas Minister for Stow', for 'two Communion Cupps wt 25 oz ... 2 drop att 7sh 6 per oz ... £9 : 7s : 6d'. 'Ingraving' cost '7s : 8d', and the box five shillings. The total came to '£10 _s 2d'.

7.25 COMMUNION CUP
FROM ST MICHAEL'S KIRK, DUMFRIES

David Coutts, Dumfries, c.1753

Mark: 'DC' (maker David Coutts)

Lent by the kirk session of St Michael's Church, Dumfries

Reference: Dobie (n.d.), p. 13

One of two cups, with deep U-shaped bowl with everted rim, with an acorn baluster stem set on a plain stepped trumpet foot; the body later engraved 'St Michael's Church / Dumfries'. Of a style common throughout Scotland in the second half of the 18th century, they were originally quite plain, with the inscription not added until July 1849, as recorded in the session minutes. However, they represent a far older tradition, being remade from much earlier cups that were 'rent and much decayed'. David Coutts, who had only been admitted as a goldsmith burgess in March 1753, was paid £3 6s 5d for them on 26 November of the same year. They are the oldest surviving examples of Dumfries-made silver.

7.26 COMMUNION CUP
FROM TRON KIRK, GLASGOW

David Warnock, Glasgow, 1762

Marks (underside of bowls): 'D.W' (David Warnock); Glasgow mark in oval punch; 'D.W'; 'S' in rectangular punch

(1) H 20.9 cm; D (rim) 11.4 cm; D (base) 10.6 cm

NMS H.1993.632; one of two, purchased from the kirk session of St George's Tron Parish Church, Glasgow, 1993; two others were purchased by St Mungo's Museum of Religion, Glasgow

7.24   7.25   7.26

7.21

...IR GENEROSUS ANDREAS GRA...

7.21

7.21 (details left)

7.22

7.24

7.26

7.27

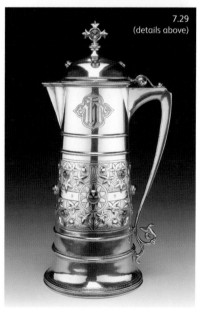

7.29
(details above)

Squat, almost straight-sided tapering bowls, baluster and knop stem on spreading, stepped foot. The inside of the bowl is gilded. The bowls are engraved with 'Donation by the Trustees of Bailie Robt: Tennants Mortification'; and the arms of Glasgow, i.e. tree, fish, bell and bird, within a cartouche signed 'IR / Sculp', with 'LET GLASGOW FLOURISH' in a ribbon above and 'MDCCLXII' in a ribbon below.

Maker David Warnock was admitted as a master of the Glasgow Hammermen in 1756, and was still in business in 1777. He made many cups for parishes in and around Glasgow, in a similar style to this.

The Tron Cup is unusual in that it has its very fine engraving signed by the artist 'IR': proof that by the middle of the 18th century goldsmiths were employing specialist engravers to finish off their vessels.

7.27 COMMUNION CUP
FROM TIBBERMORE KIRK, PERTHSHIRE

James Cornfute, Perth, 1790

Marks (on foot-rim): double-headed eagle twice (Perth); 'IC' twice (maker James Cornfute); marks (underside of foot): castle (Edinburgh); thistle (standard mark); 'J' (date-letter 1789-90)

H 27 cm; D (rim) 12.7 cm; Wt 15.99 oz

Lent by the kirk session of Tibbermore Parish Church, via Perth Museum and Art Gallery

Deep bowl on slender baluster stem, set on spreading, stepped and beaded foot; the bowl engraved 'Kirk of Tibbermore / 1790'. This style of cup became common in the late 18th and early 19th centuries.

7.28 ALMS PLATE
FROM ST PAUL'S CHURCH, ABERDEEN

George Jamieson & Sons, Aberdeen, hallmarked Sheffield, 1881-82

Marks (on rim): 'GJ&S' (maker George Jamieson & Sons); crown (Sheffield); lion passant (sterling standard mark); 'O' (date-letter 1881-82); queen's head (duty mark); 'ABDN.' (Aberdeen)

D 35.8 cm; Wt 46.16 oz

On loan to NMS from the Synod of the Diocese of Aberdeen and Orkney of the Episcopal Church in Scotland

{opposite page}

7.28 ALMS PLATE FROM ST PAUL'S CHURCH, ABERDEEN, 1881-82

Circular plate with dished centre and wide rim; centre engraved with the sacred monogram 'IHS' in a quatrefoil. The base of the plate is engraved: '1882 / Made / From the Silver of Two Cups / and Two Plates / which were / Presented to St Paul's Church / in / 1757'.

This plate perfectly illustrates one reason for the disappearance of much early church silver. Like other domestic plate, once old pieces were either too damaged or old fashioned for use they were handed over to a goldsmith and converted into a newer, more usable item. This plate is particularly heavy and no doubt used all the silver from the two older cups and plates.

7.29 COMMUNION CUP, PATEN AND FLAGON
FROM ST PAUL'S EPISCOPAL CHURCH, EDINBURGH

G. & M. Crichton, Edinburgh, 1880-81

Marks: queen's head (duty mark); thistle (standard mark); 'G&MC' (makers G. & M. Crichton); castle (Edinburgh); 'Y' (date-letter 1880-81)

Flagon: H 33.5; D (foot) 13.6 cm; L (max.) 16 cm

Cup: H 21.2 cm; D (rim) 9.8 cm; D (foot) 13.5 cm

Paten: D 21.5 cm; Wt 6.46 oz

NMS H.KJ 224, 226 and 229; purchased from St Paul's & St George's Episcopal Church of Scotland, Edinburgh, in 1975

Silver-gilt flagon with tapering cylindrical body, with band of chased and engraved vine-leaf scroll and strapwork decoration, set with cabochon garnets; two shaped panels are engraved with the Sacred monogram 'IHS' and the Lamb of God; domed hinged lid with wheel-head cross finial. Cup of chalice form on spreading octagonal foot, knopped stem, with small bowl; all decorated with bands of chased and engraved foliage, set with cabochon garnets. Plain circular dished paten, the centre engraved with the Sacred Monogram 'IHS'.

Part of a matching set of two cups, three patens and a flagon, given to St Paul's Episcopal Church in Edinburgh by Sir David Anderson of Moredun in 1881. The ornate 'neo-gothic' design was in keeping with the then current vogue for looking back to the Church's medieval past, promoted within the Church of England, and to a lesser extent the Episcopal Church in Scotland by the 'high' church Oxford Movement.

7.27

7.28

7.29

Ceremonial and Presentation Silver

8

Introduction

Silver and gold, as precious metals, have been used for symbols of authority, and for objects that added prestige to ceremonial occasions from the earliest times. Among the earliest references to Scottish ceremonial gold and silver is in an inventory of what was taken by Edward I from Edinburgh Castle in 1291. No crown is mentioned, but he took an object called 'Aaron's Rod', probably the Scottish Sceptre in the form of a silver-gilt caduceus, as depicted in the hands of David I in the famous illumination of him with his son, Malcolm, on the foundation Charter of Kelso Abbey.

Other early accounts include several crowns, sceptres and regalia for different kings and queens, none of which has survived. The earliest items now remaining are the Honours of Scotland, consisting of the Crown, Sceptre and Sword of State. The Sword is of Italian workmanship and was given to James IV by Pope Julius in 1507. The Sceptre was originally also a papal gift, but was refashioned and augmented by Adam Leys, in Edinburgh, for James V in *c.*1540. The Crown in its present form dates from the same period, having been refashioned by James Mosman from an earlier one, the arches added by Adam Leys. The Crown is the oldest in Great Britain, pre-dating the English regalia by 120 years, and is one of the oldest in Europe.

The staff, misidentified by Sir Walter Scott as the Lord Treasurer's Mace and now kept with the Honours, is not a mace at all but a sceptre. It was made in London by Francis Garthorne. The most likely explanation is that it is the sceptre used by James, Duke of York, when he was in Edinburgh as Lord High Commissioner in the 1680s. He may have used it to touch the Acts of Parliament and Privy Council to give them the royal approval. However, there are medieval maces in Scotland that pre-date anything remaining in the Honours: those associated with the ancient Universities of St Andrews and Glasgow.

Maces belonging to universities take their origin not from the weapons of war of the same name, but from verges which are of church origin. The word used is *virga*, a verge or staff. The maces of the University of St Andrews were made to be carried before the deans of the respective faculties in religious and ceremonial processions as symbols of their authority, hence the form they take is an overtly ecclesiastical one. They resemble the staff portion of a crosier without its crook. The University of St Andrews was founded in 1413 by a Bull of Pope Benedict XIII, during the Great Schism which had begun in 1378. Scotland's allegiance to the Avignon popes cut her off for a time from most European countries, who

*... ane fair mase
to be bourne
befoir the
Provost ...*

{EDINBURGH
BURGH RECORDS: 1616}

{opposite page}
8.26 THE NEILL VASE, 1843-44

adhered to the pope in Rome. As a result, would-be students could no longer go abroad to study. Thus a Scottish university was required to make provision for their needs. In the United Kingdom only the Universities of Oxford and Cambridge are older than that of St Andrews.

Scotland reverted to allegiance with Rome in 1418, the year in which the earliest mace was made. The two earliest St Andrews' Maces [8.1 and 8.2] are among the oldest university maces in Europe and are of outstanding importance for the study of 15th-century silver in Scotland. There is a large amount of documentation, not all conclusive, which mentions the existence of the maces, beginning within a few years of when they were made. Dr Helen Rawson has recently completed a review and study of all the relevant documents, and we are indebted to her for allowing us to read her paper prior to publication.[1] All the available evidence seems to confirm that the earlier mace, which pertains to the Faculty of Arts, is the one which is commonly called the 'French' Mace; and that the later one, which pertains to the Faculty of Canon Law, was almost certainly made in Scotland, using the 'French' Mace as its model.[2]

Maces still perform the same function as they did in medieval times and are part of an ongoing tradition. One of the most significant new commissions in recent years was the mace for the new Scottish Parliament made by Michael Lloyd in 1999. Curiously, this is actually an innovation for the Scottish Parliament, as the pre-Union Parliament, unlike that of England, does not seem to have had a ceremonial mace. The Honours of Scotland served to lend authority to the sitting of Parliament, and although maces were carried in the official procession, or 'riding', when the members processed up the High Street of Edinburgh to the Parliament Hall, these were 'borrowed' for the occasion from the City of Edinburgh [see 8.3] and the Law Courts.[3]

Surviving ceremonial plate displays a fascinating variety; from the unique little gold vial or ampulla used in the Scottish coronation of Charles I [8.9], the only piece of the Scottish Crown Jewels not still in the possession of the Crown, to the remarkable and no less unique Glasgow civic trumpets [8.10, 8.11].

Presentation plate was used for both reward and recognition in many spheres of pubic and private life. Academic excellence, rewards for political services rendered, and commemorations of martial endeavours, did not always simply take the form of the ubiquitous medal. The celebration of economic and agricultural improvement of the later 18th and 19th centuries produced some of the most spectacular examples of the goldsmith's art, the exuberance of which was entirely in keeping with the spirit of optimism and enterprise that lay at the bottom of many such schemes. There were also the simple, often highly personal expressions of thanks, gratitude or affection that have always provided silversmiths and goldsmiths with a large percentage of their livelihoods, whether it be that universal symbol of friendship in 18th-century Scotland, the snuff mull, or something much more uniquely personal such as a silver model of a boat to acknowledge a humanitarian sea rescue [8.19].

Notes

1   Dr Helen Rawson, PhD thesis (2007), unpublished.
2   Henry Steuart Fothringham has an apology to make concerning a misleading statement he made inadvertently in Finlay and Fothringham (1991), p. 37. It had not been his intention to suggest that the 'Scottish' mace was earlier than the 'French' one; his error was to confuse the order in which the Faculties were established, not the order in which the maces were made; this was due to the order in which they are dealt with by Ian Finlay in his original text. Let us hope that this confusion and muddle may now be allowed to pass below the horizon of receding history.
3   Dalgleish, in McCracken-Flesher (ed.) (2007), pp. 129-40.

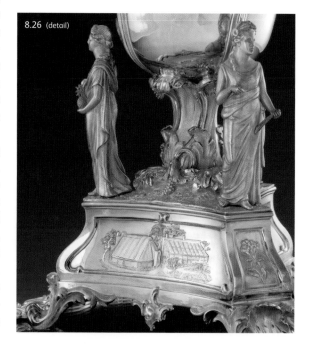

8.26 (detail)

Maces

8.1 MACE OF THE FACULTY OF ARTS, UNIVERSITY OF ST ANDREWS

Probably French, unmarked, c.1418-19

L 128.3 cm

Lent by the University of St Andrews Museum's Collection

Silver, parcel-gilt, the shaft with two wrythen knops, a swirled foot, and fitted with a wooden core. The hexagonal head is in three tiers consisting of gothic windows above, panels depicting saints in the middle and six angels below, each one bearing a shield with a coat of arms. The saints and shields still show traces of enamelling. The arms are those of the King of Scots, Archbishop Spottiswood, Bishop Wardlaw, the Earl of Mar, the Earl of Douglas, and the Duke of Albany, which fixes the date of the shields as no later than 1420 when Robert, Duke of Albany, died. The arms of Archbishop Spottiswood (Chancellor of the University, 1615-39) must have replaced a previous coat of arms in that position. It is certainly of different manufacture from the other shields and, unlike them, has never been enamelled.

It appears that this mace, though made mostly abroad by a French or possibly Flemish goldsmith, was actually brought to St Andrews to be completed. The elements which are most likely to have been done last were probably the enamelled coats of arms, for which some local knowledge would have been necessary in order to render them accurately. On 18 December 1419 a goldsmith called Robert, described as a citizen of St Andrews, was witness to a summons issued by the Abbey of Inchcolm (on the island of that name in the Firth of Forth). It is tempting to speculate whether or not this Robert may have been the Frenchman or Fleming who had recently come to St Andrews to complete the mace; perhaps he had remained there, becoming a Scottish national and taking up burgess-ship in the burgh. However, it is all mere speculation at this stage and Robert's name has not been found in any other source.

8.2 MACE OF THE FACULTY OF CANON LAW, UNIVERSITY OF ST ANDREWS

Apparently Scottish, unmarked, c.1437-57

L 125.4 cm

Lent by the University of St Andrews Museum's Collection

Silver, parcel-gilt; shaft with two knops, spreading foot, and fitted with a wooden core. The hexagonal head, clearly in imitation of the earlier mace, has a similar three-tiered arrangement of windows above, saints in the middle and angels below. In this case, however, they are not holding coats of arms. It seems clear that there were originally coats of arms to match those of the Arts Mace, but these have been removed. The halo of one of the angels has clearly been renewed at some time. On its back is stamped the mark of Patrick Gardyne, goldsmith in St Andrews in the mid-17th century. It appears from this that Gardyne was responsible for renewing the halo, and possibly for other work on the mace.

Finlay said of this mace that it is the 'first piece of medieval silverwork for the native Scots authorship of which a good case has been made out'. The head is noticeably larger than on the earlier mace, and although the workmanship appears less assured it is perfectly competent. It has, in fact, a more immediate and appealing effect than its more proficiently-made predecessor.

8.3 MACE OF THE CITY OF EDINBURGH

George Robertson I, Edinburgh, 1617-18

Marks (repeated on inner plate of head, outside of lower bell of head and on lower section of shaft): 'GR' (maker George Robertson); castle (Edinburgh); 'GC' (deacon George Crawfuird 1615-17)

L 101 cm; W (across arches) 10.5 cm; D (knop) c.9 cm; Wt 142 oz

Lent by the City of Edinburgh Council

Crown-headed mace with two-part baluster shaft, with engraved base knop; the head is supported by four scroll and caryatid figures and is applied with four moulded wire roundels – two containing applied cast representations of a three-towered castle (Edinburgh's arms), and two containing applied cast representations of a crowned thistle between the Royal initials 'I R'. Upper band of the head is applied with

8.3

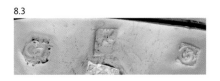

163

cast representations of a rose, a thistle, a harp and a fleur-de-lis; the crown rises from a band of moulded inverted arcading, with crosses *patée* and fleur-de-lis; the four-arched open-work crown supports an orb surmounted by a cross *patée*. Inside the head of the mace is an applied cast of the Royal Arms of James VI, and the back-plate is engraved 'I R6 / In Defence' in a ribbon above, and 'DIEU ET MON DROIT / 1617' in a ribbon below.

It is not known when a mace was first used as a symbol of civic dignity in Edinburgh, but there is a reference to a 'Macer' as a burgh official as early as February 1554. The present mace is the earliest of this type of 'bell-head' civic mace in Scotland and, unlike the ecclesiastical maces, seems to derive from the original weapon of war. It is the finest example in Scotland and a masterwork of the maker George Robertson, a young goldsmith who had only just been admitted to the Incorporation when he received the commission from the Council to 'mak ane fair mase to be bourne befoir the Proveist, of ten pund wecht of silver and to caus mak the same partiall gilt' on 18 December 1616. The mace had to be ready for King James VI's visit to the city on 25 May 1617; indeed it was carried during the official celebrations of the visit. The city treasurer's accounts show Robertson was paid £833 6s 6d for the mace, which weighed 159 ounces. The mace continues to this day to be 'borne before the Provost' and Council when they attend church and other ceremonial duties.

8.4 MACE OF KING'S COLLEGE, ABERDEEN

Walter Melville, Aberdeen, c.1650

Marks (on head): 'WM' conjoined (maker Walter Melville); 'ABD' (Aberdeen); 'WA' in monogram ('tryer' William Anderson); central knop of shaft embossed with 'Waltervs Melvil Fecit Anno 1650'

L 95 cm; Wt 55 oz

Lent by the University of Aberdeen

References: Maxwell and Dalgleish (2000), pp. 218-22; A. J. S. Brook (1891-92), pp. 492-95

Bell-head form with an imperial crown of four beaded arches supporting an orb and cross; the bowl is closed by a circular plate embossed with the Stuart Royal Arms as used in Scotland and 'God Save the King'

below. The bowl has two embossed cartouches bearing a pot of lilies (the earliest arms of the college) and the arms of the founder Bishop Elphinstone. The head is supported on a plain cylindrical shaft with two chased knops and terminating in a domed finial enriched with chased acanthus leaves.

It is possibly no coincidence the King's College Mace was, like the City of Edinburgh's Mace, made in time for a royal visit, this time that of Charles II to Aberdeen on 7 July 1650, or after his coronation on 25 February 1651. These were troubled times for the monarchy, with Oliver Cromwell leading a successful invasion of Scotland. The inclusion of the inscription 'God Save the King' (unusual on other maces) is perhaps indicative of the strength of royalist support in Aberdeen. Melville probably followed the design of an earlier King's College mace, described in an inventory of 1542 as 'the Rector's Mace of silver with the arms of the King and the Founder'.

8.5 MACE OF THE UNIVERSITY OF EDINBURGH

William Davie, Edinburgh, 1789-90

Marks (in line near rim of mace head): 'WD' script (maker William Davie); castle (Edinburgh); thistle (standard mark); 'I' (date-letter 1789-90); king's head (duty mark); marks, excepting maker's mark, repeated (much rubbed) on underside of upper knop

L (max.) 71 cm; L (head) 21 cm; D (coronet) 11.5 cm; Wt 33.3 oz

Lent by the University of Edinburgh

Reference: A. J. S. Brook (1891-92), pp. 498-501

Of bell-head form with four-arched crown, springing from coronet cresting comprising alternating crosses *patée* and fleur-de-lis and surmounted by an orb and ball; the body of the head with four roundels defined by moulded wires, the centres chased with (1) the arms of the City of Edinburgh; (2) the (newly matriculated) arms of the University of Edinburgh; (3) a crowned thistle with 'I R VI'; (4) the engraved inscription 'NOVA HAC CLAVA ARGENTEA ACADEMIAM SUAM DONAVIT SENATUS EDINBURGENSIS CONSULE THO. ELDER PRAETOR ACADEMICO GUL. CREECH, AD 1789'. The head is closed with a domed plate which is engraved with the Royal Arms of George III; the shaft of the mace is baluster-shaped and divided by a central knop, the halves chased with acanthus leaf decoration; the base finial is a stepped domed knop, chased with acanthus leaves; the shaft is connected to the head by means of a spool and knop, chased with foliate decoration.

The town's college certainly had a mace, to be carried before the Rector, as 'ane ensigne of his office',

8.4   8.5

8.1

8.2

8.7

8.3 (details below)

8.4 (details below)

8.1

8.2

8.5 (details below)

by 1640. This early mace was stolen on the night of 29 October 1787. The city magistrates immediately offered a ten-guinea reward for the apprehension of the culprits. When this failed to produce a result, the City Council presented the University with this new mace on 2 October 1789. It has been suggested that the Council were so anxious about this because public opinion at the time linked the theft of the old mace with one of their own members, the notorious William Brodie as Deacon of the Incorporation of Wrights and Masons. Brodie was later caught, tried and then executed for burglary in August 1788.

8.6 PORTRAIT OF PRINCIPAL WILLIAM ROBERTSON (1721-93)

Henry Raeburn, 1792

H 127 cm; W 102 cm / Oil on canvas

Lent by the University of Edinburgh

William Robertson, historian and leader of the Moderate Party in the Church of Scotland, was Principal of Edinburgh University at the time when the new mace was commissioned by the Town Council, and chose to be depicted with it as a symbol of his office in this fine painting by Sir Henry Raeburn. Curiously, both sitter and artist had strong connections with the goldsmiths' craft. Robertson, who was related to the Adam family of architects, was the brother of Patrick Robertson, goldsmith in Edinburgh. Raeburn (1756-1823), an orphan in Heriot's Hospital, intended to become a goldsmith, and was originally apprenticed to James Gilliland on 27 June 1772. At some point he switched careers, and went on to become one of Scotland's best-known portrait painters.

8.7 RECTOR'S MACE OF THE UNIVERSITY OF ST ANDREWS

Donald Wintersgill, Edinburgh, 2003

Marks: 'DW' (maker Donald Wintersgill); '925' (sterling standard mark); lion rampant (sterling standard mark); castle (Edinburgh) 'C' (date-letter 2003)

L 129 cm

Lent by the University of St Andrews

Ebonised wooden staff or verge, with two knops and a finial applied with symbols of the University; the cast and chased silver head in the form of a medieval monk, to represent Laurence of Lindores (1373-1437), the first Rector of the University.

Designed, made and donated to the University by Glasgow-born silversmith Donald Wintersgill, this is the latest mace in St Andrew's long tradition, upholding its reputation for finely-designed and made pieces.

Ceremonial Plate

8.8 SEAL BOX

George Cunningham, Canongate, c.1605

Marks (inside both sections): 'GC' (maker George Cunningham); stag lodged (Canongate town mark); 'XI.D' ('Eleven penny', standard mark)

D 13 cm; H 1.5 cm; Wt 9.7 oz

NMS A.L.419; lent anonymously

Silver-gilt seal box, in two halves; one engraved with the Royal Arms of James VI and I as used in England, surrounded by the mottos 'In * Defence' and 'Honni * Soit * Qvi * Male * Pense'; the other engraved with full arms and initials 'I/G/M' for John Graham, Earl of Montrose, surrounded by two lines of inscription:

8.6

8.7

'Iohne * Eril * of * Montrois * Lord Grahame &
Mvgdok / Heigh * Chancellor * of * Scotland * Anno
Do 1604'. The two halves have slits for the seal cords.

This box held the wax impression of the Great
Seal of King James VI and I, affixed to a document
appointing John, 3rd Earl of Montrose, High Commissioner for His Majesty in Scotland. Wishing to replace
Montrose as Chancellor of Scotland with the Earl of
Dunfermline, James gave him this empty but nomi-
nally higher dignity of commissionership as a sop.

8.9 GOLD CORONATION AMPULLA OF CHARLES I

Unmarked, possibly by James Denneistoun, Edinburgh, c.1633

H 12.5 cm; D (base) 4 cm; Wt 3.5 oz

NMS H.KJ 125; purchased in 1948 from the Trustees of the late
Sir George Grant Suttie, with help from the National Art-Collections
Fund and the Special Purchase Fund of the Society of Antiquaries
of Scotland

Provenance: The Sutties of Balgone, by descent to Sir George
Grant Suttie, Bt.

References: R. B. K. Stevenson, pp. 237-42; Grant (1932), pp. 16-19;
National Art-Collections Fund Review 1552 (1948); Finlay and
Fothringham (1991), p. 98-99; Clayton (1985), p. 17; Dalgleish
and Maxwell (1987), no. 12, col. pl.

Pear-shaped vial body on simple cushion foot crudely
engraved to represent ovolo decoration; the screw-on
cover has two horn-like curved spouts; the body is
engraved with a Latin inscription, stating that it is the
gold ampulla which held the sacred anointing oil for
the coronation of King Charles I, held at Holyrood on
18 June 1633.

This unique little vial is one of the earliest surviving pieces of Scottish-made gold. Although unmarked,
it may have been made by James Denneistoun, deacon
of the Incorporation of Goldsmiths at the time of the
coronation. The deacons often seem to have made
special or commemorative pieces. A contemporary
account of the coronation, a much-postponed and
controversial ceremony, by the Lord Lyon Sir James
Balfour, mentions that he carried the golden ampulla.
An earlier written form prescribed by Archbishop
Laud indicated that the vial should be of silver.

8.8

The ampulla was preserved for centuries in the
Suttie of Balgone family; and although there is no
documentary evidence, it has been suggested that it
was commissioned by the serving Edinburgh treasurer
George Suttie who retained it after use. The crude
engraving of the foot, in contrast to the accomplished
raising work, may be due to the hurry with which it
had to be completed.

8.10 TRUMPET

Thomas Moncur, Glasgow, c.1669

Marks: unmarked, except for the name on the bell, described
below

L c.75 cm; D (bell) 11.45 cm; D (knop) 9.4 cm;
Wt 31.07 oz

Lent from a private collection at Mount Stuart

Provenance: Home Sale of Arms and Armour, 29 July 1919

References: RSM (1948), no. 191; Finlay and Fothringham (1991),
p. 109, pl. 44(ii); Byrne (1966), pp. 77-78; Smithers (1988), p. 59

The trumpet is formed from a coiled tube, held in
place by a central triple knop. The bell is decorated
with two winged angel masks, looking inwards
towards the player. Between them on the one side is a
cluster of fruits, nuts and flowers; on the other side is
a vacant oval escutcheon. Near the collar, where the
bell joins the shaft, are the words: '◊ THOMAS ◊
McCVIR ◊ GLESGOVE ◊ 1669 ◊'. All the decoration
and wording are executed on a thin sheet which is
afterwards fitted over the body of the bell and held in
place with solder at the wide end. The inscription is
engraved on a stippled background; the angels, fruit,
etc., are repoussé. The central triple knop is heavily
repoussé in the same manner as the bell, including
two more winged-angel masks, flowers and fruit.

This, and the instrument below [8.11], are the sole
surviving 17th-century examples of their kind in Scotland. Ceremonial trumpeters attended numerous state
and civic occasions. They are depicted on the well-
known illustrations of the 'Downsitting and Riding of
the Scottish Parliament' of the 1680s, and a trumpet
banner bearing the Scottish Royal Arms of Charles II
is displayed in the National Museum of Scotland.

However, the present trumpets are more likely to
relate to Glasgow civic matters than to state occasions,
if only because of the prominent position of the town's
name alongside that of the makers. Like other Scottish
burghs, Glasgow did employ ceremonial musicians.
In 1669, the date of the first trumpet, the City Council
agreed to pay for a professional musician both to
serve the town and to 'instruct the youth in the airt

8.10 and 8.11
(details left)

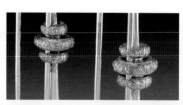

8.11

8.10

8.13

(detail below)

8.9

8.13

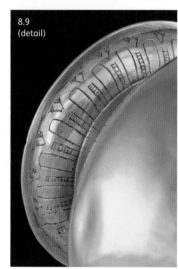

8.9
(detail)

8.12

of musick'. A trumpeter by the name of 'Walace' is specifically mentioned in 1675, when he was to have a salary of 100 merks, as that had been the pay of previous trumpeters. However, he was to get more if he had to 'ryd with the militia'. Indeed the militia were called out during the emergency occasioned by the Earl of Argyll's rebellion of 1685; the trumpeter, named Andrew Bell, received £16 16s Scots over and above his ordinary pay for attending for 44 days.

It is entirely possible that the two silver trumpets were commissioned as part of the equipping of the newly-employed city trumpeters, although they are not mentioned in the extracts of the Treasurer's Accounts, which detail such payments as 'for cloath, lace and furnishing and making of ane coat to the trumpeter of the militia troop … £101 18s' in 1682.

8.11 TRUMPET

Robert Brock, Glasgow, c.1675-80

Marks (on the widening part of the shaft towards the bell): 'RB' in monogram, five times (maker Robert Brock); in addition to his name on the bell

L c.75 cm; D (bell) 11.45 cm; D (knop) 9.4 cm; Wt 38.05 oz

Lent from a private collection at Mount Stuart

Provenance: Home Sale of Arms and Armour, 29 July 1919

References: RSM (1948), no. 191; Finlay and Fothringham (1991), p. 109; Byrne (1966), pp. 77-78; Smithers (1988), p. 59

The form and description of this instrument are almost the same as for the Moncur Trumpet [8.10], but they are not quite identical. Near the collar, where the bell joins the shaft, are tooled the words: '• ◊ • ROT

8.12 (detail)

8.13

BROCK ◊ GLASGOW'. The plain escutcheon on the bell-sleeve is almost circular, and the relief of the repoussé work is slightly bolder than on the earlier instrument.

8.12 COLLAR OF THE ANCIENT AND MOST NOBLE ORDER OF THE THISTLE

John Campbell of Lundie, c.1707-08

Unmarked, but identified from Jewel House records

D 61 cm; Wt 29.15 oz

NMS M.1992.1; purchased from Sotheby's sale, London, Wednesday 18 December 1991, lot 439, with the aid of grants from the National Heritage Memorial Fund, Coutts Bank, Bank of Scotland and Royal Bank of Scotland

Gold and enamel collar composed of 34 links of alternating thistle heads and crossed sprigs of rue. With later gold and enamel pendant badge of St Andrew by John James Eddington, London, c.1825.

This collar was issued to Cosmo George, 3rd Duke of Gordon (c.1720-52), created a Knight of the Thistle in February 1747. Subsequently the 4th and 5th Dukes of Gordon were also made knights, and the pendant badge was probably issued to the latter.

Maker John Campbell was a goldsmith-banker and founder of the bank now known as Coutts & Co. His most interesting commission was to supply the collars and badges of the refounded Order of the Thistle between November 1707 and March 1708. He produced ten collars; three have survived. The collars were originally the property of the Crown and issued to new knights, to be returned on their death.

8.13 PAIR OF TAZZE FROM GLASGOW UNIVERSITY

John Luke II, Glasgow, c.1709

Marks (on upper face of plate): 'IL' (maker John Luke); tree, bell, etc. (Glasgow); 'JL'; 'D'

(1) D 33 cm; H 10.7 cm; D (base) 13.4 cm; Wt 36 oz
(2) D 33.2 cm; H 10.7 cm; D (base) 13.5 cm; Wt 38.5 oz

Lent by The Hunterian Museum and Art Gallery, University of Glasgow

Reference: Williams (1990), no. 9

Plain circular plates with simple strengthening wire rim, on trumpet foot with wide simple foot-rim; the centre of the plates are engraved with contemporary arms for the University of Glasgow, within a wreath.

These unusually large tazze are first mentioned in the University records on 8 August 1728, and seem to have been lent outwith the University on several occasions for the payment of 'half a crown'.

8.14 BADGE OF THE OFFICER OF THE BANK OF SCOTLAND

James Welsh, Edinburgh, 1743-44

Marks (on underside of rim): 'IW' gothic (maker John Welsh); castle (Edinburgh); assay-master's mark indistinct; 'N' (date-letter 1743-44)

H 21 cm; W 14.3 cm; Wt 8.86 oz

Lent by the Bank of Scotland plc

Oval badge, cast and chased in high relief with full arms of the Bank of Scotland, motto 'Tanto Uberior' above and 'Bank of Scotland' below, all within a border of rococo scrolls, flowers and shells; the badge is convex and the rim is pierced to allow for sewing onto the arm of a dress coat.

This is one of a series of similar badges that acted as livery ensigns for the officers of various organisations, such as the Incorporations of Baxters, Surgeons and, of course, the Goldsmiths themselves [see 2.20]. This is the second such badge relating to the Bank. It originally commissioned one to be made in October 1700 from the Edinburgh goldsmith Robert Inglis at a cost of £70 16s Scots. Something happened to this first badge and the Bank ordered a new one on 5 May 1743.

Although there is no record in the Bank's minutes as to which goldsmith was chosen, it is clear from the hallmarks, and a contemporary scratched inscription on the back, that it was 'John Welsh / Fecit / 1743'. Initially the officer's badge and livery coat seem to have been worn for ordinary business, but by the 19th century it seems that the badge and a silver tipped baton were used for more ceremonial purposes.

The Bank and the Incorporation of Goldsmiths are two of the very few organisations established before the Union of Parliaments that still fulfil their original role. The Incorporation still has shares in the Bank which it bought a few days after the Bank first opened its doors for business in 1695.

8.15 SEAL BOX

James Glen, Glasgow, c.1752

Marks (on base): 'IG' twice (maker James Glen); tree, fish, bell, etc. (Glasgow); 'M'

L 12.2 cm; H 3.2 cm; W 8.7 cm; Wt 6.53 oz

Lent by The Hunterian Museum and Art Gallery, University of Glasgow; purchased at Bonham's sale, Edinburgh, 23 August 2006, lot 103, with the aid of the National Fund for Acquisitions

Oval box with domed lift-off cover; cover engraved with the arms of Glasgow University, with the motto 'VIA VERITAS VITA' in a ribbon above, surrounded by the legend 'SIGILLUM * COMMUNE * UNIVERSITATIS * GLASGUENSIS'; all surrounded by a band of chased and engraved foliage, shell and scroll decoration.

The University's archive has the original receipt, stating that the box cost £3 7s 6d. It was specially commissioned for presentation to Col. Joseph Yorke (Baron Dover) in recognition of his services to the Foulis Press and his support of the Foulis Academy. This opened at the University in 1753 and trained several eminent artists including James Tassie.

8.16 THE WHITE ROD OF SCOTLAND WITH CHAIN AND BADGE

John Clark, Edinburgh, 1758-59

Rod: L 105 cm; H (unicorn) 9.1 cm; Wt (all-in) 16.9 oz

Chain and medal: Wt (all-in) 5.7 oz

Lent from a private collection

References: J. H. Stevenson (1897), p. 165; Finlay and Fothringham (1991), pp. 167-68, pl. 92[ii]

Tubular rod in two sections which screw together, with gilt spherical knop and terminal; the head is in the form of a cast unicorn holding a shield with the Royal Arms of Scotland. Chain of office; the links are formed of 32 panels with thistle-heads in relief, suspended from which is a crowned oval badge set with emeralds, sapphires and rubies; the obverse is enamelled with the Royal Arms as used in Scotland, with the mottoes 'Honi Soit Qui Mal Y Pense' and 'Hostiarij Parliamenti Insigne'; the reverse has an enamelled badge of St Andrew, surrounded by the mottoes 'Nemo Me Impune Lacesset' and 'Quem Virga Semel Candida'.

The chain and jewel are remarkable pieces of work. The enamelling is superb and quite the equal of London work of the period. The choice of John Clark as the maker was a wise one, as few in Edinburgh at that time would have been capable of such

8.14

8.15

fine and detailed work. Clark specialised in mathematical instruments, microscopes and other precision items, and was admirably suited to the work in hand.

When the Parliament of Scotland was prorogued in 1707, the Honours of Scotland were laid up in a chest in the Crown Room in Edinburgh Castle. The insignia of the Usher of the White Rod, however, was the personal property of the Usher, so it was not stashed away with the regalia. By the time Alexander Coutts of Redfield, a close cousin of the banking family of that name, purchased the ushership from the bankrupt Alexander Cockburn of Langton in 1758, the old rod had disappeared (or had perhaps been pawned or disposed of) and Coutts commissioned a new rod and chain. His arms (matriculated 15 December 1758), included a depiction of the White Rod. He carried the rod and wore the chain and badge at the coronation of George III in 1761, walking by the side of Black Rod, the equivalent usher of the Parliament of Great Britain at Westminster (the only coronation at which this particular rod has been used).

Coutt's tenure of office was brief as he sold the ushership in 1766 to James Cockburn, heir of Alexander Cockburn of Langton from whom he bought it; however he held onto the insignia. The ushership eventually passed to the Walker Trust, a charity endowed for the Episcopal Church of Scotland, with whom the office now resides.

8.17 CEREMONIAL KEYS OF THE CITY OF PERTH

Robert Keay II, Perth, *c*.1842.

Marks: 'RK' (maker Robert Keay II, Perth); 'K' (date-letter 1841-41); castle (Edinburgh); thistle (standard mark); queen's head (duty mark)

(1) L 23.5 cm; W 7.5 cm

(2) L 15.7 cm; W 4.4 cm

Lent by Perth City Museum and Art Gallery

Large and smaller ceremonial keys, the smaller with elaborate pierced head, the larger with applied cast arms of the Burgh of Perth featuring the double-headed eagle. These keys were presented by the town's Lord Provost, Charles Graham Sidey, to Her Majesty Queen Victoria during her first state visit to Perth in 1842. She recorded the presentation in her journal and noted that 'the town (which is very pretty) was immensely crowded, and the people very enthusiastic'.

Presentation Silver

Academic Recognition

8.18 THE STRATHNAVER CUP

Walter Melville, Aberdeen, *c*.1653

Mark (under rim): 'WM' conjoined twice (maker Walter Melville); 'ABD' (Aberdeen); 'WA' in monogram ('tryer' William Alexander); assay-scrape

H 23.2 cm; D (rim) 11.2 cm

Lent by the University of Aberdeen

Reference: James (1981), pl. 2

Deep bowl, engraved with two sets of full arms of George Gordon of Strathnaver, set within elaborate mantling and foliate strap-work swags; with a lobed baluster stem, set on a trumpet and stepped cushion foot engraved with stylised leaves and scrolls. Beneath the rim is engraved the inscription: 'D Georgius Gordonius Strathnaverinae Dominus, hoc poculum in educationis et amoris tesseram Collegio Marescallano donavit, Anno 1653'.

George Gordon was born in 1633 and was served heir to his father, the Earl of Sutherland, in 1637, on the death of his elder brother. He attended Marischall College and, as seems expected of graduates, presented

8.16 (obverse)

8.16 (reverse)

8.16

8.17

8.13

8.20

8.17

8.14

8.15

8.19

8.22

8.18

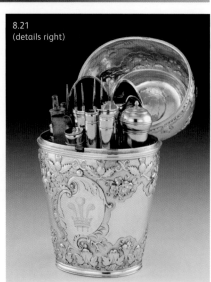

8.21
(details right)

this cup for the use of the college. On leaving the college he and his younger brother Robert undertook an extended visit to London from 1654 to 1656. He eventually succeeded his father as 14th Earl of Sutherland in 1679, and died in 1703.

Personal Story

8.19 MODEL BOAT

Robert Bruce, Edinburgh, 1710-11

Marks (on base): 'RB' (maker Robert Bruce); castle (Edinburgh); 'EP' (assay-master Edward Penman); 'F' (date-letter 1710-11)

L 13.9 cm; W 7.9 cm; H 4.2 cm

Lent by Aberdeen Museum and Art Gallery

Simple oval boat-shaped dish, with simple rim wire; one side is engraved with the arms of Bruce within a circular scroll cartouche, with the motto 'Fides Servata Didat' below. Around the rim is engraved the inscription: 'This silver boat is gifted to John Shiphird by Robert Bruce goldsmith for the kindness he shew'd to his sone David Bruce and Others After they were Six days and Six nights at sea without meat or drink / And by Providence thrown in at Earn Heugh near his House on 25 August 1711'.

This is a relic of a remarkable story. On 19 August 1710 a group of seven boys, all about 15 years old and possibly students at St Andrews University, set out from St Andrews harbour in a small rowing boat. They lost their oars and were swept out to sea, where they survived for six days and nights without food or water. Eventually their boat came ashore some four miles south of Aberdeen, where they were helped by the local laird John Shepherd. He sent to Aberdeen for a doctor, but tragically two of the youngest died. As a token of his gratitude for helping his son David survive, the Edinburgh goldsmith Robert Bruce presented Mr Shepherd with this silver boat.

Political Machinations

8.20 BOX FOR A BURGESS TICKET

John Rollo, Edinburgh, 1736-37

Marks (on base): 'IR' (maker John Rollo); castle (Edinburgh); 'AU' (assay-master Archibald Ure); 'G' (date-letter 1736-37)

L 26.5 cm; W 15.8 cm; H 2.2 cm; Wt 30.38 oz

NMS A.1958.237; purchased in 1958 from Messrs Adamson, Edinburgh, with the aid of the National Art-Collections Fund

Provenance: by descent in the family of Sir John Barnard; sold at Sotheby's sale, London, 6 March 1958, lot 135

References: Dalgleish and Maxwell (1987) no. 33; Finlay and Fothringham (1991), pp. 144-45, pl. 77(ii)

Simple rectangular box to take a folded parchment burgess ticket; with lift-off cover, the centre with a raised oval panel, engraved with the arms of the City of Edinburgh within an acanthus wreath; the corners flat-chased with elaborate shell and foliage sprays. The burgess ticket confers the Freedom of the City of Edinburgh on Sir John Barnard, Member of Parliament for the City of London.

This box is mentioned in John Rollo's Account Ledger [4.45] where he charged the 'Good Toun' £14 15s 5d, including the substantial sum of two guineas for the engraving. Sir John Barnard was granted the Freedom of the City in gratitude for opposing a bill in Parliament which sought to punish Edinburgh for the Porteous Riot. This was the result of popular opposition to the Government's taxation regime. Prime Minister Walpole was infuriated at this outburst of anti-government violence.

8.21 TRAVELLING CANTEEN

Ebenezer Oliphant, Edinburgh, 1740-41

Marks (on bases of outer cover and beakers): 'EO' (maker Ebenezer Oliphant); castle (Edinburgh); 'GED' (acting assay-master Dougal Ged); 'L' (date-letter 1740-41)

H 16.5 cm; W 10.5 cm; Dp 8.5 cm; Wt (all-in) 40.22 oz

NMS H.MEQ 1584; purchased in 1984 from D. S. Lavender, London, after an export licence deferral, with the help of the Glenmorangie Distillery Company, National Heritage Memorial Fund, Hugh Fraser Foundation, and contributions from over 600 businesses and members of the public

References: Dalgleish and Mechan (1985), pp. 4-7; Dalgleish (1988), pp. 168-84; Dalgleish and Maxwell (1987), no. 34; Finlay and Fothringham (1991), pp. 142-43, pl. 72(ii)

8.18

8.19

8.20

Silver travelling canteen of demountable cutlery for two, which sits in a wooden block, which in turn sits within two nesting beakers, all of which are contained in an outer case with a hinged lid. The outer case is elaborately chased in the rococo manner with bands of linked thistles, void panels and a central cartouche engraved with the three-feathered badge of the Prince of Wales; the domed hinged lid is also chased with bands of linked thistles, and a central badge with a figure of St Andrew, surrounded by the motto 'Nemo Me Impune Lacesset', all representing the collar and badge of the Most Noble Order of the Thistle.

This canteen was made, possibly as a 21st birthday gift, for Prince Charles Edward Stuart in 1741, and is decorated with his insignia as Prince of Wales and a Knight of the Thistle (at least in Jacobite eyes). He brought it with him to Scotland during the ill-fated 1745 Rebellion; and it was captured, with the Prince's baggage wagon, at the battle of Culloden on 16 April 1746. The victorious Government commander, William, Duke of Cumberland, then presented it to his *aide-de-camp*, George Kepple, Viscount Bury, later 3rd Earl of Albemarle, who was entrusted with taking the news of the victory back to Cumberland's father, George II, in London. The canteen remained in the Albemarle family until it was sold by Christie's London in 1963.

The maker, Ebenezer Oliphant, was an obvious choice for this commission. He was a member of the staunchly Jacobite family of Oliphant of Gask, whose father and brother were 'out' during the Rebellion.

8.22 PAIR OF CANTEEN BEAKERS

James Ker, Edinburgh, 1737-38

Marks (on base of both beakers): 'I.K' (maker James Ker); castle (Edinburgh); 'AU' (assay-master Archibald Ure); 'H' (date-letter 1737-38)

(1) H 9.5 cm; W (rim) 9 cm; Wt 3.4 oz

(2) H 9.6 cm; W (rim) 8.6 cm; Wt 3.49 oz

NMS K.2004.207.1 and 2; purchased in 2004

Provenance: Sotheby's sale, Gleneagles, 29 August 1978, lot 392

Reference: Dietert (2007), p. 30

Plain tapering oval form, one with everted rim to fit inside the other; both engraved with full coat of arms with motto 'SPARE NOUGHT' in a ribbon below, for John Hay, 4th Marquess of Tweeddale.

These beakers may originally have also held travelling cutlery like no. 8.21. Ironically, they were made by a Whig goldsmith, James Ker, for one of the main figures in the Hanoverian Scottish Government that opposed Prince Charles Edward's Jacobite Rising. John Hay, 4th Marquess of Tweeddale, was an ambitious politician who was made Principal Secretary of State for Scotland in 1742, and was in office at the time of the '45. He was not particularly effective in dealing with the Jacobite threat and demitted office (which itself was scrapped) in 1747. On the death of the Duke of Argyll he was appointed Lord Justice-General of Scotland in 1761 and died in London in December 1762.

8.23 DUMFRIES FREEDOM BOX

Alexander Gardner, Edinburgh, 1792-93

Marks: 'AG' below Prince of Wales feathers on an applied pad (maker Alexander Gardner); castle (Edinburgh); thistle (standard mark); 'M' (date-letter 1792-93); king's head (duty mark)

H 19.9 cm; W 12.2 cm; Dp 1.9 cm; Wt 20.45 oz

NMS H.1991.10; purchased in 1991 from Spink & Son, London, with the aid of the National Heritage Memorial Fund, the National Art-Collection Fund, the Worshipful Company of Goldsmiths of London, and the Incorporation of Goldsmiths of the City of Edinburgh

Provenance: family of Henry Dundas, by descent; Habsburg Feldman sale, Geneva, 15 November 1989, lot 52/259

Reference: Dalgleish (2001[i]), pp. 100-110

Rectangular box, with lift-off cover pierced to show gilt inner cover, the interior of the box gilt. The cover is engraved with the seal of the Burgh of Dumfries surrounded by parcel gilt wreath and floral swags; the pieced border has trophies of arms and four oval panels, two engraved with ships and two with the arms and supporters for Dundas. The underside of the base is finely engraved with two oval vignettes: the top one depicting coal being landed at a quay and carried up to a cottage; the bottom one depicting a family scene inside the cottage with coal being burned

8.22	8.23	8.24	8.25
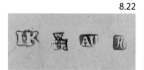			

on a fire. Between the two is an extensive inscription indicating that the box and freedom of the Burgh of Dumfries were presented to Henry Dundas of Melville, Secretary of State, for his role in removing the duty on water-borne coal.

Henry Dundas (1742-1811) was one of the most important and powerful politicians at the end of the 18th century, who 'managed' Scotland for William Pitt's Tory Government in London. The occasion for the presentation of this and the following box, containing honorary burgess tickets for Dumfries and Montrose, was his role in removing a punitive tax on coal transported by sea. His reasons for doing so were not entirely altruistic, but involved an attempt to remove a grievance contributing to widespread radical and anti-government agitation. The peat harvest of 1792 was exceptionally poor, driving up prices. Since peat was still a major source of fuel for most people, Dundas saw this as a threat to stability; in June 1793 he revoked the coal tax in an attempt to bring down prices and curb agitation. Although it was extraordinarily popular with many burgh communities, it ultimately did little to halt demands for political reform.

Gardner was a good choice of maker for Dumfries; as well as being a talented craftsman, he is recorded as being a staunch supporter of the Government establishment. On the wedding of the Prince Regent (later George IV) in 1795, he decorated his shop window in Parliament Close with lights in the shape of the Prince of Wales feathers, to emphasise that he had been made 'Jeweller to His Royal Highness'.

8.24 MONTROSE FREEDOM BOX

Gold, Benjamin Lumsden, Montrose, c.1793.

Marks: rose (Montrose); 'B.L' (maker Benjamin Lumsden); rose (Montrose)

L 8.7 cm; W 5.5 cm; H 1.9 cm; Wt 3.21 oz

Lent by Montrose Museum; purchased at Christie's sale, Scotland, 5 March 1985, lot 91

Plain oval box, with hinged lid; engraved on upper face of the lid with arms of the Burgh of Montrose, within a bright-cut circle, with a four-arched bridge in the background. Inner face of the lid is engraved: 'A Token of Gratitude / from the Town of Montrose to / Secty. Henry Dundas / for the Abolition of the Tax on / Coals in Scotland'. [See notes on 8.23 for its political significance.]

As many as 50 towns and burghs sent their appreciation to Henry Dundas, many contained in gold or silver boxes. At least four, and possibly many more, of these still survive: Aberdeen, Kirkcudbright, Dumfries and Montrose.

Celebrating Improvement

8.25 PUNCH BOWL AND LADLE

Andrew Wilkie, Edinburgh, 1831-32

Marks: 'AW' (maker Andrew Wilkie); castle (Edinburgh); thistle (standard mark); 'Z' (date-letter 1831-32); king's head (duty mark)

Bowl: D (rim) 31 cm; D (foot) 18 cm; H 18 cm; Wt 59.09 oz

Ladle: L 40 cm; W 8.6 cm

Lent from a private collection

Deep, almost hemispherical bowl, set on a stepped cushion foot. The body of the bowl is chased with a detailed topographical scene depicting the route of the aqueduct and the parallel road leading from the Crook of the Moss to the town of Auchterarder. In the centre is a scroll cartouche engraved with a presentation inscription to 'Captain M C W Aytoun of the Royal Artillery' from the inhabitants of Auchterarder, for devising and implementing a scheme for bringing fresh water from springs at the Crook of the Moss into the town of Aucherarder, September 1832.

Captain Aytoun of Purin was a local landowner. Using engineering skills gained in the Royal Artillery, he constructed an aqueduct from nearby springs which 'by his kind and scientific exertions ... has been made to pour in 72 gallons every minute, of the most excellent water, which has been taken into many houses; and baths have been fitted up in some ...' (as described in the New Statistical Account for his parish). This was very much in keeping with the drive for rural 'improvement' in the 18th and early 19th centuries, and had a major effect on the development of the town. The Auchterarder town hall is named after Captain Aytoun in recognition of this.

The chasing on his punch bowl is excellent and presents a detailed and accurate picture of the area. The road shown on the bowl is now basically the route of the modern A9, past Gleneagles Hotel.

8.26 THE NEILL VASE AND STAND

Mackay & Cunningham, Edinburgh, 1843-44

Marks: queen's head (duty mark); thistle (standard mark); 'JMc' (maker James Mackay, for Mackay & Cunningham); castle (Edinburgh); 'L' (date-letter 1842-43)

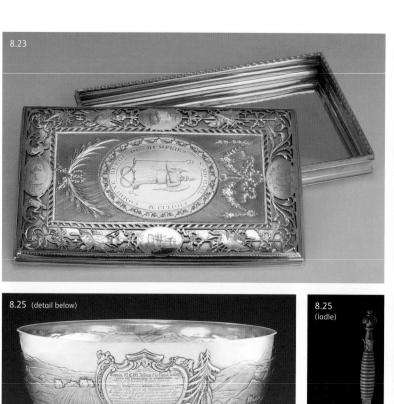

8.23

8.24

8.25 (detail below)

8.25
(ladle)

8.26

8.28
(detail right)

8.27

Vase: H 51.5 cm; W (max.) 30 cm; D (stand) 45.5 cm

NMS A.1878.50; presented in 1878 by James MacNab, Royal Botanic Garden, Edinburgh

References: Byrom and Dalgleish (2001), pp. 33-42

Body of inverted pear form, set on a triangular pedestal, supported by three cast female figures representing Flora, Pomona and Ceres; domed cover with cast figure of Britannia as a finial; body with applied wreaths and bands of flowers, fruit and foliage, representing actual plants first introduced into Britain by Dr Neill, and first cultivated in his garden at Canonmills, Edinburgh; the pedestal base has chased representations of glasshouses, horticultural implements and a bust of Dr Neill; the upper body is engraved with an extensive inscription indicating that the vase was presented to Dr Patrick Neill LLD, FRSE as a token of gratitude by 'six hundred practical gardeners, natives of Scotland' on 22 June 1843.

Patrick Neill is best remembered as a highly influential, innovative horticulturalist and natural historian, and a founding member and secretary for many years of the Caledonian Horticultural Society. He published extensively on horticultural matters, and his own garden at Canonmills was a haven for all those interested in the subject. He was also prominent in civic affairs and responsible for the scheme converting the drained Nor' Loch into West Princes Street Gardens.

This silver vase was presented to him at a testimonial dinner held in June 1843, organised by his friend and pupil James MacNab, who went on to become keeper of the Royal Botanic Garden in Edinburgh. It was attended by, among many others, 'Mr MacKay, the jeweller'. MacNab raised contributions from over 600 Scottish gardeners for this massive piece of plate.

It is also more than likely that MacNab, a talented botanical illustrator, actually designed the form and decoration of the vase. On Neill's death in 1851 the vase was left to MacNab, who in turn presented it to the Edinburgh Museum of Science and Industry in 1878, a year before his own death.

Military Valour

8.27 BEER MUG OF THE BANFFSHIRE LOCAL MILITIA

John Keith, Banff, 1810

Marks (on base): 'M'; 'IK' (maker John Keith); 'B' (Banff); outline head mark (very rubbed)

H 14 cm; L (over handle) 14 cm; D (rim) 9.6 cm; Wt 20.13 oz

H NMS K.2003.932; purchased at Lyon & Turnbull sale, Edinburgh, The Murray Collection, 20 August 2004, lot 244

Bellied body with two reeded bands above and below the engraved inscription to front: 'To / Captn. James Reid / Adjutant / in Testimony of their respect / From / The Noncomd. Officers / and Privates of the / Banffshire Local Militia 1810.', with simple rounded angular handle and simple rim and foot mouldings.

Local auxiliary military units were an important feature during the Napoleonic War, and normally officered by local lairds or gentry. The gifts of presentation pieces of silver were very common, but this beer mug is slightly unusual. Like most other 'tokens of esteem', which took the form of elaborate swords or pieces of ready-made or designed plate, this item has clearly been made to order, locally, with the character of the recipient very much in mind. This reveals, in a telling way, the regard in which Reid was held, and something of the close bonds that existed in such locally organised military units during a period of conflict, particularly in the small, close-knit communities of the north-east.

8.28 PRESENTATION SWORD

James Mackay, Edinburgh, 1858-59

Marked (on hilt and all scabbard mounts): 'JMc' (maker James Mackay of Mackay & Cunningham); castle (Edinburgh); thistle (sterling standard mark); 'B' (date-letter 1858-59); queen's head (duty mark); blade engraved 'Mackay & Cunningham'

L 100 cm; L (scabbard) 84.6 cm

Presented to Major William Drummond Stewart VC in 1859

Lent by a private collection

The hilt and scabbard-mounts are of silver gilt. The hilt is elaborately cast with scrolling foliage in which

8.26

8.27

8.28

is set the coat of arms of the recipient, Major William George Drummond Stewart. Below his arms hangs a representation of his Victoria Cross, which he won at the relief of Lucknow, during the Indian Mutiny. The original crimson velvet scabbard is replete with silver-gilt mounts bearing a trophy of arms and Highland accoutrements, the family crest, and an inscription in raised lettering which reads: 'Presented / to / Major W. G. Drummond Stewart V.C. / on his return from service in the / Crimea & India / as a token of the pride & interest / taken in his gallant discharge of duty / by the tenantry on the / estates of his father / Sir W. Drummond Stewart / of Grandtully Bart. August 1859'.

Major Stewart was born in 1831. At the age of 17 he joined the 93rd Highlanders as an ensign and was promoted to lieutenant in 1852. Two years later he found himself in the Crimea and took part in the famous 'Thin Red Line' engagement. He was promoted to captain on 29 December 1854. Within a few months of his safe return he was once more dispatched abroad, this time to take part in quelling the Indian Mutiny. It was at the relief of Lucknow on 16 November 1857 that he won the Victoria Cross. The very brief and underplayed citation reads: 'In leading an attack upon and capturing two guns by which the Mess House was secured. Elected by the officers of the Regiment'. This laconic understatement does less than justice to what Stewart actually did. According to an eye-witness, he took several men from his company and charged up a long level road straight at the two enemy guns, which had been pouring a withering fire into the British position; he 'dashed forward in a most gallant style, captured the guns at the point of the bayonet and turned them on the fleeing rebels'. All the Sepoys who had manned the guns were killed. He received his Victoria Cross from his commanding officer at Umbeyla on 6 December 1858. Promoted to major, he later retired from active service on half pay, and died near Southampton on 18 October 1868, aged only 37.

This is believed to be the only such sword to have been made in Scotland, and the only one made for, and presented to, a winner of the Victoria Cross in the Indian Mutiny.

8.29 MEDAL OF ELGIN AND LOSSIEMOUTH VOLUNTEERS

Possibly William Smith, Elgin, c.1869
Marks: 'WS' (maker William Smith, Elgin)
H 6 cm; W 5.2 cm; Wt 1.32 oz
Lent by a private collection

Oval medal with cast acanthus wreath border with ornate suspension loop; obverse is engraved '1st Elgin / Artillery Volunteers / Lossiemouth / Challenge Medal / 1869; reverse is engraved 'Won By / Corpl. A Milne'.

Local Volunteer units were raised for national defence in response to the threat of a French invasion in the middle of the 19th century. Shooting competitions were encouraged to improve skill with firearms, and this is one of many medals awarded as prizes for such competitions.

8.29 (obverse)

8.29 (reverse)

8.29

{opposite page}

8.23 DUMFRIES FREEDOM BOX, 1792-93

Sporting Glories

John Burnett and George Dalgleish

Introduction

Scotland is unique among the countries of the United Kingdom in having so many surviving early prizes and trophies for various sports. Obviously vessels of silver and gold made highly appropriate rewards where sporting success also involved financial gain. Most horse-races, for example, put up 'a piece of plate' worth a certain amount of hard cash for the winner. The surviving examples of this type are referred to as 'prizes' in the following discussion. However, in some sports the resultant fame was deemed reward enough, with the winner receiving only temporary custody of a trophy, generally to be returned for the next holding of the competition, after having a medal attached to record the victor's success. These terms, 'prize' and 'trophy', while used in this very specific way here, were not always so definitively used in the past.

Scotland is also fortunate in the sheer variety of types of surviving prizes and trophies, so there is no endlessly dull line of identical cups. Ranging from silver arrows to broadswords, from silver bells to silver balls, the following examples provide a unique collection of these early examples of the goldsmith's art. The King's Prize for Leith Races [see 9.16] provides a fine illustration of the humour that attended many sporting events in the past: whether unintentional or deliberate design, there is a splendid sense of Scottish irony in the fact that the main prize at the races on Leith Sands, one of the biggest mass bacchanalian excesses in 18th-century Scotland, was a gold teapot.

Although they all existed earlier, horse-racing, archery and shooting with guns all produced their earliest surviving Scottish prizes during the reign of James VI. Sport was not merely a competition, it was part of a larger social occasion which might include wearing one's best clothes, walking or riding to the venue, the sport itself, drinking during the competition, and a dinner afterwards. It was not the kind of event which appealed to the more thorough-going Presbyterians – King James therefore positively encouraged it! Although there seem to be no direct links between the King and horse-racing and archery competitions, they can be regarded as demonstrations of political loyalty. During the Civil Wars and Commonwealth periods in the 1640s and '50s, virtually all sports were frowned upon, and consequently reinvigorated with gusto upon the restoration of the monarchy.

Burgh sports competitions were common all over Europe, organised either by burgh authorities themselves, or by guilds and incorporations within them. Silver trophies offered by these groups gave status to a

There is a large Silver-piece of Plate ... to be Run for ...

{RULES FOR THE HORSE-RACE AT LEITH: c.1680}

(opposite page)
9.18 KING'S PRIZE GOLD CUP, 1751

burgh, in the same way handsome communion silver gave status to a kirk. Scotland's tradition is different from England's, where the cup as a prize becomes common in the 18th century. In Scotland a far greater variety of types of trophies and prizes exist, and it is not until the 19th century that the two-handled prize cup is ubiquitous. It seems that the explanation for the greater number of early prizes in Scotland is that money prizes were more usual in England. For example, the 1619 rules for the race at Kiplingcoats (near Market Weighton, Yorkshire) shows it was a sweepstake.[1] At Lancaster in 1773 all three races were for purses.[2] Although purses of hard cash did exist in Scotland, it was much more usual for the prize to be a piece of silver, or an appropriate item such as a saddle. This no doubt stimulated the trade of the goldsmith, and it is no coincidence that many of the most important burgh prizes and trophies were made by the deacons of the appropriate incorporations. As well as being leaders of their individual crafts, deacons sat on the town or burgh councils, and had a hand in supporting and regulating the sporting competitions.

There were three common types of trophy and prize. (1) Replicas, often in miniature, of a piece of equipment from the sport (e.g. Dumfries and Kirkcudbright 'siller guns' [9.1 and 9.2], numerous silver arrows, and the Rattray silver ball [9.10], all fall into this category). (2) The apparatus of sociability, with prizes such as silver monteiths, trays, drinking cups, snuff boxes or ultimately gold teapots, all highly fashionable indicators of both the status of the victory and the victor. And (3) things to be worn to denote the victor's success, like prize swords, sashes for horse-racing or archery, silver quoits and medals. It is probable that even the 'siller guns' were originally intended to be worn on a ribbon; and the Rattray ball has a suspension loop.

The practice of each winner attaching a silver token to the trophy can be seen as part of an exchange: the club (or whatever) gave him the status of victor, and he in return enhanced the status of the club by giving it a small piece of silver. The following collection of trophies and prizes illustrates all the above types and hopefully presents a unique glimpse of Scotland's rich early sporting heritage.

Archery and Shooting

It is ironic that two surviving Scottish shooting prizes are older than any extant archery prize. The longbow was invented c.8000 BC, and the first guns which could be fired from the hand or shoulder appeared in Europe around AD 1400 (the first mention of a 'culverin' in Scotland was in 1489). Early shooting competitions were, like horse-races, associated with burghs, and the prizes were as important as symbols of civic pride than as rewards for marksmanship. Later accounts show that the guns were highly inaccurate and many of the competitors were intoxicated; the competitions were really games of chance. Shooting competitions were found particularly in south-west Scotland, and as well as the 'siller gun' trophies at Dumfries and Kirkcudbright, the burghs of Irvine and Kilmarnock gave cash prizes.

Success at archery was a matter of skill. This skill was encouraged by King James I in 1424, when he required every man over 14 years old to practice after Mass. Although the bow ceased to be a weapon of war in the Lowlands in the 16th century, archers continued to enjoy their sport, and bowyers and fletchers to work at their crafts. Around 1600 the practice of the Low Countries, where guilds owned silver arrows as trophies, was adopted by the burghs, presumably through direct trading and cultural links. Charles II had been in exile in the Low Countries, where he became a member of the Ghilde St-Sebastiaan at Bruges.[3] Catherine of Braganza was also a keen archer. It was presumably their leadership in the sport which gave rise in Yorkshire to the Scorton Arrow (1673), a rare example of an English silver arrow, and to the Company of Scottish Archers. In contrast with shooting, the 17th-century archery prizes are all from the east of Scotland.

The Company of Scottish Archers, founded in 1676 (becoming the Royal Company about 1710), was an amalgam of the Scottish burgh archery tradition and the European tradition of archery guilds. Its membership has always been noble and military. In time, burgh competitions failed and the Royal Company took over their prizes and arranged competitions for them. Early in the 18th century the Royal Company was the only active archery society in Scotland, and it took on the role of employing a bow maker, importing arrows from Flanders, and keeping a supply of yew wood.

9.1 THE KIRKCUDBRIGHT SILLER GUN

Unmarked, c.1587

L 17.7 cm

Lent by the Stewartry Museum, Dumfries and Galloway Council

References: *Sporting Glory* (1953), p. 34, fig. 1; Finlay and Fothringham (1991), pp. 97-98; Dobie (1998), pp. 44-45; Dobie (2001[ii]), pp. 177-78, figs 2 and 3; *Scot. Nat. Mem.* (1890), p. 204, fig. 147; J. Burnett (2000), pp. 151-55

A silver model gun in the form of a 'culverin' barrel, engraved 'T Mc 1587', probably for Sir Thomas MacLellan, Provost of Kirkcudbright (1582-96); a single badge or medal is attached, with the arms of the MacLellan family

This is the earliest extant sporting trophy in the United Kingdom, and is still competed for by the Six Incorporated Trades of Kirkcudbright, to mark special local or national occasions. It is likely to have been presented to the Incorporated Trades by the Provost to encourage the use of firearms in the defence of the burgh. It was first mentioned in the town's minutes in 1590, when it was clear that it was to be shot for annually and returned by the winner. It is probable that it was intended to be worn as a badge.

9.2 THE DUMFRIES SILLER GUN

Barrel unmarked, stock by David Gray, Dumfries, c.1813

Mark (on stock butt): 'DG' (maker David Gray)

L 25.9 cm

Lent by Dumfries Museum, Dumfries and Galloway Council

Finlay and Fothringham (1991), pp. 97-98; Dobie (2001[ii]), pp. 177-80; *Scot Nat Mem.* (1890), pp. 202-203; J. Burnett (2000), pp. 142-51

Silver model 'culverin' barrel, engraved 'I*M' for John Maxwell of Newlaw, Provost of Dumfries c.1583-87 and (at a later date c.1813) 'Presented by King James VI of Scotland to the Seven Incorporated Trades of Dumfries MDXCVIII [1598]'; silver butt, stock and flintlock mechanism added c.1813 by David Gray, Dumfries.

As John Maxwell's sister Grisel was married to Sir Thomas MacLellan, the two siller guns have a close family link. Leaving aside the modifications of c.1813, the two are more or less identical and are almost certainly made by the same silversmith. Despite the tradition that the Dumfries gun was given to the Trades by James VI on his visit to the Burgh in 1617, it can be confidently dated to c.1587. The fact that the two towns' provosts' initials are on guns owned by the Trades suggests they were both given by the provosts, probably as an encouragement to the 'useful' sport of shooting. However, they may have been associated with the regular 'wapinshaws', when the inhabitants assembled to prove they were able to defend the town and had sufficient skill with the necessary weapons.

Initially shot for annually by the freeman of the Seven Incorporated Trades of Dumfries, the frequency of the competition decreased. At the match in 1808 a drunken blacksmith, Alexander Kirkpatrick, seized and broke the gun. He was heavily fined and banned from associating with his fellows for 21 years. The damage seems to have led to the gun being converted to a model flintlock some years later by the Dumfries silversmith David Gray. A poem by John Mayne commemorates the match of 1777, which he expanded into a 100-page book by 1838. After the winding up of the Incorporated Trades in 1852, the gun was given into the care of the Burgh Museum.

9.2

9.1

9.2 (and detail)

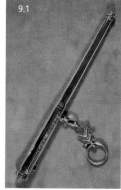

Originally the arrow had soldered loops to hold the winner's medals, but it is now displayed on a triangular wire-work stand set on an ebonised base, from which hang the hundreds of medals won since it was first shot for. The stand was made by Marshall & Sons, Edinburgh, 1885-86.

The first dated medal associated with the arrow bears the date 1603 and was won by J. Johnstone of Elphinston. However there are four other early medals, including one in the form of a bell, that do not carry any date, which may indeed record earlier competitions for the arrow. Unfortunately, as the records of the burgh of Musselburgh do not survive before 1635, there is no documentary evidence from the origin of the arrow. By 1676, the date of the founding of the Company of Scottish Archers, it had come to be shot for exclusively by members of that body. It is probable that it was originally instituted by the town to encourage the sport, as a prize for all-comers – several of the early winners were clearly not burgesses of the town. It is still shot for today by the Royal Company of Archers, each winner adding a new medal. Its stand boasts several hundred, presenting a tangible history of medallic art in Scotland.

One medal is of particular relevance to this study; the 1704 medal was added by Colin Mackenzie, goldsmith in Edinburgh, who was admitted to the Royal Company at some point before this date. His oval medal is engraved on the obverse with the arms of Mackenzie within an elaborate foliate cartouche, and on the reverse with a wreath and the inscription 'Captain / Colin MacKenzie / Goldsmith in Edr Won / this Arrow at Musselburgh, / 29 July / 1704'. Curiously, although it is unmarked, it is signed by the engraver 'Rot. Wood Sculp. Edr.'

9.4 THE UNIVERSITY OF ST ANDREWS FIRST SILVER ARROW AND SELECTED MEDALS

Unmarked and uninscribed

L 22.3 cm; Wt 1.22 oz

Lent by the University of St Andrews

References: A. J. S. Brook (1893-94), pp. 350-440; J. Burnett (2000), pp. 156-57

Two-barbed head on a nocked cylindrical shaft, with three flights engraved to represent feathers; a soldered collar has a loop from which the early medals hung. It is not known when the St Andrews University arrow was first shot for, but it is unlikely to be much before the date of the first medal, 1618. Unfortunately there is little recorded information about the competition

9.3 THE MUSSELBURGH ARROW AND MEDALS, 1603-current

Unmarked

Two-barbed head on cylindrical, nocked shaft, with three flights, engraved to represent feathers

Lent by the Queen's Bodyguard for Scotland, the Royal Company of Archers

References: Balfour Paul (1875), pp. 305-12; J. Burnett (2000), pp. 156-57

until the 18th century, but it probably followed the lines of the other burgh archery competitions that developed in the 17th century, except confined to the students of the University. Like the Musselburgh Arrow [9.3], the winners' medals were originally small and simple, but they developed into large, highly elaborate pieces of plate, made by some important goldsmiths. Later, other arrows were needed to accommodate the medals: there are now three arrows and 70 medals.

Medals

9.4 (a) Won by John Cunningham, 1618

Unmarked; 2.6 cm x 1.7 cm

Small medal in form of a shield, engraved with arms and initials
Medal no. 1 [The numbering system here and below is that used by A. J. S. Brook in his descriptive article on the St Andrews arrows]

The first surviving medal attached to the St Andrews arrow.

(b) Won by James Graham, Earl of Montrose, 1628

Unmarked; 7.5 cm x 5.4 cm

Oval, engraved with Montrose's arms and the figure of an archer
Medal no. 8

Initially a Covenanter, Montrose successfully led Charles I's army in the wars. Eventually defeated at the battle of Philliphaugh, he was executed in 1650.

(c) Won by Alexander Yeaman;
made by Thomas Lindsay, Dundee, 1684

Marks: 'TL' (maker Thomas Lindsay); pot of lilies (Dundee)
14.3 cm x 10.7 cm

Shaped oblong; engraved, with arms of Yeaman and figure of archer

Medal no. 19

(d) Won by Alexander Robertson of Struan;
made by James Penman, Edinburgh, 1687

Mark: 'JP' in monogram twice (maker James Penman)

17.1 cm x 11.7 cm

Octagonal; obverse engraved with the arms of Robertson; reverse embossed in high relief with figure of an archer

Medal no. 23

Robertson was a committed Jacobite, 'out' in the 1715 Rebellion, and a talented poet.

(e) Won by Andrew Gallaway;
made by William Burton, Edinburgh, 1701

Marks: 'WB' twice (maker William Burton)

11.5 cm x 8.1 cm

Oval, with chased laurel border, engraved with arms of Gallaway and figure of an archer

Medal no. 33

(f) Won by William Murray, Marquess of Tullibardine;
made by Patrick Murray, Edinburgh, 1706

Marks: 'PM' in monogram, twice (maker Patrick Murray); scratch weight on reverse 'Wh u/9 d/10' (9 ounces, 10 drop)

17.3 cm x 11.9 cm

Cartouche-shaped oval with mainly embossed obverse with mask, floriated scrolls and shell, enclosing oval shield bearing the arms of the Marquess of Tullibardine; reverse engraved with figure of archer on plinth

Medal no. 39

(g) Won by Adam Murray; made and engraved by
Archibald Burden, Edinburgh, 1718

Unmarked, but engraved on obverse 'A Burden Fecit et Sculp'

8.8 cm x 6.8 cm

Oval; engraved with arms of Murray and figure of archer

Medal no. 49

9.5 THE SELKIRK ARROW

James Fairbairn, Edinburgh, 1660

Date of first medal, 1660

L 30 cm; W (across barbs) 3.6 cm; W (across feathers) 3.5 cm; Wt 3.88 oz

Stand marks (cap): 'H&I' (maker Hamilton & Inches); thistle (sterling standard mark); castle (Edinburgh); 'D' gothic (date-letter 1959-60)

Stand: H 48 cm; (base) 33 cm x 33 cm

Lent by the Queen's Bodyguard for Scotland, the Royal Company of Archers

References: Balfour Paul (1875), pp. 348-49; Craig-Brown (1886), vol. II, p. 64

Two-barbed head set on solid circular, nocked shaft, with three flight feathers engraved to represent fletching. Unmarked, but maker identified by contemporary document commissioning its manufacture. The arrow is now mounted on a wire-work frame set on a triangular black wooden stand; frame has loops to suspend winners' medals (in total 37 medals, 1660-74 and 1818-2001 [intermittent]) and terminates in a domed cap, with band of chased 'Celtic' ornament, mounted with a silver and enamel shield with the Burgh of Selkirk's arms ('The Virgin with Child').

A letter from the town clerk of Selkirk (now in the Walter Mason Collection, Selkirk Museum), makes it clear that this was the first arrow provided as a prize by the town and that they commissioned it from 'Captain' James Fairbairn in Edinburgh in July 1660 (James Fairbairn was both deacon of the Incorporation and captain in the city's trained bands at this time). Selkirk burgh officials confiscated 'a quarter pound of silver plate which was selling by ane Egyptian [a gypsy]' and 'always, since we had a mind to buy ane silver arrow ... wherefore [we] agree with Capt Fairbairne to make it for the towns use'. The document also indicated that it would remain the town's property and whoever won it each year would add their arms on a medal. They demanded that the goldsmith 'make it with four rings or the like to hang the arms upon'.

It was shot for and won intermittently between 1660 and 1674, when it seems to have been stored and forgotten about in the town's charter chest until rediscovered by Sir Walter Scott in 1818. The magistrates then arranged for a grand shooting competition attended by the Royal Company of Archers, and the Arrow eventually came into their care. It is now returned annually to Selkirk for display in the Museum.

9.5 (and hallmarks)

9.5

9.6 THE ABERDEEN GRAMMAR SCHOOL SILVER ARROW AND MEDALS, c.1664-99

Unmarked

L 33.7 cm; Wt 1.9 oz

Lent by Aberdeen Grammar School

Reference: A. J. S. Brook (1893-94), pp. 444-68

The Arrow has two-barb head and three flights, engraved to represent feathers, two flights engraved 'AV' and 'CM'. Fourteen medals are associated with the arrow, dating c.1664-99. The first, won by George MacKenzie, was made by Walter Melville, goldsmith in Aberdeen, who engraved his mark 'WM' conjoined. It is possible that he made the arrow as well.

Other medals also bear Aberdeen goldsmiths' engraved marks: no. 3 won by John Bannerman, no. 5 won by Adam Gordon in 1670, and no. 11 won by William Keith, 9th Earl Marischall, in 1677, were all made by William Scott. No. 6 won by John Gordon of Breachly in 1672, no. 7 won by James Moir of Stoneywood in 1673, no. 8 won by John Skene in 1674, no. 9 won by Walter Lord Deskford in 1675, and no. 12 won by Alexander Fraser of Strichen in 1678, were all made by Alexander Galloway. Engraved makers' marks, although rare, are not unknown, and indeed appear on another important sporting trophy – the Lanark Race Bell [9.11].

Although there are no early records relating to this arrow and its medals, it is clear from later documents and the identities of the winners that it was shot for by senior pupils of Aberdeen Grammar School from 1664 onwards. It may have originally been presented by the Town Council, to encourage the sport amongst the students, as was the case with other archery trophies; and like these other competitions the participants were generally sons of the aristocracy, gentry or wealthy burgesses. Some of the medals bear similarities to those from St Andrews University [9.4], although they are cruder in execution and may have been influenced by the badges and medals of the sporting guilds of the Low Countries. One medal, no. 10 won by John Udny in 1676, depicting Orpheus charming the beasts, may have been a cast copy of a Dutch original.

9.7

9.7 THE BURGH OF STIRLING ARCHERY PRIZE BOX

Maker 'IH', c.1698

Mark: 'IH' in a heart-shaped punch

L 9.5 cm; W 7.7 cm; H 2.9 cm; Wt 3.75 oz

NMS Q.L.1981.10; on loan from a private collection

Oval box with lift-off lid; the body and lid decorated with repoussé-work bands of winged heads, animals and flowers; a plain oval in the centre of the lid is crudely engraved with a representation of the Burgh of Stirling's arms ('a wolf on a crag'); the underside of the base is engraved with a figure of an archer shooting at a target, with the inscriptions: 'The Burgh of Sterlings Pryze for Archerie 1698', and (in a much more accomplished hand) '18 Day of Octr / Won Be Mr Wm Dundas Ad- / -vocat and Given Be him To / Anna Dundas his Daughter/ Spouse to Lt Coll. Jo. Erskine Lieut. / Governour of Stirling Castle'. This was possibly intended as a box to hold grease for seasoning the archer's bow-string, or was a snuff or tobacco box.

An archery competition was revived in Stirling in 1676, with the town supplying a prize worth initially £24. In September 1698 this box was bought from a merchant called John Allane who also arranged for the town's arms to be engraved on it. Given that the maker's mark is in a heart-shaped punch, this may possibly be a rebus of his name, suggesting someone called J. Hart.

9.8 THE ROYAL COMPANY OF ARCHERS PRIZE MONTEITH

William Ged, Edinburgh, 1719-20

Marks (on base around centre point): 'WG' in shaped punch (maker William Ged); castle (Edinburgh); 'EP' (assay-master Edward Penman); 'P' (date-letter 1719-20)

H 25 cm; D (rim) 34 cm; D (base) 17.7 cm

Lent by the Queen's Bodyguard for Scotland, the Royal Company of Archers

References: Dalgleish and Maxwell (1987), no. 30; Finlay and Fothringham (1991), p. 122, pl. 63(ii); Lee (1978), p. 102; Balfour Paul (1875), pp. 321-28

Deep, hemispherical bowl with scalloped rim, set on a simple stepped foot. Two applied moulded wires around the body are pierced to suspend the annual prize gold medals; the lower body is engraved with four wreath-girt roundels showing St Andrew; two figures of bowmen below a tree with 'The Common Seal of the Royal Company of Archers at Edin.'; an angel with a bow, and a warrior with a sword and shield with 'In Peace and War' above; a dedicatory inscription 'Edr 20 June 1720 / The Council of the Royal Company of Archers ... Ordered this piece of Plate to be furnish'd / out of the Stock of the Company & to be shot / for as an annual Prize at Rovers by the said Company ...'.

This monteith was also supplied with a silver ladle by William Ged, made from native Alva silver [2.5], which suggests it was certainly intended as a practical punch bowl as well as a trophy. In 1751 the monteith was enlarged, at the cost of £9 7s 6d, to provide space for further medals. The bowl is now set on a stepped, ebonised wooden stand also hung with prize medals.

9.9 ROYAL COMPANY OF ARCHERS KING'S PRIZE TRAY

HcHattie & Fenwick, Edinburgh, 1800-01

Marks: 'M&F' (makers McHattie & Fenwick); castle (Edinburgh); thistle (standard mark); 'u' (date-letter 1800-01); king's head (duty mark)

L 43.7 cm; W 36 cm; H 4 cm, Wt 65 oz

NMS H.1992.102; purchased from How of Edinburgh, 1992

References: Balfour Paul (1875), p. 107; RSM (1948), no. 80; *Empire Exhibition* (1938), no. 14, pl. 8

Rectangular tray with cut corners; everted rim with reeded wire, set on four shell feet; inner edge engraved with a band of guilloche and the centre engraved with the Scottish Royal Arms of George III, the seal of the Royal Company of Archers, the Arms of the Hope family, and the inscription: 'The King's Prize / to / The Royal Company / of Scottish Archers / Gained 21st July 1800 By / Thomas Charles Hope MD&P'.

The King's Prize, although of 17th-century origin, was revived in 1787 as a piece of plate worth at least £20. Unlike other Royal Company trophies, it was retained by the winner, in this case Dr Thomas Charles Hope (1766-1844), a major medical and scientific figure, who succeeded Joseph Black as Professor of Chemistry at Edinburgh University in 1800. Like many Enlightenment luminaries, Hope played a full part in the social and cultural life of Edinburgh; he was a keen sportsman, winning many other archery competitions.

The Rattray Ball Game and its Relations

The Rattray Ball was the prize for a parish match at a game rather like real tennis[4] and is a unique survivor in Scotland. James I was unable to escape from his murderers at the Dominican Friary in Perth in 1437; his exit route had been blocked up, to prevent balls being lost down it when playing 'at the paume'. In the next hundred years the game became more complex and an important part of it was the irregular, asymmetrical court. After seeing it in Paris, James V had a real tennis court built at Falkland Palace in 1539-41. The Rattray game was a folk version of it, and it was played on the north side wall of the church. In the Royal game the ball is served onto the 'penthouse', the sloping roof above the spectators' gallery, and play was started by a player throwing a ball onto the roof.

The Rattray game seems to have been unique in Scotland, but derivatives of real tennis were played in southern Europe. Scotland had 'caich' or handball, in which a ball was repeatedly struck against a wall. At Arbroath, and St Andrews University, there are leather-covered balls stuffed with rags; the Rattray balls are likely to have been similar.

9.10 THE RATTRAY SILVER BALL

Thomas Ramsay, Perth, *c*.1612; medals dated 1639-1766

Marks: 'TR' in monogram (maker Thomas Ramsay); lamb and cross (Perth)

D 5.5 cm

Lent by Perth Museum and Art Gallery

References: Rodger (1992), pp 403-11; J. Burnett (1998[i]), pp. 1101-04

The ball is made from two soldered hemispheres, each with makers' and town marks. It is engraved with the initials 'AH', 'GH' and 'IC', possibly for members of the first winning team. Accompanying it are 15 silver medals or badges, dating from 1639 to 1766, each engraved with the date and a number of initials, again possibly relating to the members of the winning team. A second, replacement ball (unmarked) was presented in 1751. There is a gap in the medals from 1640 to 1661, corresponding to the civil wars and Cromwellian interregnum. Most medals relate to the period 1662-1700, when sport was being actively encouraged by the Restoration regime.

9.9   9.10

9.6

9.9

9.7

9.7

9.9
(detail)

9.8

9.10

9.10

2.5

This is the earliest surviving example of marked Perth-made silver. Its maker, Thomas Ramsay, was admitted to the Perth Hammermen in 1597 and remained active until at least 1614. He also made another of the three trophies associated with the parish of Rattray: the Silver Arrow (1612). Along with a silver curling stone (now missing), they were reputedly given to the parish by James VI. It is more likely, however, they were presented by the incumbent local minister, Silvester Rattray of Nether Persie. The second son of a local laird, he was educated at St Andrews University, graduated in 1582, and admitted to the charge of Rattray Parish in 1591. He married Mary Stewart, daughter of George Stewart of Cardney, in 1609 and died in 1623. He may have presented the ball at any time during his incumbency, but as the arrow has the date 1612, and Ramsay disappears from the record in 1614, it is likely the ball dates to *c*.1612.

Horse-racing

Horse-racing in Scotland was probably widespread, if not regular, in the period before the 17th century, but lack of evidence makes it impossible to elaborate on the origins of racing as an organised sport. The first reference to a silver bell as a prize is at Peebles in 1569,[5] and there is a scatter of other references to horse-racing in the 16th century (e.g. Leith in 1504 and 1591, Haddington in 1553, and Ayr in 1576). It is possible that the later burgh prizes were put up for races which already existed.

In the early 17th century the sport began to emerge into the light of historical record as the sport of monarchs, noblemen and lairds. It was promoted by James VI and his son Charles I, more so once they moved to London. Major races were associated with some of the burghs: Lanark has the earliest surviving Scottish racing trophy, the Silver Bell (1608-10) [9.11]; Paisley had a race by 1608; Dunfermline by 1610, again with a bell as the trophy; and Jedburgh by 1625. In this regard Scottish burghs were operating in the same way as their English counterparts: Carlisle, for example, has the oldest horse-racing bell trophies in Britain, dating to 1590 and 1597. By the middle of the 17th century, Scottish horse-racing had a common system of organisation which included entry fees, the use of weights, and a system of cautions to ensure the return of the trophy.[6]

The political and religious troubles of the mid-17th century seem to have severely restricted the growth of the sport; little further is heard of it in Scotland until after the Restoration of 1660. Like other sports, however, it emerged with renewed vigour. The introduction of prizes to keep, rather than trophies, can be interpreted as adopting an English practice when it was politically desirable to show loyalty to the crown. At Alnwick the borough had a 'plate' (trophy) which was sold in 1696; the interest on the money raised was used to buy a small plate each year.[7]

Although horse-racing was organised by the burghs, the horses were owned by the gentry, and the burgh's office-holders were often local gentry.[8] But horse-racing is unique in that although it was organised by the gentry, for the gentry, it was still enjoyed by the people *en masse*. It became highly popular in the 1820s, a decade when all forms of popular culture were doing well.[9]

9.11 THE LANARK SILVER BELL

Hugh Lindsay, Edinburgh, 1608-11

Marks (engraved on shoulder): 'RD' in monogram (deacon Robert Denneistoun, 1608-10); 'XI D' (11 penny fine standard); 'HL' in monogram (maker Hugh Lindsay); assay-scrape to left of marks; assay-scrape also visible on underside of mouth closure

Bell: H 12.5 cm; D (mouth) 10.2 cm; Wt 5.86 oz

Medal stand: H 14.7 cm; D (outer ring, max.) 23 cm

Lent by South Lanarkshire Council

References: Dalgleish and Maxwell (1987), no. 5; A. J. S. Brook (1890-91), pp. 174-88; Finlay and Fothringham (1991), pp. 98, pl. 34(i)

Bell-shaped body, closed mouth with cross-shaped sound opening; four equally spaced holes in the rim, which originally held rings for suspending the medals/badges. The top of the bell has an applied suspension ring and oak-leaf decoration; the face is engraved with the burgh arms of Lanark in a scroll shield (double-headed eagle with a bell in sinister talon and a fish in the dexter, between two lions rampant, all within a foliate wreath); arms and wreath parcel gilt. The bell now rests on a circular wire-frame stand, made by T. Smith & Son, Glasgow, 1896, and from which all the prize medals hang. The earliest surviving medal is of a simple shield shape, engraved on the obverse, 'VIN * BE * ME * / SIR * IOHNE * / HAMILTON / OE [*sic*.] TRABRO/VN * 1628 *'; with Hamilton arms on the reverse. The next medal is dated 1852, with annual medals thereafter until 1977.

While local legend says that the Lanark Races were instituted in 1166 by King William, this bell, probably created as a trophy for the first running of the races, makes it clear that they did not start until the reign of James VI.

9.12 THE SELKIRK RACE PRIZE SILVER CHOCOLATE POT

Patrick Murray, Edinburgh, 1720-21

Marks: 'PM' conjoined (maker Patrick Murray); 'q' (date-letter 1720-21); 'EP' (assay-master Edward Penman); castle (Edinburgh)

H 23.7 cm; D (base) 10.8 cm; L (max.) 18 cm; Wt 27.45 oz

NMS H.MEQ 1065; purchased from H. S. Fothringham, Grantullly Castle Antiques, 1972

Reference: Finlay and Fothringham (1991), p. 142, pl. 68(ii)

Pear-shaped body, the front engraved with the arms of the Burgh of Selkirk ('the Virgin and Child') surrounded by the motto 'The Seal of the Burgh of Selkirk', on a circular pedestal foot; with beak-spout and S-shaped handle with ivory insulators and an S-shaped wire retaining clip for the simple domed lift-off lid, with a ball finial on a swivel disc hinged to cover the molinet hole.

This is one of only two known Scottish 18th-century chocolate pots [see 4.11 for the other], and was a particularly fashionable piece of domestic plate to offer as a race prize. Selkirk Races were instituted in 1715 by the Burgh Council to promote the advantages the town would gain by 'the great confluence of gentlemen that would resort thereto'. The Council provided a piece of plate worth £10 sterling to be run for yearly on the last Tuesday of April.

This chocolate pot is the only surviving 18th-century example of a Selkirk prize. Curiously, an account with the same maker, Patrick Murray, for a prize for the year 1724 survives. He charged the Burgh £9 19s 1½d for a piece weighing 24 ounce 12 drop at 5s 4d the ounce, and an extra six shillings for engraving the arms. Unfortunately he omits to say what form the prize took.

9.13 THE CUPAR RACE PRIZE SILVER TANKARD

Unknown maker, Edinburgh, 1726-27

Marks (on base): castle (Edinburgh); 'EP' (assay-master Edward Penman); 'W' (date-letter 1726-27); maker's mark lacking (blank space where it should be)

H 24.2 cm; D (lip) 12.7 cm; D (body) 14 cm; D (foot) 13.4 cm; Wt 47.7 oz

Lent from a private collection at Mount Stuart

Slightly bellied body with everted rim, on apron foot; the stepped domed lid with shaped peak, acorn finial and shaped acanthus and scroll thumb-piece; the S-scroll handle with dog-nose terminal and elongated moulded rat-tail. Body engraved with the inscription: 'Coupar Plate won by Sir Alexr Murrays Horse Small Hopes Keneth Wright Rider / 11 Apr 1727'. Above the inscription an oval shield is engraved with a coat of arms with exuberant scroll mantling, and the motto 'SUPERNA VENABOR'.

The Burgh of Cupar in Fife had one of the earliest horse-races, starting in 1610. Although it fell into abeyance in the mid-17th century, it was revived in 1661, the date being set as the second Tuesday in April. It is extremely unusual to have the name of the rider as well as the owner recorded on a prize.

9.14 CUP AND COVER

Robert Gray & Son, Glasgow, 1821-22

Marks (cover underside): king's head (duty mark); tree, fish, bell, etc. (Glasgow); 'RG/&S' (maker Robert Gray & Son); lion rampant (Glasgow sterling standard mark); 'C' (date-letter 1821-22); stamped order no. 152 on underside of foot

H (overall) 40 cm; D 24.8 cm; W 33.2 cm; Wt (all-in) 138.9 oz

Lent by Glasgow Museums & Art Galleries; purchased by C. J. Vander, London, 1988

Reference: McFarlan (1999), pp. 216-17, pl. 7

Bell-shaped body based on Greek *krater* form, with applied band of cast and chased fruiting vine, two vine stem handles and chased acanthus leaves on lower body and cover. The centre of the body is applied with relief casts of two racing horses and riders. The stepped domed cover is chased with bands of acanthus leaves and an acanthus finial.

9.12

9.13
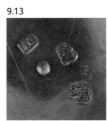

9.11

9.14

Leith Races

Although there is a tentative early reference to horse-racing at Leith from 1504, it was not until 1665 that they emerged as the most important races in Scotland. This is the date of the first published set of rules for the conduct of the races issued by Edinburgh Town Council. The races were promoted by the Council as a means of attracting business and money to both towns, in the form of big-spending aristocrats and gentry who owned and ran the horses. From the outset it was clear the races were intended to appeal to a far-flung constituency – the values of the prize plates were advertised in sterling, at a time when all the Council's other financial affairs were conducted in pounds Scots. The races were aimed at drawing participants from at least the north of England, if not from further afield, and they were certainly successful in this; many of the winners were eventually to come from Northumberland and Yorkshire.

The course was on the extensive sands immediately to the east of the mouth of the Water of Leith and extended over two miles. As each race seems to have involved several circuits of the course and at least three heats, the winning horse had to run some twelve miles over very heavy going, occasionally splashing through the incoming tide. Strength and stamina rather than speed were necessary to win at Leith Races.

Originally held in March of each year, this seems to have changed to August or September by the second half of the 18th century. The town initially supplied one prize worth £20 to £25, rising to £30 and then £50 in the 18th century, usually in the form of a piece of silver plate made by the current deacon of the Goldsmiths. That so few prizes have actually survived suggests that they were fairly rapidly converted back into hard cash by most winners. The actual type of silver plate was not specified, and all manner of currently fashionable objects are mentioned in the Council records: monteiths, casters, posset cups, candlesticks and tea kettles all make their appearance. As the races took hold of the popular imagination, more prizes were added, and they grew into a week-long jamboree of racing, gambling, balls, assemblies and drinking. The excitement and fun of the occasion are wonderfully evoked in Robert Ferguson's long poem 'Leith Races', first published in 1773.

To the town's silver prizes were added a much more important reward sometime before 1721: the Kings' Gold Prize. Unfortunately it is not yet clear when this was actually instituted, but it may have had its origins in the aftermath of the 1715 Jacobite Rebellion. In September 1717 the Town Council, in an outburst of loyalty to the Hanoverian dynasty, proclaimed that they had changed the date of their annual race at Leith from March to October 'in Commemoration of the City's Deliverance from the Army of Highland Rebels, upon the 13th Day of October 1715, by the Vigilance of his Grace the Duke of Argyle'.[10] A prize of £50 was to be run for on 14 October. Not to be outdone by the town, a group of like-minded 'Loyal Gentlemen, hearty Friends to our Sovereign King George, and to the Protestant Succession, in the most Illustrious Family of Hanover', proposed a second race to be run on the '30th Day of October next; being the Birth Day of his Royal Highness George Prince of Great Britain and Wales, Electoral Prince of Brunswick and Lunenburgh, Duke of Cornwall and Rothsay, … Lord of the Isles, and Steward of Scotland'. The Prince of Wales' Birthday Plate was set at £100 and took the form of a gold quaich, or 'quaff' as it was described in a newspaper of the day, engraved with the Prince's crest and motto, and this inscription: '*Octobris Dici zomo celebrando / Dicatum. / Quem diem Natalem agnoscet / Georgius Cambriae Pinceps / Scotiae Seneschallus, / Domus Regiae Britannicae, / Populique Britanni / Spes, decus & Columen / Anno AEiae Christi MDCCXVII.*'[11]

The Gold Quaich was won by a horse owned by one Colonel Guest, the Prince's health was drunk by all, flags were flown, and a volley fired by the City Guard.

This outburst of loyalty seems to have had the effect of spurring the Crown itself into supporting the racing at Leith, as it had done at Richmond and York. By 1721 a gold 'King's Prize' worth 100 guineas was now one of the inducements, and this is recorded by the other bard of the Races, Allan Ramsay, this time by means of an inscription on the actual prize for the year, a gold teapot: '*Inscription on the Gold Tea-pot, gain'd by Sir James Cunningham of Milncraig, Bart / After gaining Edinburgh's Prize / The Day before with running thrice, / Me Milncraig's Rock most fairly won, / When thrice again the Course he run: / Now for Diversion 'tis my Share / To run three heats, and please the Fair.*'[12]

This is the first mention of a gold teapot as a prize for the races, but it was not the last. Two King's Prize teapots actually survive [see 9.16 and 17], and are no doubt a reflection of the status of this vessel at the time as the appropriate premier prize at Scotland's main race meeting.

Leith Races thrived throughout the 18th century, with more and more prizes being added to the card. They were attended by many thousands of people – possibly attracting the largest ever public crowds in Scotland in the days before the railways heralded mass attendance at sporting events.[13] By the early 19th century, however, horse-racing was becoming more specialised, with speed rather than endurance becoming the goal of the racing fraternity: the valuable thoroughbred racehorse was coming into its own, rather than the sturdy hunters that could handle the heavy going on the sands of Leith.

This led many of the leading lights in racing to seek a new, purpose-built turf race track. This, combined with proposals to develop docks on the east sands at Leith, meant that the days of racing on the sands were numbered. A new site, Musselburgh Links, was chosen and the first races took place there in 1816. This was not the complete end of racing on Leith sands, but it did herald a change in character. The eventual building of the East Docks finally removed the site of this ancient course. However, racing at Musselburgh still continues to this day, as a lineal descendant of the famous, or the infamous, Leith Races.

9.15 TOWN'S PRIZE: SILVER SPOUT CUP AND COVER

Walter Scott, Edinburgh, 1706-07

Marks: 'WS' in shaped punch (maker Walter Scott); castle (Edinburgh); 'JP' in monogram (assay-master James Penman); 'C' (date-letter 1707-08)

H 30 cm; W 30.3 cm; D (base) 14.7 cm; Wt 67.1 oz

NMS MEQ 1206; purchased at Christie's sale, Silver of the Marquess of Linlithgow, 15 June 1977, lot 137

Provenance: won by Charles, 1st Earl of Hopetoun, and by descent

Reference: Finlay and Fothringham (1991), p. 142, pl. 65(ii)

This was the Town's Plate Prize for 1708; the engraved arms of the city were probably copied from the arms at the top of a printed handbill that circulated advertising the running of the Leith Races. This cup was in the collection of the Marquesses of Linlithgow for many years, and was won by one of their ancestors, Charles, 1st Earl of Hopetoun.

The maker, William Scott, was commissioned by the town of Edinburgh to make a piece of plate not exceeding £20 sterling for the Leith Races on 25 February 1708, and was paid for it, along with a pair of candlesticks he also furnished for the second race, on 28 April 1708. As generally the case, Scott was deacon of the Goldsmiths when he was asked to supply the race prize. It was probably a perk of the office, but also practical; the deacon sat on the Town Council and was aware when the race was going to be announced.

The Earl of Hopetoun was an avid horseman, and in the Hopetoun archives is an authograph 'account of all the horse matches ever I ran', listing more than 45 races he participated in, often riding himself. He won many prize plates, including two other pieces of silver from Leith Races which have survived but are currently untraceable: and a set of three casters by Patrick Turnbull, won in 1716, and a small plain monteith by an unknown maker, weighing just over 49 ounces.

9.16 KING'S PRIZE GOLD TEAPOT

James Ker, Edinburgh, 1736

Mark (on base): 'IK' (maker James Ker)

H 14.1 cm

Lent by Manchester City Galleries

Provenance: Anthony de Rothschild Collection; Michael Noble Collection; Edgar Assheton Bennett Collection

References: Dalgleish and Maxwell (1987), no. 52(a); *An Exhibition of Sporting Art* (1984), no. 42; Finlay and Fothringham (1991), p. 135; Jackson (1911), p. 954; E. A. Jones (1907[i]); E. A. Jones (1907[ii]), pl. xxii; Grimwade (1951[i]), p. 10; Clayton (1985), pp. 295; RSM (1948), no. 119; *Empire Exhibition* (1938), no. 29, pl. 14

Compressed spherical or 'bullet' shape, with straight tapering spout and wooden scroll handle, flush hinged lid with ball finial; the 'mouth' is flat-chased with a band of rococo shells and scrolls; the body engraved with the Scottish Royal Arms to one side and a representation of a racehorse and rider with 'Legacy / 1736' beneath on the other. This was the King's Plate Prize for 1736, won on 2 August by a black six year-old mare called 'Legacy', owned by a Mr Croft from England. The Town's Plate for this year was won by Sir James Cunningham's horse 'Bonny Lass', prompting Allan Ramsay to write his poem 'Leith Races'.

9.15

9.16

9.17 KING'S PRIZE GOLD TEAPOT

James Ker, Edinburgh, 1737-38

Marks (on base): 'IK' (maker James Ker); castle (Edinburgh); 'AU' (assay-master Archibald Ure); 'H' (date-letter 1737-38)

H 16 cm; L 24.5 cm; Wt 19.41 oz

Lent from a private collection

Provenance: sold to present collection by Crichton Bros, London, 1908

References: Dalgleish and Maxwell (1987), no. 52(b); Finlay and Fothringham (1991), p. 135, pl. 76(ii); Jackson (1911), p. 954; E. A. Jones (1907[i]); E. A. Jones (1907[ii]) pl. XXII; Grimwade (1951[i]), p. 10; Clayton (1985); RSM (1948), no. 120

Compressed spherical or 'bullet' shape, with straight tapering spout and wooden scroll handle, flush hinged lid with ball finial; the 'mouth' deep chased with a band of rococo scrolls foliage and fruit; the body is engraved with the Scottish Royal Arms; the leaf strainer is pierced in the form of a crowned thistle.

The King's Plate Prize for 8 August 1738 was competed for by three horses: a mare called 'I will if I can' belonging to Lord Cranston; a gelding called 'Keelman' belonging to John Fenwick of Northumberland; and a stoned horse called 'Cyprus', property of William Carr of Northumberland. As the *Caledonian Mercury* newspaper declared with resignation, it was 'carried over the Tweed as usual, by Mr. Carr's Cyprus'.

9.18 KING'S PRIZE GOLD CUP AND COVER

Ker & Dempster, Edinburgh, 1751

Marks: 'K&D' in rectangular punch, twice (makers Ker & Dempster); 'K&D' in engrailed punch, twice

H 21.5 cm; W 22 cm; Wt 21.21 oz

NMS H.1993.55; purchased with the aid of grants from the National Heritage Memorial Fund and the National Art-Collections Fund

Provenance: by descent to the collection of J. T. D'Arcy Hutton, Marske Hall, Richmond; Christie's sale, London, November 1950; Sir Alan Caird Collection

References: Finlay and Fothringham (1991), p. 159, pl. 85(ii); Grimwade (1951[ii]), pp 85-86; *Apollo* (November 1950), p. 158; Clayton (1985), p. 295

Bell-shaped body with central rib, set on stepped circular foot, with two opposed double scroll handles; upper section of the body deeply chased with S-band of flowers, scrolls and cartouches, one of which is engraved with the arms and motto of the City of Edinburgh; lower part of body is engraved with full Royal Arms as used in England. One curious feature is that the engraved Royal Arms are the version for use in England, whereas the correct Scottish version is used on the teapots. The stepped cover is chased with a band of flowers and scrolls and has a cone finial.

The King's Plate Prize, 1751, was won on Monday 12 August by a horse called 'Traveller', owned by a Mr Colesworth from Yorkshire. He may have been the ancestor of J. T. D'Arcy Hutton of Marske Hall, Richmond, Yorkshire, in whose collection this was until 1950. The makers were the partnership of James Ker with his son-in-law William Dempster.

Like the 1736 teapot, this is marked with the maker's mark only. This was probably because James Ker, the senior partner in the firm, was both deacon of the Goldsmiths and deacon convenor of the Trades on the City Council for this year (as well as being the sitting Member of Parliament for the city).

9.19 KING'S PRIZE GOLD CUP AND COVER

William Gilchrist, Edinburgh, 1752-53

Marks: 'WG' (maker William Gilchrist); castle (Edinburgh); 'HG' (assay-master Hugh Gordon); 'x' (date-letter 1752-53)

H 27 cm; Wt 24 oz

Lent by The Metropolitan Museum of Art, The Jules S. Bache Collection, 1949

Provenance: sold by Messrs Crichton Bros, London, to Jules S. Bache

References: Grimwade (1951[ii]), pp. 85-86; Finlay and Fothringham (1991), pp. 158-59, pl. 85(i)

Bell-shaped body with central rib set on stepped circular foot, two ebonised wooden scroll handles with acanthus leaf and double volute terminals, with a stepped domed cover with vase-shaped finial. The entire cup is deeply chased with a mass of exuberant rococo flowers, scrolls and leaves, on a matted ground; two cartouches are engraved with the Royal Crest and Motto, and the arms and motto of the City of Edinburgh.

This was the King's Prize for 1753, won on Thursday 16 August by a mare called 'Lady's Thigh', the property of a Mr Fenwick (presumably the same gentleman from Northumberland who had unsuccessfully competed for the King's Prize in 1738) [see 9.17];

9.17   9.18

9.19

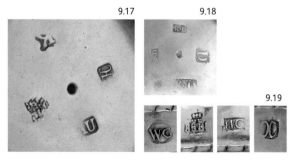

she won the first and second heats against six other horses and therefore won the cup.

The maker William Gilchrist was once again the deacon of the Incorporation at the time. Although a relatively long-lived craftsman, unfortunately very little of his work survives, particularly as this cup and the following tea-kettle show that he was an extremely skilled goldsmith.

9.20 TOWN'S PRIZE: SILVER TEA KETTLE AND STAND

William Gilchrist, Edinburgh, 1753-54

Marks (on bases of kettle and burner): 'WG' (William Gilchrist); castle (Edinburgh); 'HG' (assay-master Hugh Gordon); 'y' (date-letter 1753-54)

H (max.) 41 cm; W (across spout) 23.5 cm; D (base of stand) 21 cm; Wt 70.08 oz

Lent by City of Edinburgh Museums and Galleries; purchased at Lyon & Turnbull's sale, Edinburgh, 25 May 2006, lot 338, with help from the National Fund for Acquisitions

Provenance: Sir John Stirling Maxwell of Pollok's Collection

References: Finlay and Fothringham (1991), p. 158, pl. 84; RSM (1948), no. 146; Empire Exhibition (1938), no. 16, pl. 9

Body of inverted pear shape, the upper part heavily chased with rococo flowers, fruit and foliage; two cartouches, one void, one engraved with full arms of the City of Edinburgh motto above in ribbon 'NISI DOMINNUS FRUSTRA', and below in ribbon 'Insignia Civitatis Edinburgensis'; hinged domed lid and swing handle with S-scroll supports top of handle encased in basket work; scroll spout; kettle with simple collet base which locates into a stand on three cabriole legs, shell feet, cast swags of flowers and foliage, central burner; hinge with removable pin to secure the kettle.

This kettle had been known about for many years, in the collection of the Stirling Maxwells of Pollok, as a rare example of William Gilchrist's work. Its significance as a Leith Race prize, however, was overlooked until it was recently sold at auction (principally because it was always illustrated showing the side with the void cartouche). The Edinburgh City arms and mottoes make it clear that it was the Town's Prize for 17 September 1754, worth £30, and won by a chestnut horse called 'Thistle Whipper', owned by a Mr William Bates of Morpeth.

9.20

9.21 OLD LEITH RACES

Oil on canvas, signed by William Reed (c.1844-84)

H 90 cm; W 154 cm

Lent by City of Edinburgh Museums and Galleries

Reference: J. Burnett (2000), pp. 136-38

This was probably painted to commemorate the final race run on Leith Sands on 22 September 1859. The last of the 'Subscription Races', it had been reinstituted on the Sands in 1838 after racing had been removed to the purpose-built turf track at Musselburgh in 1816. The 'subscribers' were local shopkeepers and traders keen to bring back the level of business to the port that had been encouraged by the old races. However, as they were no longer supported by Edinburgh Town Council, and the gentry preferred the more specialised course at Musselburgh, the 'new' races were never entirely successful. Their disorderly conduct now attracted the condemnation of various kirk sessions, and they were eventually wound up in 1859. Reed's depiction of the last race shows a scene that was probably little different from the races of the late 18th century.

Huntly Races

Huntly Races in Aberdeenshire were held intermittently between 1695 and 1749. They were promoted by George, 1st Duke of Gordon (succeeded 1653-1716), and his son Alexander, 2nd Duke (succeeded 1716-28). Since they were Roman Catholics and Jacobites, it appears the races were a less than covert way of expressing support for the exiled House of Stuart. In 1695 the Scots Parliament granted a fair at Huntly, to be called Charles Fair, to run for three days from the second Tuesday in September: this was the day of the race. The name was a gesture of respect to the deceased Charles II; the initials 'CR' below a Royal Crown on the Huntly Prize Sword hilts emphasise this connection.

Curiously all three swords are associated in some way with either the Rebellions of 1715 or '45. The 1701 sword [9.23] was won by James Drummond of Drumquhany, a Jacobite officer captured at the battle of Sheriffmuir (or Dunblane as it was known at the time) in 1716, who lost his sword there, as recorded on the pommel. The 1713 sword [9.24] (won by

9.15

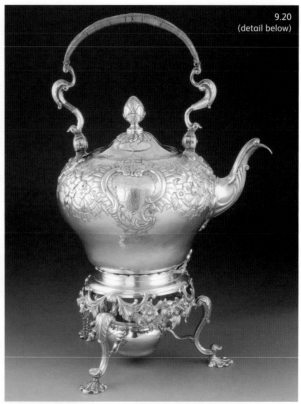

9.20
(detail below)

9.11

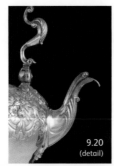

9.20
(detail)

9.12

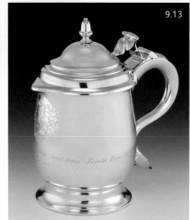

9.13

9.13 (detail)

9.13 (detail)

9.14
(details right)

9.25

George Gordon of Glestiren who was 'out' in 1715-16), and the 1727 sword [9.26], both appear to have ended up in the collection of William, Duke of Cumberland, the victor at the battle of Culloden, where presumably Cumberland acquired these quintessentially Jacobite weapons.

Races of this kind were scattered across Scotland in the 17th and 18th centuries, often held once every few years, and most of them associated with burghs. What is unusual about the Huntly Race is that it had such substantial prizes, and that it was organised by a nobleman. The existence of the Huntly Race may explain why there were no horse-races at Aberdeen in the same period.

9.22 PRIZE THISTLE CUP

William Scott, Banff, 1695

Marks (on base): 'VS' (maker William Scott); 'BANF' (Banff mark)

H 8.3 cm; D (rim) 7.9 cm; D (base) 4.5 cm; Wt 4.9 oz

NMS H.1996.275; purchased in 1996 from S. J. Shrubsole, New York

Reference: J. How (1983), p. 491, figs 210 and 211

'Thistle'-shaped cup, with flaring rim, central applied moulding wire and applied lobed base calyx; it has a double scroll strap handle and an applied collet foot. Base is engraved 'Hountlie Coup 95' and 'H/AA'; front of cup originally engraved with initials 'IH/EG'. Unfortunately, the cup is not in its original condition; the foot-rim has been renewed, the calyx lobes have been replaced, and engraved initials on the body have been removed when the cup was 'improved' by an unknown 'restorer' between 1981 and 1995.

The earliest surviving Huntly Race prize would have been a fashionable piece of domestic plate, very much in line with the sorts of prizes that were being won at Leith Races.

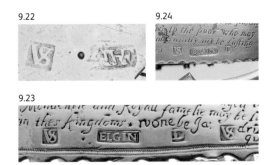

9.22

9.24

9.23

9.23 PRIZE SILVER-HILTED SWORD

William Scott, Elgin, 1701

Marks (on forward knuckle-guard): 'VS' in monogram (maker William Scott); 'Elgin' (Elgin); 'D'; 'VS' repeated

L 98.6 cm

NMS H.LA 158; purchased at Christie's sale, London, 21 December 1977, lot 261

Reference: J. How (1983), pp. 491-92, fig. 212

Silver hilt of conventional form, with gadrooned flattened oval bars, and two pierced side panels in the form of crowned shields, one with the initials 'CR', the other 'II' for King Charles II; the main forward knuckle-guard is engraved with the inscription: 'Att Huntly Castle the second fryday of Septr 1701 Wonne at King Charles the 2nd fare all horses not exceeding ane 100 merks pryce were admitted the riders staiking crouns which was given to the poore who were obligded to pray that the Monarchie and Royall famelie may be lasting and Glorious in thes kingdoms Wonne by Ja drummond in drmma quhance'. Around the pommel is engraved: 'Taken at Dunblain by one of Evan's Dragoons'. The blade is German, from Solingen, probably early 18th century.

The injunction on the remaining Huntly prizes for the Poor to pray for the Monarchy and Royal family, although ostensibly loyalist in sentiment, leaves no doubt for which family God's favour was being sought.

9.24 PRIZE SILVER-HILTED SWORD

William Scott II, Elgin, 1713

Marks (on forward knuckle-guard): 'VS' in monogram (maker William Scott II); 'Elgin' (Elgin); 'D'

L 103 cm

Lent by Her Majesty The Queen/The Royal Collection

Provenance: The Duke of Cumberland's Collection

References: J. How (1983), pp. 494-95, fig. 213; The Swords and the Sorrows (1996), exhibition, 1:31; Lankaster (1994), pp. 271-72

Silver hilt of conventional form, with two pierced side panels in the form of crowned shields, one with initials 'CR', the other 'II' for King Charles II; two bands below shields carry inscriptions 'praemium hoc ab illomo.dno Alexro / Marchione: de Huntly oblatum' and 'quod adeptus est geo: Gordon de Gleshrin / haeredibus suis transmitti jubet'. The forward main knuckle-guard has a virtually identical inscription to the 1701 prize sword above, except for the date which reads 'the second Tusday of september 1713'. The blade is German, from Solingen, probably early 18th century.

This sword is clearly by William Scott younger, as his father was dead by this date; however, the marks are identical to those on the 1701 sword and on the Huntly Sporran [see 5.38], which may be about the same date. It is fairly certain that the letter 'D' cannot be a date-letter, as it appears on pieces with widely varying engraved dates.

9.25 PRIZE CUP AND COVER

Robert Cruickshank, Old Aberdeen, c.1725

Marks (on base and inside cover): 'RC' (maker Robert Cruickshank); 'OABD' (Old Aberdeen); 'C'; maker's mark on the base is double-struck

H 17.8 cm; W (across handles) 23.8 cm; D (lip) 13.4 cm; D (foot) 8.8 cm; Wt 24.2 oz

Lent from a private collection at Mount Stuart

Reference: J. How (1983), pp. 496-97, fig. 214

Two-handled cup and cover; the bucket-shaped body with very slightly everted and caulked rim, tucked in on plain domed base, with two opposed simple plain-capped scroll handles, the one-stepped flat cover with ball-and-button finial and simple locating flange. The body is engraved: '*Given by the Duke of Gordon and / winn at Huntly Castle the third thursday / of September. 1725 years. All Horses not ex : / : ceeding ane hundred merks of price are ad : / : mitted to runn the Riders stakeing Crowns / a piece. Which are given to the Poor that / they may pray that the Monarchy & Royall / family may be lasting and Glorious in / these Kingdoms.*

In this instance, a piece of plate 'most useful in a family', as the Duke's factor described it, was acquired from Robert Cruickshank in Old Aberdeen. In the years preceding the 1725 cup further sword hilts were acquired, this time from James Tait, goldsmith in Edinburgh.

9.26 PRIZE SILVER-HILTED SWORD

Robert Cruickshank, Old Aberdeen, 1727

Marks: (on stool towards blade): closed crown in oval; 'RC' (maker Robert Cruickshank); 'OABD' (Old Aberdeen); 'C'

L 100.2 cm

Lent by Her Majesty The Queen/The Royal Collection

Provenance: probably Duke of Cumberland's Collection which passed to King George III's Collection

References: How (1983), pp. 497-98, fig. 215; *The Swords and the Sorrows* (1996), 1:31; Lankaster (1994), pp. 271-75, pl. 2(a, b)

Silver hilt of conventional form, with two pierced side panels in the form of crowned shields, one with the initials 'CR', the other 'II' for King Charles II; the broad main knuckle-guard is inscribed: 'Given by the Duke of Gordon and Winn at Huntly Castle the / Second Thursday of Septr. 1727 years all Horses not exceeding 13 hands / and 2 inches high are admitted to runn and the winning Horse to be sold / for ane Hundred merks if required by the Judge of the Race. The / Riders staiking Crouns a piece which are given to the Poor to / pray that the Monarchy and Royal Family may be lasting and Glorious in these Kingdoms'.

The blade is German, from Solingen, possibly second half of the 17th century.

Notes

1 Fairfax-Blakeborough (c.1950), p. 141.
2 Ibid, p. 153.
3 Vanhoutryve (1998).
4 Rodger (1992), pp. 403-11; J. Burnett (1998[i]), pp. 1101-04.
5 Williamson (2001-02), p. 31.
6 Ibid., p. 39.
7 Fairfax-Blakeborough (c.1950), p. 21.
8 J. Burnett (1998[ii]), pp. 55-75.
9 Golby and Purdue (1984).
10 *The Scots Courant* (Friday 13 September 1717). We wish to express our deep gratitude to Mr William Fortescue for giving me unfettered access to his extensive research into Edinburgh city newspapers of the period. He discovered this and the following references to the Gold Prize at Leith, and has generously made them all available to us.
11 *The Scots Courant* (Friday 1 November 1717).
12 Curiously, although this teapot is no longer extant, it is not the last time it makes an appearance in the records. When Sir James Cunningham of Milncraig died in 1747, his plate was rouped publicly at Goldsmiths Hall, and amongst the pieces to be sold the only item to be singled out for special mention was a gold teapot. It seems certain that it was the teapot he won in 1721.
13 Burnett (2000), pp. 105-09.

9.25

9.26

9.16

9.17

9.19

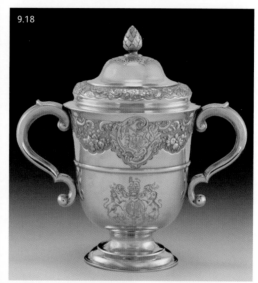

9.18

9.23

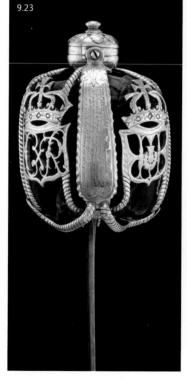

9.23

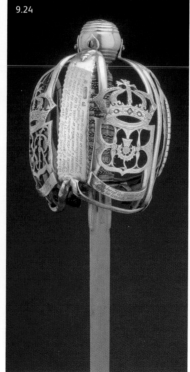

9.24

9.26

Silver Now

Amanda Game

10

Introduction

What role is there for the silversmith in the 21st century? The reverence formerly given to the silver punch bowl or grand silver salver in the discerning household has been replaced by reverence for the Alessi kettle (stainless steel, Italian) or a Philippe Starck lemon squeezer (acrylic, French). The silversmith in Scotland has to compete today in a contemporary world, which is global, driven by mass consumption, and increasingly fuelled by the virtual imagery of the Internet. Is making things in silver, in small studios, a hopeless anachronism of hard craft in the modern world; or does it seem to be a flourishing, imaginative art, that has become more ambitious, more exciting and less trammelled by the whim of conservative patrons than in the immediate post-war period?

Looking at the St Andrews University Mace [10.1], designed in 1949 by the Scottish architect Pilkington Jackson with enamels by Edinburgh-born Elizabeth Kirkwood, one sees a beautifully made object of fairly traditional design. Created in the same year as the Scottish Craft Centre in Edinburgh, as part of a well-documented era of reconstruction placing the making of things at the heart of the post-war world, the mace both celebrates handskill and higher education. If there were to be a mantra for the post-war period it would be 'education, education, education', as the art colleges gained money, pupils and specialist courses as part of the high-minded drive towards a newer, better world. From the early 1960s Graham Hughes, as the art director of the Worshipful Company of Goldsmiths in London, actively encouraged the silversmiths to commemorate the founding of a burgeoning number of new universities. The St Andrews University Mace can be seen as an early example of such collaboration.

Contrast then the collection known as 'Silver of the Stars', commissioned in 2006/07 by the Incorporation of Goldsmiths of the City of Edinburgh under the dynamic direction of Michael Laing, who became deacon in 1993. This project, linking ten silversmiths with ten Scottish celebrities in order to create a collection to tour worldwide to promote the craft, is clearly a product of a very different era to the mace. The objects are interesting, witty, beautifully made and sometimes extraordinary, but here ideas of design are clearly subsumed to the ubiquitous 21st-century consumer demand for celebrity as an endorsement of cultural artefacts.

In the intervening period between these two commissions, there have been a number of significant shifts of influence. Most notably, as the traditional industries continued to decline, the main training ground for the silversmith shifted more comprehensively to the art school. Bernard

Harrington established a specialist metalwork course in Dundee in 1943, and J. Leslie Auld returned from the war to develop what remains one of the most enduring and important silversmithing courses in the United Kingdom at Glasgow School of Art.

Edinburgh also developed its art college in this period. Ian Davidson had taken up the reins in 1961, followed in 1985 by Dorothy Hogg. Hogg has presided over an exceptional standard, in particular of contemporary jewellery at Edinburgh, making it one of the leading colleges in Europe. Silversmithing has also continued to have an important presence, with the able assistance of William Kirk who had become a staff member at Edinburgh in 1961. Kirk is an important figure in education in both Glasgow and Edinburgh. He taught at Glasgow from 1961 to 1978, and at Edinburgh from 1961 until his retirement in 1999. After Kirk's retirement, Edinburgh continued to develop silversmithing with the assistance of the young Glasgow graduate Grant McCaig. Both Coilin O'Dubhghaill and Sara Hutchinson, participants in the 'Silver of the Stars project', were Edinburgh graduates.

At Aberdeen the specialist metal course, run successfully for a number of years by David Hodge, became, under the leadership of Eric Spiller, a product design course, with a strong emphasis on exploring CAD/CAM and other new design technologies. Although silversmithing was less active under Spiller, the Dunblane silversmith Graham Stewart graduated from there in 1978. Under the current direction of Gordon Burnett, himself a Gray's School of Art graduate some 30 years previously, new design technologies and silversmithing have been linked in interesting ways. The clock Burnett made for the Bute House collection is an example of this.

One of the advantages of having a high-calibre course at Glasgow School of Art is that it attracted good quality tutors from elsewhere. One such was John Creed, who joined the staff at Glasgow in 1971. Creed's formidable hands-on silversmithing skills are evident in the jewel box he was commissioned to make in 1983 for the Scottish Crafts Collection. His open imagination, visible in this work, was to take him forward later that decade for a period of sabbatical study with the distinguished American architectural metalworker, Albert Paley; and his current work spans both architectural metalwork and commemorative and exhibition silver.

Roger Millar, who became course leader at Glasgow in 1984, following a successful period running silversmithing and jewellery at Dundee, was himself a Glasgow graduate. His subsequent studies at the Royal College of Art in the mid-1960s, and a period of workshop experience with the jeweller Andrew Grima in London, had introduced Millar to a wide range of innovative activity. The breadth of Millar's early experience created a teacher and course leader of exceptional standing, which has contributed significantly to maintaining silversmithing as a creative force in Scotland. Helen Marriott, who is currently a part-time tutor at Glasgow, was a pupil of Millar.

Besides direct education, demonstrable example has been important for the development of silversmithing in contemporary Scotland. For Millar this was in part contact with individuals such as Robert Welch and David Mellor, but there were different small studios in Scotland and elsewhere which were successful and influential. Prime among small studios established in Scotland is that of Malcolm Appleby. Appleby moved north from London, attracted less by the opportunities in education and more by the possibility of establishing a workshop, relatively economically, in a beautiful and inspiring rural location. In 1969 he set up his studio near Crathes, Kincardineshire, moving to his current workshop in Perthshire in 1997.

Appleby's formidable engraving skills, rich imagination and keen intelligence have made him one of the most extraordinary and prolific silversmiths of our time. From relatively remote rural locations, he has run a very successful silver studio, overturning the preconception that the maker has to live and work near his or her urban markets. Appleby's markets are local, but they are also national and international courtesy of the quality of his work. As well as creating a body of commissioned work ranging from the Victoria and Albert Museum Seal to silver for both Downing Street and Bute House, Appleby has also created a vast range of smaller items for the wider market. He has also offered workshop experience to a host of young people and students, many of whom, like Graham Stewart, have gone on to forge successful careers as silversmiths.

What Appleby demonstrates is that silver can be used to create a highly individual form of art. Patrons may continue to commission and give silver to commemorate private and public occasions, and a number of the forms – spoons, tumbler cups, etc. – may seem a direct descendant of traditional historic forms.

However the appearance of contemporary silver, as the small collection demonstrates, is far more varied. Forms are chosen and surfaces created to express best the ideas of the maker, rather than the desire of the patron. An example might include the way that Appleby, with his extraordinary 'Centrepiece for Bute House' [10.15], uses engraving to create a dynamic texture inspired by geology and the natural world.

Graham Crimmins moved from Birmingham to establish a studio in Edinburgh in the early 1970s. By the latter part of the decade silver had become increasingly expensive, courtesy of the Bunker Hunt monopoly which set the price of the raw material at an astonishing $47 per ounce. This high material cost, when linked with strong political developments in art schools of the 1970s which allied silversmithing with an unacceptable luxury taste, effectively side-lined the craft as a realm for imaginative study in many colleges for well over a decade. Although this was in part regrettable, it nevertheless offered new freedoms to experiment, which bore fruit in different ways. Makers increasingly created bodies of work which explored colour, form and ideas in different metals – eschewing both the function and precious-ness of silversmithing. Crimmins' spun, patinated bowls with their small silver details were an imaginative response to these new social times for the silversmith.

Michael Lloyd moved to rural south-west Scotland in the mid-1980s. Although he experimented with chasing and patinating copper, his attraction to the physical properties of silver has always kept him close to the material. Lloyd was commissioned in 1999 to make the mace for the new Scottish Parliament. The finished work has the traditional shape necessary to its function, but is in every other way a different, more personal creation than many of its ceremonial predecessors.

Another maker who was interested in finding a more personal language for silver, which transcended the historic markers of value and status, is Adrian Hope. Hope was born in Edinburgh, but studied at Sheffield before establishing a studio in Edinburgh in 1980. Influenced in part by the fluid contemporary designs of Scandinavian silver, Hope explores the way in which surface and form can be integrated to create imaginative objects for modern domestic life. Hope, like Lloyd, and London-based silversmiths such as Simone ten Hompel, share a concern with exploring new ways of interpreting domestic silver. Surfaces are often left unplanished, unpolished, and are patinated or whitened; function is more suggested than defined; design and creation seek to express the less formal, more fluid structures of the modern household.

The traditional craft and incorporations – such as the Worshipful Company of Goldsmiths in London, the Incorporation of Goldsmiths of the City of Edinburgh and the Incorporation of Hammermen in Glasgow – continued to have importance as patrons in this period. Grants and awards to students, such as the Young Designer Silversmith Award in London (won on no fewer than eight occasions in twelve years by Glasgow students) and Precious Metal Bursaries have continued to support newcomers to the craft.

Other developments which have provided opportunities for silversmiths have included the founding of groups such as the Association of British Designer Silversmiths, now celebrating its tenth anniversary, which include a number of Scottish makers. In the mid-1980s Roger Millar in Glasgow had established an independent exhibiting group called Flux, to try to expand opportunities for silversmiths to meet patrons, but also to exhibit different kinds of artistic work. The Scottish Craft Centre, which had started with such high ideals, increasingly failed to support and encourage excellence in crafts. By the mid-1980s it was moribund, and by the early 1990s it had closed its doors.

Another element of influence in the craft in the past 20 years has been the increase in the numbers of art galleries and museums showing and collecting modern silver. The Scottish Gallery (Aitken Dott Ltd), Edinburgh, known for its long-standing support of Scottish painters, added silversmithing to the exhibition programme with the 'Metal Vessel' in 1987. In addition to curating some 20 exhibitions of modern Scottish, British and international silver, The Scottish Gallery has also hosted exhibitions curated by others, such as '100% Proof' (versions 1 and 2) curated by Dorothy Hogg, and 'Field of Silver' curated by Simone ten Hompel. Elsewhere, galleries such as Rodger Billcliffe in Glasgow, under the particular direction of Lynn Park, herself a Glasgow graduate, and museums such as Aberdeen Art Gallery in particular, under the informed curatorial eye of Christine Rew, have brought high quality Scottish silver to a wider audience with a range of exhibitions. Aberdeen, for example, worked with Malcolm Appleby to create a major show of his work in 1993, which brought together for the first time many of his privately-commissioned as well as public works.

Museums also collect objects, and the great majority of the post-war objects illustrated in this exhibition belong to National Museums Scotland. Both contemporary Scottish silver and contemporary international silver have been actively collected by the Museum in the past 20 years, which gives both direct support to the maker, in a financial sense, but also considerable support in terms of the prestige and exposure it offers to a wide audience. Occasionally the Museum has also commissioned works, as in the examples of the 'Cup and Cover' by Malcolm Appleby and the 'Leopard Vase' by Maureen Edgar.

Other initiatives which have stimulated the craft in Scotland include the Inches Carr Trust, established ten years ago, which has awarded a number of professional development grants to makers in all disciplines. Silversmiths who have benefited include Malcolm Appleby, John Creed and Michael Lloyd. The Trust was of course established through the generous support of the late Deirdre Inches Carr, whose family used to own and run the prestigious Hamilton & Inches workshop and shop in Edinburgh. Hamilton & Inches continues to function under Scottish ownership, and young silversmiths, such as Sarah Cave, are currently working with the firm. The Scottish Arts Council established a department for Crafts in 1994, taking over the role from the Scottish Development Agency, and has offered set-up grants to young makers establishing first workshops in Scotland. And a final mention must be given to the Makower Trust in Oxfordshire, whose project to help young silversmiths at Bishopsland, through giving them low rent workshop space for one to two years after graduating, together with strong tutor input, has had a very positive impact on the development of the craft. A number of Scottish-trained students, such as Angela Cork, have found places there and gone on to successful studio practice in London.

To sum up, the last 50 years of considerable social change in Scotland seems to have opened up new opportunities for the talented silversmith. The visibility of modern masters, such as Malcolm Appleby, the demonstrable example he and others have provided, the role of art colleges and, in particular, the dedication of a few outstanding teachers, as well as the support and encouragement of museum curators, gallerists, private patrons and traditional craft guilds, have kept a small but extremely vibrant flame alive. The art of the silversmith in 21st-century Scotland seems to express a very particular, very powerful beauty. Beauty and all forms of art may be contested territories in the 21st century, but silver, which continues to be the means through which many of us still celebrate the joy of being human – birth, marriage, anniversaries, etc. – seems a material which has an enduring power in the modern world.

10.1

204

10.1 MACE OF THE SCHOOL OF MEDICINE, UNIVERSITY OF ST ANDREWS

Designed by Charles d'Orville Pilkington Jackson; enamels by Elizabeth Kirkwood; made by Hamilton & Inches, Edinburgh, 1949

L 130 cm

Lent by the University of St Andrews

Reference: *The Mace of the School of Medicine, University of St Andrews* (1950)

On a cylindrical shaft with four knops, with a hexagonal head with open crown-work symbolising the fountain of healing, surmounted by a figure of St Andrew; lower faces of head have cast angels bearing enamelled shields with the arms of the University Chancellor (Duke of Hamilton); the founding Pope Benedict XIII; the Rector (Sir George Cunningham); the founder of the first chair of medicine (the Duke of Chandos); and the Principal and Vice-Chancellor (Sir James Irvine). The head is also decorated with medical symbols and a Greek inscription reading: 'In purity and holiness will I guard my life and my art.' The collar of the lower knop or fleuron is engraved with a Latin inscription which translates as: 'The sculptor Charles d'Orville Pilkington Jackson conceived this mace in his mind. It was made in Edinburgh in AD 1949, in the workshop of the jewellers, Hamilton & Inches, by the silversmith Edward Robert Key Hamilton and the chaser William Samuel, and in her workshop by the enamellist Elizabeth Henry Kirkwood, and in his workshop by the engraver James Anderson.'

The gift of an anonymous benefactor, it was commissioned by St Andrews University for the School of Medicine in 1948. Charles Pilkington Jackson was invited to design it with the instruction that '… while the new mace should conform in size and general design to the older Maces [8.1 and 8.2] with which it would come to be associated in the ceremonies of the University, it should be in no sense a copy but as frank and sincere an expression of the craftsmanship of the age in which it was made as the medieval Maces were of theirs'.

10.2 TEA AND COFFEE SERVICE

Designed by Bernard Harrington; made by Ian Davidson, 1952

Marks: 'BH' (sponsor's mark Bernard Harrington); thistle (standard mark); castle (Edinburgh); 'W' (date-letter 1952-53); queen's head (coronation mark)

Tray: L 57.5 cm; W 38.1 cm

Teapot: H 20.6 cm; L 24.3 cm

Coffee pot: H 31.2 cm; L 23 cm

Hot water pot: H 28 cm; L 17.3 cm

Sugar bowl: H 13.6 cm; L 12.8 cm

Sugar spoon: L 11.5 cm

Milk jug: H 12.5 cm; L 11.8 cm

Total Wt: 173.5 oz

NMS K.2006.400.1-7; purchased at Lyon & Turnbull's sale, Edinburgh, 8 November 2006, lot 217

Six-piece tea and coffee service, comprising teapot, coffee pot, hot water pot, two-handled sugar bowl with spoon, cream jug and two handled tray; each of planished ovoid form, on domed circular foot, the teapot, coffee pot, hot water pot and tray with carved rosewood handles and matching tapered finials to the domed lids.

Both Bernard Harrington and Ian Davidson are important in the history of silversmithing education in Scotland in the post-war period. Harrington established silversmithing and jewellery as an independent department at Duncan of Jordanstone College of Art in Dundee in 1943 and continued to teach there until 1974. Amongst his many successful graduates was Maureen Edgar, the contemporary Scottish enameller. Ian Davidson taught at Edinburgh from 1961 to 1985.

10.3 CENTREPIECE, GLASGOW UNIVERSITY GENERAL COUNCIL

Designed and made by J. Leslie Auld, Glasgow, 1979

Marks: 'JLA' (maker J. Leslie Auld); castle (Edinburgh); lion rampant (sterling standard mark); 'E' (date-letter 1979)

D (bowl) 49 cm; H (max.) 30 cm; Wt 'over 18 lbs'

Lent by the University of Glasgow

Reference: Williams (1990), no. 8

Deep bowl with central column with sculptural representation of arms of the University of Glasgow surmounted by a tree; inset with an annulus with nine cups and nine trigonal pinnacles.

The entire composition represents the cycle of university life: the tree representing knowledge, the pinnacles rising aspirations, and the cups aspects of the University's traditions. It was a gift made on behalf of members of the University General Council to cele-

10.2   10.3

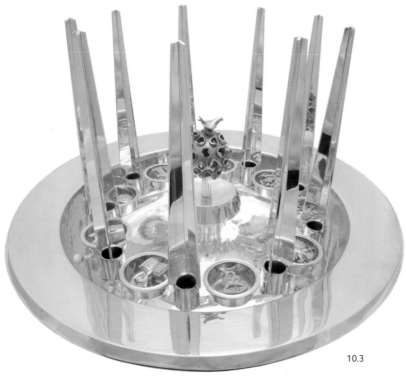

10.3

brate the centenary of the new buildings at Gilmourhill.

This centrepiece was J. Leslie Auld's last major commission prior to his retiral from the art school.

10.4 RAISED SILVER BOWL

Designed by Malcolm Appleby, 1975

Marks: 'MA' in monogram (maker Malcolm Appleby); lion rampant (sterling standard mark); castle (Edinburgh); 'A' (date-letter 1975)

D 6.8 cm; H 3.6 cm

NMS A.1977.240; purchased from the British Craft Centre, London, 1977

Silver bowl with a flattened hemispherical bowl with incurved rim; engraved on the exterior with irregular running scroll-work.

This early bowl illustrates Appleby's capacity for animated work in an informal style. See also the 'Cup and Cover' commissioned by National Museums Scotland in 1987 [1.12], and the Bute House Table Centrepiece [10.15].

10.5 JEWEL BOX

Designed and made by John Creed, 1983

Marks: 'JC' (maker John Creed); castle (Edinburgh); lion rampant (sterling standard mark); 'I' (date-letter 1983)

L 35 cm; W 24.5 cm; H 9.5 cm

NMS A.1991.440; acquired as part of the Scottish Crafts Collection in 1991

Jewel box with hemispherical lid of silver, partly gold-plated and decorated with marine invertebrates, fitted into an outer carrying case. The design of the box was inspired by aquatic imagery, but also deliberately demonstrates different techniques including spinning, handraising, chasing and shagreen. The shagreen (shark skin) was from the Cooper workshops.

The Scottish Crafts Collection commissioned this piece through a competition run with funds from the Scottish Development Agency and Johnson Matthey Metals Limited. The aim of the commission was to add a major work of contemporary Scottish silver to the collection and thus stimulate the craft.

10.6 A PAIR OF SPUN BOWLS

Designed and made by Graham Crimmins, 1986

Marks: 'GC' (maker Graham Crimmins); castle (Edinburgh); lion rampant (sterling standard mark); 'M' (date-letter 1986)

D 9 cm; L 12.5 cm; H c.4.8 cm

NMS A.1991.493; Edinburgh; acquired as part of the Scottish Crafts Collection in 1991

Small fine-spun silver bowls, with a tapering crescent-shaped piece of sterling silver with a patterned surface attached to the rim.

10.7 A GROUP OF THREE SPUN BOWLS

Designed and made by Graham Crimmins, early 1990s

Mixed metals, so no hallmark

9 cm x 3.5 cm

Lent by the artist

This important body of work was inspired by the fusing techniques of traditional Sheffield plate, as well as the decorative traditions of patination in Japanese metalwork. The pieces were spun in Birmingham by Ray Newey, with the silver fused to the centre and then returned to Edinburgh to be chemically patinated and finished.

10.8 TEA CADDY

Designed and made by Adrian Hope, 1987

Marks (on base): 'AKAH' (maker Adrian K. A. Hope); lion rampant (sterling standard mark); castle (Edinburgh); 'N' (date-letter 1987)

H 12.9 cm; W (base) 9.8 cm; Dp 8.7 cm

NMS H.MEQ 1603; purchased from the artist, 1987

Oval in plan with domed, hinged lid. The body and lid are made up of eight panels, textured by milling the silver sheets between watered paper.

This tea caddy is an early example of Hope's exploration of integrated surface through paper-embossing techniques.

10.6

10.4

10.5

10.8

10.9 LEOPARD VASE

Designed and made by Maureen Edgar, 1989/1990

Marks (on base): 'ME' (Maureen Edgar); lion rampant (sterling standard); castle (Edinburgh); 'P' (date-letter 1989)

H 23.5 cm; D (rim) 21 cm; D (inner rim) 12 cm; D (base) 7 cm

NMS H.MEQ 1616; commissioned from the artist, 1989

Silver enamelled vase; the main body cylindrical, funnelling out in a 'V' form and ending in a wide, curved everted rim. The silver body was spun from a single sheet of specially milled silver. The main body and the upper face of the rim are enamelled in *cloisonné* (with pure gold wires) and free-hand styles with a running pattern of two leopards (black and white), foliage and flowers in yellow, greens and browns, reserved against a golden yellow background. Inset within the vase is a similarly shaped black glass liner, specially blown by Lindean Glass, Lindean Mill, Selkirk.

This highly decorative *cloisonné* enamel vase was commissioned by National Museums Scotland in 1989 for the permanent collection in order to represent the world-class enamel work of Edgar.

Sadly Edgar took early retirement from her enamel studio on health grounds in 2001.

10.10 CHOCOLATE POT AND TEAPOT

Teapot: designed and made by Roger Millar, 1999

Chocolate pot: designed and made by Roger Millar, 2006

Teapot: 26 cm

Chocolate pot: 14 cm x 18 cm

Lent by the artist

Fabricated sterling silver with Corian handles.

Roger Millar's work is characterised by elegant, bold design and outstanding workmanship. The surface of both of these items is matt rather than highly polished, creating greater definition to the simple forms. Corian, a kind of resin, has replaced the traditional ivory to stop heat conductivity on the handle and finial. See also Millar's 'Silver for the Stars' commission (p. 214).

10.11 PAIR OF CANDLESTICKS

Designed and made by Roger Millar, 1996

Lent from a private collection

These candlesticks are made of sterling silver and stainless steel.

Although the significant patrons for imaginative modern silver in the post-war period have been the Worshipful Company of Goldsmiths, from the early 1990s the Crafts Council in London began a more active engagement with silver, with two important projects: one of which was a major show of contemporary silver; the other was 'Living Silver', a catalogued exhibition.

The aim of 'Living Silver' was to stimulate the creation of a competitively priced collection of modern silver hollow ware which would be catalogued and promoted to a new, design-literate younger public. This design by Millar was one of the objects chosen for the 'Living Silver' collection. Although the collection did tour, to Edinburgh at The Scottish Gallery and elsewhere, the project did not finally have a significant impact on either making or retailing silver, although it did result in the formation of the Association of British Designer Silversmiths, who have just celebrated their tenth anniversary with a show in Birmingham.

10.12 BOWL AND PAIR OF TUMBLER CUPS

Designed and made by William Kirk, 1997

Marks: 'WK' (maker William Kirk); lion rampant (sterling standard); castle (Edinburgh); 'X' (date-letter 1997)

Bowl: D 20 cm; H 7 cm

Cups: D 7.4 cm; H 5 cm

NMS K.1998.44-6; purchased from The Scottish Gallery, Edinburgh, in 1998

Exhibition: 'Silver from Scotland', Aberdeen Art Gallery and Museum (1997), and The Scottish Gallery, Edinburgh (1997)

The bowl and cups are made from hand-raised sterling silver. William Kirk's extraordinary raising skills are shown here in the traditional tumbler cup and bowl form that can be directly compared to tumbler cups and communion cup bowls of the 17th century.

10.9

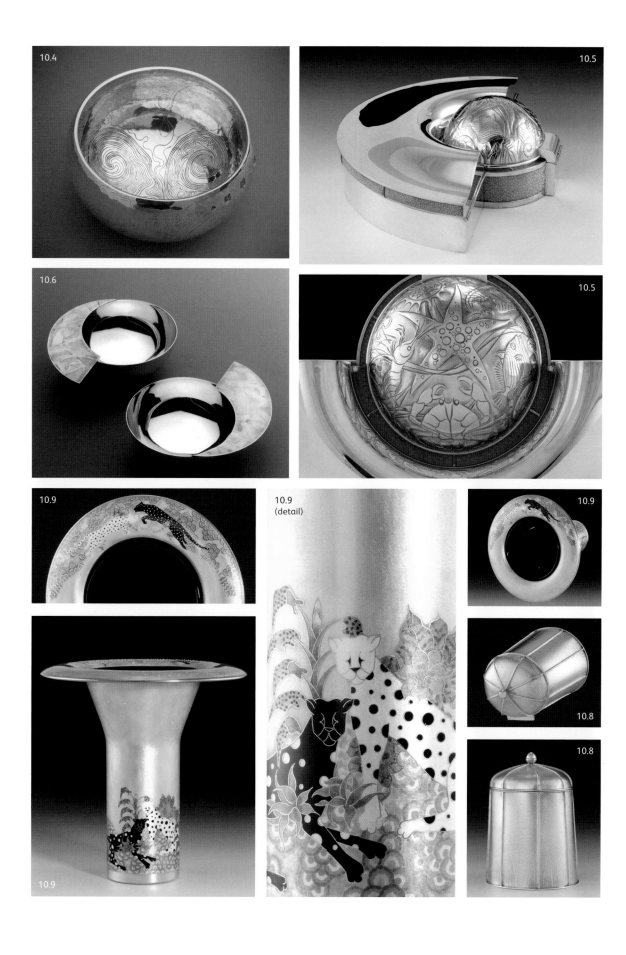

10.4

10.5

10.5

10.6

10.9

10.9
(detail)

10.9

10.9

10.8

10.8

10.13 COCKTAIL SHAKER AND TWO BEAKERS

Designed and made by Marion Kane, 2000

Marks: 'MK' (maker Marion Kane); lion rampant (sterling standard); castle (Edinburgh); 'A' (date-letter 2000); '2000' in cross (millennium mark)

Shaker: H 30.5 cm; D 10 cm / Beakers: H 16 cm; D 4.75 cm

NMS K.2001.4.1-3; purchased from The Scottish Gallery, Edinburgh, in 2001

Fabricated sterling silver with satinised surface and etched detail; gilded internally.

In 2000 the Incorporation of Goldsmiths in Edinburgh, together with their sister companies in England, struck a special commemorative hallmark for the Millennium. Two major commissions were organised in Edinburgh to celebrate this special hallmark, the first of which came through The Scottish Gallery in Edinburgh, who selected ten silversmiths working in Scotland and gave them an open brief, and sum of money, to create a piece of their choice. The ten pieces were catalogued and exhibited in Edinburgh and London as 'Collection 2000', when pieces were subsequently sold. National Museums Scotland acquired this piece by Marion Kane, who had recently graduated from Glasgow School of Art. The second major commission was the Millennium Commission for Bute House.

10.14 'DIALOGUE ONE'
TABLE CENTREPIECE IN FABRICATED SILVER AND FORGED STEEL

Designed and made by John Creed

Marks: 'JC' (maker John Creed); lion rampant (sterling standard); castle (Edinburgh); 'A' (date-letter 2000); '2000' in cross (millennium mark)

49 cm x 46 cm

Lent by The Scottish Gallery, Edinburgh

'Dialogue One' was another of the works commissioned by The Scottish Gallery and represents an early example of John Creed combining his two interests in forged steel and silverwork.

A successful period of study in America resulted in a number of larger scale commissions for Creed, including most recently a magnificent pair of gates for the newly refurbished Kelvingrove Art Gallery (2006). However, in addition to this larger scale use of steel, Creed also became interested in using steel structures in combination with silver. This commissioned example was followed by similar experiments for Bute House and 'Silver of the Stars'.

The Millennium Collection for Bute House

The second major millennial commission in Scotland was undertaken by the Incorporation of Goldsmiths of Edinburgh themselves through the Scottish Goldsmiths Trust (established 1999). The Bute House Silver commission was inspired by a commission some five years earlier, organised by the Silver Trust in association with Goldsmiths Hall, London, which resulted in a collection of magnificent modern table silver for use at civic functions in Downing Street.

With the establishment of the devolved Scottish Parliament in 1999, the Incorporation saw the opportunity to celebrate Scottish silversmithing through a similar commission. The collection is entirely practical and used when the First Minister entertains at his official residence, Bute House in Edinburgh. It comprises a 26-setting canteen of cutlery, a table centrepiece, and 13 other pieces for use in the dining-room. When not in use, it is regularly toured to venues around the world to celebrate the art of the silversmith in Scotland. For a detailed catalogue of the entire collection, see *The Millennium Collection for Bute House, Scotland* (2000).

10.15 TABLE CENTREPIECE

Designed and made by Malcolm Appleby

H. 9 cm to 20 cm; W 9 cm to 23 cm; L 9 cm to 42 cm

Lent from the Millennium Collection for Bute House by the Incorporation of Goldsmiths of the City of Edinburgh

Fabricated sterling silver

10.13

210

This spectacular and versatile centrepiece can be adapted to suit a table set for a variable number of guests. The central sections draw inspiration from the cliffs of Scotland's coast, and feature engraved representations of Edinburgh hallmarks. The candlesticks and posy holders are also inspired by the boulders and stacs of the Scottish coast.

10.16 TABLE SETTING

Designed and made by Adrian Hope

Lent from the Millennium Collection for Bute House by the Incorporation of Goldsmiths of the City of Edinburgh

Sterling silver and gold

Comprising first course knife and fork; soup spoon; table knife and fork; dessert knife, fork and spoon; coffee spoon. Each piece is inset with a representation of the Edinburgh castle town mark. There are 26 complete place settings in the collection.

10.17 WATER JUG

Designed and made by Michael Lloyd

H 32 cm; D 13 cm

Lent from the Millennium Collection for Bute House by the Incorporation of Goldsmiths of the City of Edinburgh

One of a pair, decorated with Lloyd's characteristic chasing and surface techniques.

10.18 CONDIMENT SET

Designed and made by Sarah Cave

H 7 cm; D 9 cm

Lent from the Millennium Collection for Bute House by the Incorporation of Goldsmiths of the City of Edinburgh

Hand-raised sterling silver and gilding

Comprising salt, pepper and mustard pot with spoon. Traditionally condiment sets are gilded to protect the silver against the corrosive effects of salt and mustard.

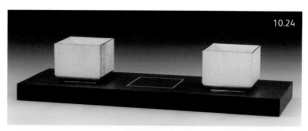

10.24

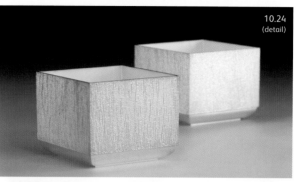

10.24 (detail)

10.23

10.23 (detail)

10.13

10.13 (detail)

10.15

10.19 CANDLESTICKS

Designed and made by Helen Marriott, Glasgow

H 31 cm; L 10 cm; W 10 cm

Lent from the Millennium Collection for Bute House by the Incorporation of Goldsmiths of the City of Edinburgh

Fabricated sterling silver with shagreen detail

Helen Marriott's bold fabricated forms, with highly polished surfaces, are typical of the undecorated formal dynamism of the Glasgow School, influenced by the teaching and design ethos of Roger Millar.

10.20 CLOCK

Designed and made by Gordon Burnett, Aberdeen

H 73 cm; L 61 cm; D 35 cm

Lent from the Millennium Collection for Bute House by the Incorporation of Goldsmiths of the City of Edinburgh

Clock made from fabricated sterling silver and cast glass.

10.21 CONDIMENT SET

Designed and made by Linda Robertson, London

Salt and pepper: H 15 cm / Mustard: H 6 cm; D 6 cm

Lent from the Millennium Collection for Bute House by the Incorporation of Goldsmiths of the City of Edinburgh

Fabricated sterling silver inlaid with gold.

10.22 FRUIT BOWL

Designed and made by Grant McCaig, Edinburgh

D 36 cm; H 18 cm

Lent from the Millennium Collection for Bute House by the Incorporation of Goldsmiths of the City of Edinburgh

Fruit bowl of fabricated sterling silver.

Grant McCaig was the youngest maker to be commissioned for the Bute House Collection. His sculptural fruit bowl shows a typical influence of natural forms allied with a bold, free-making style.

* * *

10.23 CHALICE

Designed and made by Michael Lloyd, Castle Douglas, hallmarked Edinburgh, 2004

Marks: 'MKL' (maker Michael Lloyd); '958', Britannia (Britannia standard marks); castle (Edinburgh); 'D' (date-letter 2004)

H 20 cm; D (base) 15 cm

NMS K.2004.282; purchased from The Scottish Gallery, Edinburgh, 2004

Chalice is of raised and chased Britannia Silver with gilding.

Michael Lloyd has made a number of pieces of church plate, firstly for Lichfield Cathedral and subsequently a set of four millennial chalices for York Minster. In 1999 he was commissioned to make the Mace for the newly-inaugurated Scottish Parliament, a commission which directly relates to this chalice. Using some reserve funds from the Mace commission, Michael designed and made this 'Chalice for New York' in the hope that the Scottish Parliament would take the piece and present it to a New York church to celebrate the healing power of craft in the aftermath of 9/11. The chalice, however, remained with the artist and was subsequently shown in a joint exhibition of Michael's work with his wife, the woodcarver Mary Lloyd, at The Scottish Gallery in Edinburgh in 2004.

10.24 SQUARE SILVER CONTAINERS ON SLATE BASE

Designed and made by William Kirk, Edinburgh, 2003

Marks: 'WK' (maker William Kirk); lion rampant (sterling standard mark); castle (Edinburgh); 'C' (date-letter 2003)

Containers: H 4.7 cm; W 5.5 cm (square)

Slate base: L 30 cm; W 10 cm

NMS K.2004.32; purchased from The Scottish Gallery, Edinburgh, 2004

Fabricated sterling silver with chased detail resting on carved and gilded slate base.

As well as a long career as a silversmith, William Kirk also undertook numerous commissions for cut, lettered stone. An exhibition at The Scottish Gallery in 2004 demonstrated his sensitive understanding of different materials, through a series of objects which combined both slate and silver using the matt tactile surface of polished slate as an effective foil to the reflective surfaces of the hand-raised silver vessels.

10.25 ENGRAVED SILVER BOWL

Designed and made by Graham Stewart, Dunblane, 2008

D 20 cm

Lent by the artist

Raised, hand-engraved, Britannia silver with parcel gilt bowl. This bowl is similar to a work commissioned by members of the Caledonian Club to celebrate the opening of the new wing in 2006, and presented to Her Majesty The Queen and His Royal Highness Prince Philip, Duke of Edinburgh. It belongs to a series of simple silver vessels Stewart has created which act as a canvas for his engraved letter-forms. Together with his older contemporary William Kirk, he shares a love of poetry and the spoken word, and translates this, lyrically, into his lettered silver.

10.26 RELIQUARY

Designed and made by Adrian Hope, 2007

Marks: 'AKAH' (maker Adrian K. A. Hope); lion rampant (Sterling standard mark); castle (Edinburgh); 'G' (date-letter 2007)

12.6 cm x 10.8 cm

Lent by the Artist

Adrian Hope has made boxes for a number of years, [cf. Tea Caddy, 10.8], interested in ways that these archetypal forms can be reinterpreted in contemporary silver. In 1989 National Museums Scotland hosted a touring exhibition, 'The Work of Angels – Masterpieces of Celtic Metalwork'. Amongst many powerful objects in this exhibition, which Hope visited, were a series of early reliquaries in the form of lidded boxes. The directness and power of these early religious artefacts were still evident to a contemporary eye. Adrian Hope's fabricated, paper-embossed modern silver 'Reliquary' captures something of those qualities. In so doing, he offers renewed possibilities for the silversmith to create objects in a personal way for the contemporary world, which celebrate the ceremonial and the memorial.

Spoons for Today

Spoons are one of the oldest and most enduring functional forms for silversmiths. They continue to be both made and purchased to celebrate births and other special occasions. From stirring tea to scooping jam to ladling soup, spoons still have an active use in our modern domestic lives. These six Scottish silversmiths offer a few examples of both the tradition and innovation still extant in the form of a spoon. All pieces bear Edinburgh marks, unless otherwise stated.

CADDY SPOON

Malcolm Appleby, 2006

Hammered and engraved silver

L 8.5 cm

SERVING SPOON

John Creed, 2000

Forged, oxidised silver

L 30 cm

PAIR OF PICKLE SPOONS

Graham Crimmins, 2007

Hammered forged silver

L 16 cm

SCOOP WITH WOODEN HANDLE

Grant McCaig, 2007

Sterling silver, found wood

L 34 cm

SERVING SPOON WITH DRIFTWOOD HANDLE

Grant McCaig, 2007

Sterling silver, driftwood

L 33 cm

SET OF FOUR COFFEE SPOONS

Linda Robertson, 1999

Silver inlaid with 18-carat gold

L 12 cm

LARGE SERVING LADLE WITH ACRYLIC HANDLE

Linda Robertson, hallmarked London, 2001

Silver and acrylic

L 37.6 cm

All the above: NMS K.2007.332-338

10.23   10.24

'Silver of the Stars' Collection 2007

As the boost to silversmithing received at the time of major commissions to commemorate the Millennium began to recede, members of the Scottish Goldsmiths Trust Contemporary Committee worked hard with the deacon Michael Laing to develop another, different, project to sustain and develop profile within the craft. 'Silver of the Stars' is the result. Ten high-profile Scottish celebrities were invited to choose their favourite drink, for which ten silversmiths were then invited to create a container. The exhibition has toured to major museums internationally, creating new audiences for this 'lovable craft' through the association with celebrity. For a detailed description of this innovative commission, see the separate catalogue, *Silver of the Stars* (2007).

HOT CHOCOLATE POT

Roger Millar for Scottish violinist
Nicola Benedetti

WHISKY SET

Grant McCaig for the actor
Robbie Coltrane

QUAICH

Michael Lloyd for the actor Sean Connery

TEAPOT

Coilin O'Dubhghaill for the actor and
comedian Billy Connolly

TEAPOT

Linda Robertson for the singer Lulu
(top image)

CLARET JUG

Sarah Cave for the promoter
Cameron Mackintosh

COFFEE POT AND MUGS

Marion Kane for the actor
Ewan MacGregor

ABSINTHE GOBLET

Graham Stewart for fashion designer
Alexander McQueen

IRN BRU SET

John Creed for novelist Ian Rankin
(image below)

TEAPOT

Sarah Hutchinson for singer
Sharlene Spiteri

Featured 'Stars' photographs
© Alastair Devine

TEAPOT

Sarah Hutchinson for singer
Sharlene Spiteri

CLARET JUG

Sarah Cave for the promoter
Cameron Mackintosh

Biographical Notes

The following listing is not a 'write all you know' exercise. It merely provides some notes on the lives of some of the goldsmiths (and a few others) whose names appear in the catalogue. Each heading (except for those of living goldsmiths) is followed by the place or places of work and by the individual's working dates, so far as they may be known. For our treatment of surnames, see p. viii. In this list, 'M' comes before 'Mac' and its equivalents.

- To save space, 'freeman' and 'deacon' in an Edinburgh context mean freeman and deacon of the Incorporation of Goldsmiths of the City of Edinburgh; in other burghs they mean freeman and deacon of the Incorporation of Hammermen (by whatever name) in that place. Similarly, 'deacon-convener' means deacon-convener of the incorporated trades in the burgh where the goldsmith worked, and 'burgess' means burgess of that burgh.
- George Heriot's Hospital is the original name for the institution now known as George Heriot's School.
- The Greyfriars burial ground referred to is the one in Edinburgh.
- The date when an apprenticeship started is given when known; otherwise we state the date when it was booked (i.e. registered in a book); this may sometimes be considerably after the actual date of the indenture.

AITCHISON, ALEXANDER (I):
Edinburgh, 1746-80s

Baptised 21 May 1717. Educated at George Heriot's Hospital 1726-33. Booked apprentice to Hugh Gordon 2 April 1733. Freeman 12 August 1746.

ALLAN, COLIN: Aberdeen, 1748-74
Son of John Allan, farmer at Mastrick. Apprenticed to George Cooper 24 November 1736 for 6 years. Burgess 5 October 1748. Deacon 1761-62, 1763-64, 1764-65 and 1767-68; deacon-convener 1763-65. Burgess of Old Aberdeen 2 January 1762 but remained in Aberdeen. Buried 9 December 1774.

ANDERSON, HEW: Aberdeen, 1610-c.39
Burgess 1610. Deacon 1617-18, 1620-21; deacon-convener 1622-24. Master of Trades' Hospital 1634-36. Member of Aberdeen Council of War 1639. Died in or by 1643. The Fintray Cup is only known surviving work.

ANDERSON, ROBERT:
Inverness, 1755-92

Freeman 23 April 1755. Trades' councillor 1784-85. Active in the Hammermen's affairs until 1791. Died 1792.

ANDERSON, WILLIAM:
Aberdeen, c.1630-c.62

Freeman c.1630. Deacon eight times between 1636-52; four times deacon-convener between 1646-52. Appointed by Town Council as 'tryar' (assayer) of the wrought silver made in the burgh 7 November 1649. His monogrammed initials are found in that capacity on the work of other goldsmiths. Died 17 February 1662.

APPLEBY, MALCOLM
Born 1946. Studied at Central, Sir John Cass and Royal Colleges of Art. First studio at Crathes (1969), then at Grandtully (1996). Leading metal-engraver, versatile designer and goldsmith.

AUCHINLECK, ALEXANDER:
Edinburgh 1536-c.70s

Son (and presumed apprentice) of Matthew Auchinleck II, goldsmith. Burgess 6 September 1536. Died in or shortly before 1581.

AULD, JOHN LESLIE MILLER:
Glasgow, 1964-96

Silversmith and jeweller. Registered first mark in Edinburgh 28 May 1964, last mark 26 January 1996; registered previously with Glasgow Assay Office. Influential teacher at Glasgow School of Art 1950-79. Died 1996.

AYTOUN, WILLIAM: Edinburgh, 1718-54
Born 1691, son of Alexander Aytoun, laird of Inchdairnie in Fife. Apprenticed to William Ged 13 December 1706. Freeman 13 June 1718. Deacon 1724-26 and 1730-32. Died 12 October 1754.

BAILLIE, JOHN: Inverness, 1727-53

Burgess 1727. Freeman 13 September 1735; deacon and deacon-convener 1744-45; trades' councillor 1749-50. Died 1753.

BENDY, CHARLES: Edinburgh, c.1820-c.27

Apprenticeship details unknown; may have come from England. An unfreeman, he sent work for assay 1820-27. Work consisted almost entirely of hollow ware. One of the goldsmiths who supplied goods to John Hay in Leith.

BILSINDS, JOHAN GOTTLEIFF: Glasgow, 1716-70

Born c.1684. Possibly immigrant from Germany or low countries. Apprenticed in Edinburgh to Alexander Kincaid in 1709. Moved to Glasgow. Burgess 18 June 1716. Freeman 20 July 1717. Buried 13 March 1770 aged 86. Possibly worked as journeyman to another master after c.1750.

BLAIR, CHARLES: Edinburgh, 1707-c.52

Son of James Blair, Laird of Gasclune. Apprenticed to a merchant before switching careers, becoming apprenticed to George Yorstoun, goldsmith, 23 March 1697. Freeman 31 December 1707. Died 1752.

BOOG, DAVID: Edinburgh 1653-82

Son of John Boog, merchant. Apprenticed to James Fairbairn 14 February 1642. Freeman 3 August 1653. Retired from business 1681. Died June 1694.

BOYD, JAMES: Glasgow, 1707

Son of James Boyd, mason. Burgess 5 June 1707. Freeman 8 August 1707.

BROCK, ROBERT: Glasgow, 1673-c.1717

Apprenticed to Thomas Moncur. Freeman 22 July 1673. From 1685-97 he was laird of Possil. A man of short temper, in 1693 he blasphemed the provost and called him 'ane villaine, ane rascall, ane cheat, ane knave, void of all religion and fear of God, ane woolfe in sheepes clothing ...'. Deceased by 12 August 1717.

BROOK & SON: Edinburgh, 1891-c.1950

Partnership of Alexander James Steel Brook (1856-1908) and son William Brook (d.1941). Successors to William Marshall & Sons 1891. In 1939-40 directory, firm is stated as goldsmiths to the late King George V and the King's Bodyguard for Scotland (Royal Company of Archers). A. J. S. Brook was a major figure in revealing the history of Scottish goldsmiths and wrote the appendix on goldsmiths and marks at the end of Burns' *Old Scottish Communion Plate* (1892).

BROWN, THOMAS LUMSDEN: Cupar, 1887-1935

Born in Leith, trained Edinburgh; moved to Cupar in 1887. Registered punch at Edinburgh Assay Office 1889, and sent silver for assay until 1935.

BRUCE, ROBERT: Edinburgh, 1688-c.1716

Apprenticed to James Cockburn on 11 October 1673. (Cockburn's second wife was Robert Bruce's sister.) Appears to have died in 1716.

BURDEN, ARCHIBALD: Edinburgh, c.1712-c.18

Third son of James Burden (Burdon), 2nd Laird of Feddall. Apprenticed to John Seatoun 28 November 1694. Worked as journeyman goldsmith and engraver after apprenticeship until he became a burgess by right of former master, gratis, 12 November 1712. Principally a silver engraver; surviving work as a goldsmith is rare. His next oldest brother, Francis, was apprenticed to David Penman, pewterer in Edinburgh, 7 October 1693.

BURNETT, GORDON

Born 1951. Trained at Gray's School of Art, Aberdeen. Returned there as lecturer in design. Main influences in his work are time, order and colour, specialist interest in CAD/CAM technologies. Other work includes the Mace of Robert Gordon University, Aberdeen and a Freedom Casket for Nelson Mandela.

BURRELL, ANDREW: Edinburgh 1642-61

Born 1618, son of Andrew Burrell, lorimer. Apprenticed to John Scott 5 November 1632. Freeman 23 February 1642. Deacon 1653-55 and 1659-61. Died late 1661 or early 1662.

BYRES, WILLIAM: Banff, 1778-1806

Freeman 1778. Deacon 1781-82. By 1806 he had moved to Aberdeen.

CAMERON, ALEXANDER: Dundee, c.1818-46

Recorded as goldsmith, jeweller and watchmaker. Sent work to Edinburgh and Newcastle for hallmarking. Accused by Edinburgh Incorporation of selling below standard work with forged marks.

CARMICHAEL, LADY GIBSON: Enameller, Edinburgh

Née Mary Helen Nugent, married 1886 Sir Thomas Gibson Carmichael, 1st Baron Carmichael, Liberal politician and art collector. Talented artist and enameller who taught technique to Phoebe Traquair.

CAMPBELL, JOHN: London, c.1692-1714

Second son of Sir Colin Campbell of Lundie, 1st Baronet. His grandfather was Colin, younger brother of Archibald Campbell, 7th Earl of Argyll. John Campbell was apprenticed to John Threipland 28 May 1679. Never became a freeman or burgess in Edinburgh and by 1692 he had established himself in London as a goldsmith and banker. Founder, with his son-in-law, George Middleton (b.1688), of the bank that eventually became Coutts & Co. In his testament, dated 12 August 1714, his executors are stated as his son-in-law and Robert Bruce, the Edinburgh goldsmith.

CAVE, SARAH

Born 1965. Studied at Edinburgh College of Art. Artist in Residence at Edinburgh College of Art. Working at Hamilton & Inches.

CLARK, JOHN: Edinburgh, 1751-71

Apprenticed to Patrick Murray 1734. Worked as journeyman to James Gillieland before becoming a freeman 24 June 1751. Took six apprentices but none of them became a freeman. For a while he specialised in making scientific instruments, including his own patent silver microscopes, and he excelled as a jeweller. After a short spell working in Lisbon he returned to Edinburgh 1770. For financial reasons he gave up his own business, 1771, and returned to the status of journeyman before beginning a new venture as an optician. It appears that although he was exceptionally skilled as a craftsman he was not a good teacher or businessman. Appointed joint assay-master with George Auld 30 July 1781; continued until his death in 1798.

CLEGHORNE, EDWARD (I):
Edinburgh, 1649-81

Son of Thomas Cleghorne I, goldsmith. Booked apprentice to his father 14 October 1637. Freeman 23 March 1649. Deacon 1663-65, 1671-73 and 1679-81. Represented Edinburgh in the Convention of Royal Burghs, 1679-81, and was a Commissioner to Parliament in the latter year. Died 1682.

CLEGHORNE, GEORGE:
Edinburgh, 1641-59

Son of George Cleghorne, minister of Dornock (Dumfriesshire). Apprenticed to Thomas Cleghorne 21 June 1630. Freeman 26 May 1641. Died March 1659.

CLEGHORNE, THOMAS (I):
Edinburgh, 1606-53

Apprenticed to Daniel Crawford 26 September 1591. Freeman 24 December 1606. Deacon 1640-42. Died 1653.

CLEGHORNE, THOMAS (II):
Edinburgh 1665-74

Born 1646, son of George Cleghorne, goldsmith. Booked apprentice to Patrick Borthwick, 9 September 1659. Freeman 11 March 1665. Deacon 1673-74. Left Edinburgh 1674.

CLERK, WILLIAM: Glasgow, 1693-1725
Freeman 12 July 1693. Deacon 1713-15 and 1718-20. Died 1725.

COCKBURN, JAMES:
Edinburgh, 1669-1700

Born 1648, eldest son of John Cockburn, tailor in Canongate. Booked apprentice to David Boog 15 July 1661. Freeman 17 July 1669. Deacon 1686-88. While deacon, he was appointed deputy-master of the Mint

1687. His third wife was Margaret, sister of his former apprentice, Robert Bruce. Prolific craftsman and successful businessman, he was among the first subscribers to the newly-founded Bank of Scotland in November 1695, committing some £20,000 Scots. Appointed Treasurer and a Director of the Bank in 1699, but died in November 1700. The Bank's Accountant reported the death thus: 'I am ordered by the Directors to acquaint you that yesterday about 3 in the afternoon it pleased God to call our Treasurer by Death; the loss of whom it cannot be enough regretted by his friends and all those who had occasion to know him'. Buried in Greyfriars Kirkyard 6 November 1700.

COK/COKKIE, WILLIAM:
Edinburgh, 1561-c.90s

Second son (presumed apprentice) of James Cokkie I. Freeman 1 November 1561. Deacon 1577-79 and 1592-93.

COK/COKKIE, JAMES (II):
Edinburgh 1557-73

Son (presumed apprentice) of James Cokkie I. Freeman 1 May 1557. Deacon 1563-65. Hanged for treason 1573.

COK/COKKIE, JAMES (III):
Edinburgh, 1574

Second son (presumed apprentice) of James Cokkie II. Freeman 15 February 1574.

COLQUHOUN, MATTHEW:
Ayr, c.1682-c.91

Apprenticed to Thomas Moncur in Glasgow for 5 years and then his servant for 2 years. Apparently in Ayr by c.1682. Deacon and deacon-convener 1690-91.

COOPER, GEORGE:
Aberdeen, 1728-65

Apprenticed to George Robertson c.1707-08. Freeman 16 August 1728. Deacon 1743-44. Buried 12 February 1765 aged 74.

CRAIG, ADAM:
Edinburgh, 1562-92

Eldest son (and presumed apprentice) of Robert Craig, goldsmith. Freemen

8 December 1562. Deacon 1572-74; acting-deacon 1576-77; deacon again 1587-89. Died 1592.

CRAW, WILLIAM: Canongate, 1760-69
Apprenticed in Edinburgh to Alexander Aitchison I, 24 January 1753. Freeman of Hammermen of Canongate 1760. Moved to Dumfries 1769. From the marks he is deduced to have been in partnership with James Hill for some of his time in Canongate but documentary evidence for this has not yet been found.

CREED, JOHN
Born 1938. Studied at Liverpool College of Art and in workshop of Francis Cooper in Kent. Moved to Glasgow 1970 and lectured in silversmithing and jewellery at the art college there. Also works in forged steel and other metals. At one time or another he has been mentor to most of the younger leading goldsmiths working in Scotland today.

CRICHTON, JOHN (III):
Edinburgh, 1882-1927

Born 21 February 1860, son of Michael Hewin Crichton, goldsmith. Apprenticed to uncle, George Crichton I, 10 August 1875, but transferred to George Crichton II, 24 November 1879. Freeman 24 August 1885. Deacon 1891-93, 1903-04, 1911-13 and 1924-26. Died 7 January 1927.

CRIMMINS, GRAHAM: Edinburgh, 1974
First mark registered 18 January 1973. Studied at Birmingham College of Art. Established studio in Edinburgh 1974.

CUMMING, THOMAS:
Glasgow, 1682-1729

Apprenticed in Edinburgh to Alexander Reid 21 August 1678. Freeman in Glasgow 5 August 1682. Listed in 1689 Draft Letter.

CUNNINGHAM, GEORGE:
Canongate, 1589-c.1635

Deacon 1593-94. Testament dative registered 12 July 1637. Son James apprenticed to George Robertson, Edinburgh in 1624.

CUNNINGHAM, WILLIAM & PATRICK (I): Edinburgh, c.1778-1807

Brothers, William (b.1743) and Patrick (b.1747), were sons of Patrick Cunningham, wright. William apprenticed to Lothian & Robertson and Patrick to Patrick Robertson alone. Opened the first silver-plating mill in Scotland in 1786. The firm ended on William's death, 19 June 1807.

DAVIDSON, ANDREW: Arbroath, c.1825-46

In Arbroath directories as a jeweller 1825-37. In the 1841 census stated to be aged 40. Died in 1846, aged 45.

DAVIE, WILLIAM: Edinburgh, 1740-c.1785

Apprenticed to James Tait 3 January 1724. Freeman 7 August 1740. Deacon 1774-76 and 1778-80. The Goldsmiths' minutes tell us that by December 1785 he was, through ill-health, 'unfit to manage his own affairs'. Died 1788. Not clear whether his business continued after 1785.

DEMPSTER, WILLIAM: Edinburgh, 1742-92

Son of a brewer. Apprenticed first to Charles Dickson I, 8 June 1732. After Dickson's death his indentures were transferred to James Ker 6 July 1739. Freeman 9 June 1742, and ran his own shop until 1751. In January that year he married Violet Ker, a daughter of his second master, and entered into partnership with his father-in-law as Ker and Dempster. This lasted until Ker's death in 1768. Deacon 1768-70 and 1786-88. Continued in business on his own until he took his son, James, into the business in 1775. This lasted until James' early death in 1790. William Dempster continued the business until his own death on 23 December 1792, after which his whole stock was bought by George Christie, goldsmith.

DENNEISTOUN, ANDREW: Edinburgh, 1636-54

Born 1610, only son of Robert Denneistoun, goldsmith. Apprenticed to James Denneistoun. Freeman 16 November 1636. Engraver at the Mint 1646. Died 1654.

DENNEISTOUN, JAMES: Edinburgh, 1598-1660

Son and apprentice of David Denneistoun, goldsmith. Freeman 15 April 1598. Deacon 1613-15, 1619-21, 1631-33 and 1642-44 (during 1642-44 John Fraser acted for him). Died April 1650.

DENNEISTOUN, ROBERT: Edinburgh, 1597-c.1622

Son (presumed apprentice) of David Denneistoun, goldsmith. Freeman 23 April 1597. Testament registered 1622.

DICKSON, ROBERT (II): Perth, c.1796-1846

Apprenticed to his father, Robert Dickson I, 1791. (The older man had been apprenticed to Robert Clerk in Edinburgh 1763.) He continued the family business, sometimes using the same punches as his father. Died 1846.

DOWNIE, DAVID: Edinburgh, 1770-94

Son of John Downie, watchmaker near Edinburgh. Apprenticed to William Gilchrist 2 November 1753. Freeman 20 November 1770. Briefly in partnership with brother William (watchmaker) 1775-77. Condemned to death for High Treason 1794 for his part in the anti-government Pike Plot, but sentence was commuted to banishment for life 1795. Settled in Augusta, Georgia, USA, where he took at least two apprentices. Died there on Christmas Day 1816.

DUFF, JOHN: Stirling, 1838

In King Street, Stirling, as manufacturing jeweller, 1838. Absent from 1841 census.

EDGAR, MAUREEN

Born 1949. Studied at Dundee College of Art under Bernard Harrington and Royal College of Art, London. Set up a workshop in the Borders 1980. Leads the way in enamelling, both *cloisonné* and *champlevé*. Major presentation pieces include Downing Street Silver Collection and Bute House Collection.

EDWARD & SONS: Glasgow, 1838-c.1960s; Jewellers, Buchanan Street, Glasgow

Registered 15 punches at Glasgow Assay Office. In 1958 registered three punches in Edinburgh. One of the biggest Glasgow concerns in the late 19th and early 20th centuries; started by George Edward senior in 1838, taken over by his sons David and George junior. Opened London branch in Cheapside in 1874, became a limited company in 1925; eventually sold out to Mappin & Webb in the 1960s.

ELPHINSTONE, ROBERT: Inverness, 1686-c.1704

Burgess 1686. Active in the Incorporation of Hammermen 1691-1703; deacon 1693-94 and 1702-04.

ERSKINE, JAMES: Aberdeen, 1792-c.1824

Son of James Erskine, vintner, he was apprenticed to James Smith 30 September 1781. Freeman 21 September 1792. In correspondence with John Ewan 1801-20.

EWING, THOMAS: Edinburgh, c.1540s-69

Date of freedom unknown. Deacon 1552-55, 1556-58 and 1561-62. It appears that he was effectively the first deacon-convener, c.1562, although that title is not known for certain to have been used until 1577. His testament was registered 6 January 1570.

FAIRBAIRN, JAMES: Edinburgh, 1641-60

Son of James Fairbairn from West Gordon, Berwickshire. Apprenticed to Alexander Reid I, 22 September 1630; indentures transferred to James Denneistoun 10 December 1632. Freeman 26 May 1641. Deacon 1651-53 and 1657-59. Died December 1660.

FENWICK, GEORGE (I): Edinburgh, 1800-24

Apprenticeship details unknown. Worked as an unfreeman from 1800. Freeman 20 September 1810, aged 34. In partnership with George McHattie as McHattie & Fenwick c.1800-c.07. Deacon 1819-21. Joint assay-master with John Ziegler from 1824 until Ziegler's death 1835 and then assay-master until his retirement 1853. Died 11 February 1857. Father of George Fenwick II.

FENWICK, GEORGE (II):
Edinburgh and Tobago, 1820-21

Apprenticed to father, George Fenwick I, without indentures. Freeman 23 May 1820. Emigrated to Tobago and died there a few months after his arrival, 4 September 1821.

FERGUSON, DANIEL:
Nairn, 1837-62

Established in Nairn 1837. In 1841 census as watchmaker aged 26. Moved to Inverness 1862.

FERGUSON, WILLIAM:
Peterhead, 1825-28

In business in Peterhead c.1825-c.1828. Afterwards moved to Elgin.

FERGUSON & McBEAN:
Inverness, 1880-1907

Formed by William Ferguson and brother-in-law James McBean. Specialised in 'artistic' Highland Jewellery and ornaments. Firm wound up 1907 after death of surviving partner McBean in 1905.

FORBES, ALEXANDER:
Aberdeen, 1728-53

Apprenticed to George Walker 1719-20, transferred to John Walker 1721-22. Burgess 16 August 1728. Deacon 1734-36 and 1744-46. Deacon-convener 1734-36. Buried 22 July 1753.

FORREST, MICHAEL:
Canongate, 1770-c.1776

Journeyman with James McEwan, Glasgow. Freeman in Canongate 1770. Master 1771-76.

FRASER, DONALD:
Inverness, 1804-c.1825

Apprenticed to Charles Jamieson. 1801. In directories under 'jewellers' 1821-25.

FRASER, JOHN: Edinburgh, 1624-c.53
Son of William Fraser of Killeithe. Apprenticed to Gilbert Kirkwood 13

May 1611. Freeman 15 June 1624. Acting-deacon 1642-44 in place of James Denneistoun. Testament registered 12 November 1653.

GALLOWAY, ALEXANDER:
Aberdeen, 1670-c.80

Apprenticed to Walter Melville 1657-58. Set up a booth 1670. Deacon 1674-76 and 1677-79. Master of the Trades' Hospital 1674-75. Deacon-convener 1675-76. Ceased work as a goldsmith c.1680 and became a merchant. City Treasurer 1687. Died at Hamburg 1702.

GARDNER, ALEXANDER:
Edinburgh, 1754-1803

Apprenticed to William Aytoun 23 May 1744. Freeman 19 November 1754. Appointed assay-master to the Mint 1767, in succession to Robert Gordon. Deacon 1772-74. Took his son, John, as apprentice 1773 and formed a business with him as A. Gardner & Co. 1797. On the occasion of the marriage of the Prince of Wales to Princess Caroline of Brunswick (8 April 1795), *The Caledonian Mercury* noted: 'Mr. Gardner, Jeweller to his Royal Highness for Scotland, had a beautiful representation of the Prince's feathers in small lamps on the front of his shop, which had a very fine effect, and attracted much notice.' Buried in the Greyfriars kirkyard 14 April 1803.

GARDYNE, PATRICK:
St Andrews, 1636-72

Freeman 1636 and last mentioned in the Hammermen's minutes 1662. His Communion Cups for the Town Church, St Andrews date from 1671-72. Brother of Robert Gardyne II, Dundee. Son, Patrick, born 1637, who may also have been a goldsmith in St Andrews. In 1624 he had become a freeman of the Hammermen of Dundee.

GARDYNE, ROBERT (I): Dundee, 1561
In 1561 a Robert Gardyne became a burgess of Dundee as a merchant. Supposed author of mark on Fergusson Spoon, 1576, and Coconut cup. No absolute proof and still confusion about identity.

GARDYNE, ROBERT (II):
Dundee, 1624-56

Freeman as goldsmith 1624. Testament registered 1656.

GARDYNE, ROBERT (III):
Perth, 1659-1708

Son (assumed apprentice) of Robert Gardyne II, Dundee. Freeman in Perth 1659. Deacon 1669-71 and 1673-34. Died in office as bailie in Perth 1708.

GED, DOUGAL: Edinburgh, 1734-63
Born 8 June 1701, fourth son of Robert Ged of Baldridge (Fife); nephew of William Ged, goldsmith. Apprenticed to William Aytoun 7 June 1718. Freeman 10 May 1734. Partnership with cousin, Ebenezer Oliphant, as Ged & Oliphant 1738-45. Deacon and assay-master 1740-42 and deacon 1760-62. Sold business in May 1763.

GED, WILLIAM: Edinburgh 1706-25
Son of William Ged of Baldridge (Fife), uncle of Dougal Ged, goldsmith. Apprenticed to Robert Inglis 23 December 1696. Freeman 16 August 1706. Virtually gave up business as a goldsmith in 1725 to devote himself to perfecting of his invention of stereotyping. Died in poverty 19 October 1749.

GILBERT, MICHAEL (II):
Edinburgh c.1549-90

Presumed son and apprentice of Michael Gilbert I. Burgess of Edinburgh 10 October 1549. Date of freedom not recorded. Deacon 1558-59. Elected deacon 1576-77 but refused to serve, Adam Craig being appointed acting-deacon in his place. Appointed King's Goldsmith 1579. Died as one of the richest men in Edinburgh 24 September 1590.

GILCHRIST, WILLIAM:
Edinburgh, 1736- c.55

Apprenticed to James Tait 19 November 1718. Freeman 26 February 1736 (his essay included a silver tea kettle and lamp); deacon 1752-54.

GLEN, JAMES: Glasgow, 1743-56
Son of John Glen, merchant in Glasgow. Apprenticed in Edinburgh to Ebenezer Oliphant, 10 March 1738.

Burgess of Glasgow 14 September 1743. Deacon 1752-54. Buried 13 December 1756, aged 40. Business briefly continued by widow, Margaret Murdoch.

GLENNIE, ALEXANDER:
Stonehaven, 1841

In 1841 census aged 35. Afterwards moved to Arbroath.

GORDON, PATRICK: Banff, 1732-c.41
Freeman 1732. Mentioned until 1741.

GRAHAM, ADAM: Glasgow, 1763-c.1818
Burgess as goldsmith 1763. Appears in the trade directories from 1787 till 1818, when he gave up business. He appears to have died in 1821.

GRAHAM, WALTER: Canongate, 1693
Apprenticed to Robert Brock, Glasgow, 1683. Burgess in Canongate in 1693. Afterwards moved to London.

GRAY, DAVID: Dumfries, 1810-41
Apprenticed in Edinburgh, working in Dumfries by 1810; opened shop there 1814. Probably most important Dumfries silversmith.

GRAY, JAMES: Canongate, c.1550s-c.84
Evidently working in Canongate by the 1550s. Die-sinker at the mint 1567 and was confirmed in that post 1581. Demitted office as die-sinker 1584.

GRAY & SON, ROBERT:
Glasgow, 1802-52

Robert Gray began work in Glasgow 1776 when he became freeman. Formed new business as Robert Gray & Son, 1802; lasted until 1852. Founder member of the Glasgow Goldsmiths' Company 1819 and was its chairman until 1824. Firm used Edinburgh Assay Office until 1819, after which their work was assayed exclusively in Glasgow.

HAIRT, EDWARD: Edinburgh, 1575-91
Apprenticed to James Cokkie, probably c.1560. Worked for a time as a journeyman in London with John Clerke, becoming a freeman of the Worshipful Company of Goldsmiths there 2 October 1570. Freeman in Edinburgh 22 December 1575. Deacon

1579-81, 1582-83 and briefly in 1585. Acting deacon-convener 1582. Died suddenly 'at the pleasour of God' 1591.

HAMILTON & INCHES:
Edinburgh, 1866 to the present

Partnership of Robert Kirk Inches and his uncle James Hamilton established at 90 Princes Street, 1866, replacing Mackay Cunningham & Co. there. Moved to present shop at 87 George Street in 1887, and incorporated clockmaking firm of Robert Bryson & Sons. Robert Kirk Inches became sole partner, was elected Lord Provost of Edinburgh and knighted in 1915. Firm continued in family hands until 1992 when sold to Aspreys of London. Now independent after management buy-out. Only Scottish manufacturing goldsmiths company to survive from 19th century.

HANNAY, WILLIAM:
Paisley, 1794-1838

Booked as journeyman to James Wyllie, Glasgow, 1791. Freeman in Paisley 1794. Sent silver to Edinburgh for assay until 1819, thereafter to Glasgow. A founder member of the Glasgow Goldsmiths' Company 1819. In directories until 1838.

HART, JAMES:
Canongate, c.1610-24

Dates imperfectly known, but already a freeman 1613. Keyholder of common box in 1615-16. Master 1617-18 and 1621-22 and deacon 1622-24. He probably continued work for some years thereafter.

HAY, JOHN: Leith, c.1812-c.50
Unfreeman in Edinburgh. Married there 25 April 1812; burgess 12 November 1817. Registered his last punch with the Edinburgh Assay Office 1849.

HERIOT, GEORGE (II):
Edinburgh, 1563-1610

Born c.1540; assumed to have been apprenticed to father, George Heriot I. Burgess 4 August 1562. Deacon on numerous occasions between 1565 and 1608. Deacon-convener 1606-08. Died 1610, aged 70, and was buried

in the Greyfriars kirkyard in an elaborate tomb which can still be seen there.

HERIOT, GEORGE (III):
Edinburgh, 1588-1624

Son and apprentice of George Heriot II, born June 1563. Freeman 28 May 1588. Elected a trades' councillor 21 September 1591. Deacon-convener 1593-95. Appointed goldsmith to the Queen (Anne of Denmark) 17 July 1597 and jeweller to the King (James VI) 4 April 1601. Foundation of his large fortune derived from the profligate extravagance of the queen. The king succeeded to the throne of England in 1603 and moved to London, Heriot following him shortly afterwards. Died in London 12 February 1624. His fame rests not on his work but on the fact that he left a large sum of money to the City of Edinburgh with which to found George Heriot's Hospital (now George Heriot's School), originally for the education and maintenance of orphaned children and grandchildren of the burgesses of Edinburgh.

HOPE, ADRIAN
Born Edinburgh 1953. Studied at Sheffield and Edinburgh Colleges of Art. Set up first workshop in Edinburgh 1980 and then in the Borders 1995. Studied in Denmark 1995 and is influenced by the Danish style of clean lines and surface-decoration.

HOWDEN, FRANCIS:
Edinburgh, 1781-1848

Son of John Howden, farmer in Hermiston, born 1758. Apprenticed to Alexander Aitchison II in or before 1773. Freeman 24 February 1781. For about three years in 1782-84 he was in business with John Taylor, a partnership which ended when Taylor died. Deacon 1811-13 and prime mover in establishing the Incorporation's Widow's Fund, for which service he was, in 1817, presented by his fellow freemen with a piece of plate worth 20 guineas. Died 14 September 1848, aged about 90.

HUTCHINSON, SARAH
Born 1982. Studied at Edinburgh College of Art; won Goldsmiths Company

New Designer Award for silver-smithing 2004; Dewar Arts Award 2006.

INNES, ROBERT: Inverness, 1708-c.22
Freeman 1708. Said to have died 1722.

JAMIESON, WILLIAM:
Aberdeen, 1806-41
Freeman 1806. Sent silver for assay in Edinburgh until 1840. Died 1841. Succeeded in business by son, George.

JAMIESON & NAUGHTEN:
Inverness, c.1813-c.23
Partnership mentioned in the Hammermen's minutes and apprentice register 1813-23. Partnership of Charles Jamieson and Robert Naughten (or Naughton).

JOHNSTON, ALEXANDER:
Dundee, 1739-c.1750
Apprenticed to Charles Dickson; Jacobite, 'out' in 1745-46; served in Price Charles Edward's Life Guards at Falkirk and Culloden.

JORGENSEN NICHOLAS:
Canongate 1638-44
Presumably of European origin; freeman 12 October 1638 (essay a gold ring and silver needle); master 1641-42. Died 1644.

KANE, MARION
Born 1975. Trained at Glasgow School of Art. Teaches at Edinburgh College of Art. Often uses contrasting matt, polished and textured surfaces.

KEAY, ROBERT (II): Perth, 1825-56
Freeman 1825. Partner with uncle, Robert Keay I, as R. & R. Keay 1825-39. Ran the business on his own 1839-56. Sent work to Edinburgh for assay until 1854. Died 1856, aged 56.

KEITH, JOHN: Banff, c.1794-c.1824
Silversmith 1794. Master 1798-1801. Deacon 1804-05. Became a freeman in Elgin 1808. Mentioned until 1824.

KER, JAMES: Edinburgh, 1723-68
James Ker of Bughtrig, son and apprentice of Thomas Ker, goldsmith, born 1700. Many family connections with titled and landed families in Lothians and Borders. Mother related to the Earls of Haddington; second wife (married 1750) was Elizabeth, daughter of Lord Charles Ker, Director of Chancery, second son of Robert Ker, 1st Marquess of Lothian. Freeman 31 May 1723. Deacon 1734-36, 1746-48 and 1750-52. Member of Parliament for Edinburgh 1747-54; considered by many to have become vain, haughty and contemptuous, he was not nominated to stand in general election of 1754 and lost his parliamentary seat. Died at Drumsheugh 24 January 1768.

KER, THOMAS:
Edinburgh, 1694-1714
Born 9 March 1667, 4th son of Andrew Ker in Barnhouse, whose father was Sir Thomas Ker of Redden, younger brother of 1st Earl of Ancrum. Apprenticed to James Penman 9 July 1685. Freeman 27 March 1694. Deacon 1708-10. Died of a decay 12 December 1714. Father of James Ker, goldsmith.

KER & DEMPSTER:
Edinburgh, 1751-68
Partnership between James Ker and his son-in-law, William Dempster.

KIRK, WILLIAM
Born 1933. Trained with Charles Creswick in Edinburgh. Founded a business as designer-silversmith letter-cutter and engraver 1961. Lecturer in silversmithing and jewellery at Glasgow School of Art and Edinburgh College of Art until 1999.

KIRKWOOD, ELIZABETH HENRY:
Edinburgh, 1929-65
Chaser and enameller, sent work for assay 1929-65.

KIRKWOOD, GILBERT:
Edinburgh, 1609-45
Son of Patrick Kirkwood, blacksmith in Colinton, and Elspeth Foulis. Booked apprentice to mother's relative, George Foulis, 19 September 1598. Freeman 13 September 1609. Second wife (married c.1618) was his kinswoman, Margaret, daughter of his former master. Deacon and deacon-convener 1623-25. Bought Pilrig estate 1634 and built Pilrig House by 1638. Died 1645 during outbreak of plague in the city. He was the master, but not the father, of Thomas Kirkwood, goldsmith.

KIRKWOOD, JOHN:
Glasgow, 1616-40
Freeman 1616. Deacon in 1629-30, 1632-33 and 1639-41.

KIRKWOOD, R. & H. B.:
Edinburgh, 1872 to the present
In 1872 firm of die-sinkers and medallists registered a punch. For a time 'conjoined' with Wilson & Sharp, but separated again. Original partnership was between Robert and Henry Bruce Kirkwood.

LAMB, ADAM: Edinburgh, 1619-c.47
Apprenticed to Robert Denneistoun 5 January 1609. Freeman 3 June 1619. Deacon 1627-29, 1635-37 and 1644-46. His testament was registered 24 August 1647.

LAW, ANDREW: Edinburgh, 1694-c.1703
Son of William Law, goldsmith. Apprenticed to his uncle, John Law, 11 September 1683. Freeman 27 March 1694. Deacon unusually early in his career 1696-98. In 1698 imprisoned for a debt of £300 Scots, having invested unwisely in the disastrous Darien Scheme; the Incorporation of Goldsmiths bailed him out. Stated to have been deceased by 10 September 1703.

LEITH, GEORGE (possibly): Banff
Mentioned in Inverness 1708. It is speculated that he may have returned to Banff after a period in Inverness. Documentary evidence lacking.

LESLIE, JOHN: Aberdeen, 1773-c.1824
Apprenticed to James Wildgoose 1769-70. In correspondence with John Ewan 1773-78. Freeman 2 November 1774. Burgess 4 October 1782. Deacon 1784-86 and 1802-03. Master of the Trades' Hospital 1795-97. Deacon-convener 1802-03. Retired c.1824. Died 24 May 1837, aged 88.

LEYS, ADAM: Edinburgh c.1519-c.40

Maker of the Hammermen's seal in 1519 and was deacon 1524-26. Made the arches for the Scottish crown and also recast and augmented the sceptre. It has been surmised as a tentative theory that he may have been the maker of the Watson Mazer, but this is not yet substantiated.

LINDSAY, THOMAS (II):
Dundee, 1662-c.88

Burgess by right of father, Alexander Lindsay, goldsmith 1662. Freeman 1663. Mentioned in the journeymen's book 1663-88. Four times deacon from 1664-65 to 1668-69.

LINDSAY, WILLIAM (I):
Montrose, c.1665-83

In parish records from 1665. Burgess 1666. Mentioned in the Register of Deeds 1672 and 1679. Died 1683. Father of William Lindsay II (c.1688-c.95).

LLOYD, MICHAEL

Born 1950. Trained at Birmingham School of Silversmithing and Royal College of Art. Set up a studio in south-west Scotland 1988. Specialises in raising and chasing; inspired by 'a homage' to the natural world. Other work includes Mace of the Scottish Parliament.

LUKE, ROBERT:
Glasgow, 1721-52

Freeman 1721. Treasurer of the City of Glasgow 1730-31. Many business interests outside goldsmith's workshop, including a brewery and a soap factory. Died 1752.

LUMSDEN, BENJAMIN:
Montrose, 1788

Son of Benjamin Lumsden, goldsmith in Aberdeen. Apprenticed to James Gordon & Co., Aberdeen, 26 September 1782 for 4 years. In Montrose by 1788.

LYLE, JOHN: Ayr, c.1900

Registered several punches at Glasgow Assay Office, all without dates, probably either side of 1900.

LYMEBURNER, PETER:
Glasgow, c.1558-c.1610

Mentioned several times in the books of town clerks of Glasgow from 1558 onwards. Deacon 1606. Died c.1610.

MARRIOTT, HELEN

Born 1958. Studied at Glasgow School of Art and the Royal College of Art, London. Set up her studio in Glasgow 1984. Often uses contrasting materials in her work.

MELVILLE, WALTER:
Aberdeen, 1649-c.1670

Burgess 10 October 1649. Master of the Trades' Hospital 1656-58. Deacon and deacon-convener 1662-63. Retired by c.1670. Died in Edinburgh 1698.

MILL, WILLIAM: Montrose, 1811-c.38

Apprenticed to James Cornfute, Perth, 1777. Freeman in Montrose 1811. Sent work to Sheffield for assay 1838.

MILLAR, ROGER

Born 1942. Studied at Glasgow School of Art and the Royal College of Art, London. Took over from Bernard Harrington at Dundee. Head of silversmithing and jewellery at Glasgow School of Art 1979-2005. Major influence in teaching of silversmithing.

MILNE & CAMPBELL:
Glasgow, c.1757-c.1783

Partnership between George Milne and John Campbell. Established c.1757. Last mentioned 1783. Innovative goldsmiths: advertised in 1761 that he 'had engaged a workman from London for chasing … all kinds of plate, being the first of that profession in this place'.

MITCHELSON, JAMES:
Edinburgh, 1706-57

Son of John Mitchelson of Middleton. Apprenticed to George Main 25 March 1696. Freeman 31 May 1706. Deacon and deacon-convener 1722-24. Treasurer of the Trades' Maiden Hospital 1741-57. Died 8 December 1757.

MONCUR, THOMAS:
Aberdeen, 1643-c.57

Probably Thomas Moncur born in Aberdeen to Thomas Moncur and

Margaret Anderson; baptised there 4 November 1619. Apprenticed to Hew Anderson. Moncur married Janet Findlay and son, Thomas, born in 1641. Burgess 20 September 1643. Deacon 1649-50. Last mentioned in Aberdeen 1657. Probably father of Thomas Moncur, freeman goldsmith in Glasgow.

MONCUR, THOMAS:
Glasgow, 1665-c.70s

Probably Thomas Moncur who was born in Aberdeen to Thomas Moncur and Janet Findlay, baptised 6 January 1641. Burgess in Glasgow 29 December 1664, having been an apprentice in Aberdeen and journeyman in Edinburgh. Took Matthew Colquhoun (afterwards goldsmith in Ayr) as his apprentice 1675. Also took Robert Brock as apprentice. Commissioned to make many pieces of Glasgow town plate.

MUIRHEAD & SON, JOHN:
Glasgow, 1858 to the 20th century

An important and prolific firm. John Muirhead became a freeman 1858. Sons, Robert and Lewis, became freemen in 1868 an 1872 respectively.

McCAIG, GRANT

Born 1974. Trained at Glasgow School of Art. Lecturer in silversmithing and jewellery at Edinburgh College of Art. Other work includes a commemorative link for the chain of office of the Lord Provost of Edinburgh.

MacGREGOR, DAVID:
Perth, 1863-1909

Goldsmith, jeweller and engraver. Born 1839; trained with Begbie & Lee and Thomas Haliday, engravers in Edinburgh. Started work in Constable & MacGregor (successors to Magdalene MacGregor see below) Perth, 1863. Continued business under his own name 1875. Royal warrant from Queen Victoria 1893; Lord Provost of Perth 1899-1901; died April 1909.

MacGREGOR, MAGDALENE:
Perth, 1848-65

Widow (née Currie) of Robert McGregor; continued to use her

husband's maker's mark from 1848. Called lapidary and jeweller to Her Majesty 1856. Registered a punch in her deceased husband's name 1864. Died 1865 aged 59. Business was continued by Albert McGregor.

McHATTIE, GEORGE:
Edinburgh, 1806-28

Son of Alexander McHattie, merchant. Working as an unfreeman by 1806. Freeman 28 May 1811. In partnership with George Fenwick as McHattie & Fenwick c.1800-c.1807. Died April 1828.

McHATTIE & FENWICK:
Edinburgh, c.1800-c.1807

Partnership between George McHattie & George Fenwick.

MACKAY, JAMES:
Edinburgh, 1796-c.1865

Apprenticed to Alexander Gardener, 1783. Freeman 13 August 1793. Burgess 1 September 1796. Listed as jeweller and goldsmith 40 South Bridge from 1805. In partnership with David Cunningham by 1825.

MACKAY, JOHN RIDDLER:
Elgin, 1859-63

Apprenticed to William Ferguson, Elgin. Took over his premises in 1859. Retired through ill health 1863.

MACKAY CUNNINGHAM & CO.:
Edinburgh, c.1824-c.1930s

Partnership of James Mackay and David Cunningham established sometime before 1824 at 40 South Bridge. Became Mackay Cunningham & Co., 'Goldsmiths to the Queen', by 1856, now at 54 Princes Street. In 1873 recorded as 'Goldsmiths to the Queen, HRH Prince of Wales, watchmakers, and manufacturers and designers of Scottish jewellery'. Taken over by James Hardy & Co. Ltd by 1912.

McKENZIE, COLIN:
Edinburgh, 1695-c.1720s

Apprenticed to James Penman 21 July 1686. Freeman 23 July 1695. Fined for employing goldsmiths in Canongate 1695. Member of Royal Company of Archers by 1704. Mentioned until 1735.

McKENZIE, SIMON: Inverness, 1708-57

Apprenticed to Robert Elphinstone. Freeman 1708. Paid dues for an apprentice and a journeyman 1712.

MacKENZIE, WILLIAM: Tain, 1841-79

In 1841 census aged 20. Sent gold to Edinburgh for assay 1858-75. Died 1879. His mark as a retailer of silver appears always to be overstriking that of other goldsmiths.

McLEAN, WILLIAM: Inverness, 1702-14

Apprenticed to Robert Elphinstone 1696. Freeman 1702. Last mentioned in the Hammermen's minutes 1714.

NAUGHTEN/NAUGHTON, ROBERT:
Inverness, 1814-57

Freeman 1814. In partnership with Charles Jamieson as Jamieson & Naughten c.1814-c.23. Burgess 1824. Sent work to Edinburgh for assay 1839-56. Died 1857.

O'DUBHGHAILL, COILIN: Glasgow

Born 1974. Studied at Edinburgh College of Art, graduated 1996; Tokyo National University of Fine Arts and Music, 2000-05. Goldsmiths Company Designer Silversmith Award 1996. Taught at Glasgow School of Art and Sheffield Hallam University.

OLIPHANT, EBENEZER:
Edinburgh, 1737-c.66

Born 7 March 1713, 8th son of James Oliphant, 5th of Gask. Booked apprentice to James Mitchellson 13 September 1727. Freeman 26 August 1737. May have retired from business in 1766. Died 26 October 1798.

PALMER, DAVID:
Edinburgh, 1578-c.1615

Apprenticed to George Heriot II, 3 May 1564. Freeman 8 January 1578. Deacon 1611-13. Died 1615.

PENMAN, JAMES:
Edinburgh, 1673-1733

James Penman, 4th son of John Penman, merchant, baptised 9 November 1649. Booked apprentice to Edward Cleghorne 22 May 1666. Freeman 1 September 1673. Married his former master's daughter, Margaret Cleghorne, 20 April 1676. Deacon 1684-

86, 1692-94; assay-master 1697-1708; promoted to be assay-master at the Mint 1708. Died 21 February 1733.

PEARSON, JOSEPH:
Dumfries, 1794-1816

Started business in Dumfries 1794. Made wide range of work, especially Old English pattern flatware. In 1810 advertised that everything he sold was manufactured in his own premises. Sold business 1816.

PILKINGTON-JACKSON, CHARLES D'ORVILLE: Sculptor, b.1887-d.1973

Born in Cornwall 1887. Studied at Edinburgh College of Art. Made many public sculptures all over Scotland, including Robert I, the Bruce, at Bannockburn 1964.

RAEBURN, SIR HENRY:
Edinburgh, portrait painter, b.1756-d.1823

Born 4 March 1756, younger son of Robert Raeburn, mill-owner. Parents both died when he was six years old; brought up by older brother, Thomas. Educated at George Heriot's Hospital between 9-15 years of age. Booked apprentice to James Gillieland, goldsmith, 16 November 1771. During apprenticeship his talent as an artist became apparent; turned to portraiture. Gillieland introduced him to David Martin, at that time Scotland's most distinguished portrait painter; career developed from there. Knighted by George IV in 1822. Died 8 July 1823.

RAMSAY, JAMES:
Dundee, c.1894-1960s

Shop in high street by 1894. Produced work for major English retailers. Marks registered in London, Sheffield, Glasgow and Edinburgh.

REID, ALEXANDER (II):
Edinburgh, 1660-c.99

Son of John Reid, wright. Apprenticed to Nicoll Trotter 18 December 1644. Freeman 7 January 1660. Deacon 1669-71, 1674-75, 1677-79. Deacon-convener 1677-79. Still living in 1700.

REID, ALEXANDER (III):
Edinburgh, 1677-89

Baptised 17 July 1660, son of Alexander Reid II, goldsmith. Booked apprentice to his father 5 December 1668. Freeman 4 April 1677. Died October 1689.

RITCHIE, WILLIAM: Perth, 1796-1815

Freeman 1796. Sent work to Edinburgh for assay 1799-1805. Deacon 1806-08. Died 1815, aged 42.

ROBB, WILLIAM: Ballater, c.1880-1926

Apprenticed in Aberdeen, moved to Kincardine O'Neil, Lumphanan and finally Ballater. Sent silver to Edinburgh Assay-Office from all these places. Produced Mark from Brook & Son, Edinburgh and Jamieson, Aberdeen. Prolific producer of 'Celtic revival' and Highland 'souvenirs'.

ROBERTSON, GEORGE:
Aberdeen, 1708-26

Third son of Alexander Robertson, town clerk of Aberdeen. Apprenticed to William Lindsay 1696-97. Journeyman with Alexander Forbes 1703. Burgess 11 September 1708. Buried 29 September 1727.

ROBERTSON, GEORGE:
Edinburgh, 1616-c.42

Apprenticed to George Crawford 27 December 1607. Freeman 6 December 1616. Held office in the Incorporation of Goldsmiths until 1642.

ROBERTSON, JOHN:
Canongate, 1773-90

Freeman 1773. Master 1774-76. Died 1790.

ROBERTSON, LINDA

Born 1965. Studied at Glasgow School of Art, followed by a Master's degree at the Royal College of Art, London. Since 2000 working in London. Often combines slate, soap-stone, nickel and other materials in her work.

ROBERTSON, PATRICK:
Edinburgh, 1751-90

Born 6 August 1729, 3rd son of Mr William Robertson, minister of Borthwick parish, later of Old Greyfriars:

Edinburgh. Oldest brother was Dr William Robertson (b.1721-d.1793), distinguished historian and Principal of University of Edinburgh. Family related to Robert Adam, distinguished architect. Patrick Robertson booked apprentice to Edward Lothian 10 October 1743. Freeman 24 June 1751. Entered business partnership with former master until at least 1776. Deacon 1754-56, 1764-66. Member of the Royal Company of Archers 14 July 1755. Trades' councillor 1763-64 and 1766-68. Imported ready-made goods from England, notably from Boulton & Fothergill, Birmingham; copied their designs in his own workshop. Died in Harrogate 8 September 1790 while taking the waters.

ROBERTSON, ROBERT: Cupar, 1815-77

Apprenticed to his uncle in London, 1807. Moved to Cupar 1815, taking over the business of George Constable. Sent work to Edinburgh for assay 1825-75. Semi-retired and formed business with his son, George Brunton Robertson as R. & G. B. Robertson 1857. Died 1877. Also Officer of Weights and Measures for the County of Fife.

ROLLO, JOHN: Edinburgh, 1731-37

Born 1708, 3rd son of Robert, 4th Lord Rollo. Apprenticed to Henry Bethune 20 November 1723. Freeman 28 July 1731. Deacon 1736-37. Retired from business in 1737, to become customs officer in Fife, then in Banff (1745) and Cullen (1749) (while remaining a freeman of the Incorporation). Succeeded his brother, Andrew, as 6th Lord Rollo 1765. Died 26 March 1783.

ROSS, HUGH (I): Tain

Doubt as to his starting date, perhaps c.1710. Where his work ends and his son's begins is uncertain. Father of Hugh Ross II.

ROSS, HUGH (II): Tain, c.1755-c.78

Born c.1733, son, apprentice and eventual partner of his father, Hugh Ross I. He, or his father, died 1778. May have been other generations of Hugh Ross goldsmiths in Tain before and after the dates mentioned.

SCOTT, ALEXANDER:
Edinburgh, 1649-77

Son of John Scott, goldsmith, possibly born c.1627. Apprenticed to his father 14 October 1637. Freeman 23 March 1649. Married Agnes Wauchope, dowager countess of Linlithgow, 29 July 1652. Died 1677.

SCOTT, JOHN: Edinburgh, 1621-c.49

Son of John Scott, indweller in Canongate. Apprenticed to Thomas Cleghorne I, 17 September 1611. Freeman 7 December 1621. Deacon 1637-39 and 1646-48. Died between September 1648 and February 1649.

SCOTT, JOHN: Perth, 1808-58

Freeman 1808. Sent work to Edinburgh for assay 1838. Died 1858 at 79.

SCOTT, WILLIAM [I]:
Aberdeen, Banff and Elgin, 1666-1702

Admitted to Aberdeen Hammermen 1666. Arrived in Banff in 1688. Burgess there 1690. Burgess of Elgin 1700 but continued to live and work in Banff. Died c.1702. Father of William Scott II.

SCOTT, WILLIAM [II]:
Aberdeen, Banff and Elgin, c.1693-1741

Mentioned in Banff 1693-1741. Burgess of Elgin with his father 1700. Died in Banff 1748. Son of William Scott I.

SCOTT, WILLIAM: Dundee, 1788-99

Freeman by 1778. Died 1799. Business assets and tools taken over by his apprentice Edward Livingston.

SEATOUN, JOHN:
Edinburgh, 1688-c.1728

Baptised 20 October 1661, youngest child of Alexander Seatoun, merchant. Apprenticed to Alexander Reid II, 17 March 1677. Freeman 19 September 1688. Still active in the Incorporation 1728.

SELLAR, JOHN: Wick

In directories 1825-36 as watch and clockmaker and jeweller. Previously in Forres and Tain, afterwards in Elgin.

SORLEY, R. & W.:
Glasgow, 1877-1964

Original partners were Robert & William Sorley; succeeded Jaffray(?) in 1877. In directories from 1888 as watch and clockmakers, gold and silversmiths, dealers in precious stones, silver plate, etc. Registered 23 punches in Glasgow. Registered punches in Edinburgh 1964.

STALKER, WILLIAM:
Glasgow, 1607-d.1644

Apprenticed to his father, also William Stalker, in Edinburgh, 7 February 1590. Freeman in Edinburgh 9 May 1600. Moved to Perth by 1605. Settled permanently in Glasgow 1607 when he became burgess as goldsmith. Deacon 1626-27 and 1638-39. Died 1644.

STEVEN, JOHN: Dundee 1746-75

Apprenticed to William Aytoun, Edinburgh October 1737. Freeman in Dundee September 1746. Died September 1775 aged 51. He is possibly Dundee's finest 18th century goldsmith.

STEWART, GRAHAM

Born 1955. Studied at Gray's School of Art, Aberdeen with Malcolm Appleby. Established workshop in Dunblane in 1978. Particular interest is in inscriptive and lettering work.

SYMONTOUN, JAMES:
Edinburgh, 1645-c.82

Eldest son of William Symontoun, merchant. Apprenticed to Robert Gibson 2 April 1635. Freeman 5 June 1645. Deacon 1665-67. Last mentioned in the Goldsmiths' minutes 1682.

TAIT, JAMES:
Edinburgh, 1704-c.1751

Baptised 3 July 1679. Apprenticed to his uncle, George Yorstoun, 14 March 1694. Freeman 3 June 1704. Still alive in 1751 but died soon afterwards and his widow, Katherine Lamont, continued the business for a short while.

TRAQUAIR, PHOEBE ANNA:
Enameller, Edinburgh

Born Phoebe Anna Moss, daughter of William Moss, surgeon in Dublin, 24 May 1852. Trained at Royal Dublin Society Art School. Following marriage in 1873 to Scots palaeontologist, Dr Ramsay Heatley Traquair (1840-1912), they moved to Edinburgh 1874. By c.1900 she had taken up enamelling and developed her skill to a high degree. Ceased work c.1925 due to failing eye-sight. Died 4 August 1936.

VEITCH/VAICHE, JOHN:
Edinburgh, c.1517-c.1540s

Burgess 27 July 1517. Appears in the burgh records 23 October 1520 when he valued some silver and gold work. His name is sixth in the Nominal Roll of Edinburgh freemen goldsmiths on 31 January 1526. It is not known for how long he worked.

WALKER, GEORGE:
Aberdeen, 1685-1743

Burgess 3 June 1685. Trades' councillor 1716-17. Deacon and deacon-convener 1721-23. Died 20 September 1743, aged about 80. Father of John Walker.

WALKER, JOHN: Aberdeen, 1713-27

Son (and presumed apprentice) of George Walker, goldsmith. Freeman 1713. Deacon and deacon-convener 1723-25. Died 1727.

WEEMS, JAMES: Edinburgh, 1738-86

Baptised 30 June 1711, son of Thomas Weems, advocate. Apprenticed first to Edward Penman 8 July 1727 and transferred after his master's death in 1729 to William Aytoun. Freeman 6 March 1738. His shop was robbed on the night of 9 October 1786 and he seems to have lost heart and given up business from that time. Died a few years later.

WELSH, JAMES: Edinburgh, 1746-c.85

Baptised 4 April 1721, eldest son of John Welsh, vintner. Apprenticed to James Mitchell 19 October 1736. Freeman 13 November 1746. Deacon 1756-58. His business seems to have continued until c.1785. He was still living, though in ill health, in 1791.

WILKIE, ANDREW: Edinburgh, 1811-62

Son of James Wilkie, cabinet-maker. Booked apprentice to John Ziegler 23 September 1805. Worked as unfreeman from c.1811 or earlier. Freeman 1813 (precise day of his admission not minuted). Died 30 December 1862.

WILKIE, RICHARD MAXWELL:
Tain, c.1834-38

Made silver for the Ross of Pitcalnie family 1834. In directory as silversmith 1837. Moved to Glasgow 1838 and was in business there until c.1860. In 1841 census returns in Stirling. Confined to an asylum in Aberdeen 1871. Died 1880 and buried in Tain. For a short time in partnership with William Innes as Innes & Wilkie.

WILSON, ADAM: Edinburgh, 1599-1609

Apprenticed to John Mosman 18 April 1589. Freeman 8 April 1599. He appears to have left Edinburgh by January 1609.

YORSTOUN, MUNGO:
Edinburgh, 1702-21

Born 1677. Apprenticed to John Seatoun 15 April 1691. Freeman 7 March 1702. Died October 1721.

ZIEGLER, ALEXANDER:
Edinburgh, c.1762-1817

Son of George Ziegler, glover, born c.1729. Booked apprentice first to Alexander Campbell 10 October 1747; transferred to William Aytoun 13 February 1753 because Campbell was about to leave Edinburgh. By or before 1762 he was working on his own account as an unfreeman. Freeman 24 May 1791. Died 1817 aged 88.

Selected Glossary

APPRENTICE: One bound, usually by indentures, to a master, to learn a craft or business.

ASSAY: The testing of precious metals to establish their purity and the proportion of added baser metals.

ASSAY-MASTER: The first assay-master in Edinburgh was John Borthwick, appointed in 1681. The assay-master's duty is to assay, or oversee the assaying of, the work of all who send their wares to Edinburgh for assay. In modern times the assay-master is also the hands-on manager of the Assay Office and employees.

ASSAY-MASTER'S MARK: From 1681 until 1758 the assay-master's mark consisted of his initials, the same as his maker's mark. In 1758 his mark was changed to a thistle. The assay-master's mark continued to be a thistle until 1 January 1975, from which date a lion rampant has been used as a standard mark in its place.

ASSAY OFFICE: The first assay office in Scotland was set up in Edinburgh, probably in the 1680s, at the west end of the Tolbooth, before which time the deacon assayed goldsmiths' work either in his shop or theirs. In 1701 the first Goldsmiths' Hall was established in the Parliament Close and the assay office was moved to the same building then or shortly thereafter.

BALUSTER: A form of circular section of smooth double-curved outline, slender above and swelling below, as often used for the bodies of casters, coffee pots, mugs and similar items in the 18th century. An essential part of the standard repertoire of basic designs.

BAROQUE: Originally a jewellers' term describing a rough natural pearl. A vigorous, exuberant decorative style arising in the Renaissance and popular throughout the 17th century.

BRIGHT-CUTTING: A type of engraving involving the cutting away of the surface to achieve a series of contrasting facets, resulting in a bright and light effect.

BURGESS: A burgess is a freeman or citizen of a Scottish burgh, deriving both responsibilities and benefits from his/her burgess-ship. Minimum age for receiving a burgess ticket was usually 21.

CASTING: A basic construction technique where metal is melted down and poured into a mould which has an impression of the piece to be made. Moulds can be used more than once, and this technique is used to make multiple copies of items like spouts, feet and handles.

CHASING: Covers all types of decoration which use punches to push metal into a pattern. Flat-chasing, where punches are lightly hammered to produce low-relief designs, is done from the front.
See also REPOUSSÉ and EMBOSSING.

COAT OF ARMS: Main part of a heraldic device, depicted within a shield.

CREST: In heraldry the crest, sometimes issuing from a coronet or resting on a helmet or wreath, is placed above the coat of arms. The term 'crest' is not a synonym for a coat of arms and should never be employed as such. The two are different.

DATE-LETTER MARK: Annually-changing letter of the alphabet, denoting assay-year in which an item was assayed and marked. Introduced in Scotland in 1681.

DEACON: The office of deacon, or elected leader of a given craft, was first provided for by an Act of Parliament in 1424. Originally his task was merely to oversee the work of his fellow craftsmen and ensure it was satisfactory. In Edinburgh, from 1458, he was to assay and mark all the silver-work within his jurisdiction; this task was passed to an assay-master in 1681. The deacon had many other responsibilities including serving on the Town Council and being a governor of the Trades' Maiden Hospital. Today the deacon is the managing director and chairman of the Incorporation.

DENDRILS: 'Tree-like' veins of silver found in some locations in Scotland.

DENTICULATION (OR DENTILLATION): A term borrowed from architecture, originally describing a row of tooth-like structures (denticles or dentils) in the moulding of a cornice or column. In the context of silver design, a series of short vertical lines of decoration fancifully resembling a row of narrow teeth.

DUTY/DUTY MARK: In 1784 a duty of six pence per ounce was imposed on silver at the time of assay. The rate varied (always upward) from time to time and was abolished after 106 years in 1890. A mark consisting of the monarch's head was applied at the assay office to denote that the duty had been paid. From 1784 all silver made in Scotland was supposed to be sent to the assay office so that the duty could be collected, but not every goldsmith complied.

EMBOSSING: Decoration raised from behind with punches.

ENGRAVING: Uses sharp tools (gravers or burins) to cut away thin slivers of metal to form decorative designs, cipher, armorials, initials, etc. In skilled hands this decorative technique can produce stunning works of art.

ESSAY: A set-piece of work wrought by a journeyman as part of his entry to become a freeman. Most essays included a gold ring. In early records the word is often spelt 'assay', but it has nothing to do with the assaying process.

FORGING: Produces a shape by hammering a piece of sheet metal into a die or mould cut with the required pattern. Used widely for making flatware such as spoons, forks and knives.

FREEMAN: A full member of an incorporated trade. Any qualified journeyman, usually over the age of 21, could apply for freedom of his incorporation. He was required to make a satisfactory essay and to pass an oral examination.

GOLDSMITH: Term in use in Scotland from at least the twelfth century onwards, it encompasses all workers in gold, silver and jewellery. Goldsmiths were often employed in various capacities at the Mint, and many of them were also bankers, money-lenders, pawnbrokers and financiers.

GUILLOCHE: Decoration consisting of intersecting arcs or circles, or of curved bands enclosing circles.

HALLMARK: Mark struck on wrought gold or silver at an official assay office. Marks struck in any other place are not hallmarks. Since there were no assay offices in Scotland except in Edinburgh (and from 1819 till 1964 in Glasgow), it follows that all marks struck locally by goldsmiths working elsewhere in Scotland are not hallmarks (see LOCAL MARKS). By convention the maker's (or sponsor's) mark is also usually deemed to be a hallmark, though struck by the maker or sponsor himself.

INCORPORATION: Body of craftsmen in a burgh, legally constituted usually by a seal of cause from the town council and recognised as having an official standing in the burgh, with particular responsibilities and exclusive privileges. It was not a trade guild, but an incorporation, and the term 'guild', which applies to the body of merchants in a burgh, is not a correct synonym for 'incorporation' in Scotland.

INCORPORATION OF GOLDSMITHS OF THE CITY OF EDINBURGH: In existence as a body corporate at latest by 1492 when its first recorded deacon, Patrick Forester, sat with the other deacons on the Town Council. It still exists today to administer the Edinburgh Assay Office.

INCORPORATION OF HAMMERMEN: Incorporation embracing the arts of blacksmith, coppersmith, tinsmith, lorimer, pewterer, armourer, belt-maker, clockmaker, watchmaker, etc. In burghs other than Edinburgh the goldsmiths usually belonged to the hammermen.

JOURNEYMAN: Originally one who was paid a daily wage. By the late 15th century the term had come to mean a workman who had completed his apprenticeship and was working as the employee of a master. His status is thus distinguished from, and lies between, that of an apprentice and a master. Because of their lower status they are usually not as fully documented as freemen.

LOCAL MARKS: The marks struck by provincial silversmiths on their locally-made work. These are not hallmarks and should not be referred to as such.

MAKER'S MARK: The maker of a piece was required to put his mark on his work before submitting it for assay. This was so that the authorities would know who was responsible for it if it proved to be insufficient or substandard. In 1975 the terminology changed and the mark became known as the sponsor's mark.

MASTER: Term with ordinarily two different meanings: (1) The master of an apprentice; (2) A freeman of an incorporation, whether or not he had any apprentices or journeymen under him. There were other specialised meanings also.

OFFICER: A paid servant of the incorporation, usually a retired or out-of-work journeyman, but sometimes a superannuated freeman. His duties included summoning the freemen to their meetings, looking after the premises and assisting the assay-master.

OLIGODYNAMIC: The purifying effect of silver (and some other metals) caused by the metal ions killing certain bacteria. Possibly the scientific reason why silver was traditionally thought to have healing and purifying properties.

OVOLO: In silver design a term rather different from the architectural meaning, referring principally to a band of raised ovals, often alternating with other elements.

RAISING: Traditional method of producing a hollow item. A flat sheet of metal is cut to a basic shape, then hammered up, first into a hollow block, then over a series of shaped stakes, or anvils, into the final shape. On earlier pieces the marks of the hammers can still be seen, giving a very pleasing hand-worked finish.

REPOUSSÉ: A decorative technique that combined embossing and chasing to produce high detail and definition.

RESTORATION, THE: Restoration of King Charles II to the throne of Great Britain in 1660. He had been crowned King of Scots at Scone on 1 January 1651, but was then in exile on the Continent until 1660.

ROCOCO: A decorative style more free and frivolous than the baroque (from which it derived), in which the decoration is both profuse and unrelated to the form being decorated. It is based on the representation of rockwork, scrolls, asymmetrical curves, shells, foliage, flowers and fruit. To these are sometimes added cherubs or *putti* with garlands of grapes, etc.

SPONSOR'S MARK: Since 1 January 1975 this is the correct name for what was previously called the maker's mark. This change was made to reflect the fact that the person or business whose mark was struck was frequently not the actual maker of the object.

SOLDERING: Joins different parts to form the final complete item. Silver solder is a mixture of silver and zinc or brass which has a lower melting point than the silver pieces it is used to join together. The solder is melted and runs into the joint between the separate parts. Great skill is required to produce a neat joint.

TOWN MARK: Mark signifying the burgh in which something was made. In the case of Edinburgh this was, and is, the castle, as found in the City's coat of arms. In most burghs the town mark usually consists of either some element of the town's arms or else the town name (often abbreviated), or both. With few exceptions, each provincial goldsmith had his own marks which were not held centrally by any overseeing authority and were not hallmarks.

UNFREEMAN: A goldsmith with his own business but who was not a freeman of any incorporation. The freemen often referred disparagingly to such a workman as 'unfreeman', 'silversmith' or 'pretended goldsmith', reserving the term 'goldsmith' for themselves only. From the 1780s onwards the number of unfreemen grew until, by about the mid-19th century, they outnumbered the freemen in Edinburgh, Glasgow and elsewhere. Once exclusive privileges were abolished in 1846, the term gradually fell out of use.

Bibliography and References

- This bibliography supersedes that which appeared in Finlay and Fothringham (1991). It does not include manuscript sources or works on other subjects with only passing reference to the subject in hand, e.g. burgh histories, burgess rolls, gazetteers and the like.
- Numbers in Roman numerals have been converted to Arabic numerals here, except where they form part of a title, or where page numbers and same-year publications require to be differentiated.

ANDERSON, JOSEPH (1880): 'Notice of an Ancient Celtic Reliquary exhibited to the Society by Sir Archibald Grant, Bart., of Monymusk', in *PSAS*, vol. 14 (1879-80), pp. 431-35.

ANDERSON, JOSEPH (1889[i]): 'Notice of the Quigrich or Crosier, and other Relics of St Fillan, in possession of their hereditary Keepers, or Dewars, in Glendochart, in 1549-50', in *PSAS*, vol. 23 (1888-89), pp. 110-18.

ANDERSON, JOSEPH (1899[ii]): 'Notice of a Highland Brooch in Silver, ornamented with Niello, exhibited by Mr T. S. Omond; and of other Highland Brooches in Silver and Brass', in *PSAS*, vol. 33 (1898-99), pp. 57-67.

ANDERSON, JOSEPH (1909): 'The Architecturally Shaped Shrines and other Reliquaries of the Early Celtic Church in Scotland and Ireland', in *PSAS*, vol. 44 (1909-10), pp. 259-81.

ANDERSON, REV. WILLIAM JAMES (1965): 'David Downie and the "Friends of the People"', in *The Innes Review*, vol. 16, part 2 (Autumn 1965), pp. 165-179, 2 plates. [See also JOHNSTON (1980).]

An Exhibition of Sporting Art (1984): exhibition catalogue (Manchester City Art Galleries (1984).

ANON (1795): *The Trial of David Downie, for High Treason, before the court, under the special commission of Oyer and Terminer, held at Edinburgh. Taken in short hand by Mr Blanchard, revised by the Counsel on both sides, and published with permission of the Court* (Edinburgh: printed for William Brown, 1795), 297 pp. [David Downie, goldsmith in Edinburgh, was found guilty.]

ANON (1853): 'Notice of an Ancient Celtic Brooch, the property of William Rose Campbell, 28th Regt., Madras Native Infantry, Esq. of Ballochyle (Holyloch, Cowall), Argyllshire', in *PSAS*, vol. 1 (1852-53), p. 170.

ANON (1946): 'Victor Cumming Collection of Silver', in *Scottish Arts Review*, vol. 1 (1946), no. 3, pp. 24-25.

ANON (1990): 'Appleby's Latest Masterpiece. A silver cup commissioned by the National Museums of Scotland', in *Silver Society Journal* 1 (1990), p. 24.

ANON (2001[i]): 'New Silver Standards', in *Pride and Passion* (2001). [The Millennium Collection for Bute House.]

ANON (2001[ii]): 'A Bright Future: Edinburgh's Assay Office is re-invented for the new challenges ahead', in *Pride and Passion* (2001).

Applied Art through the Alphabet (Aberdeen Art Gallery and Museum).

APS = Acts of Parliament of Scotland.

ARMET, H. (1966): 'A Dispute Between Guild Brothers', in *Book of the Old Edinburgh Club* [*BOEC*], vol. 32 (1966), pp. 218-21. [Dispute between Gilbert and Thomas Kirkwood, goldsmiths of Edinburgh.]

ASSAY OFFICES OF GREAT BRITAIN (2001): *Hallmarks on Gold, Silver & Platinum* (Assay Offices of Great Britain, London, Birmingham, Sheffield & Edinburgh, 2001).

ASSAY OFFICE SCOTLAND, THE (2003): *European Draft Directive on Hallmarking* (Edinburgh, 2003), 11 pp.

ATKINSON, STEVEN (1825): *The Discoverie and Historie of the Gold Mynes in Scotland, Written in the Year M.DC.XIX.* [1619], Bannatyne Club (Edinburgh, 1825).

AULD, ALASTAIR A. (1968): 'Silver – Some Recent Acquisitions' [by Glasgow City Art Galleries and Museums], in *Scottish Arts Review*, vol. 11, no. 3 (Glasgow, 1968), pp. 22-23.

BAIN, EBENEZER (1887): *Merchant and Craft Guilds. A History of the Aberdeen Incorporated Trades* (Aberdeen: J. & J. P. Edmond & Spark, 1887), 360 pp.

BALFOUR, SIR J. PAUL (1875): *The History of the Royal Company of Archers, the Queen's Bodyguard for Scotland* (Edinburgh, 1877).

BAKER, MALCOLM (1970): 'Quiet Splendour of Kirk Silver', in *Country Life*, vol. 148 (13 August 1970), pp. 386-87.

BAKER, MALCOLM (1973): 'Patrick Robertson's Tea Urn and the late eighteenth-century Edinburgh Silver Trade', in *Connoisseur*, vol. 183 (August 1973), pp. 89-94.

BANISTER, JUDITH (1964): 'No more Glasgow Hallmarks', in *Scotland's Magazine* (October 1964), pp. 21-23.

BARROW, GEOFFREY W. S. (1998): 'The Social Background to the Bute Mazer', in Fawcett [ed.] (1998), pp. 122-32 and plates.

BEARD, CHARLES R. (1933): 'The Monymusk Reliquary', in *Connoisseur*, vol. 92 (November 1933), pp. 182-83.

BELL, A. S. [ed.] (1981): *The Scottish Antiquarian Tradition. Essays to mark the bicentenary of the Society of Antiquaries of Scotland and its Museum, 1780-1980* (Edinburgh: John Donald Publishers Ltd, 1981), 286 pp.

BELL, JOHN (1964): *Aberdeen, Scottish Antiquities Fair*, catalogue (Aberdeen, 1964).

BLACK, Dr GEORGE F. (1991): *The Surnames of Scotland* (Edinburgh: Birlinn, 1991; first published by the New York Public Library, 1946).

BERTIE, D. (2001): 'Banff Silver' (Banff Museum pamphlet, 2001).

BOARD OF TRADE: *Report of the Departmental Committee on Hallmarking. Presented to Parliament by the President of the Board of Trade by Command of Her Majesty, March 1959* (London: HMSO, 1959), 138 pp.

BOEC = *Book of the Old Edinburgh Club*

BREADALBANE, MARQUESS OF (1855): *The Black Book of Taymouth, with other Papers from the Breadalbane Charter Room* (Edinburgh, 1855), pp. 346-48. [For BREADALBANE SILVER, see DOWELL LTD (1935).]

BREMNER, D. (1869): *The Industries of Scotland* (Edinburgh, 1869).

BROOK, ALEXANDER J. S. (1888[i]): 'Notice of a silver Brooch with Black Letter Inscription and Ornamentation in Niello, the property of Miss Steven of Bellahouston, and of a large brass Highland brooch with incised ornamentation, the property of Mrs W. R. Mitford', in *PSAS*, vol. 23 (1888-89), pp. 192-99.

BROOK, ALEXANDER J. S. (1888[ii]): 'Additional Notes on the Silver Chain known as "Midside Maggie's Girdle"', in *PSAS*, vol. 23 (1888-89), pp. 445-52.

BROOK, ALEXANDER J. S. (1889): 'Technical Description of the Regalia of Scotland', in *PSAS*, vol. 24 (1889-90), pp. 49-141.

BROOK, ALEXANDER J. S. (1890-91): 'Notes on the Silver Bell of Lanark, a Horse Racing Trophy of the Seventeenth Century', in *PSAS*, vol. 25 (1890-91), pp. 174-88.

BROOK, ALEXANDER J. S. (1891-92): 'An Account of the Maces of the Universities of St Andrews, Glasgow, Aberdeen and Edinburgh, the College of Justice, the City of Edinburgh, etc.', in *PSAS*, vol. 26 (1891-92), pp. 440-514.

BROOK, ALEXANDER J. S. (1892): 'Old Scottish Hall-Marks', in BURNS (1892), pp. 533-97.

BROOK, ALEXANDER J. S. (1893-94): 'An Account of the Archery Medals belonging to the University of St Andrews and the Grammar School of Aberdeen', in *PSAS*, vol. 28 (1893-94), pp. 343-469.

BROOK, WILLIAM (1930): 'Note on the Boss of the Bute Mazer', in *PSAS*, vol. 65 (1930-31), pp. 252-53.

BROWN, IAIN GORDON (1987): *The Clerks of Penicuik, Portraits of Taste and Talent* (Edinburgh, 1987), p. 7.

BRYDEN, D. J. (1969): 'Three Edinburgh Microscope Makers: John Finlayson, William Robertson and John Clark', in *BOEC*, vol. 33, pp. 165-76 (Edinburgh, 1969).

[BUCCLEUCH and HOPETOUN Silver Sale, see SOTHEBY & Co. (1953)].

Burke's Landed Gentry of Great Britain: The Kingdom in Scotland, 19th edition, vol. 1 (2001).

BURNETT, CHARLES (ROSS HERALD) (2003): 'The Honours of Scotland', a lecture to the Friends of Innerpeffray Library, summarised in FOIL-facts, no. 30 (July 2003), pp. 10-11. [Also available on cassette.]

BURNETT, CHARLES J. and CHRISTOPHER J. TABRAHAM (1993): *The Honours of Scotland: The Story of the Scottish Crown Jewels* (Historic Scotland: 1993).

BURNETT, JOHN (1998[i]): 'A note on the Silver Ball of Rattray', in *PSAS*, vol. 128(i) (1998), pp. 1101-04.

BURNETT, JOHN (1998[ii]): 'The sites and landscapes of horse racing in Scotland before 1860', in *Sports Historian*, vol. 18 (1998), pp 55-75.

BURNETT, JOHN (2000): *Riot, Revelry and Rout* (Edinburgh, 2000).

BURNS, REV. THOMAS (1892): *Old Scottish Communion Plate* (Edinburgh: R. & R. Clark, 1892). Limited to 675 copies, of which 175 are on large paper. [Includes A. J. S. BROOK (1892).]

BURNS, REV. THOMAS (1906): 'The Benefice Lectures', Edinburgh, George A. Morton (1906). [Includes 'Sacramental Vessels and Church Furniture', pp. 134-82.]

BYRNE, MAURICE (1966): 'The Goldsmith-Trumpet-Makers of the British Isles', in *Galpin Society Journal*, 19 (April 1966), pp. 77-78.

BYROM, CONNIE and GEORGE DALGLEISH (1991): 'A Massive and Handsome Vase', in the journal of the Royal Caledonian Horticultural Society, 1991, pp. 33-42.

BYROM, CONNIE and GEORGE DALGLEISH (2001): 'All that Glitters', in *The Caledonian Gardener* (2001) (the journal of the Royal Caledonian Horticultural Society), pp. 20-36. [Silver prizes awarded by the Society, including wine labels.]

CALDWELL, DAVID [ed.] (1981): *Scottish Weapons and Fortifications, 1100-1800* (Edinburgh: John Donald, 1981).

CAMPBELL, SUSAN (1986): *Scottish Provincial Domestic Silver*, published to accompany an exhibition at the Crawford Centre for the Arts, University of St Andrews (24 October to 23 November 1986) (St Andrews, 1986).

CARSON, R. A. G. [ed.] (1971): *Mints, Dies and Currency: Essays dedicated to the Memory of Albert Baldwin*, 336 pp., frontispiece and 23 photographic plates (London: Methuen & Co. Ltd, 1971).

CASEBOW, BEVERLEY (2003): 'Strawberry Dish', in 2002 Review of The National Art-Collections Fund (London, 2003), p. 84. [Item 5101, Strawberry Dish, Edinburgh, 1717-18, by Mungo Yorstoun.]

CHAMBERS, WILLIAM and ROBERT CHAMBERS (1836): 'The Siller Gun of Dumfries', in *Chambers' Edinburgh Journal*, vol. 5, no. 205 (12 March 1836), p. 52.

CHAMBERS, WILLIAM and ROBERT CHAMBERS (1836): 'Gold and Silver', in *Chambers' Edinburgh Journal*, vol. 5, no. 205 (12 March 1836), pp. 180-81.

CHEAPE, HUGH and GEORGE DALGLEISH (*et al.*) (1984): *At Home: Ten Years' Collecting from Historic Scotland* (Edinburgh, 1984).

CHRISTIE'S (1983): *The Shaw Collection of Important Scottish Silver and Pistols*, sale catalogue (29 March 1983).

CHRISTIE'S (1984[i]): *Scottish Provincial Silver from the David Morris Collection*, sale catalogue (3 July 1984).

CHRISTIE'S (1984[ii]): *Scottish Provincial Silver from the David Morris Collection*, sale catalogue (9 October 1984).

CLARKE, D. V., T. G. COWIE and ANDREW FOXON (1985): *Symbols of Power at the time of Stonehenge*, exhibition catalogue (Edinburgh: National Museum of Antiquities Scotland and HM Stationery Office, 1985).

CLAYTON, MICHAEL D. G. (1968): 'Archery Prizes and Medals', in *Proceedings of the Society of Silver Collectors*, no. 11 (London, Autumn 1960), pp. 17-21.

CLAYTON, MICHAEL D. G. (1971): *The Collector's Directory of Gold and Silver*, 19th edition (London, 1971).

CLAYTON, MICHAEL D. G. (1985): *Collector's Dictionary of Silver & Gold*, second edition (Antique Collectors' Club, 1985).

COLSTON, JAMES (1891): *The Incorporated Trades of Edinburgh with an introductory chapter on the Rise and Progress of Municipal Government in Scotland* (Edinburgh: Colston & Co., 1891), 237 pp.

COMSTOCK, H. (1939): 'Edinburgh Teapot of 1726', in *Connoisseur*, vol. 104 (9 December 1939), pp. 298-99.

CRAIG-BROWN, T. (1886): History of Selkirkshire (Galashiels, 1886).

CRAMOND, REV. WILLIAM (1889): 'Clockmakers, Watchmakers, Gold and Silversmiths, and Jewellers who have carried on business in the City of Elgin from the years 1697 until and after the years 1820-1838', in *Scottish Antiquary*, vol. 3 (Edinburgh, 1889), pp. 48-49.

CRAW, J. HEWAT (1928): 'Gold in Scotland and Ireland', in *PSAS*, vol. 63 (1928-29), p. 188.

CRICHTON, LIONEL A. (1930): 'On the Provenance of the Bute Mazer', in *PSAS.*, vol. 65 (1930-31), pp. 251-52.

CUMMING, E. (1993): *Phoebe Anna Traquair*, exhibition catalogue (Scottish National Portrait Gallery, 1993).

CUMMING, VICTOR J. (1938): 'Old Scottish Silver', in *Apollo*, vol. 28 (July 1938), pp. 10-12.

CUTHBERT, ALEXANDER (c.1960): 'Scottish Wine Labels and Scottish Provincial Marks', in *The Wine Label Journal* (n.d. [c.1960]), pp. 141-46.

DALGLEISH, GEORGE (1984): 'Silver & Pewter', in CHEAPE and DALGLEISH (1984).

DALGLEISH, GEORGE (1985): 'Prince Charlie's Canteen', in *The Antique Collector* (October 1985), pp. 66-71.

DALGLEISH, GEORGE (1988): 'The Silver Travelling Canteen of Prince Charles Edward Stuart', in FENTON and MYRDAL [eds] (1988), pp. 168-84.

DALGLEISH, GEORGE (1990): 'Bonnie Prince Charlie's Canteen', in *The Highlander*, vol. 28, no. 2 (March/April 1990), pp. 1, 4 and 6. [Reprinted (with variations) from *Antique Collector*.]

DALGLEISH, GEORGE (2001[i]): 'Burning Images: Illustration of a coal-burning hearth in the Dumfries Freedom Box', in WOOD [ed.] (2001).

DALGLEISH, GEORGE (2001[ii]): 'Collection of Silver Communion and Baptismal Plate', in 2000 Review of The National Art-Collections Fund (London, 2001), p. 106. [Item 4850, the Holy Trinity Church Sacramental Plate.]

DALGLEISH, GEORGE (2007): 'Of Maces, Medals and Monarchy: Symbols of Authority (and otherwise) and the New Scottish Parliament', in McCRACKEN-FLESHER [ed.] (2007).

DALGLEISH, GEORGE and D. MECHAN (1985): *'I am Come Home': Treasures of Prince Charles Edward Stuart* (Edinburgh, 1985).

DALGLEISH, GEORGE and STUART MAXWELL (1987): *The Lovable Craft, 1687-1987*, exhibition catalogue (Royal Scottish Museum, Edinburgh, 1987).

DENARO, VICTOR F. (1969): 'The Canongate, Edinburgh, and Maltese Silver', in *PSAS*, vol. 102 (1969-70), pp. 237-40.

DIETERT, RODNEY and JANICE DIETERT (2007): *Compendium of Scottish Silver II* (Lansing, NY: Dietert Publications, 2007).

DOBIE, KIRKPATRICK H. [n.d.]: *Dumfries Silversmiths* (Dumfries, n.d., c.1984).

DOBIE, KIRKPATRICK H. (1992): 'Scottish Provincial Silver, Dumfries Silversmiths', part 1, in *The Finial* (St Austell, July 1992).

DOBIE, KIRKPATRICK H. (1998): 'The Siller Gun', in *Silver Society Journal*, no. 10 (1998), pp. 44-45.

DOBIE, KIRKPATRICK H. (2001[i]): 'A Medallion for the "Siller Gun"', in *Silver Society Journal*, no. 13 (2001), p. 61.

DOBIE, KIRKPATRICK H. (2001[ii]): 'The Dumfries Silver Gun', in *Transactions of the Dumfries and Galloway Natural History and Antiquarian Society*, vol. 75 (2001), pp. 177-80.

DONALDSON, G. (1970): *Scottish Historical Documents* (Edinburgh, 1970).

DOWDEN, JOHN (1899): 'The Inventory of Ornaments, Jewels, Relicks, Vestments, Service-books, etc., belonging to the Cathedral Church of Glasgow in 1432, illustrated from various sources, and more particularly from the inventories of Aberdeen', in *PSAS*, vol. 33 (1898-99), pp. 280-329.

DOWDEN, JOHN [ed.] (1903): *Chartulary of the Abbey of Lindores, 1195-1479*. Edited from the original manuscripts at Caprington Castle, Kilmarnock, with translation and abstracts of the charters, illustrative notes and appendices (Edinburgh: Scottish History Society, 1903), series 1, vol. 42.

DOWELL'S LTD (1935): *The Breadalbane Collection of Silversmiths' Work*, sale catalogue, 30/31 May 1935 (Edinburgh: Dowell's Ltd, 1935).

DRYSDALE, WILLIAM (1857): 'Notice of an ancient gold Seal in the Possession of J. W. Williamson Esq. of Kinross', in *Archæologica Scotica*, vol. 4, pp. 420-21.

EASSON, D. E. and ANGUS MacDONALD (1938): *Charters of the Abbey of Inchcolm* (Edinburgh: Scottish History Society, 1938), series 3, vol. 32, pp. 46 and 162.

EDWARDS, A. J. H. (1939): 'The Mary Queen of Scots Pendant', in *PSAS*, vol. 74 (1939-40), pp. 137-38 and plate 54.

EELES, FRANCIS C. (1920): 'The Methuen Cup: A Piece of Sixteenth-Century Scottish Plate', in *PSAS*, vol. 55 (1920-21), pp. 285-89.

EELES, FRANCIS C. (1934): 'The Monymusk Reliquary or Breckbennoch of St Columba', in *PSAS*, vol. 68 (1933-34), pp. 433-38.

EGM (2006): *Edinburgh Goldsmiths' Minutes* [see FOTHRINGHAM, HENRY STEUART (2006)].

Empire Exhibition (1938): *Empire Exhibition, Glasgow, May to October 1938: Old Scottish Silver, Catalogue of Loan Collection in Scottish Historical Pavilion* (Glasgow, 1938).

English and Scottish Silver (Edinburgh: Royal Scottish Museum, 1954).

FAIRFAX-BLAKEBOROUGH, JOHN (c.1950): *Extinct Race Meetings* (London: c.1950).

FAIRLEY, J. A. (1925): *Lauriston Castle the Estate and its Owners* (Edinburgh, 1925).

FAWCETT, R. [ed.] (1998): *Medieval Art and Architecture in the Diocese of Glasgow* (British Archaeological Association Conference Transactions, 23, 1998).

FELL, H. G. (1939): 'Scottish Silver at Stratton Street' [Messrs How of Edinburgh], *Connoisseur*, vol. 103 (Feb. 1939), pp. 107, 109.

FENTON and MYRDAL [eds]: *Food and Drink and Travelling Accessories* (Edinburgh, 1988), pp. 168-84.

FINLAY, IAN (1939): 'Old Scottish Silver in Scottish Churches', in *Connoisseur*, vol. 104 (August 1939), pp. 64-70.

FINLAY, IAN (1946): 'Scottish Silver', in *Apollo*, vol. 44 (December 1946), pp. 145-48.

FINLAY, IAN (1947[i]): 'Scottish Silver', in *Apollo*, vol. 45 (February 1947), pp. 31-36.

FINLAY, IAN (1947[ii]): 'Scottish Silver', in *Apollo*, vol. 45 (March 1947), pp. 67-70.

FINLAY, IAN (1948[i]): *Art in Scotland* (Oxford, 1948).

FINLAY, IAN (1948[ii]): *Scottish Crafts* (London: George G. Harrap & Co. Ltd, 1948), 128 pp.

FINLAY, IAN (1948[iii]): 'The Watson Mazer', in *Apollo*, vol. 48 (November 1948), pp. 101-02.

FINLAY, IAN (1948[iv]): 'Scottish Silver in Edinburgh', in *Connoisseur*, vol. 122 (December 1948), pp. 88-93.

FINLAY, IAN (1949): 'Scottish Silver', in *Antiques*, vol. 56 (October 1949), pp. 271-73.

FINLAY, IAN (1951[i]): 'Some Silver and Gold Work recently acquired by The Royal Scottish Museum', in *Apollo*, vol. 53 (March 1951), pp. 69-72.

FINLAY, IAN (1955): 'The Milne Davidson Collection', in *Connoisseur*, vol. 125 (May 1955), pp. 173-77.

FINLAY, IAN (1956[i]): 'Old Scottish Sporting Plate', in *Country Life* (12 January 1956), pp. 68-69.

FINLAY, IAN (1956[ii]): 'Scottish Ceremonial Plate', in *Apollo*, vol. 63 (January 1956), pp. 6-8.

FINLAY, IAN (1956[iii]): 'Scottish Ceremonial Plate', in *Apollo*, vol. 63 (February 1956), pp. 48-50.

FINLAY, IAN (1956[iv]): *Scottish Gold and Silver Work* (first edition, London: Chatto & Windus), 96 illustrations. [For second edition, see FINLAY and FOTHRINGHAM (1991).]

FINLAY, IAN (1959[i]): 'Silver in the Royal Scottish Museum', in *Connoisseur*, vol. 143 (June 1959), pp. 9-13.

FINLAY, IAN (1959[ii]): 'The Finest Age in Scottish Silver', in *Country Life* (27 August 1959), pp. 130-33.

FINLAY, IAN (1959[iii]): 'Silver Seal Case of the Earl of Montrose', in *Burlington Magazine*, vol. 101 (November 1959), pp. 404-07.

FINLAY, IAN (1963): 'Masterpieces of Scottish Silver', in *Country Life* (22 August 1963), pp. 443-44.

FINLAY, IAN and HENRY FOTHRINGHAM (1991): *Scottish Gold and Silver Work*, second edition, extent increased (Stevenage: Strong Oak Press, 1991). [For first edition, see FINLAY (1956[iv]).]

FOTHRINGHAM, HENRY STEUART (1972): 'Scottish Silver: Marks are not Everything', in *Antique Finder* (December 1972), pp. 14-15.

FOTHRINGHAM, HENRY STEUART (1973): 'Small Inverness Quaichs c.1760-c.1840', in *Antique Collector* (April 1973), pp. 73-76.

FOTHRINGHAM, HENRY STEUART (1976): 'Some Inverness Goldsmiths and their Marks', in *Antique Finder* (December 1976), pp. 12-15.

FOTHRINGHAM, HENRY STEUART (1994[i]): 'The Records of the Incorporation of Goldsmiths of the City of Edinburgh', in *Silver Society Journal*, no. 5 (Spring 1994), pp. 187-94.

FOTHRINGHAM, HENRY STEUART (1994[ii]): 'Silver appearing before the Reviewing Committee on the Export of Works of Art from 1953 to 1993', in *Silver Society Journal*, no. 6 (Winter 1994), pp. 302-22.

FOTHRINGHAM, HENRY STEUART (2001[ii]): 'The Darnley Jewel', in *Silver Society Journal*, no. 13 (2001), pp. 52-60.

FOTHRINGHAM, HENRY STEUART (2001[iii]): 'The Strathmore Silver Inventory of 1695', in *Silver Society Journal*, no. 13 (2001), pp. 81-93.

FOTHRINGHAM, HENRY STEUART (2002): 'Scottish Goldsmiths' Apprenticeships', in *Silver Society Journal*, vol. 14 (2002), pp. 79-86.

FOTHRINGHAM, HENRY STEUART (2003[i]): 'St Eloi', in *Silver Society Journal*, vol. 15 (2003), pp. 7-11.

FOTHRINGHAM, HENRY STEUART (2003[ii]): 'Scottish Goldsmiths' Weights', in *Silver Society Journal*, vol. 15 (2003), pp. 68-72.

FOTHRINGHAM, HENRY STEUART (2006): *Edinburgh Goldsmiths' Minutes 1525-1700*, 407 pp., series 5, vol. 29 (Edinburgh: Scottish Record Society, 2006).

FRANK, D. (1985): 'Gazing into Arcadia', *Country Life* (April 1985).

GEDDES, J. (2000): *King's College Chapel, Aberdeen 1500-2000* (Aberdeen, 2000), pp 218-22.

Glamis Book of Record (1890): A diary written by Patrick first Earl of Strathmore, 1684-1689, edited by A. H. Millar (Scottish History Society, 1890), series 1, vol. 9.

GLENN, VIRGINIA (2003): Romanesque and Gothic Metalwork and Ivory Carvings in the Museum of Scotland (Edinburgh: NMSE – Publishing, National Museums Scotland, 2003), pp. 34-38.

GOLBY, J. M and A. W. PURDUE: *The Civilization of the Crowd: Popular Culture in England 1750-1900* (London, 1984).

GOW, IAN (1989): 'The Northern Athenian Teapot', in *The Burlington Magazine* (1989), pp. 353-55.

GRANT, SIR FRANCIS (1932): 'State Ceremonials in Edinburgh in the Olden Time', in *BOEC*, vol. 18 (Edinburgh, 1932), pp. 11-32.

GRIMSHAW, M. E. (1981): *Silver Medals, Badges and Trophies from Schools in the British Isles 1550-1850* (Cambridge: M. E. Grimshaw, 1981), 64 pp.

GRIMSHAW, M. E. (1989): *Silver Medals from Scottish and Irish Schools before* 1872 (Cambridge: M. E. Grimshaw, 1989), 56 pp.

GRIMWADE, ARTHUR (1951[i]): 'A New List of Old English Gold Plate, Part I', in *Connoisseur*, vol. 128 (1951), pp. 10-16.

GRIMWADE, ARTHUR (1951[ii]): 'A New List of Old English Gold Plate, Part II', in *Connoisseur*, vol. 128 (1951), pp. 83-89.

HALLEN, A. W. CORNELIUS (1888): 'Silver Mines at Alva, Stirlingshire', in *The Scottish Antiquary*, vol. 1 (Edinburgh, 1888), pp. 53-55.

HOLLAND, MARGARET (1971): *Old Country Silver. An Account of English Provincial Silver, with Sections on Ireland, Scotland and Wales* (Newton Abbot: David & Charles, 1971), 240 pp.

HOLMES, NICHOLAS M. McQ. (1982): *Weill Wrocht and Cunyeit: the Edinburgh Mint and its Coinage* (Edinburgh: City of Edinburgh Museums and Art Galleries, 1982).

HOPETOUN ARCHIVES: catalogued by National Register of Archives, Scotland (NRAS 888), National Archives of Scotland.

HOW, G. E. P. (1933): 'Scottish Teaspoons', in *Connoisseur*, vol. 92, Supplement (1933), p. 30.

HOW, G. E. P. (1934[i]): 'Scottish Standing Mazers', in *Connoisseur*, vol. 93 (May 1934), pp. 313-19.

HOW, G. E. P. (1934[ii]): 'Scottish Standing Mazers', in *PSAS*, vol. 68 (1933-34), pp. 394-411.

HOW, G. E. P. (1935): 'Early Scottish Spoons', in *PSAS*, vol. 19 (1934-35), pp. 138-57.

HOW, G. E. P. (1936[i]): 'Early Scottish Spoons', in *Connoisseur*, vol. 98 (December 1936), pp. 341-46.

HOW, G. E. P. (1936[ii]): *How of Edinburgh Ltd, Silver Exhibition at 15 Stratton Street, London, W1, 1936* (London: How of Edinburgh, 1936).

HOW, G. E. P. (1937): *How of Edinburgh Ltd, Silver* Exhibition *at 15 Stratton Street, London, W1, 1937* (London: How of Edinburgh, 1937).

HOW, G. E. P. (1939[i]): 'Scottish Silver Teapots', in *The Antique Collector* (May 1939), pp. 108-11.

HOW, G. E. P. (1939[ii]): 'Canongate Goldsmiths and Jewellers', in *Burlington Magazine*, vol. 74 (June 1939), pp. 283-88 and 2 plates.

HOW, G. E. P. (1941): 'Scottish Silver', in *Notes on Antique Silver*, no. 1 (London: How of Edinburgh, 1941).

HOW, G. E. P. (1942): 'Sentiment for Sale', in *Notes on Antique Silver*, no. 2, pp. 7-11 (London: How of Edinburgh, 1942).

HOW, G. E. P. (1947): *A Coconut Cup by Thomas Lindsay of Dundee, c.1600* (London: How of Edinburgh, 1947), 6 pp.

HOW, G. E. P. (1949): 'The Watson Mazer, A Criticism', in *Apollo*, vol. 49 (1949), pp. 16-17.

HOW, G. E. P. and JANE PENRICE HOW (1952): *English and Scottish Silver Spoons, Medieval to late Stuart, and Pre-Elizabethan Hallmarks on English Plate*, vol. II (London: How of Edinburgh, 1952-57).

HOW, JANE (1983): 'The Huntly Race and its Trophies', in O'CONNOR and CLARKE (1983).

HUNT, COLIN A. (1889): *The Perth Hammermen Book (1518-1568)* (Perth: printed for the Incorporation by James H. Jackson, 1889), pp. cxxii, 106.

HUTCHESON, A. (1893): 'Old Communion Plate, Dundee', in *The Scottish Antiquary*, vol. 7 (Edinburgh, 1893), pp. 6-9.

HYMAN, JOHN A. (1997): 'Scottish Drinking Vessels', in *Antiques* (June 1997).

HYMAN, JOHN A. (1998): 'Further Reflections on Scottish Silver', in *Antiques* (August 1998).

INCORPORATION OF GOLDSMITHS OF THE CITY OF EDINBURGH (1820): *A Collection of Royal Grants and other Documents, Relative to the Constitution and Privileges of the Incorporation of Goldsmiths, 1483-1687* (Edinburgh: printed for the Incorporation by George Ramsay & Co., 1820), 44 pp.

INCORPORATION OF GOLDSMITHS OF THE CITY OF EDINBURGH (1826): *Laws of the Incorporation of Goldsmiths of Edinburgh. Revised by T. W. Baird Esq. Advocate. Ratified by the Magistrates and Town-Council, 12 April 1826* (Edinburgh, printed for the Incorporation by John Pillans, 1826), 37 pp.

JACKSON, SIR CHARLES JAMES (1905): *English Goldsmiths and their Marks* (first edition, London 1905; second edition, London 1921; Dover edition 1964). [See also PICKFORD (*et. al*) (1989).]

JACKSON, SIR CHARLES JAMES (1911): *An Illustrated History of English Plate, ecclesiastical and secular, in which the Development of form and decoration in the Silver and Gold Work of the British Isles from the earliest known examples to the latest of the Georgian Period is delineated and described*, in 2 vols (first edition, London, 1911; reprinted, London: The Holland Press Ltd, 1967).

JAMES, I. E. (1981): *The Goldsmiths of Aberdeen, 1450-1850* (Aberdeen: Bieldside Books, 1981), 156 pp.

John Bell of Aberdeen Collection (1961): *Silver Teapots from the John Bell of Aberdeen Collection, 20 November – 16 December, 1961*, exhib. catalogue (Glasgow: The Ceylon Tea Centre, 1961).

JOHNSTON, CHRISTINE (1980): 'David Downie: A Reappraisal', in *The Innes Review*, vol. 31, part 2 (Autumn 1980), pp. 87-94. [See also W. J. ANDERSON (1965).]

JONES, BRUCE (2003): 'Caledonian Horticultural Society Labels (Part 2: 1820-1836)', in *Journal of the Wine Label Circle* 11/05 (Autumn 2003), pp. 149-155, illustrated.

JONES, E. ALFRED (1907[i]): *Catalogue of the Collection of Old Plate of Leopold de Rothschild Esq.* (1907).

JONES, E. ALFRED (1907[ii]): *Old English Gold Plate* (London: Bemrose, 1907).

JONES, E. ALFRED (1930): 'Collection of Sir J. H. B. Noble: Old English, Scottish and Irish Silver', in *International Studio*, vol. 96 (May 1930), pp. 48-52; (June 1930), pp. 20-24.

JONES, E. ALFRED (1933): 'Some Old Scottish and English and Plate of the Marquess of Linlithgow, K.T.', in *Apollo*, vol. 18 (September 1933), pp. 153-61.

JONES, E. ALFRED (1936[i]): 'Collection of Plate of Sir John Stirling Maxwell, Bart., K.T.', in *Apollo*, vol. 23 (February 1936), pp. 96, 99-104; (April 1936), pp. 207-14.

JONES, E. ALFRED (1936[ii]): 'Binning Collection of Old English and Scottish Plate', in *Burlington Magazine*, vol. 68 (March 1936), pp. 118-125.

JONES, E. ALFRED (1937): 'Some Scottish and English Plate at Castlemilk', in *Burlington Magazine*, vol. 71 (December 1937), pp. 278-83.

JONES, E. ALFRED (1938): 'Old Silver in Scottish Churches', in *Connoisseur*, vol. 101 (June 1938), pp. 316-20.

JONES, E. ALFRED (1939): 'Silver at the Exhibition of Scottish Art', in *Burlington Magazine*, vol. 74 (1939), pp. 71-72 and plate.

KNOX, JOHN (1565): *The Forme of Prayers and Ministration of the Sacraments … approved and received by the Churche of Scotland* (1565).

KNOX, JOHN: *1st Book of Discipline*, in DONALDSON (1970).

LAING, MICHAEL (2002): 'The New Silver Collection at Bute House', in *Goldsmiths' Review* (2001/02) (London: The Worshipful Company of Goldsmiths, 2002), pp. 24-29, illustrated.

LANKASTER, PHILIP J. (1994): 'Notes on some Scottish silver-hilted Swords and related Swords', in *Journal of the Arms and Armour Society*, vol. 14, no. 5 (March 1994), pp. 268-315.

LEE, GEORGINA E. assisted by RONALD A. LEE (1978): *British Silver Monteith Bowls including American and European examples* (Byfleet: Manor House Press, 1978), 70 illus., 114 pp.

LENMAN, BRUCE P. (1995): 'Jacobean Goldsmith-Jewellers as Credit-Creators: The Cases of James Mossman [*sic*], James Cockie [*sic*] and George Heriot', in *Scottish Historical Review*, vol. 74.2: 198 (October 1995), pp. 159-77.

LESLIE, JOHN (2004): *John Leslie, 18th Century Aberdeen Goldsmith* (Aberdeen: Aberdeen City Council, 2004).

Loan Exhibition of Scottish Art and Antiquities, at 27 Grosvenor Square, London, February 5th – March 1st 1931, exhibition catalogue (1931).

LUMSDEN, HARRY and P. HENDERSON AITKEN (1915): *History of the Hammermen of Glasgow: A Study typical of Scottish Craft Life and Organisation* (second edition, Paisley: Alexander Gardner, 1915).

LYON & TURNBULL: *The Murray Collection of Silver and Sheffield Plate*, 'single owner' sale catalogue (20 August 2003). [Important collection, including 72 lots of Scottish silver.]

MacARTHUR, E. MAIRI (2003): *Iona Celtic Art: The Work of Alexander and Euphemia Ritchie* (Iona: The New Iona Press, 2003), 80 pp.

MacBEAN, L. (1908): *Extracts from Kirkcaldy Burgh Records* (Kirkcaldy, 1908), pp. 314-15.

McCLENAHAN, RICHARD L. (1955): *Some Scottish Quaichs*, in 2 volumes (Skokie, Illinois, 1955/68).

McCLENAHAN, RICHARD L. (1969): 'Some Scottish Quaichs', in *Antiques* (September 1969).

McCRACKEN-FLESHER [ed.] (2007) *Culture, Nation and the New Scottish Parliament* (Lewisburg: Bucknell University Press, 2007).

MacDOUGALL, MARGARET O. (1970s): 'Inverness Silversmiths' (Inverness: Inverness Museum and Art Gallery, n.d., 1970s).

McFARLAN, GORDON (1999): 'Robert Gray & Son, Goldsmiths of Glasgow', in *Silver Society Journal*, no. 11 (1999), pp. 211-22.

McINNES, C. T. (1944): 'An Addendum to Brook's Account of Scottish Maces', in *PSAS*, vol. 78 (Edinburgh, 1943-44), pp. 126-28.

MacPHERSON, NORMAN (1886): 'Notice of Communion Cups from Duirinish, Skye, with Notes on other Sets of Scottish Church Plate, of which Specimens were Exhibited', in *PSAS*, vol. 20 (1885-86), pp. 398-446.

MacPHERSON, NORMAN (1888): 'Notice of a finely ornamented Chalice of Silver, parcel-gilt, the property of R. B. Æ. MacLeod, Esq. of Cadboll', in *PSAS*, vol. 22 (1887-88), pp. 423-32.

MacROBERTS, DAVID (1967): 'Some Post-Reformation Chalices', in *The Innes Review*, vol. 18, part 2 (Autumn 1967), pp. 144-46. [Discusses the Forsyth Chalice.]

MacROBERTS, DAVID (1976): 'Bishop Kennedy's Mace', in David

MacRoberts [ed.]: *The Medieval Church of St Andrews* (Glasgow: Burns, 1976), pp. 167-71.

MacROBERTS, DAVID and CHARLES OMAN (1968): 'Plate made by James II & VII for the Chapel Royal of Holyrood in 1686', in *The Antiquaries Journal*, vol. 48, part 2 (1968), pp. 285-95.

Mace of the School of Medicine, University of St Andrews, The (1950): printed for the University Court (Edinburgh: R. & R. Clark Ltd, 1950).

MALCOLM, C. (1945): *The History of the Bank of Scotland* (Edinburgh: R. & R. Clark, 1945).

MARSHALL, ROSALIND K. and G. DALGLEISH (1991): *The Art of Jewellery in Scotland* (1991).

MAXWELL, STUART (1954): 'The Galloway Mazer', in *PSAS*, vol. 88 (1954-55), pp. 227-28 and plate 45.

MAXWELL, STUART (1959): 'The Queen Mary Jewel', in *PSAS*, vol. 93 (1959-60), pp. 244-45 and plate 14.

MAXWELL, STUART (1964): 'An Embossed Silver Standing Dish of 1667-9', in *PSAS*, vol. 98 (1964-65), p. 325 and plate 45.

MAXWELL, STUART (1967): 'A Silver Coffee Pot and Hot Milk Jug by Colin McKenzie, 1713', in *PSAS*, vol. 100 (1967-68), pp. 199-200 and plate 24.

MAXWELL, STUART (1981): 'Letters from Walter Allan, Armourer in Stirling, to Colin Mitchell, Goldsmith in Canongate, 1741-1750', in CALDWELL [ed.] (1981), pp. 408-18.

MAXWELL, STUART (1983): 'Quaichs', in O'CONNOR and CLARKE (1983).

MAXWELL, STUART (1987): 'The Incorporation of Goldsmiths of the City of Edinburgh', in *University of Edinburgh Journal*, 33, no. 1 (1987).

MAXWELL, STUART and GEORGE DALGLEISH (2000): 'The Mace of King's College', in GEDDES (2000).

MILLAR, A. H. [ed.] (1890): *The Book of Record: A Diary written by Patrick First Earl of Strathmore and other Documents Relating to Glamis Castle 1684-1689* (Edinburgh, Scottish History Society, 1890), series 1, vol. 9, 194pp.

Medallic Illustrations (1885): *Medallic Illustrations of the History of Great Britain and Ireland*, vol. 1 (London, 1885).

Millennium Collection for Bute House, The (2000): catalogue (Edinburgh: Incorporation of Goldsmiths of the City of Edinburgh, 2000).

MILNE-DAVIDSON, J. (1938): 'The Scottish Quaich', in *Antique Collector* (1 September 1938).

MORETON, STEPHEN (2007): *Bonanzas and Jacobites: The Story of the Silver Glen* (Edinburgh: Clackmannan Field Studies Society and NMS Enterprises Limited – Publishing, 2007), p. 65.

MOSS, G. P. (1994): *Provincial Silversmiths of Moray and their Marks* (London: Quartet Books, 1994), 114 pp.

MOSS, G. P. and A. D. ROE (1999): *Highland Gold and Silversmiths* (Edinburgh: National Museums of Scotland Publishing, 1999), 214 pp., with 285 monochrome illustrations. [Includes brief bibliography.]

NAS = National Archives of Scotland: Mar and Kellie Papers (GD 124/3/37); Breadalbane Papers (GD 112).

NOBLE, JOHN (1959): *Exhibition of Scottish Silver from the Collection of John Noble, Chairman of the Scottish Craft Centre, 24 August – 12 September 1959*.

NORMAN-WILCOX, G. (1961): 'The Methuen Cup', in *Bulletin of the Art Division of the Los Angeles Museum of Art*, vol. XIII: 3 (1961), pp. 10-15.

NORMAN-WILCOX, G. (1965): 'Some Jacobite Silver', in *Los Angeles Museum of Art Bulletin*, vol. 17, no. 4 (1965), pp. 13-15.

North East Silver (Peterhead Museum, 1988).

NRAS = National Register of Archives, Scotland.

O'CONNOR, ANNE and D. V. CLARKE (1983): *From the Stone Age to the 'Forty Five: Studies presented to R. B. K. Stevenson, Former Keeper, National Museum of Antiquities of Scotland* (Edinburgh: John Donald, 1983), 621 pp.

OMAN, CHARLES C. (1939): 'Scottish Silver at the Royal Academy', in *Connoisseur*, vol. 103 (February 1939), pp. 70-75.

Palace of History Catalogue of Exhibits: Scottish Exhibition of National History, Art, & Industry, Glasgow (1911), 2 volumes (Glasgow, Edinburgh and London: Dalross Ltd, 1911).

PENZER, N. M. (n.d.): 'The Tree, the Bird, the Fish and the Bell', in *The Wine Label Journal* (n.d.), pp. 92-95.

PICKFORD, IAN (1983): *Silver Flatware, English, Irish and Scottish 1660-1880* (Woodbridge: Antique Collectors' Club, 1983), 231 pp., highly illustrated. [Flatware; spoons.]

PICKFORD, IAN (*et al.*) [ed.] (1989): *Jackson's Silver and Gold Marks of England, Scotland and Ireland* (Woodbridge: Antique Collectors' Club, 1989), 768 pp., with 400 black and white illustrations and *c*.15,000 marks.

PITTOCK, MURRAY G. H. (2004): 'John Law's Theory of Money and its roots in Scottish culture', in *PSAS*, vol. 133 (2003), pp. 391-403.

Pride and Passion: Scottish Jewellery 2001. Published by rj magazine, with the Incorporation of Goldsmiths of the City of Edinburgh (Edinburgh, September 2001).

PSAS = Proceedings of the Society of the Antiquaries of Scotland. Published in Edinburgh at or after the end of the season stated.

QUICK, ESTELLE (1997): *A Ballance* [sic.] *of Silver: the story of the silversmiths of Tain*, exhibition catalogue (Tain, 1997).

QUICK, ESTELLE (2001): 'Silver Thistle Cup', in 2000 Review of The National Art-Collections Fund, London (2001), p. 122. [Item 4877, Tot Cup by Hugh Ross, Tain.]

QUICK, ESTELLE (2007): Tain Silver in Tain & District Museum (Tain, 2007), p. 7.

RABINOVITCH, BENTON SEYMOUR (1991): *Antique Silver Servers for the Dining Table* (Joslin Hall Publishing, 1991).

REID, DAVID WILSON (1957): 'Six Pieces of Silver Plate', in *The College Courant*, Glasgow University (Whitsun 1957), pp. 118-23.

Renaissance Decorative Arts (1959): *Renaissance Decorative Arts in Scotland, 1480-1650*, exhibition catalogue (Edinburgh, 1959).

RENWICK, ROBERT (1897): *Abstracts of Protocols of the Town Clerks of Glasgow*, vol. v of *Henry Gibsone's Protocols* (1555-68).

RCEWA = Reviewing Committee on the Export of Works of Art

RCEWA (1954): 'The Galloway Mazer by James Gray', in First Report, 1953-54 (R1,e. April 1954) (London: HMSO, 1954), pp. 11-12.

RCEWA (1959): 'Mary Queen of Scots Cameo Jewel', in [Sixth] Report, 1958-59 (R6,c. October 1958) (London: HMSO, 1959), pp. 8-9.

RCEWA (1960): 'Pair of Scottish Silver Tankards', in Seventh Report, 1959-60 (R7,e. April 1960) (London: HMSO, 1960), pp. 9-10.

RCEWA (1969): 'A Silver Quaich', in Sixteenth Report, 1968-69 (R16,j. January 1969) (London: HMSO, 1969), p. 11.

RCEWA (1970[i]): 'A William III Silver Monteith Bowl', in Seventeenth Report, 1969-70 (R17,c. August 1969) (London: HMSO, 1970, p. 7.

RCEWA (1970[ii]): 'The Cadboll Cup', in Seventeenth Report, 1969-70 (R17,g. December 1969) (London: HMSO, 1970), p. 10.

RCEWA (1973): 'A Pair of Charles I Scottish Silver Communion

Cups, Edinburgh 1645', in Twentieth Report, 1972-74 (R20,i. February 1973) (London: HMSO, 1974), p. 14.

RCEWA (1978): 'A George II Oval Cake-Basket by James Ker, 1740', in Twenty-Fourth Report, 1977-78 (R24,vii. September 1977) (London: HMSO, 1978), p. 15.

RCEWA (1984): 'A George II Monteith', in Thirtieth Report, 1983-84 (R30,ii. July 1983) (London: HMSO, 1984), p. 9.

RCEWA (1985): 'A 17th [sic.] century canteen of Prince Charles Edward Stuart', in Thirty-First Report, 1984-85 (R31,ix. August 1984) (London: HMSO, 1985), pp. 15-16. ['17th' error for 18th.]

REW, CHRISTINE (2002): 'Silver at Aberdeen Art Gallery & Museums', in Goldsmiths' Review 2001/2002 (London: The Worshipful Company of Goldsmiths, 2002), pp. 10-13, illus.

RODGER, ROBIN H. (1992): 'The Silver Ball of Rattray: a unique Scottish sporting trophy', in PSAS, vol. 122 (1992), pp. 403-11.

RODGER, ROBIN H. and FIONA SLATTERY (2001): Perth Silver: A Guide to Perth Silver and Silversmiths and [sic.] illustrated by the collections of Perth Museum and Art Gallery (Perth: Perth Museum and Art Gallery, 2001 [pub. 1 February 2002]), 50 pp.

ROMANES, ROBERT and JAMES CURLE (1897-98): 'Letter to the Secretary, presenting the silver Chain known as 'Midside Maggie's Girdle' to the National Museum of Antiquities; with Notes upon the Story of the Girdle and its Owners', in PSAS, vol. 32 (1897-98), pp. 195-204, and illustration.

RSM = Royal Scottish Museum

RSM (1948): Catalogue of the Exhibition of Scottish Silver, Royal Scottish Museum, August– September 1948 (Edinburgh, 1948).

RSM (1985): French Connections: Scotland and the Arts of France, exhibition catalogue (Edinburgh: HMSO and Royal Scottish Museum, 1985).

RUSSELL, JOHN (1938): 'The Builder of Pilrig House', in BOEC, vol. 22, pp. 160-66. [Gilbert Kirkwood.]

SALTER, J. R. (1980[i]): Goldsmiths and Silversmiths of the Royal Burgh of Banff, 1600-1850.

SALTER, J. R. (1980[ii]): Goldsmiths and Silversmiths of Forres, 1600-1860.

SALTER, J. R. (1980[iii]): Incorporation of Hammermen in Paisley and its Silversmiths.

SALTER, J. R. (1980[iv]): Tain Silversmiths, 1650-1850.

SANDERSON, JAMES H. (1861): 'An Account of the Plate-Marks used in Scotland since the year 1457, and Chronological list of those of Edinburgh from 1681; to which is added a Note of those used in Glasgow', in PSAS, vol. 4 (1861-62), pp. 541-48; plates 19 and 20.

SCHRODER, T. (1986): 'Decorative Arts of the Renaissance', in Apollo, vol. 124 (November 1988), pp. 406-08.

SCHRODER, T. (1988): The Gilbert Collection of Silver and Gold, Los Angeles County Museum of Art (London: Thames & Hudson, 1988).

Scot. Nat. Mem. = Scottish National Memorials (1890): A record of the historical and archaeological collection in the Bishop's Castle, Glasgow, 1888, J. Paton [ed.] (Glasgow: Maclehose, 1890).

SCOTTISH CRAFT CENTRE (1977): Important Scottish Silver 1952-1977. An exhibition to commemorate the twenty-fifth anniversary of the Queen's Accession (Edinburgh: The Scottish Craft Centre, 1977), 16 pp.

SETON, WALTER (1923): The Penicuik Jewels of Mary Queen of Scots (London, Philip Allan & Co., 1923), 55 pp.

SHARP, ANDREW (1924): 'Notes on Stuart Jewellery', in PSAS, vol. 58 (1923-24), pp. 160-84.

SHAW, NICHOLAS (2004): Antiques Catalogue of Fine & Rare Antique Silver (2004), p. 93.

Silver of the Stars (2007): catalogue (Edinburgh: Incorporation of Goldsmiths of the City of Edinburgh, 2007).

SIMPSON, JAMES YOUNG (1860): 'Notes on some Scottish Magical Charm-stones, or Curing-Stones', in PSAS, vol. 4 (1860-61), pp. 211-24. [Also printed in Simpson's collected Archæological Essays, 2 volumes, edited by John Stuart (Edinburgh: Edmondston & Douglas, 1872).]

SLATTERY, FIONA (2003): 'Perth Museum & Art Gallery', in Silver Society Journal, vol. 15 (2003), pp. 170-72. [Acquisition of church plate of St John's Kirk, Perth.] [See also RODGER and SLATTERY (2002).]

SLATTERY, FIONA (2004): 'Perth Museum & Art Gallery: St. John's Kirk Plate', in National Art-Collections Fund Review 2003, no. 5293 (NACF, 2004).

SMART, A. (1999): Allan Ramsay. A complete catalogue of his paintings (Yale University Press, 1999), no. 296.

SMITH, DAVID B. (1990): 'Medals of Curling – "Scotland's Ain Game"', in The Medal (Spring 1990).

SMITH, JOHN ALEXANDER (1873): 'Notice of a Silver Chain or Girdle, the Property of Thomas Simson, of Blainslie, Esq., Berwickshire; Another in the possession of the University of Aberdeen, and of other ancient Scottish Silver Chains', in PSAS, vol. 10 (1872-73), pp. 321-47, pls 12 and 13.

SMITH, JOHN ALEXANDER (1880): 'Notices of Silver Chains found in Scotland', in PSAS, vol. 15 (1880-81), pp. 64-70.

SMITHERS, D. L. (1988): The Music and History of the Baroque Trumpet before 1721 (second edition, Burin, The Netherlands: Uitgeverij Frits Knut, 1988), p. 59.

SOCIETY OF ANTIQUARIES OF SCOTLAND (1892): Catalogue of the National Museum of Antiquities of Scotland, 2nd edition, illustrated. Printed for the Society (Edinburgh, 1892), 380 pp.

SOTHEBY & CO. (1953): Catalogue of Highly Important English, Scottish and Continental Silver, the Property of His Grace the Duke of Buccleuch … and the Hopetoun Estate Company, sale catalogue (25 June 1953). [Buccleuch and Hopetoun Silver Sale.]

Sporting Glory (1992): The Courage Exhibition of National Trophies at the Victoria and Albert Museum (exhibition catalogue) (London, 1992).

STANNARD, BRUCE (2003): 'Malcolm Appleby', in Scots (being the Journal of the Scots Heritage Society [of Australia]), no. 20 (May 2003), pp. 73-77.

STEVENSON, J. H. (1897): 'The Usher of the White Rod', in The Scottish Antiquary, vol. 11 (Edinburgh, 1897), pp. 158-70 .

STEVENSON, J. H. (1931): 'The Bannatyne or Bute Mazer and its carved bone cover', in PSAS, vol. 65 (1930-31), pp. 217-55.

STEVENSON, R. B. K. (1947-48): 'Charles I's Coronation Ampulla', in PSAS, vol. 82 (1947-48), pp. 237-41.

STEVENSON, R. B. K. (1961): 'The Kames Brooch', in PSAS, vol. 95 (1961-62), pp. 308-09 and plate 59.

STEVENSON, R. B. K. (1968): 'A Mint Account 1632-3', in The Scottish Historical Review, vol. 47 (1968), pp. 199-202. [Reference: Gilbert Kirkwood and Nicholas Briot.]

STEVENSON, R. B. K. (1971): 'The Cadboll Cup', in PSAS, vol. 104 (1971-72), pp. 306-08. [See also McKERRELL (1971) and MacPHERSON (1887).]

STEVENSON, R. B. K. (1972): 'The Financing of the Cause of the Covenanters, 1638-51', in The Scottish Historical Review, vol. 51 (1972), p. 90.

STEVENSON, R. B. K. (1974): 'The Hunterston Brooch and its Significance', in *Medieval Archæology*, vol. 18, pp. 16-24 (1974).

STEVENSON, R. B. K. (1983): 'Further Notes on the Hunterston and 'Tara' Brooches, Monymusk Reliquary and Blackness Bracelet', in *PSAS*, vol. 113 (1983), pp. 469-77.

STEVENSON, R. B. K. and STUART MAXWELL (1958): *Brooches in Scotland* (Edinburgh, 1958).

STEWART, IAN HALLEY [now LORD STEWARTBY]: *The Scottish Coinage* (London: Spink & Son Ltd, 1955).

STEWART, IAN HALLEY (1971): 'Scottish Mints', in R. A. G. Carson [ed.] (1971), (q.v.), pp. 165-273 and plates 15-19.

STEWART, IAN HALLEY (1981): 'Two Centuries of Scottish Numismatics' [with ten-page bibliography of Scottish numismatics, including historical and commemorative medals], in A. S. Bell (1981), pp. 227-65.

STUART, JOHN [ed.] (1872): *Records of the Monastery of Kinloss, with illustrative documents* (Edinburgh: Society of Antiquaries of Scotland, 1872).

STUART, JOHN (1874): 'Notice of two ancient silver Chalices and a silver Basin belonging to the parish of Forgue, Aberdeenshire, and of their donors, James Crichton of Frendraught, and his son, the Viscount Frendraught', in *PSAS*, vol. 10 (1872-74), pp. 91-109.

STUART, JOHN (1878): 'Historical Notices of St Fillan's Crosier, and of the Devotion of King Robert Bruce to St Fillan', in *PSAS*, vol. 12 (1876-78), pp. 134-82.

STÜCKLIN, AMANDA (2003): 'A Jewel in Scotland's Crown: The renaissance of Hamilton & Inches', in *Goldsmiths' Review*, *2002/2003* (London: The Worshipful Company of Goldsmiths, 2003), pp. 44-48.

SWEENY, PETER J. (1983): *The Coinage of Scotland, a select bibliography* (Glasgow: Scottish Library Association, 1983), 47 pp.

TAYLOR, JOAN J. (1983): 'An Unlocated Scottish Gold Ore Source or An Experiment in Alloying?', in O'CONNOR and CLARKE (1983).

THOMSON, THOMAS [ed.] (1815): *A Collection of Inventories and other Records of the Royal Wardrobe and Jewelhouse; and of the Artillery and Munition in some of the Royal Castles M.CCCC.LXXXVIII. – M.DC.VI.* (Edinburgh: 1815), 359 pp.

TODD, M. (2002): The Culture of Protestantism in Early Modern Scotland (Yale University Press, 2002).

Treasures from Scottish Houses, exhibition catalogue (Royal Scottish Museum, 1967).

TULLOCH, VERY REV. (1882): 'Notice of three Silver Vessels belonging to St Mary's College, St Andrews', in *PSAS*, vol. 17 (1882-83), pp. 141-44.

VANHOUTRYVE, ANDRE (1998): Ghilde van myn heer Sint-Sebastiaan die d'archiers houden binnen de Stede van Brugge (Bruges, 1998).

WATERSTON, CHARLES DEWAR (2004): 'Robert Keay (1766-1839) and Nephews, Silversmiths', in *The Scottish Genealogist*, vol. 51, no. 3 (September 2004), pp. 113-20.

WATT, ROSEMARY [n.d.]: 'Ten Years of Silver Purchases for Kelvingrove', in *Scottish Arts Review*, vol. 15, no. 2, pp. 16-21 [n.d.].

WHYTE, JOY SCOTT (1966): 'Scottish Silver Teaspoons', in *Scottish Arts Review*, vol. 10, no. 4 (1966), pp. 8-13, 29-30.

WHYTE, JOY SCOTT (1967): 'Scottish Silver Tablespoons', in the *Scottish Arts Review*, vol. 11, no. 2 (1967) pp. 12-17, 27 and 29.WILLIAMS, JOAN (1990): *The Silver of the University of Glasgow* (Glasgow: University of Glasgow, 1990), 48 pp.

WILLIAMSON, ELIA (2001-02): Horse-racing in Scotland in the sixteenth and early seventeenth centuries', in *Review of Scottish Culture*, vol. 14 (2001-02), 31-42, p. 31.

WOOD, DR MARGUERITE (1933): 'The Hammermen of the Canongate: Part I', in *BOEC*, vol. 19 (Edinburgh 1933), pp. 1-30.

WOOD, M. [ed.] (2001): *The Hearth in Scotland* (Scottish Vernacular Buildings Working Group, 2001).

YOUNG, H. [ed.] (2002): *Elegant Dining* (London: Victoria and Albert Museum, 2002).

YOUNGS, SUSAN [ed.] (1989): *The Work of Angels. Masterpieces of Celtic Metalwork, 6th – 9th Centuries AD* (London: British Museum Publications Ltd, 1989), 223 pp. [Includes a bibliography.]

Exhibitions

'A Ballance of Silver: the story of the silversmiths of Tain' (1997), in Tain.

'An Exhibition of Sporting Art' (1984), at Manchester City Art Galleries.

Elizabethan Exhibition (1933), at Grosvenor Place, London.

Empire Exhibition (1938) (May to October), in Glasgow.

'Exhibition of Scottish Art'(1939), at the Royal Academy of Arts London.

'Exhibition of Scottish Silver from the Collection of John Noble, Chairman of the Scottish Craft Centre' (1959) (24 August to 12 September), in Edinburgh.

'Exhibition of Scottish Silver' (1948) (August to September), at the Royal Scottish Museum, Edinburgh.

'French Connections: Scotland and the Arts of France' (1985), at the Royal Scottish Museum, Edinburgh.

How of Edinburgh Ltd, Silver Exhibition (1936), at 15 Stratton Street, London, W1.

How of Edinburgh Ltd, Silver Exhibition (1937), at 15 Stratton Street, London, W1.

'Important Scottish Silver 1952-1977. An exhibition to commemorate the twenty-fifth anniversary of the Queen's Accession' (1977), at The Scottish Craft Centre, Edinburgh.

Loan Exhibition of Scottish Art and Antiquities (1931) (5 February to 1 March), at 27 Grosvenor Square, London.

'Palace of History: Scottish Exhibition of National History, Art, & Industry' (1911), in Glasgow.

'Phoebe Anna Traquair' (1993), at the Scottish National Portrait Gallery, Edinburgh.

'Renaissance Decorative Arts in Scotland, 1480-1650' (1959), in Edinburgh.

'Scottish Provincial Domestic Silver' (1986) (24 Oct. to 23 Nov.), at the Crawford Centre for the Arts, University of St Andrews.

'Silver from Scotland' (1997), at Aberdeen Art Gallery and Museum, and The Scottish Gallery, Edinburgh.

'Silver Teapots from the John Bell of Aberdeen Collection' (1961) (20 November to 16 December), at The Ceylon Tea Centre, Glasgow.

'Sporting Glory: The Courage Exhibition of National Trophies' (1992), at the Victoria and Albert Museum, London.

'Symbols of Power at the time of Stonehenge' (1985), National Museum of Antiquities, Edinburgh.

'The Lovable Craft, 1687-1987' (1987), at the Royal Scottish Museum, Edinburgh.

'The Swords and the Sorrows' (1996): An exhibition to Commemorate the Jacobite Rising of 1745 and the Battle of Culloden 1746 (Edinburgh: National Trust for Scotland, 1996).